JEWISH FAITH

AND THE

NEW COVENANT

JEWISH FAITH

AND THE

NEW COVENANT

Enlarged and Improved Edition

by
Ruth Specter Lascelle

𝔅

Bedrock Publishing
Arlington, Washington

Library of Congress Cataloging-in-Publication Data
Jewish Faith and the New Covenant *(enlarged and improved
edition)* / Ruth Specter Lascelle.

Includes bibliographical references and Index. Duane
Bagaas, Editor; Wuffy Evans, Associate Editor.

1. Fundamentals of Judaism. 2. New Testament interpretations of Jewish Customs, Holidays and Ceremonies.
3. Hebrew alphabet. 4. Gematria. 5. Messianic prophecies
and fulfillments. 6. Charts and Diagrams. 7. Scripture
Studies.

Library of Congress Catalog Card Number: 98-070019
ISBN 0-9654519-6-8

Cover design by Bedrock Publishing

Printed in the United States of America
by
Gorham Printing
Rochester, Washington

Dedicated to the memory of my
precious sister, Fay (Feygala)—

and to the memory of my
dear husband, Wallie Lascelle—

both who ministered to my Jewish
people for Messiah Jesus
through the Rock of Israel
Ministries.

Books by Ruth Specter Lascelle

A Dwelling Place for God

God's Calendar of Prophetic Events: "Leviticus Twenty-Three"

Hanukkah and Christmas

How Shall They Hear? (With Hyman Israel Specter)

Jewish Faith and The New Covenant

Jewish Love for a Gentile: "Story of The Lascelles"

My Jewish People

New Covenant Passover Haggadah: "Remembering The Exodus of Deliverance"

On What Day Did Christ Die? "The Last Week of Christ"

Pictures of Messiah in The Holy Scriptures

That They Might be Saved: "Eight Lessons in Jewish Evangelism"

The Global Harvest

The Passover Feast

Two Loaves—One Bread: "Jew and Gentile in the Church"

We Have a Great High Priest: "A Brief Study of The Book of Hebrews"

No longer in print:
  Mission to Haiti
  Sent Forth by God
  The Bud and The Flower of Judaism

HASSIDIC RABBI LIPEH SALTZMAN
(My Great-grandfather)
(See Explanation of Frontispiece on p. 323.)

ORIGINAL TITLE OF THIS VOLUME

The first edition of this book was entitled "The Bud and the Flower of Judaism" under my maiden name (Specter) and was announced in the following advertisement:

"This volume is full of interesting facts, not often known by Christians, concerning the religious life of modern orthodox Jewry. Miss Specter writes from intimate acquaintance as a Jewess with the fundamentals of Judaism, the rituals and symbols of the Jewish religion. A most striking feature is the unfolding of the analogies between Christianity and Judaism, even in its modern perverted and abbreviated form. Lord Beaconsfield declared: 'Christianity is incomprehensible without Judaism, just as Judaism is incomplete without Christianity.' Thus, Miss Specter develops the Old Covenant as the 'bud' of the divine redemptive plan into the 'flower' of full blown Christianity. Interestingly illustrated."

—*Pentecostal Evangel*, Gospel Publishing House
Springfield, Missouri, 1955

AUTHOR'S PREFACE

From the former title of this book (*The Bud and the Flower of Judaism*) comes this volume which is renamed *Jewish Faith and the New Covenant*. This title is more appropriate to the contents of the book which has been enlarged and improved. As I studied extensively I discovered that Judaism (contrary to popular belief) was not the religion of ancient Israel! Rather, Judaism was a development out of the Jewish faith found in the First Testament (OT) with a combination of interpretations contained in the *Talmud* and the *Shulkan Arukh* (see Chapter I: Fundamentals of Talmudic Judaism).

The existence and arrangement of the synagogue as well as the entire synagogue ritual from the beginning to the end of the year, the prayers, the phylacteries, the "tallit," the "yarmulkah" (or "kipa"), the "mezuzah," the sabbath candles and sabbath prayer, the ceremonies of Rosh Hashanah, Yom Kippur and Pesach, the reading from a scroll instead of a book, the dietary laws (Kashrut), etc., are all taken from the Talmud's interpretation of the T'nakh (OT).

The term *Judaism* itself is not mentioned in the Hebrew Scriptures (neither in the New Covenant Scriptures), but appeared first in II Maccabees 2.21, a Greek work composed at the end of the pre-Christian Second Century. It bears the mark of having been coined in antithesis to the term Hellenism. Lightfoot's conjecture of the title (Judaism) may be correct:

> "Though perhaps originally coined by the heathen and, as used by them, conveying some shadow of contempt, it would, when neutralized among the Jews themselves, lose this idea and even become a title of honor. The case of [Christian], likewise a term of reproach in the first instance, is a parallel. Its incorporation into the Hebrew idiom dates from the Middle Ages. The Talmud still speaks of the Jewish faith as '*Dat Moshe*' (the law of Moses), and of popular Jewish piety as '*Dat Jehudit*'."[1]

The law of Moses is **not** called *Judaism*, but "the Jews' religion" in Galatians 1:13-14. The ending *-ism* signifies a *system;* the word *religion* signifies a *faith* which can be Jewish or any other kind of faith. Judaism in its various branches is a development after 70 AD; it is a *sequel* to the religion of ancient Israel. (Christianity is also a sequel.)

Today orthodox Judaism in Israel is seeking to revert to the Mosaic and Rabbinical regulations without a temple. Reform Judaism in America is adapting itself to the second generation, American-born, university-educated Jew. How much of the Mosaic law, and of the Talmud, and of the Shulkan Aruch, should be retained? This is the great battleground in Judaism today.

Jewish *religious* activity in Bible days centered about three requirements: the *Temple*, the *Sacrifices*, and the *Priesthood* which Judaism does not require today. Ancient Israel lived by the Covenant (agreement) made by God with

---

[1]Harris Franklin Rall, *Christianity and Judaism Compare Notes, Part II*, p. 3.

the Hebrew people at Mount Sinai. But it is an impossibility to abide by it today because of the destruction of Jerusalem in 70 AD and also because of God's pronouncement in Jeremiah 31:31-34 which states that *that Covenant was broken* and a *New Covenant* promised.

Judaism cannot be the religion (faith) of ancient Israel for various other reasons: (1) It insists upon the absolute oneness of God whereas the true *Jewish faith* in the Bible had a triune conception of Deity. (2) It has no mediatorial access to God as we find is the requirement of the ancient Jewish faith. God instructed His people through the five books of Moses that they were to come to Him through the Aaronic priesthood and by virtue of the sacrifices offered. [Moses was the mediator between God and men in some instances.] (3) In today's *system* of Judaism there is no blood sacrifice as was commanded of Israel in the Hebrew Scriptures in order to atone for sin, etc.

One thing, however, that can be said of Judaism (the orthodox form) in relation to the Jewish faith found in the T'nakh is that it *is Messianic* since its faith accepts the doctrine of the Messiah's coming (but not His coming in the Person of Jesus). Jews who follow the *system* of (Talmudic) Judaism at the present time deny that Jesus was the Messiah and expect their Redeemer to come some time in the future.

Both Judaism *and* Christianity were developed from the **true Jewish faith** found in the First Covenant Scriptures. Christianity did *not* spring from Judaism as commonly supposed but is based upon the *New Covenant* and is the fulfillment of and necessary sequence of the *faith* of ancient Israel.

Christianity fulfills the Jewish *faith* found in the Old Testament for, according to the requirements of the law, it has *a Temple, a Sacrifice,* and a *Priesthood* such as in the following list.

1: The Temple is composed of the bodies of believers and is indwelt by God, the Holy Spirit.

2: Jew and Gentile approach God by virtue of a Supreme Sacrifice, the Messiah Jesus: redemption is through His blood (life) which He gave on Calvary's Altar (see Ephesians 1:7).

3: Instead of the special *human*-appointed priesthood, the New Covenant Scriptures teach the *priesthood of all believers* and the eternal *Priesthood* of the *Messiah* as predicted in Psalm 110:4.

Since Christianity is based on the New Covenant and was developed out of the *Jewish faith* found in the Hebrew Scriptures, it accepts the doctrine of the composite unity (*echad*) of God, the mediatorial ministry of the Messiah Jesus, and His blood atonement (Leviticus 17:11) for the sins of all who receive Him into their hearts.

Furthermore, a believing Jew is said (by some) to be a part of a movement within *Judaism*. This is in direct conflict with the Word of God. A believing Jew is *not* a part of Judaism which calls for attendance at the Jewish synagogue for purposes of identification. Judaism also does not accept Jesus as Messiah, nor does it believe in the shedding of His blood for the remission of sin. *Judaism* believes in conforming to the traditions of men but the *Bible* teaches transforming to the image and likeness of Messiah Jesus.

The concept that a descendant of Abraham through Jacob and Judah who accepts Christ is part of a movement within *Judaism* is not exactly true. I repeat: Rabbinical and modern-day Judaism does not accept Jesus as Messiah nor does it believe in the shedding of His blood for the remission of sin, whereas a Jew who has accepted Jesus as the Christ (Messiah) *does* believe these things.

On the other hand, believing Jews who are members of Bible-believing churches are a positive influence to stir these churches toward a witness to Israel. Jewish believers are not pressed into observing the customs of long ago. Much that passes for Jewish tradition was not instituted by God in the T'nakh (OT), but was the creation of Jewish leadership, which had long before rejected the person and work of Messiah Jesus.

Most American Jews are not particularly religious. After they accept Jesus as Messiah, the major problem is not so much cultural as it is *psychological*. It has been said: "By giving to new Hebrew Christians what can only be termed a 'pseudo' culture, they will in the long run only complicate the problems because this new culture will not square with the Word of God!"

All the foregoing is given to explain the reason for the Title of this book. The reader will discover here many customs, holidays, rituals and ceremonies of *Judaism* today. These have been taken and interpreted from the Hebrew Scriptures with many descriptions, added laws, and many rituals from many Rabbis in the *Mishnah-Gamara* (the Talmud). However, the ***true Jewish faith*** (not *Judaism*) is contained in both the T'nakh and the New Covenant Scriptures–which I have endeavored to show in this volume (see Appendix I: *Is Christianity the Offspring of Judaism?, p. 351*).

PURPOSE OF THIS BOOK

1. To honor and bless God, my Savior.

2. To inform believers in Yeshua (Jesus) as Messiah concerning their beginnings in the faith of Abraham, Isaac, and Jacob.

3. To call God's people back to the teachings in His Holy Word consisting of the First and New Covenant Scriptures.

4. To unite the body of Messiah composed of both Jewish and Gentile believers with a better understanding and love for one another.

5. To be used as a "tool" in the hands of God's people to win Jews to their own Messiah.

The above ®1996 graphic
(on the cover of this book)
was designed by Ruth Specter Lascelle
and developed by Duane Bagaas.
The *Menorah* represents the *T'nakh* (OT)
and *Ichthus* (Fish) the *Brit Chadasha* (NT),
also Jew and Gentile in Messiah Jesus.

ANU ECHAD

We are ONE!

Table of Contents

Chapter One–Fundamentals of Talmudic Judaism 1
The Thirteen Articles of Faith 1
Explanation of Synagogue Diagram 6
The Synagogue 8
The Priestly Benediction 11
Separation of Men and Women 12
The Veil of the Temple 14
Maaser (Tithe) 15
Kosher (Dietary Laws) 17
Ritualistic Slaughtering 23
Mezuzoth 27
Tefillin (phylacteries) 29
Tallit (Prayer Shawl) 32
Tzitzith (Fringes) 34
The Shema (God is One) 41
The Trinity of God 46
The Talmud 47
Oral and Written Law 48
A Few Teachings From the Talmud 48
The Six Orders of the Mishnah 50
The Shulkhan Arukh (Shulchan Oruch) 51
Talmudical Lore in the Light of the Bible 52

Chapter Two–Jewish Customs and Ceremonies 59
Mizrach (East) 59
Jerusalem is East 61
The Ultimate Prayer 61
Shalom, Jerusalem! 63
Death and Resurrection 68
Death of Moses 71
Resurrection After Death 71
Brit Milah 75
Supplemental Note on Circumcision 78

Pidyon Ha-Ben (Redemption of the Son) 79
Mikvah (Ritual Bath) 82
The Jewish Wedding 87
  The First Marriage 88
  The Shadchan (Shadkhan) 89
  The Bride 91
  The Wedding Garments 92
  Hupah (Wedding Canopy) 94
  The Ceremony 96
  The Ring 98
  The Seven Benedictions 98
  Breaking the Glass 99
  Conclusion of the Wedding 101
  Dancing 102

Chapter Three—Jewish Holy Days 105
  Shabbat (Sabbath) 105
    The Sabbath Commandment 115
    Observing the Biblical Sabbath 115
    The Eighth Day 116
    The Lord's Sabbath 119
  Pesach (Passover) 120
    The Haggadah 123
    Seven-Branched Light 126
    Hametz (Leaven) 126
      Mekihirat Hametz (Sale of Leaven) 127
    Matzah (Unleavened Bread) 129
    The Jewish Man 132
    The Special Guest 134
    Seating Arrangements (in Bible Days) 136
    The Four Cups 137
      Wine 138
    Ancient Hebrew Music 145
    Ka'arah (Seder Dish) 147
      The Shankbone of a Lamb 150
      God's Division of the Lamb 154
    The Afikoman (Aphikoman) 156
    The Three Matzot 159
    The Jewish Passover 165

Christ Our Passover (Poem) 165
Chart of Jewish Calendar 167
Easter and Passover.. 167
Rosh Hashanah 179
The Shofar 180
Sounds of the Shofar in the Synagogue 181
Yom Kippur (Day of Atonement) 186
Fasting 187
The High Priest's Cleansing 189
Order of Capuroth (Kapporos) 190
Kol Nidre 192
Blowing the Shofar 194
Casting of Lots 198
Kematslif?.. 199
The Blood-Way of Approach to God 200
Sukkot (Booth or Tabernacles) 202
Booths 204
Seven 207
The Land During the Millennium 209
Why I Believe in a Millennium 209
The Consummation of God's Plan...................... 210
Feasts of the Lord in Leviticus 23 212
Shimcas Torah... 213
Tisha B'Av (The Ninth of Av)............................... 215
Purim (Feast of Lots) 217
The Divine Name in the Book of Esther 218
Anti-Semitism 219
Hanukkah (Dedication).. 225
Dedication... 228
The Driedel Game 228
Does the Bible Speak of Christmas?................... 231
My Note on the Christmas Date 232

Chapter Four—Messiah of Israel 235
Messiah in the Hebrew Scriptures 235
One Solitary Life 237
Speaking the Name "Jesus Christ".......................... 238
Two Messiahs 239

Prophecy and Fulfillment 239
  False Messiahs 240
  The True Messiah.. 241
Date of Messiah's Coming 242
To be of the Tribe of Judah 244
Two Genealogies of Jesus, the Christ 245
Messiah's Two Genealogies (chart)........................ 248
  The Law of Moses 250
Scriptural Proof Jesus was a Jew 250
  Jesus and the Law.. 251
  Jesus and Tzitzit (Fringes) 251
  Jesus, the Jew 252
To be Born in Bethlehem 252
  Tower of the Flock 254
To be the Son of God 255
  God in Human Form 256
To be Born of The Virgin 258
Almah and Bethulah 259
To be Prophet, Priest and King.............................. 262
To be Like Moses 264
  Jerusalem in the Life of Messiah 267
To Enter Jerusalem Humbly 267
To be Despised and Rejected of Men 267
To be Betrayed.. 268
To be Sold for 30 Pieces of Silver 269
To be Crucified 270
To Suffer 270
  Who was Responsible for Messiah's Death? 273
  The False Arrest and Illegal Trial 277
  The Guilty One 284
To be Buried in a Rich Man's Tomb...................... 285
To Rise From the Dead 285
To Come a Second Time 286
  The Coming of His Feet (poem) 289
  Scars of Crucifixion 289
  Sign of the Red Heifer 291
  Rejected Stone Becomes Chief Cornerstone 292

To Reveal Himself to Israel, to Forgive and
    Defend Them 292

Chapter Five—Related Jewish Items 294
    Luach (Calendar) 294
    Some Important Dates in Jewish History 296
    Declaration Establishment of the State of Israel 297
    Flag of Israel 300
        Flags of Israel in the Bible 300
        The Mogen David in the Flag of Israel 302
    Jerusalem Covenant 304
        Jerusalem 306
    The Five Books of Moses, the Torah 307
    The Scroll of the Law and Israel's High Priest 307
    The Completion of the Old Testament 307
    The Hebrew Bible 308
    The Hebrew Scriptures 309
        Outline Lesson of the Hebrew Scriptures 310
        Canon of Scripture 311
        Interesting Facts Concerning the Scriptures 312
        The Word of God 313
        A Bit of Chronology 314
        The Most Important Chapter in the Bible 315
        God Wrote a Book 317
    Explanation of Frontispiece 323
    The Hasidic Movement 324
    The Story of the Alphabet 326
        Hebrew (Ivreit) 327
        Pictograph of Aleph-Resh-Tav 333
        Gematria 334
        Pictograph Forms of the Hebrew Alphabet 335
        The Hebrew New Testament 338
        The Resurrection of the Hebrew Language 338
        Rabbis and the Tetragram 342
        Some Definitions of the Tetragram 344
        Messiah and the Tetragrammaton 345
        The Lord That Healeth 347
        Healing by the Tongue 349

Appendix I:
   Is Christianity the Offspring of Judaism? 353
Appendix II:
   Jacob, the Jew 354

Bibliography 358

General Index 360

Sketches by Howard Morlock
(developed into graphics by Duane Bagaas)

A Jewish Synagogue.. 6
Synagogue Diagram 6
Mezuzoth (Doorpost symbols) 27
T'fillin (phylacteries) 29
Rabbi Wearing Tallit (prayer shawl) 32
Tzitzit (Fringes with system of wrappings).................... 35
Tabernacle in *Mogen David* with *Shema* 40
Rabbi With "Shin" Formation in His Hands 46
Eastern Plaque (Mizrach) 59
Bar Mitzvah (Son of Commandment) 85
The Hupah (Chuppah) Wedding Canopy........................ 87
Woman in Sabbath Prayer.. 105
The First Passover 121
Ka'arah Plate With Passover Symbols 147
Rabbi Blows the Shofar (Trumpet) 179
Kapporas Schlagen (Sacrifice for Atonement).............. 186
Sukkot (Feast of Tabernacles) 202
Shimcas Torah (Rejoicing of the Law) 213
Purim (Feast of Lots) 217
Esther Before the King 222
Father Using "Shammas" of the Hanukkah Menorah .. 225
Moses and the Two Tablets of the Law 264
Flag of Israel and National Emblem 300
Hasidim in Worship 324

Illustrations

Rabbi Lipeh Saltzman ....Frontispiece
Louis and Anna Specter (author's parents) 104
Song, "Hineh Ma Tov" for Sabbath 113
Illustrated Haggadah Page 124
Seating Arrangement (in Bible Days) 136
A Door is Opened for Elijah from Haggadah 146
Hanukkah Driedels 228
Elijah Heralding the Messiah (ancient woodcut print
    from the Haggadah) 267
Kosher (Cow) 291

Charts and/or Diagrams by Author
(edited, developed by Duane Bagaas)

The Three Matzoth of the Passover Seder 163-164
Jewish Calendar—Passover to Pentecost 168
Feasts of the Lord in Leviticus 23 212
The Divine Name in the Book of Esther 219
Tracing Messiah's Genealogy 248-249
Pictograph of Aleph-Resh-Tav 333
Pictograph Forms of the Hebrew Alphabet 335

DEFINITION OF TERMS

BC—*Before Christ* (Ante Christum)

AD—Anno Domini, *After Christ*

BCE—Before the Common Era (Before the Christian Era)

CE—Common Era (Christian Era)

OT—Old Testament. Throughout this book I have used the complete term "Old Testament" at times as an accommodation to popular reference, as a tool of convention to facilitate communication. But more times the symbol "OT" is used.

NT— New Testament

T'nakh תנ״ך—Torah, Neviim, Ketuvim, three sections of the Hebrew Bible composed of the Law of Moses, the Prophets and the Writings—the Hebrew OT.

Brit Hadasha—ברית חדשה = The New Covenant (Testament, NT)

YHWH, JHVH = the sacred Tetragram transliterated into English as "Yahweh" or "Jehovah." The Hebrew is יהוה (yod, hei, vav or waw, hei). Whenever, in the English King James Version of the Bible, the word "Lord" is capitalized it is not to show emphasis but is the translator's code to indicate the Tetragram, the יהוה (YHWH).

LXX (seventy)—*Septuagint*. The Greek translation of the Hebrew OT. The Hebrew term is *Targum Ha-Shibim*, "Translation of the Seventy." (However, there were *seventy-two* translators of the Hebrew OT into Greek.)

TWO TESTAMENTS

"The New Testament [NT] can be understood and properly interpreted *only* against the background of the Old Testament [OT]." As Dr. A.T. Pierson has said:

> "The two Testaments are like the two cherubim of the mercy seat, facing in opposite directions, yet facing each other and over-shadowing with glory one mercy seat; or again, they are like the human body bound together by joints and bands and ligaments; by one brain and heart, one pair of lungs, one system of respiration, circulation, digestion, sensory and motor nerves, where division is destruction ..."[2]

THE TEN WORDS

Popularly called "The Ten Commandments," the Bible itself calls them *Aseret ha-Debrot* which means "The Ten Words" (see Deuteronomy 4:13 and 10:4). "Ten Words" is also called by the name *Mitsveh* ("Mizvah") which means "observance," "good deed," includes 613 commands in the Hebrew Scriptures. The 613 are divided into 248 positive commands (*Mitsvos aseh*) and 365 negative commands (*Mitsvos lo-saaseh*).

---

[2]A.T. Pierson, *Knowing the Scriptures*, 1910, pp. 54-55.

CHAPTER ONE

FUNDAMENTALS OF TALMUDIC JUDAISM

THE THIRTEEN ARTICLES OF FAITH
(Thirteen Credos)

Moses Maimonides (called *Rambam* from the initials of his name: Rabbi Moses Ben Miamon), was one of the greatest Jewish philosophers that ever lived. He was born in Cordova, Spain, on March 30, 1135, and died in Israel in 1204. He was perhaps the greatest Rabbinical scholar of his day, and is well known as a philosopher, physician, astronomer, Talmudist, and prolific writer. He formulated the following Thirteen Articles of Faith which many Jewish people have considered an important part of their religious belief. (The *centered portions* are the scriptural applications and notes which I have compiled.)

I.   **I BELIEVE WITH A PERFECT FAITH, THAT GOD, BLESSED BE HIS NAME, IS THE CREATOR AND RULER OF EVERYTHING THAT HAS BEEN CREATED, AND THAT HE ALONE HAS MADE, DOES MAKE, AND WILL MAKE ALL THINGS.**

> *"In the beginning God created the heaven[s] and the earth"* (Genesis 1:1).

> Wisdom (Messiah) is speaking here:

> *"The LORD possessed me **in the beginning** of his way, before his works of old. I was set up from everlasting, **from the beginning**, or ever the earth was. When there were no depths, I was brought forth; when there were no fountains abounding with water. Before the mountains were settled, before the hills was I brought forth: When he prepared the heavens, I was there: ... when he appointed the foundations of the earth:"* (Proverbs 8:22-25, 27, 29).

> Jewish commentators have said that this *Wisdom* is personified in the *Messiah*.

II.   **I BELIEVE WITH A PERFECT FAITH, THAT THE CREATOR, BLESSED BE HIS NAME, IS THE ONE AND ONLY GOD; HIS UNITY IS UNLIKE ANY OTHER UNITY OF WHICH WE CAN HAVE ANY IDEA; AND THAT HE ALONE IS OUR GOD, WHO WAS, IS, AND WILL BE.**

> *"And God said, Let us make man in **our** image, after **our** likeness:"* (Genesis 1:26. See *The Shema*, p. 41.)

III. I BELIEVE WITH A PERFECT FAITH, THAT THE CREATOR, BLESSED BE HIS NAME, IS NOT MORTAL, AND THAT HE IS FREE FROM ALL THE ACCIDENTS THAT ARE LIKELY TO HAPPEN TO A MORTAL BEING, AND THAT HE HAS NOT ANY FORM WHATSOEVER.

(See "Messiah of Israel," "God in Human Form," p. 256.)

IV. I BELIEVE WITH A PERFECT FAITH, THAT THE CREATOR, BLESSED BE HIS NAME, IS THE FIRST AND THE LAST OF ALL BEINGS.

"Do you know," said Rabinowitz, a former Rabbi, "what questioning and controversies the Jews have kept up over Zechariah 12:10, *'They shall look upon me whom they have pierced'*? Hence the dispute about the WHOM; but do you notice that this word is simply the first and the last letters of the Hebrew alphabet—Aleph, Tav? Do you wonder, then, that I was filled with awe and astonishment when I opened at Revelation 1:7, 8 and read these words of Zechariah quoted by John *'Behold, he cometh with clouds; and every eye shall see him, and they also which pierced him'*; and then heard the glorified Lord saying, *'I am Alpha and Omega,'* the *first* and the *last* letters of the Greek alphabet? Jesus seemed to say to me, 'Do you doubt who it is *whom* you pierced? I am the *Aleph-Tav* the *Alpha-Omega*, Jehovah, the Almighty'."

—The Moody Monthly

V. I BELIEVE WITH A PERFECT FAITH, THAT TO THE CREATOR, BLESSED BE HIS NAME, AND TO HIM ALONE, IT IS RIGHT TO PRAY, AND THAT IT IS NOT RIGHT TO PRAY TO ANY BEING BESIDES HIM.

"And it came to pass, that, as he [Yeshua-Jesus] *was praying in a certain place, when he ceased, one of his disciples said unto him, Lord, teach us to pray, as John also taught his disciples"* (Luke 11:1).

"And when thou prayest, thou shalt not be as the hypocrites are: for they love to pray standing in the synagogues and in the corners of the streets, that they may be seen of men. Verily I say unto you, They have their reward. But thou, when thou prayest, enter into thy closet, and when thou hast shut thy door, pray to thy Father which is in secret; and thy Father which seeth in secret shall reward thee openly. But when ye pray, use not vain repetitions, as the heathen do: for they think that they shall be heard for their much speaking. Be not ye therefore like unto them: for your Father knoweth what things ye have need of, before ye ask him. After this manner therefore pray ye: Our Father which art in heaven, Hallowed be thy name. Thy kingdom come. Thy will be done in earth, as it is in heaven. Give us this day our daily bread. And forgive us our debts, as we forgive our debtors. And lead us not

into temptation, but deliver us from evil: For thine is the kingdom, and the power, and the glory, for ever. Amen" (Matthew 6:5-13).

Thus did Yeshua (Jesus) instruct his disciples to pray to God, not to be seen and heard of men.

VI. I BELIEVE WITH A PERFECT FAITH, THAT ALL THE WORDS OF THE PROPHETS ARE TRUE.

*"And beginning at Moses and **all the prophets**, he [Messiah] expounded unto them in all the scriptures the things concerning himself"* (Luke 24:27).

The words of *all* the prophets are true and each one of them spoke of the Messiah. David called him, "Lord" (Matthew 22:45).

The Anointed One said to the Jews: *"Your father Abraham rejoiced to see my day: and he saw it, and was glad"* (John 8:56).

VII. I BELIEVE WITH A PERFECT FAITH, THAT THE PROPHECY OF MOSES, OUR TEACHER, PEACE BE UNTO HIM, WAS TRUE, AND THAT HE WAS THE CHIEF OF THE PROPHETS, BOTH OF THOSE THAT WERE BEFORE AND OF THOSE THAT CAME AFTER HIM.

The Messiah said: *"For had ye believed Moses, ye would have believed me: for he wrote of me"* (John 5:46).

VIII. I BELIEVE WITH A PERFECT FAITH, THAT THE LAW, NOW IN OUR POSSESSION, IS THE SAME THAT WAS GIVEN TO MOSES, OUR TEACHER, PEACE BE UNTO HIM.

Paul, who was a Hebrew of the Hebrews, wrote:

"Behold, thou art called a Jew, and restest in the law, and makest thy boast of God, Thou therefore which teachest another, teachest thou not thyself? thou that preachest a man should not steal, dost thou steal? Thou that sayest a man should not commit adultery, dost thou commit adultery? thou that abhorrest idols, dost thou commit sacrilege? Thou that makest thy boast of the law, through breaking the law dishonourest thou God? For circumcision verily profiteth, if thou keep the law: but if thou be a breaker of the law, thy circumcision is made uncircumcision" (Romans 2:17, 21-23, 25).

IX. I BELIEVE WITH A PERFECT FAITH, THAT THIS LAW WILL NOT BE CHANGED, AND THAT THERE WILL NEVER BE ANY OTHER LAW FROM THE CREATOR, BLESSED BE HIS NAME.

*"Behold, the days come, saith the LORD, that I will make a **new covenant** with the house of Israel, and with the house of Judah: Not according to the covenant that I made with their fathers in the*

day that I took them by the hand to bring them out of the land of Egypt; which my covenant they brake, although I was an husband unto them, saith the LORD:" (Jeremiah 31:31-32).

X. **I BELIEVE WITH A PERFECT FAITH, THAT THE CREATOR, BLESSED BE HIS NAME, KNOWS EVERY DEED OF THE CHILDREN OF MEN, AND ALL THEIR THOUGHTS, AS IT IS SAID: IT IS HE THAT FASHIONETH THE HEARTS OF THEM ALL, THAT GIVETH HEED TO ALL THEIR DEEDS** (Psalm 33:15).

"The eyes of the LORD are in every place, beholding the evil and the good" (Proverbs 15:3).

XI. **I BELIEVE WITH A PERFECT FAITH, THAT THE CREATOR, BLESSED BE HIS NAME, REWARDS THOSE THAT KEEP HIS COMMANDMENTS, AND PUNISHES THOSE THAT TRANSGRESS THEM.**

"For God shall bring every work into judgment, with every secret thing, whether it be good, or whether it be evil" (Ecclesiastes 12:14).

"For there is nothing covered, that shall not be revealed; neither hid, that shall not be known" (Luke 12:2).

"Therefore judge nothing before the time, until the Lord come, who both will bring to light the hidden things of darkness, and will make manifest the counsels of the hearts: ..." (1 Corinthians 4:5).

"For the wages of sin is death; but the gift of God is eternal life through Jesus Christ our Lord" (Romans 6:23).

XII. **I BELIEVE WITH A PERFECT FAITH IN THE COMING OF THE MESSIAH, AND THOUGH HE TARRY I WILL WAIT DAILY FOR HIS COMING.**

"I believe, I believe, I believe, Sincerely, firmly and devoutly
In the coming of the Messiah. I believe in the Messiah,
And, though He tarry, No less firmly, I believe.
And though He tarry longer still,
Nevertheless, I believe in the Messiah.
I believe, I believe, I believe." (Song of the Ghetto Martyrs)

(See "Messiah of Israel," pp. 235-293.)

I believe in perfect faith in the coming of the Messiah. And though He tarries. I will wait daily for His coming.

אֲנִי מַאֲמִין בֶּאֱמוּנָה שְׁלֵמָה בְּבִיאַת הַמָּשִׁיחַ ׳ וְאַף
עַל פִּי שֶׁיִּתְמַהְמֵהַּ עִם כָּל־זֶה אֲחַכֶּה־לּוֹ בְּכָל־יוֹם שֶׁיָּבֹא ׃

XIII. I BELIEVE WITH A PERFECT FAITH, THAT THERE WILL BE A RESURRECTION OF THE DEAD AT THE TIME WHEN IT SHALL PLEASE THE CREATOR, BLESSED BE HIS NAME, AND EXALTED BE THE REMEMBRANCE OF HIM FOREVER AND EVER. "FOR THY SALVATION! I HOPE, O LORD! I HOPE, O LORD FOR THY SALVATION! O LORD, FOR THY SALVATION, I HOPE!"

(See "Death and Resurrection," pp. 68-74.)

Philip Birnbaum in his *A Book of Jewish Concepts* makes the following summation of the **Thirteen Credos** of Maimon:

1) There is a Creator.
2) He is One.
3) He is incorporeal.
4) He is eternal.
5) He alone must be worshiped.
6) The prophets are true.
7) Moses was the greatest of all prophets.
8) The entire Torah was divinely given to Moses.
9) The Torah is immutable.
10) God knows all the acts and thoughts of Man.
11) He rewards and punishes.
12) Messiah will come.
13) There will be a resurrection.

A JEWISH SYNAGOGUE

EXPLANATION OF SYNAGOGUE DIAGRAM

1. The TORAH (Scroll of the Law)

The Torah, a hand-written parchment scroll which contains Words of God given to Moses on Mount Sinai, is considered by Jews to be the most sacred of their religious objects. To them it is the pillar of faith since it contains the expression of God's Will and the Ten Commandments.

2. The ORON HA-KODESH (The Holy Ark)

The Jewish Synagogues today have what is called "the Holy Ark." It is supposed to be similar to the "Ark of the Testament (Covenant)" which was in the Holy Temple. (It is usually decorated with the Ten Commandments and with

Inside the Synagogue

lions on either side to guard them.) This Ark, holding the Torah (Scroll of the Law), the most sacred spot in the synagogue, is so placed that when the congregants face it in prayer they also face Jerusalem. In the Holy City itself, the congregation always face the site of the original Holy Temple. When the Ark Curtain is opened, it is customary for the congregation to rise.

3. The POROCHES *(parekhet)* (Curtain).

In the Holy Temple, a curtain or veil of "blue, purple, scarlet and fine twisted linen" separated the Holy of Holies from the rest of the Sanctuary. Now, during most of the year, a blue, purple or scarlet curtain performs that very same function by separating the Holy Ark from the rest of the Synagogue. During the High Holiday season, a white *Poroches* is used, symbolic of forgiveness and purity. During *Tisha B'Av,* a time of mourning, the Poroches is removed entirely, as a sign of bereavement. A crown, symbolizing the majesty of Torah in Jewish life, is usually found on the Poroches.

The Poroches

4. The MENORAH (Candelabrum).

It is forbidden to have or use an exact replica of the golden solid-hewn, intricately designed Menorah that was in the Holy Temple–however, there is, in every Synagogue, a symbolic reminder of this seven-branched candelabrum. To the Jewish people, the Menorah generally means the "light" representing the **Torah,** and the soul of man.

5. The NER TAMID (Eternal Light).

According to Jewish tradition, the lamps on the branches of the Menorah (Candelabrum) in the Holy Temple were filled with the same amount of oil. In six of these lamps the oil lasted only until morning but in the seventh lamp the oil lasted until the following evening when it was time to light the others again. This continuous light represented the Divine Presence. Today, the *Ner Tamid* ("perpetual light") placed over and in front of the *Oron Hakodesh* in every Synagogue, symbolizes that seventh lamp.

6. The OMUD (Reading Stand).

The *Omud* is the place "before the Ark" where the Cantor or Reader stands to lead the congregation in prayer. Frequently the words: "Know Before Whom You Stand" is inscribed on this Omud as also another phrase: "I Place the Lord Constantly Before Me."

7. The BIMAH (Platform).

The *Bimah* is a raised platform in or near the center of the Synagogue. This is used primarily for the reading of the Torah but occasionally it is the place from which the "Cantor" (singer) leads the congregation in prayer. It represents the Altar in the Holy Temple. "The 'special person' called to the *Bimah* to read the Torah on the Sabbath ascends by the shortest way to it and descends by the longest to demonstrate his eagerness to be called to read the Torah and his reluctance to leave."[3]

---

[3]*Encyclopedia Judaica, Vol. 15*, Article, *Reading the Torah*, p. 1254.

8. The MACHZOR (Holiday Prayer Book).

The *Machzor* (literally "cycle") is a compilation of the standard and special prayers for each major Jewish holiday. It contains many *piyutim* or poems (poetic writings of a very complex Hebrew literary style) which have been composed by individual Rabbis as late as the Middle Ages. (The standard prayers in the *Machzor* were written and arranged some 2,000 years ago.)

* The SHOFAR (Ram's Horn).

The Shofar, not shown in the illustration, is usually set on the Reading Stand. To the Jewish people the Sounding of the Shofar refers to a variety of symbolisms. Some of these are: a call to repentance, an expression of fear and trembling before the Lord on this Day of Judgment, a memorial of the binding of Isaac upon the altar by his father, Abraham, with a ram to substitute for him, and the promise of God for the final redemption of Israel by the Messiah. The Shofar (as God's Voice) calls to remembrance before the Jew his past, present and future. (See illustration of the Shofar with "Rosh HaShanah," pp. 179 and 194.)

THE SYNAGOGUE

"Synagogue" is a Greek word for "an assembly," "a gathering together" (for religious purposes) and was coined about the middle of the Third Century BC in Alexandria, where the Jews first came in contact with Grecian culture and adopted Greek as their daily speech. As the term implies, the synagogue is the house of worship for the Jews and is considered the means for the preservation of the Jewish religion. Stress is placed upon the congregation to respect the synagogue and therefore, laughing and loud talking is forbidden within its walls. The origin of the Jewish synagogue is probably to be assigned to the time of the Babylonian Exile. Having no Temple, the Jews assembled on the Sabbath to hear the law read, and the practice continued in various buildings after the Return. (Compare with Psalm 74:8.)

God calls His House (Temple or Church Building) *The House of Prayer for All Nations.* (See Isaiah 56:7. The Hebrew rendering is *"the house of my prayer."*) It is the meeting place for believers whom God seeks to worship Him in spirit and in truth. The assembly of the righteous gather together not only to meet with the Most High, but to encourage one another in the Lord and to preserve their faith in Him. They are exhorted to gather together "even more so" as they see the day approaching when the "church age" will end because of the return of the Messiah (see Hebrews 10:25).

What Maimonides had to say about the Synagogue is found in the following words:

> "In every place where there are ten Jews it is incumbent upon them to establish an institution where men may enter to pray on every occasion for prayer—and such an institution is called *Beth ha-Knesset*. And the Jews in the community compel one another to build for themselves a synagogue and to acquire a Torah. And when a synagogue is built it should be built on a high place in the city, and it should be taller than all the buildings in the community."

The majority of Jewish synagogues are built facing Jerusalem so that when the people of the congregation stand to pray before the platform where the "Oron Hakodesh" ("Holy Ark") is located, they are praying toward the City of Jerusalem. This opportunity for the worshipers is given because of the Scriptural injunction:

> *"... and pray unto thee **toward their land**, which thou gavest to their fathers, the city which thou hast chosen, ..."* (1 Kings 8:48).

There is a total absence of all images, portraits and statues in the Jewish house of worship because of the second commandment:

> *"Thou shalt have no other gods before me. Thou shalt not make unto thee any graven image, or any likeness of any thing that is in heaven above, or that is in the earth beneath, or that is in the water under the earth:"* (Exodus 20:3-4).

This commandment is so ingrained in the heart of some Jews that even to him who receives Yeshua as his Messiah, there is still an aversion, not only in the church but also in the home and other places, to portraits, etc., which attempt to show a likeness to the Lord! However, inscribed on the walls, are some Scriptural passages glorifying God and His House in one way or another to keep the interior from being too plain. In some instances the decorations are costly.

> "Services in the Jewish house of worship are conducted twice daily, in the morning a little after sunrise, and in the evening shortly before the sunset. On the Sabbath and on holidays, services are conducted on the eve of the day, the morning, the afternoon, and the evening." [4]

In most of the synagogues we find no musical instruments. This apparently is to preserve the thought of mourning for the destruction of the temple. In *orthodox*[5] synagogues the hands are washed before entering and for this purpose a pitcher of water is placed in the

---

[4]William Rosenau, *Jewish Ceremonial Institutions and Customs*, pp. 13-14.
[5]*Orthodox* means "thinking straight" or "devout." This term was first applied to Jews by Abraham Furtado of Bordeaux while Chairman of the French Sanhedrin which was convened by Napoleon.

anteroom which corresponds to the laver before the Tabernacle and Temple of old. ("Burial from the synagogue in most localities, is forbidden because of the defilement of the holy place by the corpse.")[6]

"While in the synagogue, worshipers keep their heads covered (a practice observed also by many persons when reading any and every Hebrew text), because literature written in the so-called 'holy tongue' is considered especially sacred and its study is regarded a religious act. A not insignificant number of Jews consider it a sacrilege to go at any time with uncovered head. There is no Biblical warrant for this custom, although it is often stated, that as the high priest wore a head covering when officiating in the sanctuary, so should every Jew when praying." [7]

During religious services or functions Jewish men wear what is called *yarmulkah.* "Yarmulkah" is a word derived from the Slavic-Tartarian language and means *skull cap.* This head cover of the Jews is also called (in Hebrew) *kipah* because, as supposed, it is made in the shape of a *kipah,* "the dome of heaven." Another word for this covering is the German *kappel* or "small cap." A Jew, who follows religious tradition covers his head at all times, even when sleeping! Moses Miamonides wrote that "great men among our sages would not uncover their heads because they believed that God's glory was around and over them." A devout Jew will not pronounce God's name, recite the Shema, or read from the Book of the Law without this, or a similar covering. (See also *mitre,* which means "bonnet" in Exodus 28:39 and Leviticus 16:4.)

The orthodox Jewish women always wore (and still do) a head covering in the synagogue. It was the custom among them to shave the hair off their heads (so that it would not be seen by man) and to substitute a wig of false hair (called *sheital* or *peruk*). (My paternal grandmother observed this custom.) According to the Talmud's interpretation of Numbers 5:18-19, the woman who was suspected of adultery had her head *uncovered* because "A woman's hair is considered nudity." That is, a man should not look upon a woman's hair, therefore her hair should be covered (see 1 Corinthians 11:5, 6). According to an ancient Jewish belief, evil spirits gained power over a woman who went with her head bare! The Jewish law states that although the head is to be kept covered, the hands are to be kept uncovered; therefore gloves must be removed during devotion. "The custom is based on the synonymous use of praying with the Biblical phrase: *spreading forth the hands.*"[8]

---

[6]David Goldstein, L.L.D., *Jewish Panorama,* p. 52.
[7]Rosenau, op. cit., p. 46.
[8]Rosenau, op. cit., p. 48.

The Talmud states that the priests in ancient times, elevated their hands up to the shoulders in the giving of the benediction (see *Sotah* vii 6). When they were in the Temple they raised their hands up to the forehead. This position, they felt, was in order to follow the expression "the lifting up of the hands." In his writings the apostle Paul spoke of the worshipers as *"men lifting up holy hands, without wrath or doubting"* (1 Timothy 2:8). According to the present practice of the Rabbis, the fingers of the two hands are so joined together and separated as to form five "interstices." Interstices are "openings of things close to another, especially between the parts of the body," "a narrow crevice." (See Illustration of Rabbi with *sheen*, ["shin" שׁ] formation in his hands p. 46.)

The Priestly Benediction

The Rabbis today, with their hands in the fore-going described position, pronounce the priestly prayer found in Numbers 6:24-26:

"The LORD bless thee, and keep thee: The LORD make his face shine upon thee, and be gracious unto thee: The LORD lift up his countenance upon thee, and give thee peace."

(Blessing)

"This is known as the Aaronic Benediction: so called because Aaron was the first man whom God commissioned to use it. In form it is symmetrical as a cut diamond. Three times the word 'and' serves as a silver link between two golden lines. Each line brings in a new thought. It was spoken to the 'children of Israel.' It is meant for the congregation. But the congregation consists of individuals, hence ultimately it is meant for each individual member thereof. The Benediction is a God-inspired poem, full of grace and truth. It is a miniature symphony whose opening movement breathes divine goodness, whose motif is the grace of God, and whole finale is peace. It is really an intercessory prayer, dictated by God Himself. Its two and thirty words are like so many angels sent forth from the throne of God to guard and guide the departing worshipers on their way." (C. A. Wendell in *The Lutheran Herald.*) [In orthodox Jewish synagogues this benediction is never used to dismiss the congregation]!

Suspended immediately in front of the ark which is located behind the curtain on the platform, is the *Ner Tomid*, "perpetual lamp." It is constantly kept burning as the name indicates. It is made either of gold, silver or burnished brass. The reason for this lamp is because of the command of God:

Ner Tamid

"And thou shalt command the children of Israel, that they bring thee pure oil olive beaten for the light, to cause the lamp to burn always. In the tabernacle of the congregation without the veil, which is before the testimony, Aaron and his sons shall order it from evening to morning before the LORD: it shall be a statute for ever unto their generations on the behalf of the children of Israel."
(Exodus 27:20-21).

Separation of Men and Women

The orthodox congregation separates the women from the men in their worship. The women meet in the "court for women" and the men in the "court for men." This dates back to the times of the Temple, when the women were not permitted to enter the premises of the sanctuary for fear of distracting the men in their devotions!

"In Zechariah 12:11-14, the Rabbis found another argument for separation. There the prophet speaks of the great time of mourning which shall accompany the restoration of the Jews and says the families shall mourn apart and their wives apart. The Rabbis drew the conclusion that if they should mourn separately, they should also worship separately." —Dr. McCaul, *The Old Paths*

A public service is never begun unless the quorum fixed by tradition is present. This quorum called *Minyan* (meaning "number or required number") consists of ten men. Less than ten men is never regarded a congregation sufficiently large for public devotion.

"The oral law [Talmud] has ordained that no public worship, nor indeed any religious solemnities, can be performed, unless there be ten persons present, but from this number it has carefully excluded women, determining that 'it is necessary that all these ten be free and adult men." —*Orach Chaiim*. 55

The Talmud says:

"So that if there be ten thousand women in the synagogue, they are counted as nobody, and unless there be ten men there can be no service. According to Rabbinical law, women are disqualified from giving testimony, for it is said, 'at the mouth of two witnesses,' where the word for *witness* is of the masculine, not the feminine gender."

For the First Time, a Minyan in the Senate

WASHINGTON—For the first time in United States history, a *minyan*, the critical mass of 10 Jews needed to hold collective prayers, exists in the Senate–but only for those with a very liberal definition of who is a Jew and a very liberal idea of who qualifies to be counted in a minyan.

Last week's election of three Jews, two of them *women*,
brings the number of Jews in the Senate to 10. ...
—*Allison Kaplan* in *Jerusalem Post,* November 14, 1992

In the *Pirque Abbot* (*Pirke Abboth*), Chapter 1:5, we read that
Jose the son of Jochanan of Jerusalem said:

"Let thy house be open wide; let the poor be members of thy
housefmhold, and engage not in much conversation with a woman.
That applies to one's wife, and how much more to the wife of a
neighbor."

The Rabbis declare that since in the Temple there was a court for
women and a separate court for men, no one has a right to abrogate
this ancient custom. This, they argue, applies to small boys and girls
playing together. In this teaching, too, Yeshua ha-Meshiach (Jesus,
the Christ), by example as He talked to Martha and Mary, and in His
conversation with a woman of Samaria with whom the Jews had no
dealings, showed that He created *all* people, men and women, equal.

The Apostle Paul, who knew the law of the Pharisees, differed
with them, saying: *"There is neither Jew nor Greek, there is neither
bond nor free, there is neither **male** nor **female**: for ye are all **one** in
Christ Jesus"* (Galatians 3:28).

There is no male or female in God's sight when it involves rights
and privileges, nature, government, and dominion in the Messiah!
All believers are made kings and priests unto God. They are equal in
obligation, responsibility, destiny. Although it is required by Jewish
Talmudic law that a service can be conducted *only* if ten adult men
are present, how wonderful to know the comforting words of our
Messiah who, making no distinction between male or female, said:
*"Where **two** or **three** are gathered together in my name, there am I in
the midst of them"* (Matthew 18:20).

The auditorium generally consists of three parts, following the
pattern of the Temple in ancient Jerusalem. The first apartment (the
Court for the Children of Israel) is occupied by the congregation during
worship. The second (*The Holy Place* for the priests and their service)
is the platform with the pulpit, and the third apartment (*The Holy of
Holies* with the Ark of the Covenant) is for the Ark and the Scrolls of
the law. A curtain separates the second and third apartments.

Under the Old Covenant, the Israelites were restricted concerning
the Temple, for they were allowed *only through the Gate* or first
entrance on the East (and this was done by their representative priests),
into the Court. They were shut off from the Holy Place by the Curtain
called "the Door." Only the *priests* (*Kohanim*) were allowed through
this Door. A Jew under the first Covenant could not enter. Two sons of

Aaron were struck dead when they attempted to enter uninvited. A king tried to do so and he was afflicted with leprosy and lived the rest of his days in a leper house. But even the priests were shut off from the Holy of Holies by the Veil. One man, the High Priest, was allowed through the Veil into the Holy of Holies once a year and at that time he could not enter unless he carried the blood of the sin offering.

> (According to the ancient rites on the Day of Atonement the blood must be carried by the priests in a *mizrak*, a golden vessel used to catch the blood of the sacrifice and transport it to the Altar. The *mizrak* had a pointed bottom which guaranteed that the priest would not be able to set it down, assuring swift completion of the offering!)[9]

Moses, also, was allowed into the Holy of Holies at any time by God's appointment (see Exodus 25:22).

But something happened to change these restrictions. They were done away in the Messiah for he completed or fulfilled the Old Covenant and established the New!

The Veil of the Temple

> *"Jesus* [Yeshua], *when he had cried again with a loud voice, yielded up the ghost. And, behold, the veil of the temple was rent in twain from the top to the bottom; and the earth did quake, and the rocks rent;"* (Matthew 27:50-51).

At the moment ha-Meshiach (the Christ) died, the Veil ceased to exist. He died at three in the afternoon (our time), the ninth hour of His day (*bain-ha-arbaiim*, "between the evenings") which was the time of the evening sacrifice in the Temple. The priests were in the Holy Place in front of the Veil engaged in their duties when this happened. How awful and wonderful was the scene! They could see into the secret of the Holy of Holies. They could enter in!

It was not by the hand of any man that this work was done! According to Josephus, the great Jewish historian, this Veil was four inches thick. It was thirty feet square (some Commentators say 30 ft. wide and 60 ft. high), higher than a man could reach and stronger than a man could rip apart. It is said that a team of oxen tied to either end of the Veil and pulling in opposite directions would not have had the power to tear it. Nothing else in the building was shaken or marred in any way. It did not fall in tatters—a piece here and a piece there. It was torn in the middle in two *equal* pieces (according to some readings, *two parts*).

---

[9]From Thomas Ice and Randall Price, *Ready to Rebuild*, photograph insert after p. 140.

This "tearing of the Veil" is an allusion to the rite practiced as a sign of deepest sorrow and grief (see 2 Samuel 13:31)! Caiaphas, High Priest at that time, "tore" his clothes (unlawfully doing this according to Leviticus 21:10) at what he believed was blasphemy on the part of Messiah Jesus (Matthew 26:65; Mark 14:63). I suggest that the Veil ("the *tunic*[10] of the Temple"), representing the humanity of Messiah Jesus, was *torn* by the hand of God who was in deep "mourning" when he "bruised" His Son (see Isaiah 53:4, 10).

The Veil was rent from *top* to *bottom* in a straight line downwards and completely through. It was not jerked apart by anyone from below but cleanly cut by an *invisible* hand from *above*. Being torn from the top and not from the bottom clearly shows that *God* had been there and ripped that curtain apart, throwing the Holy of Holies open–not to the High Priest only–but to everyone whom the blood of Yeshua has cleansed! In other words, God the Father is no longer shut in alone. He can be approached. He can be met. Jew and Gentile who have come to God by the Messiah Yeshua are no longer shut off, but can now come past the Door, past the Veil into the very Holy of Holies and dwell between the Cherubim with God (see Hebrews 10:19-22)!

ᴍᴀᴀꜱᴇʀ (Tithe)

For the upkeep of the synagogue and its service, every Friday the Jewish people give a tenth of their income called *maaser*. Also this "maaser" is given to care for the poor and unfortunate, which is the reason that Jews are known for their great works of *charity* ("Tsedokeh"). This alms-giving is considered by them as one of the means whereby they can receive forgiveness.

Tsedokeh
(Charity)

The words "tithe," "tithes," and "tithing" occur in the Bible 36 times. The "tenth" occurs 67 times. In 36 of these it has reference to the proportion in "offerings." In every instance where rewards are mentioned they are temporal, financial. To the ancient law of the tithe which was paid by the Jew for the maintenance of the Temple was added a second tithe for the maintenance of the feasts. Every third year a third tithe was given for the poor.

The Jewish nation was not prosperous when the people failed to tithe, but when they did, prosperity was in evidence. Of course there were other causes both for abundance and adversity. Tithing is not

---

[10]The *Targum* written in *Aramaic* named the Veil, "the tunic of the temple."

all-inclusive, but the Bible plainly teaches that there is a very close cause and effect relation between tithing and temporal prosperity.

In studying the history of the Jewish people, we notice clearly that both their piety and their prosperity could always be measured by their observance of the "maaser" or "tithe." When they neglected this duty it was because of their spiritual, physical and financial backsliding, and every repentance was marked by its renewal. Their purses measured their religion!

The "tithe" and offerings given cheerfully express the liberal soul which shall be made fat (prosperous). *"The liberal soul shall be made fat: and he that watereth shall be watered also himself"* (Proverbs 11:25). All true giving is free-will giving. When the Temple of Solomon was built, the people brought freewill offerings to the Lord.

It has been computed that King David himself gave almost $100,000,000 reckoned in modern currency (before inflation; see 1 Chronicles 29:3-5, 9, 14, 17)!

Whenever the people of Israel were true to Moses' system, they gave *one-third of their **time** and three-tenths of their **substance*** to God and His cause!

Dr. A.T. Pierson has summarized the Old Testament teaching on *giving* as follows:

"FIRST, a poll tax of half a shekel which everyone paid whenever the numbering of the adult males took place.

"SECOND, the tithes, of which there were three: the Levitical, or tenth of all produce of the ground, flocks and herds, which went to the support of the Levites, and out of which they themselves gave a tenth for the support of those higher in office, then a second, or Temple tithe, for the festival services of the Sanctuary and every third year a tithe for the support of the poor. Josephus says this was besides the other two.

"THIRD, the first-fruits.

"FOURTH, freewill offerings. Taxes and tithes were obligatory; these were voluntary.

"This makes it evident that the faithful Jew never gave less than a fifth of his income, and some years he gave a great deal more."

A supply of pamphlets on tithing was sent to a converted Jewish Rabbi in New York who was preaching to a congregation of Jewish believers in Yeshua as Messiah. In his letter of thanks to the sender, he stated that he had given the package to a neighboring pastor as his own people did not need teaching in tithing. He said they (as Jews) had been tithers before coming to Messiah and they continued to tithe as His followers!

Under the law, Levi, *men that die*, paid tithes to Melchizedek through Abraham (see Hebrews 7:9). The people, brethren of Levi, paid tithes through Levi and Abraham to Melchizedek. So *all* paid the tithe. In the Messiah the Mosaic order was abolished and the order of Melchizedek *re-established*! This order also is supported by the tithe. The divinely inspired apostle Paul described the superiority of the New Covenant. If the Messiah (Christ) does not receive the tithe, he is not only inferior to Melchizedek but also to Levi "men who die." If Messiah does not receive the tithe, then the figure is broken and incomplete. The conclusion is that as Abraham paid the tithe, so the Messiahnist (the Christian), the anti-type, should honor the greater King of Righteousness!

The Messiah rebuked the religious leaders of His day:

> *"Woe unto you, scribes and Pharisees, hypocrites! for ye pay tithe of mint and anise and cummin, and have omitted the weightier matters of the law, judgment, mercy, and faith: these ought ye to have done, and **not to leave the other** [tithe] **undone**"* (Matthew 23:23).

Matthew 17:24-27 reads that the Messiah Himself paid the tithe: *"They that received tribute money came to Peter, and said, Doth not your teacher pay tribute? He saith, Yea."* Notice he did not say, "I think so." This "tribute money" was an annual tax called "the half-shekel" imposed by the law of Moses on every male Jew over 20 years of age, for the upkeep of the Temple (see Exodus 30:13-14).

When God's people appreciate His grace revealed in Yeshua the Messiah, and are become partakers of His Divine nature, they possess a spirit of unselfishness and liberality (see Acts 2:45; 4:34-35). The ancient offerings of Israel brought them prosperity. Just so, prosperity is closely connected with the prompt and cheerful payment of debts to God and man by the sons of the New Covenant. Among a Spirit-filled people there is no need of markets, fairs, festivals, and entertainments to raise money for the Lord's work, because they give money liberally to maintain the spread of the gospel. Selfishness and Spirit-filled lives do not go together!

𝕂𝕆𝕊𝕙𝔼ℝ (Dietary Laws)

This illustration shows some of the symbols which appear on food products that identify the *kosher* certifying agencies. *Mono* and *diglycerides* are derivatives of fat. If a symbol of a *kosher* certifying agency appears on the package, any *mono* or *diglycerides* are made from a vegetable fat source and are appropriate food. Any gelatin

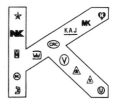

that does not carry a symbol of the Union of Orthodox Synagogues (an encircled **U**) is not acceptable as food according to the Talmud's interpretation of the Biblical dietary law.

The Leviticus 11 and Deuteronomy 14 tell of God's laws concerning the food diet which he gave to the children of Israel. They were forbidden to eat the flesh of animals whose hoofs were not cloven or which did not chew the cud, fish that had no fins and scales, birds of prey, all creeping things and insects except for certain types of locusts. It should be observed that even of those animals permitted for food, certain parts were forbidden. They are: *blood, fat* (Leviticus 7:23, Leviticus 3:3-5) and the *hind quarter.* (Deuteronomy 12:23. See also Leviticus 17:14.) Acts 15:29 instructs Gentile believers about blood, etc. What believers are to do about "Kosher" is found in 1 Corinthians 10:31. The hind quarter was to be avoided as food because of the narrative in Genesis, which, concluding the story of Jacob's wrestling with the angel (the Lord) tells:

> *"Therefore the children of Israel **eat not** of the sinew which shrank, which is upon the hollow of the thigh, unto this day: because he* [the Angel of the Lord] *touched the hollow of Jacob's thigh in the **sinew that shrank"*** (Genesis 32:32).

These dietary laws were given to the Israelites primarily for hygienic reasons to bring to their attention the importance of being clean and holy in the sight of God. Their difference from other peoples was not only to be in their religious worship but also in their eating habits. The Lord commanded:

> *"Ye shall not make yourselves abominable with any creeping thing that creepeth, neither shall ye make yourselves unclean with them, that ye should be defiled thereby. For I am the LORD your God: ye shall therefore sanctify yourselves, and ye shall be holy; for I am holy: neither shall ye defile yourselves with any manner of creeping thing that creepeth upon the For I am the LORD that bringeth you up out of the land of Egypt, to be your God: **ye shall therefore be holy, for I am holy**. This is the law of the beasts, and of the fowl, and of every living creature that moveth in the waters, and of every creature that creepeth upon the earth: To make a difference between the unclean and the clean, and between the beast that may be eaten and the beast that may not be eaten"* (Leviticus 43:47).

The primary reason for giving these food laws to Israel was to sanctify them, set them apart; i.e., or to make a difference between them and the heathen. They were to be a holy people unto God (see Leviticus 11:44; Deuteronomy 14:2-3). God gave these food restrictions to help them to be *separate* from the surrounding idolatrous nations. For almost 19 centuries, these laws have helped *to preserve the Jews as a people despite being scattered throughout the world.*

The spiritual aspect of these dietary laws is to be applied to believers in Yeshua-Jesus as Messiah. They are to be a *separated* people from the world with its thoughts, actions, and system which might be contrary to God's Word.

God called some animals and fish "clean" and some "unclean" to teach lessons by the very *nature* of these animals and fish (for their meat was good to *eat*). The "divided hoof" meant *separation*. An animal with divided hoofs is sure-footed and can climb to high places. It is not like the prohibited camel that has a padded paw with claws which leaves an indistinct mark. Hoof speaks of a careful, surefooted walk that leaves a *clean-cut* mark. The people of God are to be like the clean animal, separated from the worldly system to climb the high mountains of spiritual victory and to leave a *clear* testimony for those who follow. The fins are for propulsion, to swim against the current, to stay off the mud below. The people of God are to be like the clean fish with fins; refuse to slide along in the mud or to drift with the tide, but swim against the current. *Scales* (Hebrew word is "coat of mail") on the clean fish are for protection against muddy waters and any contamination. The people of God are to be like the clean fish with scales, though in the world, protected against all the filth of the world, encased in a "coat of mail," the Word of God!

God commanded His people to eat only the meat of those animals that "chew the cud" and had divided hooves, not one feature without the other. The Hebrew text translates "chewing the cud" as *ruminate, to muse, to ponder, to meditate.* This is a mark of the sanctified life: "to chew the cud" on the Word of God, to meditate upon it day and night. Clean spiritual food is marked by meditation. It is like the process of an animal that lies down and diligently rechews its food until it is ready to produce good meat or rich milk.

The best known example of an unclean animal (which is prohibited for food) is the pig. However, there is a Jewish tradition which tells that *even a pig* shall become *kosher* or "acceptable" for Jewish consumption when the Messiah comes! Though the pig has a split hoof, it does not chew the cud. He enjoys good food but also seems to enjoy garbage. In Isaiah's day eating "swine's flesh" had become a sign of rebellion against God (Isaiah 65:2-4).

An interesting article appeared in the Jerusalem Post concerning *kosher* meat:

> "Rabbis Examine Kashruth of 'Yaez.' Jerusalem (JCNS)— Crossbreeding a goat with an ibex, Hebrew University scientists have developed a new meat which puzzles Rabbinical authorities. The product is called 'yaez'; and a recent survey showed 70 percent of the consumers tested preferred it to lamb. But is *yaez kosher*? The animals have *cloven hooves* and *chew the cud*, but can such

crossbreeds qualify for *kashruth* approval? If *yaez* is ruled *kosher*, a major export campaign is planned, with Great Britain as a prime target." —*Message to Israel,* January/February/March 1985

Appearing in *Associated Press* of New York, 1985, was a picture of the *babirusa* animal. Beneath this picture was the following item:

> "KOSHER PIG? Investigators from the U.S. Agency for International Development think they have found what could become an important source of food for Moslems and Jews in poor countries–a kosher pig. The little-known *babirusa*, a piglike animal of Indonesia, has both an extra stomach–allowing it to chew the cud–and cloven hooves. The Old Testament says that any animal with those characteristics is edible. Neither Moslems nor Jews are permitted by their faith to eat pork."

There is significance also in the command of God which prohibits fat and blood of animals which were "clean" for food. Fat represents *abundance*. Blood signifies *life*. These belonged to the Lord. Also, the children of Israel did not eat of the "sinew that shrank" because God touched the human strength of Jacob in wrestling with him (Genesis 32:32). The sinew represents *strength* and this, too, belonged to the Lord.

"... Thou shalt not seethe a kid in his mother's milk" (Exodus 23:19). This commandment, which occurs three times in Scripture (Exodus 34:26, Deuteronomy 14:21) is a part of the dietary law of the Jewish people and is understood by them to signify the prohibition which involves the mixing of milk with meat. Dairy food is called *milchig*, meat is *fleishig*. Food neither of milk or meat is called *parve*. According to rituals made by their Rabbis, Jews are careful to observe this as one of the dietary laws of Judaism. Nothing made of milk in any form, like butter or cheese, is used by orthodox Jews together with meat or fat of any kind, the meat of fish alone being exempt. This custom is based on the Rabbinical rendering of the aforementioned Biblical passages. Jews wait six hours after a meat meal before eating any dairy food and three hours after eating dairy food to eat meat.

I remember what took place in our home at meal times: Though we lived in a Gentile community my mother, who tried to observe this command which she had been taught was a dietary law, would take us children outside the house to give us a glass of milk there. We could not have it on the table at the same time with meat nor were we allowed to butter our bread at that particular meal! On Friday evenings which was the beginning of our *Shabbat* (Sabbath), the meal included dairy food. We could then butter our bread, drink milk and, because fish was neither "milchig" or "fleishig" but "parve," we could have that! A Jewish interpretation of this milk-meat law is that basic cruelty is involved in combining the life-giving element of an animal, its milk, with the death element, its flesh.

After our family became believers in Jesus as our Messiah and we studied the Scriptures, to our surprise we found an incident in the life of Abraham, the father of the Hebrews: He did not follow the *kosher* law of today's Judaism for he served **meat with milk** to the **three** men who visited him. (Genesis 18:7-8). Also he addressed the three men as *LORD* (singular). See Genesis 18:1, 2 and 3!

We notice (in Exodus 23:19b, 34:26 and Deuteronomy 14:21) that God does not say anything about *eating* but only that the kid was not to be *boiled* in the milk. As we study the background of this law we will discover that God was very strict in commandment to Israel against the worship of "other gods." In fact, he does not want His people *even to mention their names* (Exodus 23:13)!

> "The Feasts of the Lord were to be kept to the true God and nothing was to enter into their observance that would hint at idolatry. History tells of that time that the heathen, at the end of their harvest, would seethe a kid in its mother's milk and sprinkle the broth in a magical way over the trees, gardens, etc., to make them more fruitful for the next year. This offering on the part of the idolators shows the faith they placed in their gods and of the 'feast' which was observed in their honor ... In the Ras Shamra Tablets it is stated that if one desired favor with a diety he should boil a kid in milk and present it to the diety!"
>
> —Joseph R. Free, *Archaeology and the Bible*

God repeatedly commands His people: *"Thou shalt have no other gods before me."* All their faith and obedience was to be directed to the true and only God. In other words, they were not to act, think, or worship as the unbelievers did. Their Feasts were to be kept in holiness and only to the Lord. Their harvests all were to be entrusted into the capable hands of *Jehovah-Jireh* ("The-Lord-Will-See-and-Provide") and not to the gods of the imaginative and superstitious heathen.

To God's people, then and now, the admonition is the same. In every endeavor, those who are redeemed by the great Saviour of mankind are not to follow the ways and the gods of the world. Success is to be attributed to Him who (because of His mercy) gave it and without whom nothing could be accomplished. Their "feasts" at the beginning and end of "harvest" were to be observed in honor of Him who is the First and the Last, the Beginning and the Ending, the Lord God who is *El Shaddai*, the Strong and All-Sufficient (*Many-Breasted*) One!

As we study the background of the "milk-without-meat" law we can see the significance and the truth which God was teaching His children: The heathen destroyed the kid by seething it in its mother's milk and then throwing the milk on the trees, etc. in honor of their gods. This was an act of extravagance and idol worship. God's people were not to be like the heathen. The *Jewish Commentary* on this portion states that the goat is rich in milk, that the heathen combined the kid and rich milk which is labeled as gluttonous, and gluttony is a sin. Also, milk is to strengthen and build up, not destroy. The milk is symbolic of God's Word and is to fortify, to strengthen, to nourish, and build healthy people for God, not to destroy and tear down!

Noah E. Aronstam, a medical doctor, stated:

> "The profound wisdom of the Bible...its ordinances aim at prevention. Its precepts are in accordance with the doctrines of modern sanitation, and its regulations compatible with the dictates of hygiene. The Bible is the pioneer of the sanitary sciences of today."

The word "kosher" usually means "right" ("acceptable"), "suitable," "everything in order and ceremonially clean." It has come to mean "fit" or "proper" (for food). *Kosher* is translated "right" in Esther 8:5. See also the Hebrew text of Ecclesiastes 4:4 (right) and 11:6 (to prosper). It has become a technical term describing all things, foods, vessels, etc. which are proper for Jewish use according to the rites and laws of Rabbinical Judaism.

The dietary law of Rabbinical Judaism is called *Kashrut* (Kashruth). (These laws are too involved to describe here.) *Kashrut* stems from the familiar word, *kosher* which is borrowed from the commandment of God concerning that which was "acceptable" for food.

The opposite of "kosher" is *terephah* or *treif* (trayf). It originally meant "something *torn* by wild beasts." (See Exodus 22:31, Leviticus 22:8, also Acts 15:29 for Gentile believers.) Prohibition of utensils touching unclean animals, making it "treif," is found in Leviticus 11:32-33.

Orthodox Jews have three sets of dishes, and cooking utensils: for meat, dairy and neutral (*fleishiga, milkiga, parve*). A knife which has been used for cutting *meat* and then used for *spreading butter*, would automatically become "treif," that is, *non-kosher*. A *neutral spoon* would automatically become a *milk spoon*, if used to stir the sugar in a cup of coffee with cream! (My grandparents observed the aforementioned customs.)

Not only were the Dietary Laws given to Israel by God to distinguish His people from unbelievers but they were to picture the Messiah (Galatians 3:24, Colossians 2:16-17, Hebrews 10:1). The Scriptures declare that all the law, which includes the regulation of food and drink, was a "shadow" of "things to come." It was to bring His people to Messiah and therefore they were to see pictures of Messiah in them.

RITUALISTIC SLAUGHTERING

Even of clean meats Jewish Law prescribes the animal must be slaughtered by a *shochet* (butcher) who has been ordained by a Rabbi. The "shochet" must be approved as having a good moral character and a mastery of the slaughtering laws. He must perform his task in a minutely prescribed manner with an instrument *specially designed for the purpose* called a *halof.*

The animal is killed after the shochet pronounces a proper blessing over it. The whole ritual of *kosher* slaughtering is designed to cause the animal as little suffering and anxiety as possible. Most of the blood of the animal is removed because of the commandment to "eat no blood" (see Genesis 9:4; Leviticus 3:17; Deuteronomy 12:16).

Even after the *shochet* slaughters the animal he must examine certain vital organs, particularly the lungs, for defects. He searches for adhesions, atrophied lobes, obstructions in the bronchial tubes, any one of which would render the animal unfit to eat. *This practice was followed centuries before* **Government inspection of meat**! (The only Biblical basis for *slaughtering rules* is found in Deuteronomy 12:21-24.)

Even after most of the blood of the animal is removed by the *shochet* there was to be a "ceremony" called *kashering.* This was observed by my grandmother: She would soak the meat (which my grandfather purchased in a "kosher" market) for one-half hour in cold water, salting it on all sides. She would leave the meat in the salt for one hour for the blood to drain off, then wash it again before cooking. Sometimes I would see the meat on the kitchen drainboard slanted into the sink to allow for further removal of the blood!

Orthodox Jews are very careful in their method of killing animals for food. The trachea and esophagus are severed by means of a knife (called a *halof*), entirely devoid of notches, so that the blood may flow easily out of the body through the slit made. Draining of the blood in slaughtering is not directly commanded in the Pentateuch but is based on the verse of Scripture: *"Only be sure that thou eat not the blood: for the blood is the life; And thou mayest not eat the blood with the life"* (Deuteronomy 12:23).

There are those who object to the "kosher" ritual of slaughtering for they consider it inhumane. Let us notice that in the usual *commercial* practice, animals are stunned with an electric shock, knocked on the forehead with a sledgehammer or shot between the eyes with a spring-loaded bolt before being lifted into the air with their heads down, ready for their throats to be slit. *This would be inhumane!* But in *kosher* slaughter, the Rabbi does not stun the animal because Jewish law prescribes that an animal be unblemished, unbruised and conscious before it can be killed. Otherwise, it is considered unclean.

Slaughtering, according to the Jewish method, causes instantaneous unconsciousness, and permits the greatest effusion of blood. The knife must be of a described size for each kind of animal, and of the maximum keenness, to prevent the slightest unnecessary suffering. It provides for as complete a draining as possible. In addition to this draining, the meat is soaked in water for half an hour, kept in salt for a full hour, and then thoroughly rinsed. This is the *kashering* "ceremony" taken from regulations of the Talmud. Some meat is broiled, however, without this special treatment. (Eggs, which have *blood* spots, are forbidden by Jewish law. My grandmother and mother would dispose of this kind of egg.)

A qualified *shochet* (butcher) carefully examines the animal, which after being declared fit for food or *kosher*, is slaughtered. If he finds the animal sound, he seals the parts with the mark "kosher" meaning "fit for food" in contradistinction to "terephah" meaning "unfit" or "unkosher," and originally signifying something *torn* by a wild animal. ("Terefah" or "treif," "something *torn*," has become a technical term to describe all things which are not "Kosher.") *"And ye shall be holy men unto me: neither shall ye eat any flesh that is torn of beasts in the field; ye shall cast it to the dogs"* (Exodus 22:31; also see Genesis 31:39; Leviticus 7:24; 22:8).

We find a great spiritual truth here! As all the Word of God is to be explained in its practical and natural sense, so too, it is to be defined in its *spiritual* sense as well! Every commandment of God, every ritual and ceremony relates to faith in God's Messiah! Even the ceremony of Kosher and Terephah, the removal of the blood, etc. refers to Him! Was it not cruel on the part of men to have crucified the Messiah? They stripped Him, beat Him, whipped Him until the flesh of His back was "flayed" open raw and bleeding. His blood was drained from Him for the life of the world; He was *torn* by "wild beasts," "strong bulls of Bashan" according to the prophecy (Psalm 22:12). He was made "unfit," "terephah," so that the Jewish people (*as a nation*) did not partake of Him. In prophecy they declared:

> "... when we shall see him, there is no beauty that we should desire him. ... we hid as it were our faces from him; he was despised, and we esteemed him not" (Isaiah 53:2-3).

But, according to God's Word, he was to be *cursed* for the sake of the sinner! He was to be made "unfit" that the sinner might be accepted in Him. He was made sin that all believing on Him might be made righteous! This was to fulfill the prophecies which God made concerning the Messiah of Israel, the Savior of the world!

But despite the practical value of much of this divine instruction, how weighted down with rituals and empty forms were the Israelites of the Old Covenant! How severe was the law of Moses! Many ordinances, many ceremonies did they keep and observe but their hearts were far from their God. They did not see in them the true significance or the spiritual application that would set them free. And today, these spiritually "blinded" people are still observing these and many more dietary laws which have been added by the Rabbis and religious leaders of Jewry, and are failing to grasp the deep and tender desire of Almighty God for their lives in glorious fulfillment. If only my dear Jewish people would turn to their Messiah Yeshua (Jesus) they would realize the true interpretation of all these laws and ordinances for they point to Him who is All in All, the embodiment of all wisdom!

Oh, the great spiritual truth contained in these commandments! How particular the Lord is with His "peculiar" people! How watchful he is of their every move and thought! Anything which is unclean he desires not to touch His own. That which defiles, they are commanded to put away. For he would have a holy people, pure and undefiled even as he is holy, pure, and undefiled. He has declared to His "treasure":

"Wherefore come out from among them, and be ye separate, saith the Lord, and touch not the unclean thing; and I will receive you, And will be a Father unto you, and ye shall be my sons and daughters, saith the Lord Almighty" (2 Corinthians 6:17-18).

Nevertheless, God can take that which is defiled, unclean, unholy and he can cleanse and purify it. That which was considered unfit under the Old Covenant is made worthy under the New Covenant by faith.

[Peter] *"... fell into a trance, And saw heaven opened, and a certain vessel descending unto him, as it had been a great sheet knit at the four corners, and let down to the earth: Wherein were all manner of fourfooted beasts of the earth, and wild beasts, and creeping things, and fowls of the air. And there came a voice to him, Rise, Peter; kill, and eat. Peter said, Not so, Lord; for I have never eaten any thing that is common or unclean. And the voice spake unto him again the second time, What God hath cleansed, that call not thou common. was done thrice: and the vessel was received up again into heaven"* (Acts 10:10-16).

The interpretation to this vision was revealed to Peter who explained it in the home of Cornelius, a Gentile:

"... Ye know how that it is an unlawful thing for a man that is a Jew to keep company, or come unto one of another nation; but God hath showed me [by the vision] ***that I should not call any man common or unclean"*** (Acts 10:28).

At that time the Jews claimed all the blessings and promises of God, leaving the Gentiles as "foreigners and strangers" and outside of fellowship with the Holy One of Israel. The Gentiles were considered as unbelievers, incapable of receiving anything from heaven. But the eternal purpose of God was to take from **both** Jews *and* Gentiles a people for His Name. (See my book, *Two Loaves—One Bread: Jew and Gentile in the Church.*)

Through the writings of Isaiah the *Gentiles* would be included with Israel in the Covenant.

*"The Lord GOD which gathereth the outcasts of Israel saith, Yet will I gather **others** to him, beside those* [Israel] ***that are gathered unto him"*** (Isaiah 56:8).

The Old Testament saints did not understand this mystery which was hidden to them in type and parable, in offerings and feasts. This great mystery was revealed to Paul the apostle who declared that the **Gentiles** would be *fellow-heirs* and of the *same* body and partakers of His promise in the Messiah (Ephesians 3:1-3)! The middle wall of partition was broken down, the enmity done away in the Great Sacrifice of Calvary!

When this mystery was revealed to Paul, the Jews realized that the Gentiles *also* could be partakers with them of all the benefits of the Lord! Neither *Gentile* **nor** *Jew* can be called *common*, for God can save them both by the Sacrificial Lamb! He died for *all*!

Marvelous grace of God! The gospel is for *Jew* and **Gentile**; black, white, red, yellow and brown, rich and poor; cultured and pagan; slave and free man; male and female. God accepts all who come to Him through the Messiah Yeshua!

MEZUZOTH

Mezuzah is the Hebrew word for *doorpost*, to which the ceremonial object is fastened. "Mezuzah" comes from the root *zuz* which means "to turn oneself about." Hence the meaning of the doorpost is "that upon which hinges turn." Exodus 21:6 and Deuteronomy 6:9 translates it as "posts" and in Exodus 12:7 it is "sidepost." This symbol of the Jewish profession of faith is a small wooden, glass, ceramic or metal case of from two to six inches in length containing a rectangular piece of parchment (*klaf*) inscribed with two small portions of God's Word, Deuteronomy 6:4-9 and Deuteronomy 11:13-21.

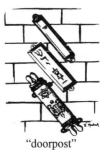

"doorpost" symbols

The paper scroll inside the case is really the "mezuzah" and the Hebrew words on it must be written by hand in ink on parchment or it is not a *true* "mezuzah." The case usually has a small opening near the top and on the front of the tube through which can be seen either the word for God, *Shaddai*, שדי or the Hebrew letter, *sheen* (ש) which also stands for God's Name, written on the back of the parchment. *Shaddai*, the personal Name of the Lord is written on the Scroll no less than ten times. Jewish interpreters believe that the three Hebrew letters which spell *Shaddai* (שדי)

The Mezuzah Scroll (klaf)

are an acronym of the phrase *Shomer Delet Israel*, "Guardian of the Door of Israel." The tube is affixed to the upper third right-hand portion of the doorpost in a slanting position pointing inside the home in obedience to the command: *"And thou shalt write them* [the words of the law] *upon the doorposts of thy house, and on thy gates"* (Deuteronomy 6:9).

A pious Jew never enters or leaves the house without reverently placing the fingertips of his right hand on the sacred word *Shaddai* and then touching his lips. This is done to be a reminder that "the Word of God was to ever be on your lips." He kisses his fingertips after he touches the Mezuzah, reciting, *"May God keep my going out and my coming in from now and forevermore"* (Psalm 121:8). This prayer connects the mezuzah to the Divine presence and Divine protection.

The mezuzah, after 4,000 years, has now become the symbol of the Jewish home. To the Jew it is a reminder of the need for sanctifying the home by means of religious teachings, and of keeping the home unpolluted from all evil. He feels that this object is an amulet which forcefully recalls the protecting charm possessed by the doorposts of the ancient Israelites in Egypt. He is reminded of the blood of the lamb sacrifice, which was struck on the doorposts by his forefathers in obedience to the command of God which kept them from death and from destruction. Religious Jews say: "The mezuzot we affix to our doorposts today are a variation of that protective lamb's blood."

In this connection Jewish people still practice the interesting custom of *dedicating their homes*, called *Hanukat Habayit*, "Dedication of the House" (see Deuteronomy 20:5, also Psalm 30 which was sung at the dedication of King David's house). Relatives and friends are invited to this, especially in the case of newly married couples and by those who move into homes of their own. Usually the ceremony begins with the *fastening of the **mezuzah** on the doorpost*. The blessing then is recited: "Blessed art thou, O Lord, our God, King of the Universe, Who hast made us holy with thy commandments and hast commanded us to fasten mezuzah." This blessing is followed by a prayer:

> "Master of the Universe, look down from Thine holy habitation and accept in mercy and favour the prayer of thy children who are here gathered to dedicate this dwelling and to offer their thanksgiving. Grant them that they may live in their homes in brotherhood and friendship."

Part of the ceremony consists of bringing bread and salt into the house as a symbol of prosperity. Refreshments, singing and fellowship follow the ceremony. Sometimes one of the guests will deliver a talk on the significance of the occasion.

Not only are the Jews to write the words of the law upon their doorposts and gates, but all who believe upon Him are commanded, in a spiritual sense however, to do likewise. For God was stressing by this statute the importance of His Word and necessity of this observance in the life of the believer. However, by the blessing of the New Covenant, the law of God is written (not upon objects of wood and stone or upon a piece of parchment) but upon the fleshly tables of the heart!

God commands that His *"words ... shall be in thine **heart**"* (Deuteronomy 6:6). It is more important to have the Word of God fixed in the heart than to have it wrapped up in a small box and nailed to the door of a house! The commandments and statutes of God then are not grievous, neither difficult to obey, but are a delight and a pleasure to the soul! The "mezuzah" attached to the "doorpost" of the believer's heart is a reminder to him of the protecting power of God's Lamb, Yeshua (Jesus) who shed His blood for all who will apply it to the door of their heart in faith. He watches our coming in and our going out, our uprising and our downsitting. Thank God, He is with us always. It is not an object of wood nor of stone which is a charm, a protection, but the real Person of the Messiah who guards us and leads us by His Spirit! Praise His Name!

TEFILLIN (phylacteries)

T'fillin is a Hebrew word taken from the singular, *t'filla* meaning "prayer." The use of the t'fillin by orthodox Jews today is based on an interpretation of the statement in the Scripture:

"And thou shalt bind them [the words of the law] *for a sign upon thine hand, and they shall be as frontlets between thine eyes* (Deuteronomy 6:8, with 11:18).

"And it shall be for a sign unto thee upon thine hand, and for a memorial between thine eyes, that the LORD's law may be in thy mouth: for with a strong hand hath the LORD brought thee out of Egypt" (Exodus 13:9).

The Hebrew word for "frontlets" in Deuteronomy 6:8 is *totaphoth*. The Greek word is *phylacteries* from *phulakterion* which means "to keep safely," "preservative." These phylacteries consist of two square wooden boxes covered with black leather, the skin of levitically clean animals. It is stitched over the box (to hold the parchment within) with 12 stitches representing the 12 tribes of Israel.

One box is worn on the left arm towards the heart, and the other worn on the forehead where the hairgrowth starts. The head box (*t'fillah shel rosh*) contains *four* compartments which hold as many bits of parchment, each inscribed with one of the four Biblical passages: (1) Exodus 13:1-10. Sanctification of the Firstborn and Feast of Unleavened Bread. (2) Exodus 13:11-16. Deliverance From Egypt. (3) Deuteronomy 6:4-9. Unity of God. (4) Deuteronomy 11:13-20. Rewards and Punishments. On the right of the box is written the 3-pronged letter *sheen* (*shin* ש) which stands for *Shaddai*, "the Almighty" and on the left a four-pronged *sheen*. And this 3 and 4-pronged letter-combination equals *seven*, the Divine number! Also the 4-pronged *sheen* shows *three* spaces in between the "prongs"– again the 3-pronged *sheen*! The box for the arm, called *t'fillah shel yad*, has one compartment with one slip of parchment upon which all four passages are written.

The boxes are one inch by one-and-a-half inches. These are fastened at the brow (the seat of *thought*) and left arm (the instrument of *action*) near the heart (the seat of *feeling*) by long leather straps attached to them. This signifies desire for obedience to the first Commandment: *"And thou shalt love the LORD thy God with all thy **heart**, with all thy **soul**, and with all thy **might**"* (Deuteronomy 6:5). So it teaches that all thoughts, feelings and actions are to conform to the will of God. The devout Jew believes that by binding one of these phylacteries on the arm and placing the other on his forehead each morning, he is truly fulfilling the Mosaic requirement! Jews who are orthodox in Judaism explain that *"t'fillin* expresses the ideal unity of the human personality." He says: "By wearing t'fillin on my arm with the box facing my *heart* and the other t'fillin on my *head* I am expressing that the actions of my hand, the emotions of my heart and thoughts of my mind are united in the single purpose of serving God and humanity."

The usual phylacteries (*t'fillin*) are quite small, but the very devout Jew makes them larger. T'fillin is reverenced as highly as the Scriptures for it contains the sacred name of the Lord (the Tetragram יהוה) not less than 23 times. One of the prayers every devout Jew repeats daily while wearing *t'fillin* is the 12th Credo of Moses Maimonides:

> "I believe with a perfect faith that the Messiah, blessed be His Name, will come speedily and though He tarry, I shall continue to wait for Him to come."

In wearing the "t'fillin," the phylactery of the arm is taken first since this is the order listed in Deuteronomy 6:8. The box is fixed firmly on the naked left arm, upon the biceps muscle (denoting strength), above the elbow, and when this is done, the worshiper recites: "Praised art Thou O Lord, our God, King of the Universe, who has sanctified us with His commandments and enjoined upon us the commandment of the phylactery."

Formed in the knot connection of the leather strap for the *hand* phylactery is the Hebrew letter *yod* (י) in the knot connection of the leather strap for the *head* phylactery is the Hebrew letter *dalet* (ד), and embossed on

Shaddai

the box for the head, the Hebrew letter *sheen* (ש). These three letters spell *Shaddai*[11], (literally, "Many-Breasted God"), the All-Sufficient and Almighty One. Also the windings around the fingers of the hand form the word: *Shaddai* as in the illustration here. On the other side of the head *t'fillah* (phylactery) there is another *sheen* embossed, but this one, strange to say, has **four** instead of three stems. This is the only place where a four-stemmed *sheen* is used. There are those who

---

[11]*Shad* means (a mother's) *breast* implying nourishment, satisfaction, contentment. *Shaddai* is the plural of *Shad*.

feel that these four stems represent the four women most prominent in Jewish history (Sarah, Rebecca, Rachel, and Leah). Others say that the four stems have reference to the four Scripture portions contained in the phylacteries (*t'fillin*) which are thought to justify the use of the t'fillin.

Returning to the phylactery of the hand (*tefillah shel yad*), its strap is wound about the arm seven times and in succession three times about the middle finger (forming the three-pronged letter *sheen*), once about the fourth, once about the middle, and finally around the whole hand. While this is done the following words are recited:

> "I betroth thee unto me forever; I betroth thee unto me in righteousness, in judgment, in kindness and in mercy. I betroth thee unto me in faithfulness and thou shalt know the Lord."

The *tefillah shel rosh* (phylactery for the head) is put on next. The box is placed on the forehead above the nose and the strap is fixed at the back of the neck exactly above the middle of the neck. The end of the straps hang down over the shoulders to the front of the body. These *t'fillin* are removed in reverse order from that in which they were put on.

While wearing the phylacteries the worshiper petitions God to consider the performance of the commandment regarding the *t'fillin* as though all 613 commandments, of which he feels the law of Moses consists, had been faithfully executed.

In the days of the Messiah, the t'fillin (phylacteries) were more in use than today. However, the Jewish youth are trying to revive this custom. I discovered this when visiting the Jewish section of Los Angeles (California) one day. In front of one of the Jewish "coffee houses" on the sidewalk was a placard with the following notice in bold print: "Have you put on your t'fillin today"? Not only among the youth, but also, the use of the phylacteries, the t'fillin, is being revived today due to the fact that the *Hasidic Movement*, as well as other Jewish revivalists, has become more widespread throughout the world.

In New Testament times the spiritual leaders who desired their religiosity to be noticed, would make their phylacteries larger than was customary. These Pharisees, Sadducees, and Hebrew scribes claimed attention so as to elevate themselves to a higher position in the eyes of the people. They made a show of their "supposed" devotion to the Lord in order that they, in turn, would receive some of that same devotion from Israel! The Messiah rebuked them for this:

*"But all their works they do for **to be seen of men**: they make **broad** their **phylacteries**, ..."* (Matthew 23:5. This is the only place in Scripture where the word "phylacteries" is found.)

How like these Jewish religious leaders have been *all* classes of people over the face of the earth! Unlike the lowly Nazarene who received not honor among men they are "broadening their phylacteries" to be seen, to be heard, to be praised even as the Pharisees of old!

TALLIT (Prayer Shawl)

"Speak unto the children of Israel, and bid them that they make them fringes in the borders of their garments throughout their generations, and that they put upon the fringe of the borders a ribband of blue: And it shall be unto you for a fringe, that ye may look upon it, and remember all the commandments of the LORD, and do them; and that ye seek not after your own heart and your own eyes, after which ye use to go a whoring: That ye may remember, and do all my commandments, and be holy unto your God" (Numbers 15:38-40).

Jewish men in the Orient customarily wore a robe, a square piece of woolen cloth (somewhat similar to the *abaye* of the Arabs) in which they used to wrap themselves. In the course of time, the Jews, adopting the costumes of the lands of their residence, no longer wore this *outer garment*, but substituted a *shawl* called the *tallit* which was worn in the synagogue and during their daily prayer as the custom is today. Among orthodox Jews from the age of 13 years, it is worn about the shoulders in the house of worship and at the time of their daily devotions which take place at nine o'clock in the morning, three in the afternoon, and after sunset around six o'clock.

At a Jewish boy's *Bar Mitzvah* he is given a large and beautiful *tallit* which he will use all his life at special occasions. At his death the tallit is wrapped around him after one of the fringes is torn to render it unfit for further religious use and it is buried with him.

"Thou shalt not wear a garment of divers sorts, as of woollen and linen together. Thou shalt make thee fringes upon the four quarters of thy vesture, wherewith thou coverest thyself" (Deuteronomy 22:11-12).

In obedience to this command, religious Jewish men today wear a shawl at their prayer times made of only *one* material, usually silk. How the Lord desires an undivided heart in our worship, an unwavering faith, not tossed about by every wind of doctrine, not mixed with the religion of the world, but *pure* and single to His honor and glory! He commands that we not make our "garments" of "divers sorts"!

Tsitzit is the name used by Jews for the *fringes* of the tallit, and it is written this way in the *Hebrew* Scriptures. To the orthodox Jew these fringes, and counting each member of their body, number 613 corresponding to 613 oral laws claimed to have been given to Moses on Mount Sinai. Because Jewish people know it is a command of God to obey His law (*mitzvah*), they feel that their obedience brings them merit. A pious Jew, according to Rabbinical regulations, is expected to keep 613 *mitzvot* (laws) daily! Since this is really impossible, the theory has grown up that the good deeds of *all* Israel put together count in making up the full number!

The Bible is a spiritual book for a spiritual people. But too often do the people of God only see its literal and not its spiritual interpretation. In the commandment concerning the *tzitzit* we want to emphasize (even as did the Master) the teaching of types and shadows:

"The woman shall not wear that which pertaineth unto a man, neither shall a man put on a woman's garment: for all that do so are abomination unto the LORD thy God" (Deuteronomy 22:5).

To understand the typical meaning hidden in this Scripture we must know something of Israel's custom of dress. In that time the under-dress and gown-coat as well as the upper robe of women was *very similar* in design to that of the men. However, there was one particular and important feature in the *man's* dress, a sign to be there at God's commandment, which made a difference from the dress of the woman. This "mark" was a *ribbon of blue*, and *fringes* in each of the four borders (corners, wings, quarters, hem) of their garments with which they covered themselves as written in Numbers 15:38-40 and Deuteronomy 22:12.

This article of clothing not only distinguished the Jews from others, testifying to the fact that they belonged to God, but also was a prophecy. It told of the Righteous Servant of Yehovah (*Yahweh*) who would wear such a garment when He came into the world. He would obey every law to the very letter which had been given to Israel!

The man, who wore the garment, being the leader in the family according to the Scriptures, speaks of the prophesied Messiah. The fringes denoted the law of God which would be fulfilled in Him, the blue signifying His heavenly origin. In marriage the man, as a type of Messiah, was in authority over the woman, a type of the Church. She was to be in subjection to the man, even as the church to Christ. Paul explains this in Ephesians 5:22-23. If the woman would put on such a holy robe, she would be "breaking the pattern" (and God is very careful of His types)! In a spiritual sense, she would be taking authority away from the man, and would be defying God's commandment. For anyone to say outright to God: "I will not have *you* to rule over me. I will take your authority away from *you* and put it upon myself," is truly an abomination in His sight! (Note: In *reformed* synagogues today a Jewish woman is allowed to wear the *tallit*.)

On the other hand (in a typical sense), for the man to wear "that which pertaineth to a woman" would be as though he were reversing the order in which God places the Church and Christ, intimating that Christ is to be in subjection to the Church, to hide His authority under the skirts of a lesser power, to disguise and put Himself (the Head of the Church) under the feet of the Redeemed, who, by this action, becomes the "ruled" instead of the Ruler. This also is an abomination to the Lord!

> "For generations, it was one of the orthodox dogmas of Judaism, the pivot of piety, that *248 positive* commandments correspond to the 248 parts of the human body, and that *365 negative* commandments correspond to the 365 sinews of the human body, according to the anatomical belief of the *Talmudic* era. The Orthodox Jewry stands on the pillar of what is *said* and what is *written* and around that conception revolves the entire *Talmudic Rabbinical* literature for the past 2,000 years. Nothing is holy if it was not written, nothing is good if it was not said before and no pious Jewish person ever dared yet to criticise [*sic., criticize*] this concept."
> —Hyman Luloff, to the Editor of *The Jewish Post*

Tzitzith (Fringes)

The fringes, which end at each corner of the *tallit*, are put in a hole about an inch from the edge of the garment. The manner of their attachment in knots and 39 windings correspond to the numerical value of the letters which spell "The Lord is One," since each letter of the Hebrew alphabet has numerical significance.

> "A long cord is wrapped, seven shorter cords first seven times, then eight, then eleven and finally thirteen, each series being separated from the others by two knots, the numbers seven and eight constituting fifteen together suggest the Hebrew letters *yod heh* (יֵה) and the number eleven, the Hebrew letters *vav* [*wau*] *heh* (הו) together they make up the name **Yahweh** (יֵהוה). The number thirteen stands for the Hebrew letters *aleph heth dalet* which spells *Echad* (אחד), the letters of which (as numerals) equal thirteen. The sentence '*Yahweh echad*' means 'Yahweh is one'." [12]

---

[12]*International Standard Bible Encyclopedia*, Vol.2, p. 1146. (Added Hebrew letters are mine.)

(The following sketch was drawn for me by my former Seattle Bible College student Howard Morlock, portraying the number system in the *Tzitzith* which was **designed by Talmudic Rabbis**. Captions are mine.)

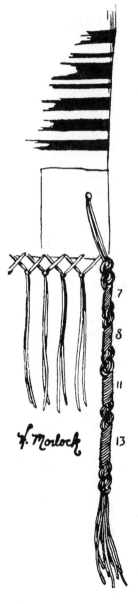

"TSITZITH" *("fringes")*
(System of Wrappings)

The Hebrew word *"Tsitzith"* in gematria (numerology) equals 600. In addition there are 8 strands plus five knots. The total is 613, which is the exact number of *commandments* in the Torah! God said to look at the *tsitzith* and "remember my *commandments."* (Numbers 15:37-41).

(See illustration on the left)

one double knot
7 wrappings
one double knot   7 + 8 = 15
8 wrappings

yod   (י) = 10
heh   (ה) =   5   י ה
                  15

one double knot
11 wrappings

vav   (ו) =   6   ו ה
heh   (ה) =   5
                  11   י ה ו ה
                        YAHWEH
one double knot   (Adonai)
13 wrappings
aleph   (א) = 1   א ח ד
cheth   (ח) = 8
daleth (ד) = 4   ECHAD
                  13   (is) ONE !

The fringes of this prayer garment in ancient times was worn in imitation of Moses who wore a veil over his face because of its radiance (some say, because the glory was fading). The fringes were drawn down over their eyes so the reader could look through the sacred veil upon the Scriptures. How significant is this to the fact that *"blindness in part has happened to Israel"* according to the prophecy. The Veil of Moses is concealing the glory of Yeshua, Jesus, as their own Messiah!

The first act of a devout Jew in his morning prayer is to put the fringes to his lips and kiss them to acknowledge the obedience of the worshiper to the whole law. (I have seen my grandfather perform this service in spite of the fact that he thought he was doing it in secret.)

> "Several prayer-books under the Ashkenazi rite include the following meditation, to be recited on putting on an under-garment or prayer-cloak with the prescribed fringes at its four corners: 'May it be thy will, O Lord, that the observance of this commandment be accounted as though I had fulfilled it in all its details and particulars and intentions, and the 613 commandments that hang on it.' ..." [13]

The Messiah rebuked the religious leaders for *"enlarging the borders of their* [prayer] *garments to be seen of men"* (Matthew 23:5). He knew what was in men and it grieved Him to see the Jewish people being swayed by their religious leaders. Some Jewish men had misused the God-given command by *enlarging* their fringes as a sign of their great spirituality. He said to these blind religionists:

> *"Woe unto you, scribes and Pharisees, hypocrites! for ye are like unto whited sepulchres, which indeed appear beautiful outward, but are within full of dead men's bones, and of all uncleanness. Even so ye also outwardly appear righteous unto men, but within ye are full of hypocrisy and iniquity"* (Matthew 23:27-28).

The Jewish prophet Isaiah said it was not enough to honor God with the lips when the heart is far from Him (see Isaiah 29:13). Not only did these Jews use their mouths to make long prayers, but also used their lips to kiss the fringes in order to impress upon the people the fact of their spirituality. What similarity to so-called worshipers of the Lord today who, to seem religious, pray loud and long in public, but have no real abiding fellowship with God in their lives! As Madame Guyon, a famous Christian leader said: "For some reason men try to love God by forms and rules. And by these very forms and rules (rituals) they have *lost* so much of that love. The simplest can know Him, and in the deepest way, *with no help from rituals or forms or theological instruction!"*

---

[13]David Daube, *The New Testament and Rabbinic Judaism*, p. 252.

God commanded the children of Israel that they *"put upon the fringes of the borders a ribband* [ribbon] *of blue."* This blue cord entwined in the fringe is the heavenly color reminding the Jews of the power and glory of God. Blue is traditionally the color of royalty because the blue dye was extremely expensive. It is said that in ancient times it took 10,000 snails to produce 1 cubic centimeter of dye. One pound of this dye cost approximately two years' wages. Lydia is mentioned in Acts 16:14 as a seller of "purple" a cloth made with this dye. It is thought Lydia was a very wealthy woman from this trade. Because of its cost, a person who wore a lot of blue was generally prominent in society. By the year 300 AD a pound of blue Sidonian silk sold for over $90,000. The use of the blue is explained in the *Talmud*: "Because this color resembles the sea; the sea resembles the sky; and the sky resembles the Chair of Glory."

Today the blue stripes or bands on the *tallit* are a reminder of the single blue thread used in each of the four tassels. No longer used today, this blue thread was part of the Torah command to include "a cord of blue." Some interpreters say blue was used because it is the color of the Mediterranean Sea, whereas others say it is the color surrounding the throne of God. Some choose a *tallit* with *black* stripes for one of several possible reasons. First, the original recipe for making the blue dye was lost with the inhabitants of Akko (Acre) in Israel. Second, when the Romans occupied Palestine, only royalty was permitted to wear the color blue. Third, it is appropriate for mourning since the destruction of the Temple in 70 AD.

The method of dyeing the threads sky blue was a secret of the people of Acre, Palestine (now Israel). After the dispersion, the art was forgotten by the Jews of the *Diaspora* (dispersion) and in view of this fact, white is used exclusively for the *tsitzit*.

The Talmud says: "Whoever has t'fillin on his head and arm, tsitzit on his garments and a mezuzah on his door, gives assurance that he will not commit sins." This statement brings to mind the desire of the Psalmist David who declared to the Lord: *"Thy word have I hid in mine heart, that I might not sin against thee"* (Psalm 119:11).

Since the Jewish religious responsibilities of the home and synagogue are upheld by the man, he feels highly honored of God and he voices his appreciation in his daily devotions. These devotions are taken from the traditional Jewish prayer book called *Siddur* founded by Talmudic Rabbis and literally means "order" or "arrangement." His prayer , while he wears the *Tallit, T'fillin* and *Yarmulkah (Kipa)* is as follows:

> *"Blessed art Thou, O Lord our God, King of the Universe, who hath not created me a **slave**. Blessed art Thou, O Lord our God, King of the Universe, who hath not created me a **heathen**. Blessed art Thou, O Lord our God, King of the Universe, who hath not created me a **woman**."*

But in Messiah, there is no distinction between the sexes regarding salvation. Both male and female come through the Door into the Sheepfold, receive the same commandments and inherit the same promises. Thank God, He created us in the Messiah to be *one* (equal) in Him!

One does not have to wear a special kind of clothing or comb the hair a certain way in order to reveal devotion to the Lord. Man looks on the outward appearance, it is true, and judges that person as to his or her spirituality by that; but God sees the attitude of the heart and this it is which determines the approval or disapproval of the Lord and the individual's final reward! Believers are under no obligation to don the *tallit* because Yeshua Messiah fulfilled this law. Instead, believers are asked to put on several other things, including the new man created in righteousness, the whole armor of God, kindness, humility of mind, meekness, longsuffering, and charity. Paul said it best: *"For as many of you as have been baptized into Christ* [Messiah] *have **put on** Christ* [Messiah]*"* (Galatians 3:27).

The *tallit* of the orthodox Jew is worn every morning throughout the year, with the exception of one; i.e., the ninth of Av, the *fast* of the 5th month (see Zechariah 7:3, 5 and 8:19), generally occurring in the month of July, which commemorates the first and second Temples. Instead of wearing it this day at morning service, it is worn before the sunset of the day, sometimes during the afternoon.

Before the garment is put on the worshiper, the fringes at the four corners are gathered, and the first two verses of Psalm 104, are repeated. A prayer is then offered, in which is repeated the text containing the words: *"That they make them fringes in the borders of their garments throughout their generations."*

Prayer for putting on the *tallit*:

> "I am here enwrapping my body in the fringed robe, so shall be enwrapped my soul and the 248 members of my body and the 365 of my veins with the light of the fringes which amount to 613. And even as I cover myself with a tallit in this world, so may I be worthy of a robe of the learned and of a beauteous tallit in the world to come, in the Garden of Eden. And through the commandment of the fringes shall be delivered my soul, and my spirit, and my prayer from outside evils; and the tallit may spread its wings over them, and deliver them as an eagle that stirreth up her nest, that fluttereth over her young. And may be counted the commandment of the

~ 38 ~

fringes before the most Holy, blessed be He, as if I had fulfilled it with all its details, and its particulars, and its meanings, and the 613 commandments that depend on it. Amen! Selah!"[14]

The garment is then thrown over the shoulders and the following prayer is offered:

> "Blessed art Thou, O Lord our God, King of the Universe, who hath sanctified us in His commandments, and hath commanded us to be covered with the fringes."

When this is done, verses 7 and 10 of the 36th Psalm are repeated. It will be observed from these latter Scriptures that the people regard the wearing of this garment as being associated with *receiving righteousness* (Isaiah 61:10), for it is written in the Scriptures: *"... it shall be our righteousness ... if we observe to do all these commandments"* (Deuteronomy 6:25). Consequently the pious Pharisee was very particular in having a *large* garment, sufficient to cover himself, with very wide borders, because the *larger* the garment, and the *greater* the border, *the more the righteousness*.

> "Thus this very object that the Lord designed to use as a means to a great end, was perverted from its purpose, and substituted for the Creator Himself! It is not at all surprising then, that the Saviour should say: *'Except your righteousness shall exceed the righteousness of the scribes and Pharisees, ye shall in no case enter into the kingdom of heaven'* (Matthew 5:20). They might have known, from the words of the prophets, that true righteousness was not found in the wearing of those objects, but in Him 'Jehovah, our righteousness'."   —Selected

Yeshua (Jesus), the Messiah is the very Righteousness of God. He observed all the commandments God gave to the Jewish people. At all times He wore a garment which covered His entire body and in its four corners was the ribbon of blue with the fringes. (It is not the garment, the *tallit* itself, but the *fringes* in the four corners that is *biblical*.) We find this recorded in Matthew 9:20 where the woman *"touched the hem* [border, corner, quarter, wing] *of His garment"* and was healed. The Greek word for "hem" (*kraspedon*) in this instance indicates that it was a *tassel* or *fringe* that she "grasped." She knew this was a true Israelite who wore the *tzitzit* in the hem of His garment without being hypocritical. It was a reminder of God's covenant of healing and His Word which healed Israel (cf. Psalm 105:37, 107:20). She acted on her faith in *Yahweh Rapha,* "The Lord That Healeth" (Exodus 15:26) and she was made whole (Mark 5:29).

---

[14]*Prayer Book For the New Year*, with a revised English translation by the Rev. Dr. A.Th. Philips, p. 20.

In the corners, borders, hem, quarters, or "wings" of Messiah's garment were the fringes or tassels which God had commanded to be there (Numbers 15:38-40). They were to bring to the remembrance of Israel the Law of God, His Word. This Jewish woman must have known the law and promise of God that there would be healing in Messiah's "wings"; *i.e.*, the wings (corners, hem) of His garment!

"But unto you that fear my name shall the Sun of righteousness arise with healing in his wings; ..." (Malachi 4:2).

The "Sun of Righteousness" refers to Israel's Messiah as we read in the words of the Jewish prophet, Jeremiah:

*"Behold, the days come, saith the LORD, that I will raise unto David a **righteous** Branch, and a King shall reign and prosper, and shall execute judgment and justice in the earth. In his days Judah shall be saved, and Israel shall dwell safely: and this is his name whereby he shall be called, **THE LORD OUR RIGHTEOUSNESS**"* (Jeremiah 23:5-6).

The woman with the disease could have grasped the garments' borders (which had the fringes with the blue ribbon) of other Jewish men standing nearby but she "grasped" the sacred fringe and the cord in *Messiah's* garment. In other words, she touched *Him who is the fulfillment of the Word* or Law, the power, glory, and righteousness of God! She believed and accepted the promise of "healing in His wings" and she was made whole! *The result of reaching out to "grasp hold" of His Word* (the borders of His garment where were the tsitzit representing His Word) *is still the same today! Praise the Lord!*

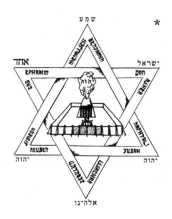

Tabernacle in center of the Mogen David
surrounded by the *Shema.*

_____

The Hebrew letters are to be read clockwise from "Shema" at the top.

THE SHEMA (God is One)

"Hear O Israel, the LORD our God is one [LORD]" (Deuteronomy 6:4).

The Chief Rabbi of the British Empire described the "Shema" as:

> "... at once the quintessential embodiment of all our philosophy, as well as chief among Israel's contributions to the everlasting truths of religion. The first prayer of innocent child-lips, the last confession of the dying, the Shema has been the watchword and rallying cry of a hundred generations in Israel. By it were they welded into one brotherhood to do the will of their Father who is in heaven. The reading of the Shema has, in Rabbinic phrase, clothed Israel with invincible lion-strength, and endowed him with the double-edged word of the spirit against the unutterable terrors of his long night of exile."
>
> —Rabbi Joseph H. Hertz (1872-1946)

The Shema receives its name from the first Hebrew word ("Sh'ma" or "Hear") in Deuteronomy 6:4. It is evident that this creed was used during and even before the New Testament era. The *Mishnah* (*Tamid* 4:3; 5:1) indicates that it was used before CE (AD) 70. Later the passages, Deuteronomy 6:5-9; 11:13-21 and Numbers 15:37-41 were added to the Sh'ma. According to the Mishnah (in *Berakhot* 1:1-2) which recites the passage in Deuteronomy 6:7, the Shema was to be recited twice a day, morning and evening: "when you lie down and when you rise."

Messiah knew the Shema and considered it with high regard. We learn this by His answer to a question about the *greatest commandment*:

> *"And one of the scribes came, and having heard them reasoning together, and perceiving that he had answered them well, asked him, Which is the first commandment of all? And Jesus answered him, The first of all the commandments is, **Hear, O Israel; The Lord our God is one Lord:**"* (Mark 12:28-29).

Then He continued:

> *"And thou shalt love the Lord thy God with all thy heart, and with all thy soul, and with all thy mind, and with all thy strength: this is the first commandment. And the second is like, namely this, Thou shalt love thy neighbour as thyself. There is none other commandment greater than these"* (Mark 12:30-31).

"Known as the *shema*, this is one of the most crucial Old Testament texts for the foundational teachings of both Jesus and Judaism. A careful investigation of early sources suggests that Deuteronomy 6:4 must have been the first portion from the Hebrew Bible that

Jesus committed to memory [in His humanity]. According to the Babylonian Talmud (*Sukkah* 42a), Jewish boys were taught this biblical passage as soon as they could speak. Since the Talmud specifies that 'the father must teach him' [the son], we may confidently assume that Joseph, Jesus' earthly [that is, in the eyes of the law, His *legal*] father, was responsible for fulfilling this task."[15]

I remember my orthodox Jewish grandfather teaching me how to pronounce the *Shema* as he would recite it every day, morning and night. With great wonderment I would repeat after him: "Sh'ma, Yisroel, Adonay Elohaynu Adonay **Echad**!" The word "echad" was held longer than the other words. He said it was very, very important that he did this, and I learned later the reason for him to do so. The Talmud (*Berach,* fol. 13, col. 2.) states: "Whosoever prolongs the utterance of the word *one* [Echad] shall have his days and years prolonged for him." (A Jewish saying to the effect that "he who utters the *Shema* is as if he held a two-edged sword." The phrase is common in classical writers.)

I also learned that Moses Maimonides, in the Thirteen Credos of Judaism which he formulated in the 12th Century of the Common Era, described God as *yachid* or absolutely *one* only. Yet my grandfather recited the Shema *from the Scriptures* that God is *Echad*, one made-up-of-parts, a compound unity. Simply: *Yachid* means *singularity* and *echad* means *unity*.

Another surprise I noticed upon hearing my *Zeydeh* ("grandfather") pronounce the Shema was that he called God by the Hebrew title "Adonai" which is a *plural* word and, although it has the meaning of *Lord*, it is not the name which is written in the Hebrew Scriptures of Deuteronomy 6:4! The Hebrew letters of the name written in two places of the Sh'ma are "Yod, Hei, Vav (or Wau) Hei" יהוה (JHVH, YHWH) which is the personal, *singular* Name translated into the English as "Jehovah," but more correctly "Yahweh." (See Chapter VI, *More Things Jewish*, "The Sacred Tetragrammaton," page 341.) Thus the *Shema* as translated and transliterated into English from the Hebrew would be: "Hear, O Israel, Yehovah our Elohim, Yehovah is one Elohim" or "Yehovah (Yahweh) our Elohim is a united Yehovah (Yahweh)." The words, Yehovah and God, have a singular and plural meaning. (A crude illustration of a word being singular and used also as plural is our English word, "sheep.")

---

[15]Marvin R. Wilson, *Our Father Abraham*, p. 123.

After becoming a believer in Messiah Jesus I learned a very interesting description of the word *Echad* in Gematria (numerology). It has **13** as the number value of the Hebrew letters *aleph, cheth, dalet* אחד (spells *echad*). א is also the number 1, ח is also the number 8. ד is also the number 4, all these adding up to **13**. According to Jewish belief there are **13** attributes of God. Torah is interpreted by means of **13** principles of Talmudic logic; Bar Mitzvah age is **13**; the poem "Who Knows One"? of the Passover Seder has **13** stanzas, ending with the **13** divine attributes!

Rabbi Simeon Ben Joachi commented on the Shema of Deuteronomy 6:4:

> "Come and see the mystery of the word Elohim: there are three degrees and each degree is by itself alone, and yet they are all one, and joined together in one, and are not divided from each other."

We see here a very good description and definition of the singularity and plurality of the *triune* nature of God!

The *Zohar*, a commentary on the Pentateuch which first appeared in the 13th Century of the Common Era, and one of the Jews' most sacred books, comments on the passage in Deuteronomy 6:4. It states:

> "Why is there need of mentioning the name of God three times in this verse? The first Jehovah is the name of the Father above. The second is the stem of Jesse, the Messiah who is to come from the family of Jesse through David. And the third one is the way which is below [meaning One who shows us the way] and these three are [*Echad*] one."

The word for *God* is used three times in the Shema. Jews use the *plural* form each time. The second word for *God* is *Elohenu*, "our God." The *nu* at the end of the word means "our" and is attached to a word to indicate that the word is *plural* since this is correct Hebrew grammar. So Moses, who wrote the Shema at God's command, knew and believed that God is a plurality! Even the Talmud, commenting on the verses in Jeremiah 23:5-7, says, "Three there are who are called by the Name God."

> "God's Names reveal the different aspects of His nature. There are not only three as in this Biblical text (Deuteronomy 6:4), but over thirty. Therefore, **Elohim** refers to the creative Deity; **Yehovah** (*Yahweh*), the covenant Deity; **El Shaddai**, the nourishing aspect of Deity; **Yehovah Yeraphah**, the healing aspect of Deity; **Ruach Elohim**, the empowering aspect; and **Yeshua**, the saving aspect (Jesus).
>
> ... All of the aspects are characteristics and/or manifestations of the one true God. There are many other names of God, revealing other aspects. An analogy would be H_2O (water) which has the

capacity to manifest itself in *three* different forms under widely varying conditions: as a *liquid* in water, as a *solid* in ice, and as a *gas* in vapor or steam. But when reduced to its ultimate, it is all H_2O. So, it is not 1+1+1=3, but 1x1x1=1. There is only ONE God in heaven, and His name is YHWH (*Yahweh*), but this one God has the capacity to manifest Himself in many different ways, on many different occasions, and for many different reasons, even to the point of taking on human flesh in order to do something for man that man could not do for himself." (Author of quote is unknown.)

As stated before: There are two words for "one" in the Hebrew language: *echad* and *yachid*. "Echad" is a compound unity ("one-made-up-of-parts") meaning several, or many in one. "Echad" is from a primitive root meaning "to unify" as, "to collect one's thoughts" and means properly, "united." *Yachid* is interpreted to mean *absolutely* and *indivisibly one*. "Yachid" is used forcefully in the Bible as an absolute one and is found twelve times in the *Tanakh* (OT) but *not once is it used to denote the **unity** of God*!

Here is an important lesson in Hebrew grammar: *Singular* nouns, verbs or adjectives must be accompanied by nouns, verbs or adjectives in the *singular* number. Likewise, Hebrew nouns, verbs or adjectives that are *plural* in number must be accompanied by nouns, verbs, or adjectives that are *plural* in number. Although plural in form, when the word for *God* is mentioned it is constantly accompanied by verbs and adjectives in the *singular*. In the first verse of Genesis, the verb *create* is singular, yet the word for *God* ("Elohim") is plural (see Genesis 1:26; 3:22; 11:7; Isaiah 6:8; Genesis 2:24)! In contrast, when the word is used of *heathen* gods, *plural* verbs and adjectives are used!

Notice these examples of compound unity: "***one*** cluster of grapes"(*eschol echad*) "the congregation was assembled as ***one*** man" (*ish echad*). Uni-plurality can be illustrated many ways: as, day and night, *one* day (*yom echad*); man and wife, *one* flesh (*bosor echad*); the shell, the white, the yolk of an egg, *one* egg; and when God (plural) said, "Let **us** make man in **our** image," He made him a *trinity*: spirit, soul, and body.

Some illustrations of Plurality in oneness are in the following suggestions:

1. Water is one substance and yet it manifests itself as a solid, a liquid, and a vapor.
2. A fork may have three prongs, yet it is a unity.
3. Every human being is a tri-unity composed of body, soul and spirit.
4. The triangle has three sides and yet it is a unity; and the Star of David (*Mogen David*)

Triangle figure with *yod* (ʾ), initial letter of God's name, "Yahweh" with its two triangles interlocked represents the Messiah who links the tri-unity of God with the tri-unity of man.

5. The Hebrew letter "shin" 𝕎 illustrates the tri-unity of God.

"To have a unity in the connotation of 'echad,' there must be a plurality, for example: When God made Adam and Eve, He stated that they shall be 'echad,' that is, a unity composed of two persons."

The Hebrew Scriptures describe the Godhead as composed of three co-eternal and co-equal Persons who are the same in substance, but distinct in subsistence. This does not imply that there are *three* Gods since God is described as a *Unity* (*Echad*). The way we can best express God's Unity is not 1+1+1=3, but 1x1x1 equals *one*. There are three names for God which include these three Persons: *Elohim*, *Adonai*, and *El Shaddai*. These names are plural. "Elohim" is used 2,500 times. "Adonai" is used 90 times. "El Shaddai" is used 48 times.

In Isaiah 48:16 we see all three persons of the Godhead:

*"Come ye near unto me, hear ye this; I have not spoken in secret from the beginning; from the time that it was, there am I: and now the Lord **GOD**, and **his Spirit**, hath sent **me**."*

In Isaiah 63:8-10–again all three Persons:

*"For he said, Surely they are my people, children that will not lie: so he was their **Saviour**. In all their affliction he was afflicted, and **the angel of his presence** saved them: in his love and in his pity he redeemed them; and he bare them, and carried them all the days of old. But they rebelled, and vexed **his holy Spirit**: ..."*

It is thrilling to note that the Hebrew letter *sheen* (shin, 𝕎), initial letter of the name for God (*Shaddai*) was formerly taken by the Jews to represent the manner of divine existence. It is composed of *three* perpendicular strokes, with *one* to unite them! In pronouncing the priestly or Aaronic benediction (Numbers 6:24-26) the Rabbis today lift their hands in blessing over the people. The hands are held with the fingers of each hand depicting three strokes, showing the letter *sheen*, which in turn represents the name of God.

As we have noted, the letter *sheen* is composed of three perpendicular strokes with one to unite them. How vividly the hands of the Rabbi (of the following illustration) in the form of the *sheen* 𝕎 symbolizes the name of God and also the Trinity, three in one, one in three! (Very striking indeed is the Hebrew language for practically all Hebrew words are built around a *3-letter root!*)

The Trinity of God

"God is a Trinity, that is, He is both one and three. But remember, He is not both one and three in the same respect. There are many things right around us that are one in one respect and three in another respect. So God is one as to His essence of being, but three as to hypotheses, persons, and modes of life and functioning ... Have you ever thought about it that in a very inner sense the human mind has a triune constitution: It is made up of the Intellect, the Sensibility, and the Will, that is, three minds, but only one mind. More than that, the mind is a unitary entity, and is not made up of parts as a lump of material

Rabbi With "Shin" Formation in His Hands.

substance is. Therefore, the Intellect is the whole mind, and the Will is the whole mind; each and all are identically of the same substance. Each in substance is equal to all, and yet all are equal to each. Thus we see again that an entity can be, in a very mysterious and profound way, one in one respect and three in another. So with the Triune God. Only God is personally Triune, not only functionally."

–Dr. Leander S. Keyser

God appeared as man in Genesis 18. There we see plainly the idea of the Tri-unity of the Lord, that is: God manifested in three different personalities. In the first verse we read: *"And the LORD* [Jehovah] *appeared unto him in the plains of Mamre,"* but when Abraham looked, *"lo **three men** stood by him,"* and although there were *three* persons, yet in verse 3 he addressed them in the *singular*, and said, *"My **Lord** (not lords) if now I have found favour in **thy** sight ..."* In this scene we notice that Jehovah appeared to Abraham as three persons. In other words, the Jehovah who appeared to Abraham and the three men that Abraham saw when he looked up were one and the same!

The Shamrock

St. Patrick gives an explanation of the Triune God. He said that God, the Father; God, the Son; and God, the Holy Spirit were Three, yet One and used the shamrock to illustrate the lesson. There are three separate leaves on the stem, yet these three are one! The New Testament relates this truth: *"For there are three that bear record in heaven, the Father, the Word, and the Holy Ghost: and these three are one"* (1 John 5:7).

The threefold constitution of *man* proclaims the Tri-personal God who created him in His own image. The Shema, expressing the Tri-unity of the Godhead, precedes the command calling upon man's threefold nature: spirit (heart), soul, and might (body) to love his Triune God! (Deuteronomy 6:5).

The *Zohar* discusses the union expressed in the *Shema* as follows:

> *"Hear, O Israel, YHVH Elohenu YHVH is one."* These three are one. How can the three Names be one? Only through the perception of Faith: in the vision of the Holy Spirit, in the beholding of the hidden eyes alone. The mystery of the audible voice is similar to this, for though it is one yet it consists of three elements–fire, air, and water, which have, however, become one in the mystery of the voice. Even so it is with the mystery of the threefold Divine manifestations designated by YHVH Elohenu YHVH–three modes which yet form one unity."[16]

The above illustration is the reproduction of a painting by the artist, Eugene Noth. It represents a venerable rabbi engaged in a study of the Talmud.

THE TALMUD

The Talmud, from *lomad*, "to teach" ("instruction" in Chaldee) is a code of laws as well as a record of Rabbinical discussions and decisions pertaining to theology, exegesis, philosophy, natural science, medical learning, ethics, political and domestic economy, etc. as these were understood during a period of 1,000 years after the Jews returned from the Babylonian exile. It is a massive compilation of 63 *massektoth* ("little books" called *tractates*). This enormous collection of literature covers subjects as diverse as biblical law, medicine, agriculture, and philosophy. It is the physical embodiment of what is called the "oral law"—a compilation of the traditions regarding Jewish

---

[16]*Zohar, Exodus,* section 43a-43b.

practices that developed over centuries and was handed down orally from generation to generation.

The Talmud consists of two main parts: the Mishna (written in Hebrew around 200 AD) and the Gemara (written in Aramaic around 400 AD in Palestine and around 500 AD in Babylonia). The Gemara is commentary to the text of the earlier Mishna. These are transcripts of symposiums that went on by some estimates, for 1,200 years, from the Fifth Century before the Christian era to the Eighth century AD. More than 2,000 scholar-Rabbi-sages conducted these debates, which were held in the great academies of the Holy Land and of Babylon. The Talmud is an almanac, a casebook, a reference encyclopedia. An English language translation runs to 35 volumes. (Interesting note: "Several of the ancient Rabbis ... including some of those who created the Talmud, traced their ancestry to *Gentiles* who had been converted to Judaism.")[17]

A Few Teachings From the Talmud

✡"The Torah begins with acts of loving and ends with kindness; it begins with God clothing Adam and Eve, and ends with God burying Moses ...The beginning and end of the Torah is performing acts of loving kindness."

✡"No more than 25 children shall be in a class."

✡"A man betrays his character through three things: his tipping, his tippling and his temper."

✡"The Lord did not create woman from man's head, so that he can command her; nor from man's foot, so that she would be his slave. God made Eve from Adam's side so that woman will always be nearest man's heart."

✡"What is hateful to you, never do to a fellowman: that is the whole law–all the rest is commentary."

✡"Give every man the benefit of the doubt."

✡"All's well that ends well."

Oral and Written Law

Most (unconverted) Jews believe that Moses received two laws on Mount Sinai, one was the *written* law, the Torah; the other was given *orally* which was **repeated** by word of mouth from Moses to Joshua, from Joshua to the elders, from the elders to the prophets, etc. as is stated in the Talmud itself. (*Pirke Aboth* 1:1. "Pirke Aboth" means "Chapters of the Fathers" or "Ethics of the Fathers.")

---

[17]Rabbi Morris N. Kertzer, *What is a Jew?*, p. 175.

It is said that the prophets handed it down orally to the "men of the Great Synagogue" and on until Ezra, when it became the possession of the spiritual leaders of that time. Rabbi Hillel*, who lived from 70 BC to 10 AD), was president of the Sanhedrin, and began to compile the Oral law so that it could be written. The President, as the 71st member of the Sanhedrin, was always the High Priest. He laid down six or seven rules for the interpretation of the Scriptures which became the foundation of Rabbinical hermeneutics and which, no doubt, was used by the Pharisees in the days of Messiah Jesus. Jesus referred to this Oral law as "tradition of the elders" in Matthew 15:1-9 and Mark 7:1-13. (In contrast to the Oral law, the True Law of God was 1,500 years old when Jesus was born.)

Since the Temple with its order of priesthood had been destroyed, there needed to be some source of authority to continue the practice of Judaism among the scattered Jewish people. Therefore a group of 148 Jewish scholars called *Tannaim* ("repeaters" or "teachers") gathered in the ancient city of Jabne, located near the present city of Lydda in Israel. By their discussions, debates and decisions they wrote down that which had been orally handed down over almost six centuries. (The *Tannaim* were scholars from the Mishnaic period up to 200 CE [AD]). The writing of the *Tannaim* was published about 200 AD under the leadership of Rabbi Judah the Prince (Judah ha-Nasi). The written form is called the *Mishnah* meaning "repetition," "duplicate" and is considered the Second Law. It was the Oral Law of the Pharisees and almost universally accepted as the authoritative legal code of Judaism.

However, since the Mishnah was not understood and there was a need for adapting it to new times and to the changing circumstances of life, a group of several hundred Rabbis, called *Amoraim* ("expounders"), scholars from the Talmudic period 200-500 CE [AD], developed the *Gemara* (Aramaic for "completion") which is a commentary on the Mishnah. The Oral law written down is called the *Mishnah* and is stated first, the commentary and application or the *Gemara* is then stated below it. This combination (Mishnah-Gemara) composed the Talmud which was completed in Babylon about 400 AD. There are two Talmuds: the Jerusalem Talmud (*Yerushalmi*) written in Jerusalem and a Babylonian Talmud (*Babli*) written in Babylon. Along with their work on the Mishnah and Gemara the Tannaim and Amoraim developed a running commentary on the actual text of the Old Testament. This is called the *Midrash*, the name coming from the Hebrew word meaning "to study" or "to investigate."

*Hillel was the grandfather of Gamaliel, who was the teacher of the Apostle Paul.

The Six Orders of the Mishnah

The First Order: Zera'im (Seeds: The Laws of Agriculture)

Berakhot (Blessings)
Pe'ah (Edge of the Field)
Demai (Doubtful Crops)
Kila'yim (Diverse Kinds)
Shevi'it (The Seventh Year [*Shemitah*])
Terumot (Heave-Offerings)
Ma'aserot (Tithes)
Ma'aser Sheni (Second Tithe)
Hallah (Dough Offering)
Orlah (Fruit of the Trees)
Bikkurim (First-Fruits)

The Second Order: Mo'ed (Festivals)

Shabbat (Sabbath)
Eruvin (Sabbath Travel Regulations)
Pesahim (Passovers)
Shekalim (Temple Taxes)
Yoma (The Day [of Atonement])
Sukkah (Booth)
Betzah (An Egg)
Rosh Hashanah (New Year Observance)
Ta'anit (Fast Day[s])
Megillah (The Scroll [of Esther])
Mo'ed Katan (Mid-Festival Days)
Hagigah (Festival Sacrifice)

The Third Order: Nashim (Women)

Yevamot (Sisters-in-law)
Ketuvot (Marriage Contracts)
Nedarim (Vows)
Nazir (The Nazirite-vow)
Sotah (The Suspected Adulteress)
Gittin (Divorces)
Kiddushin (Marriage)

The Fourth Order: Nezikin (Civil and Criminal Law)

Bava Kama (The First Gate)
Bava Metzi'a (The Middle Gate)
Bava Batra (The Last Gate)
Sanhedrin (The High Court)
Makkot (Punishment by Flogging)
Shevu'ot (Oaths)
Eduyot (Testimonies)
Avodah Zarah (Idolatry)
Horayot (Erroneous Decisions)

The Fifth Order: Kodashim (Sacred Things)
Zevahim (Animal Sacrifices)
Menahot (Flour Offerings)
Hullin (Unconsecrated Animals)
Bekhorot (Firstborn)
Arakhim (Evaluations)
Temurah (Exchanges of Sacrificial Cattle)
Keritot (Divine Punishment)
Me'ilah (Inadvertent Sacrilege)
Tamid (Daily Sacrifice)
Middot (Measurements)
Kinnim (Bird Offerings)

The Sixth Order: Tohorot (Ritual Purity)
Kelim (Vessels)
Oholot (Tents)
Nega'im (Leprosy)
Parah (The Red Cow)
Tohorot (Cleanliness)
Mikva'ot (Ritual Baths)
Niddah (The Menstruating Woman)
Makshirin (Prerequisites for Non-Kashrut)
Zavim (Bodily Discharges in Illness)
Tevul Yom (Post-Immersion Uncleanliness)
Yadaim (Uncleanliness of Hands)
Uktzin (Stalks and Ritual Uncleanliness)

—The Mishnah, Oral Teachings of Judaism
Selected and Translated by Eugene J. Lipman

The Shulkhan Arukh (Shulchan Oruch)

Since it was difficult to understand, Rabbi Joseph B.E. Caro devoted years of his life to summarizing, abridging, and codifying the Talmud for the common man. In 1564 he published his work which he called *Shulkhan Arukh* ("the prepared table"). However, there are many laws contained in the Shulkhan Arukh which have been added to the laws found in the Talmud, for example: There are 14 laws regulating the lighting of the Sabbath candles, 21 relating to the fringes on the Tallit and 26 relating to the prayer shawl itself, the Tallit. There are laws covering every conceivable thing in daily life, even as to the manner of walking, etc. Directions for the practice of present-day Judaism in the rituals and ceremonies for the holidays, Sabbaths, the Passover Seder (Table Setting), Weddings, etc. are all found in the *Shulkhan Arukh*.

Talmudical Lore in the Light of the Bible

Reverend Ernest H. Cassutto

Since my student days while preparing for the Gospel ministry in Holland I have always been interested in the Talmud, majoring in Rabbinics and in the Talmud. My New Testament professor, Dr. Van Unnik, assigned to me the task of comparing the sayings of the Lord Jesus with the sayings of the rabbis, as well as to translate and explain the Talmud treatise "Yoma," which deals with the Day of Atonement.

In dealing with the Talmud, the Christian must be careful not to give needless offense to the Jews through harsh criticism or outright condemnation. The Word of God enjoins us: *"Give none offence, neither to the Jews, nor to the Gentiles, nor to the church of God"* (1 Corinthians 10:32).

I would further recommend that the Christian worker among the Jewish people, if at all possible, become acquainted with the Talmud, so that he may have an idea of its teachings and be able to confront the views of the ancient rabbis with the message of the Word of God. Such knowledge would be particularly helpful in bringing Jews of an orthodox background to a saving knowledge of the Lord Jesus Christ.

To begin with I would like to make this foundational statement: *The Crown of the Old Testament, which the Jews call the Tenach, is not the Talmud, but the New Testament. The fulfillment of the Old Testament is not the Talmud, but the New Testament!*

It will be the purpose of this treatise to prove the above statement. To accomplish our task we shall use various statements from the Talmud to confirm the truth of the Gospel and the fact that Jesus is the Messiah of Israel. In this way we shall see the positive Bible message standing out in bright contrast to the dim twilight of the Talmud.

I would like to express my sincere thanks to Mr. Hirsch Blum who kindly verified for me all Talmud quotations in The Amsterdam Library, in the Netherlands.

The positive Bible message is based on these three basic propositions:

1. Man is sinful. This is the doctrine of sin.
2. Man obtains atonement through the shed blood of our Saviour and the Cross of Christ. This is the doctrine of grace and redemption.
3. Man keeps the commandments of God after he is saved, as an expression of his gratitude. At least he tries to do so, for in reality no one can keep the Law. Man's good works are fruits of the Holy Spirit, the result of his regeneration. Salvation is not the reward or the result

of good works, for there is no righteousness in man. But after we are saved through the righteousness of Christ, we are sanctified by the Spirit of God working in our hearts so that we may bring glory to Him.

Now that we have made this introduction let us examine the teaching of the Talmud as compared with the message of the Bible.

The Doctrine of Sin

The average Jew denies that man is sinful. He regards sin as the result of "*yetzer ha-rah,*" man's "evil inclination" or natural passions which in themselves are neither good nor bad, but become evil through the improper use which man makes of them. This is the way in which the orthodox Jewish scholar, Solomon Schechter, explains the meaning of "yetzer ha-rah," in his book "Studies in Judaism," volume I, chapter 15, pages 242-263. To the question, how is it that man makes improper use of his natural passions, Schechter provides no answer. Yet the Talmud is aware of original sin in man. And here are some quotations to support this which should be helpful to convict the Jews of sin.

Sifre 138b: "Eve was brought to her fall by the *'Nachash Ha-Kadmoon,'* the serpent of old." The pagans are called "The disciples of the ancient serpent" (see Revelation 12:9; 20:2).

Tanchuma Beresit 8: "Harsh is the evil tongue, which brought death to the first man."

Shemoth R.31: "There is no man without sin, and no creature which does not stand guilty before God."

Bereshit R.9, commenting on Job 3:17: "... even the pious ones (or: 'Saints') are, until their last breath, under the power of sin. Only after they die do they come to rest and are free from it."

Debarim R. 9: "Man, thou diest because of the sin of the first man, which brought death in this world."

Pesikta 161b: "God does not leave one debt of anyone unpaid, either here or in the hereafter."

All this confirms the Biblical message which convicts us of sin.

The Doctrine of Atonement, Redemption, Salvation

It is on the subject of atonement and salvation that the Talmud is singularly lacking in light as compared with the positive Biblical message of full salvation in the Messiah.

The Talmud teaches no atonement. It does teach "Teshuva," that is "repentance" (literally–"return to God"). The Talmud considers "repentance" as one of the good works whereby one can win God's favor. Since the Talmud rejects Christ and His atoning death, the

Talmud knows only one way—establishing one's own righteousness (salvation through works). The result is that the Talmud has no definite assurance of salvation. For who can establish his own righteousness?

The Talmud teaches these six means of attaining righteousness through which one can earn eternal life with God:

1. Torah (The Law)
2. Aboda (Ceremonies)
3. Gemiluth Chasadim (Charitable Deeds)
4. Tephilla (Prayer)
5. Teshuva (Repentance)
6. Tsedaka (literally "righteousness" but in reality, "giving of alms").

There is no need for a Mediator, nor for a Messiah. The fact of being a Jew inclines God to forgive one's sins, because of the covenant which God made with the Jewish people. The Jew provides his own atonement by being repentant.

Thus the Talmud teaches salvation through works, and eternal life through righteousness earned by man himself, denying God the glory and transferring it to man.

Nedarim 39b describes "Gemiluth Chasadim," charitable deeds to help the destitute, to feed and clothe the poor, to provide hospitality, to visit the sick, to help the immigrants, in short, works of love.

Sukka 49b says that "Gemiluth Chasadim," or "deeds of mercy" are more important than even Tsedaka ("righteousness"), because one can exercise Tsedaka by paying money, but the exercise of "Temiluth Chasadim" means personal effort and dedication.

By contrast the Bible teaches that since man is sinful, not one man can work out his own righteousness with God. We need a Mediator, who is both man, because man has sinned, and God, because only God could bear the wrath of His offended majesty and remove the curse of sin, thus bringing about perfect atonement. The Bible therefore denies salvation through works, and proclaims salvation by grace, through faith in the Messiah. "For by grace are ye saved through faith and that not of yourselves, it is the gift of God: not of works lest any man should boast" (Ephesians 2:8, 9).

Messiah in the Talmud and Messiah of the Bible
On the subject of the Messiah the Talmud is confused, because it does not know what to do with the message of the Tenach concerning the Messiah who was to come in humiliation to be our great Atonement. The Talmud teaches that the Messiah will come as a reward for

the repentance and penitence of the Jews, not to pay for their sins, but to rehabilitate the Jews as a glorious nation. The figure of the Messiah lacks the divine grace of a Saviour. *Pesikta* 163b: "If Israel, just for one day, will surrender in penitence and repentance, the redemption through Messiah will take place." *Shabbath* 118b: "If Israel would only celebrate two Sabbaths according to the ordinances, they would be redeemed right away."

But the Bible teaches that the Messiah will come as an act of love on God's part, to make atonement for our sins, as our Saviour.

"For God so loved the world, that He gave His only begotten Son, that whosoever believeth in him should not perish, but have everlasting life" (John 3:16). Biblical redemption is forgiveness of sins through atonement and the rebirth by the Holy Spirit. "But the fruit of the Spirit is love, joy, peace, longsuffering, gentleness, goodness, faith, meekness, temperance" (Galatians 5:22-23). There is no place in the Scriptures for "Moralism" but rather for the doctrine that good works are the fruit of the Spirit resulting from salvation wrought by Christ.

Neither does the Talmud know the redeeming power of the Blood of the Lamb. In the tract [Tractate] "Pesachim," (Passover) the slaughtering of the Passover Lamb and the sprinkling [striking] of its blood on the doorposts is mentioned as a historical fact, not as a symbol of the forgiveness of sins by the sacrifice of the Messiah. In the description of the Seder evening, or the Passover meal, the wine [fruit of the vine] is not mentioned as a symbol of the blood shed for the forgiveness of sins. Only the Lord made that clear to us when He took the cup, blessed it, and said, "Drink ye all of it, for this is my blood of the new testament, which is shed for many for the remission of sins" (Matthew 26:27).

The Negative and Positive Use of the Talmud

Now we face the problem: Should we condemn or attack the Talmud in our dealing with the Jews? The answer is definitely, no. Rather use the Talmud to lead the Jew to a better understanding of the New Testament as the fulfillment of the Old.

The Talmud can be used negatively and positively. *Negatively*, by asking the Jew: "What does the Talmud do with the blood in the Old Testament, as a prophecy of the blood of the Messiah, shed for our salvation?" We can point to the Bible which teaches us that there is only one way to be saved, by faith and God's grace in the Messiah, even as Isaiah prophesies so beautifully concerning Him:

"He was wounded for our transgressions, He was bruised for our iniquities: the chastisement of our peace was upon him; and with his stripes we are healed. All we like sheep have gone astray; we have turned every one to his own way; and the Lord hath laid on him the iniquity of us all" (Isaiah 53:5, 6).

Positively, we should use the Talmud to prove that Judaism does expect a Messiah and that he was to be a divine person. From there we may proceed to show that this Messiah is Jesus. We can also emphasize the love of Jesus who came as a Saviour, and not merely as a national hero.

The Person and Work of the Messiah in the Talmud
Here are some expectations of the Talmud with regard to the person and work of the Messiah:

Jalkuth Shimoni Bereshith 76: "The government, mentioned in Psalm 2 refers to the Messiah. Psalm 110:2, The scepter going out of Zion is the world government of the Messiah."

Bereshith R. 56 and 75: "Poor and riding a donkey in Zechariah 9:9 refers to the Messiah."

Bamidbar R. 13: "The Kingdom of the Messiah will be universal, without borders." Ditto 14: "The Messiah will be called God's First-born. God gives Him the right of the first born, even as He gave it to Jacob."

Aboda Zara 24b: "In the days of the Messiah all the Gentiles will count themselves as belonging to the Jews."

Shir R. 7:2: His (the Messiah) name will be the "Way" for "He will lead all the inhabitants of the world."

Midrash Tehillim on Psalm 87 "Those, who—from the Gentiles—will be brought to the Messiah, will be considered as being part of Israel. So much so, that many of them will be made into Levites and priests (according to Isaiah 66:21)."

Thus far the Talmud
Could we not use these references to build up an interest among the Jews in the Messiah? What a wonderful thing then, from there on to show the Jews:

1. That God has not chosen the Jews for their own sakes alone, but for the sake of the salvation of the whole world.
2. That God has chosen the Jews that the Messiah might be born from them to save the world.
3. That the Messiah was born of a virgin as our "Immanuel" according to the prophet Isaiah, who thus applied the word God (El) to the Messiah. Furthermore we may also point out that the name Jesus as derived from the Hebrew "Yeshua," means salvation.

The work of the Messiah is not only to make Gentiles into Jews, but to make Jew and Gentile into children of God, even as the Talmud says in *Bereshith* R.99, commenting on Genesis 49:10: "Shilo the nations will obey." We have to show the Jew that repentance is God's work in our heart. God works salvation on the Cross and salvation in our heart. We must point out that salvation means eternal life. We must also emphasize the glory of the believer when Messiah comes back to raise us from the dead.

The Resurrection and the Talmud

The Talmud does speak about the resurrection from the dead, yet considers resurrection as a reward earned by the Fathers (*Zechut Aboth*). Resurrection is a just reward for the righteous, rather than the consequence of salvation wrought by the Messiah through grace and applied to the believer by God through faith only.

Pesikta 200b: "Through the merit of the voluntary sacrifice of Isaac the Most Holy One, praised be His Name, will raise up the dead."

The resurrection, according to the Talmud, is a means in Messiah's hand to force the Gentiles to worship God (*Pesachim* 68a). But the Gospel looks upon the resurrection as being the consequence of the believer's spiritual resurrection from death and sin. So when Christ returns He will raise up the believer, body and soul, to enjoy everlasting life in Heaven in the glory of God.

Eternal Life, according to the Talmud, is a result of diligent study of the Torah (the law of God). *Mechilta* 24a: "The possession of the Torah is eternal life." The Bible, however, says that the Law cannot save us, that it convicts us of sin and the Spirit makes us accept Christ who gives us eternal life.

"For what the law could not do, in that it was weak through the flesh, God sending his own son in the likeness of sinful flesh, and for sin, condemned sin in the flesh"–Romans 8:3.

"He that believeth on the Son hath everlasting life"–John 3:36.

"This is life eternal, that they might know thee the only true God, and Jesus Christ, whom thou hast sent"–John 17:3.

The Talmud gives us no hope. For if eternal life is the study of the Law, and our delight is the Law, what good is that to us if we know, convicted of sin by the Law, that we cannot keep the Law and therefore have no propitiation or atonement for our sins?

It is here that we must contrast the Talmud with the positive Gospel message from 1 John 2:1, 2:

"My little children, these things write I unto you, that ye sin not. And if any man sin, we have an advocate with the Father, Jesus Christ the righteous: and He is the propitiation for our sins; and not for ours only, but also for the sins of the whole world."

When the Messiah returns in glory we know He will come back to bring us into the everlasting glory with the Father in the resurrection of our bodies united with our glorified souls.

John 14:2,3: "In my Father's house are many mansions ... I go to prepare a place for you ... I will come again, and receive you unto myself, that where I am, there ye may be also."

What a glorious assurance, what a glorious hope! The Talmud speaks of the "world to come"; the Bible, of "the everlasting life" which we can have here and now when we accept Christ. Indeed Jesus of Nazareth is he true Messiah, the true answer to the yearning of the Jewish soul for salvation (Zechariah 9:9; Jeremiah 23:5).

In the Talmud man makes the first step. Repentance is man's accomplishment. God's forgiveness is taken for granted. Man works out Eternal Life by studying the Law. But according to the Bible, it is God who makes the first step. It was God who called Adam first, searching for him in His mercy: "Adam where art thou?" God also took the first step when He gave His Son for our atonement.

In the Talmud (*Mishna Yoma*, last chapter) man atones for his sin through repentance and even through death. But the Bible tells us how God gave us the blood of Jesus for our atonement. Our hope is in the Lamb of God. Amen.

—Reverend Ernest H. Cassutto

CHAPTER TWO

JEWISH CUSTOMS AND CEREMONIES

Eastern Plaque

MIZRACH (East)

It is a Jewish custom to turn toward Jerusalem during the time of prayer (see 1 Kings 8:44-45). In order to indicate the direction in the home, Jews attach an artistic drawing or plaque of one or many colors on their Eastern wall. It is called "Mizrach" (originally meaning "the rising of the sun," or "east"), and always shows the name of God with the seven-branched lampstand in most cases. Jews who do not know in which direction is the East are required to direct their thoughts, at least, toward the city of Jerusalem. (The Bible contains 811 references to *Jerusalem*!) In Bible days, worshipers in the Temple in Jerusalem faced the Holy of Holies; those in the city itself turned toward the Temple Court; those in the rest of Palestine (Israel) faced in the direction of Jerusalem; those living outside of Palestine, turned toward the East. Note that when Daniel prayed three times a day to the Lord, he opened his windows toward Jerusalem (Daniel 6:10).

The Jewish National Anthem voices the love of the Jews for Palestine (Israel) and their hopes for habitation in that land. The name of this Anthem is "Hatikvah" meaning "The Hope." It was composed in 1878 by *Naphtali Herz Imber* and adopted by the Zionist movement (also by the colonists in the land) as the official song of Palestine in 1879. Since 1898 it was accepted throughout the Jewish world.

In 1957 an article appeared in the Los Angeles Herald-Express announcing an offer of $5,000 to any Israeli citizen who would compose a *new* national anthem for his country. The offer was made by George Jessel, popular U.S. Jewish entertainer and an avid backer of the State of Israel.

Mr. Jessel wanted an anthem which "will chorally crystallize the current anthem, (Hatikvah) which has nothing to do with the new democracy of Israel... We need an anthem to bespeak the new Israel as a reality, not when it was a dream," he declared. "The dream has been realized. The wish and the hope have been fulfilled," the entertainer said.

Undoubtedly Mr. Jessel had voiced the sentiments of his own Jewish people who, in the majority, are not considering the faith of their forefathers. They feel that their hopes are now realized in the establishment of the State of Israel. But only when their spiritual eyes are opened by the Spirit of God to behold their Messiah will their dreams and hopes come true!

Following is the English translation of several verses of "Hatikvah":

O, while within a Jewish breast
Beats true a Jewish heart,
And Jewish glances turning east
To Zion fondly dart.

(*chorus*)
O, then our hope—it is not dead,
Our ancient hope and true,
Again the sacred soil to tread
Where David's banners flew!

O, while the tears flow down apace
And fall like bounteous rain,
And to the fathers' resting place,
Sweeps on the mournful train.

And while upon our eager eye
Flashes the city's wall,
And for the wasted Sanctuary
The tear-drops trembling fall.

And while upon the highway there
Lowers the stricken gate
And from the ruins Zion's prayer
Upriseth passionate.

Hear, brothers mine, where'er ye be,
This truth by prophet won:
'Tis then our hope shall cease to be
With Israel's last son!

May the Lord speed the day when a new song will be placed in the mouths and hearts of the Jewish people–a song of praise to God in the Name of their Redeemer, Yeshua ha-Meshiach (Jesus, the Christ)!

JERUSALEM IS EAST

Jerusalem is one of the oldest settlements in the world being over 3,000 years in age. It is the spiritual center on the earth and is referred to in various terms over 1,037 times in the Scriptures. Prophecy tells that it will be the center of worship for the entire world:

Map of Jerusalem

"Yea, many people and strong nations shall come to seek the LORD of hosts in Jerusalem, and to pray before the LORD" (Zechariah 8:22).

The love for Jerusalem is admonished in the words of the Messiah:

"If I forget thee, O Jerusalem, let my right hand forget her cunning. If I do not remember thee, let my tongue cleave to the roof of my mouth; if I prefer not Jerusalem above my chief joy" (Psalm 137:5-6).

Jerusalem will one day be a praise to the Lord in the earth:

*"I have set watchmen upon thy walls, O **Jerusalem**, which shall never hold their peace day nor night: ye that make mention of the LORD, keep not silence. And give him no rest, till he establish, and till he make Jerusalem a **praise** in the earth"* (Isaiah 62:6-7).

God also commands prayer for this City of the great King:

*"Pray for the peace of **Jerusalem**: they shall prosper that love thee. Peace be within thy walls, and prosperity within thy palaces. For my brethren and companions' sakes, I will now say, Peace be within thee"* (Psalm 122:6-8).

THE ULTIMATE PRAYER
(Psalm 122:6)

Following is a message in outline form which my late husband, Rev. Walter (Wallie) Lascelle, gave in a Rock of Israel meeting at Philadelphia

The Kenneset (*Parliament*)-
Jerusalem, Israel

Church (Youth Center) April, 1975. Also this outline is included in my book "Jewish Love For a Gentile," pages 70-73.

Jerusalem, the City

Nineveh, Babylon, Rome! What are these cities, though ancient and commemorated, when compared with Jerusalem? Here is a city whose distinction is like the land upon which it is built. It is guaranteed for its luster in the past, but destruction and long-extended down-treading thereafter. It has a future which establishes its prestige as nothing less than the capitol of the world. This is the city of Solomon's Temple, the city of Jesus' solicitude [concern], the city of Gentile oppression, the city of the coming day of Christ enthroned!

Its Designations

2 Chronicles 6:6—God's City and for His Name. *Deuteronomy 12:5*

1 Kings 11:32—"Jerusalem, the city which I have chosen out of all the tribes of Israel."

Isaiah 66:20—"My holy mountain Jerusalem."

Its Disgrace

Jeremiah 19:8, 12, 15—"I will make this city desolate, and a hissing and even make this city as Tophet ... I will bring upon this city and upon all her towns all the evil that I have pronounced against it, because they have hardened their necks, that they might not hear my words."

Luke 21:24—"Jerusalem shall be trodden down of the Gentiles, until the times of the Gentiles be fulfilled."

Jerusalem has been besieged about 40 times, partially destroyed on 32 different occasions and two times totally destroyed.

Daniel 9:12—"For under the whole heaven hath not been done as hath been done upon Jerusalem."

Daniel 9:16—"For our sins, and for the iniquities of our fathers, Jerusalem and thy people have become a reproach to all that are about us."

Its Restoration

Isaiah 62:7—"Till he [God] make Jerusalem a praise in the earth."

Jeremiah 30:18-19—"... and the city shall be builded upon her own heap, and the palace shall remain after the manner thereof. And out of them shall proceed thanksgiving and the voice of them that make merry; and I will multiply them, and they shall not be few; I will also glorify them, and they shall not be small."

Ezekiel 48:35— "The name of the city from that day shall be, The LORD is there (*Jehovah-Shammah*)."

Revelation 20:9—"The beloved city."

Jeremiah 3:17—"At that time they shall call Jerusalem the throne of the Lord; and all the nations shall be gathered unto it, to the Name of the Lord, to Jerusalem."

(The following was added to his message, from which he made interesting comments and applications for those who attended the service.)

Why Pray for the Peace of Jerusalem?
*A Divine imperative or command
Simply because God says it, we ought to want to do it. *"If ye love me, keep my commandments"* (John 14:15). *"Why call ye me, Lord, and do not the things that I say?* (Luke 6:46).

*The resulting benefits
"They shall prosper that love thee [Jerusalem]*"* (Psalm 122:6).

*Enter into the Lord's heart feelings
Matthew 23:37—"O Jerusalem, Jerusalem ... how often would I have gathered thy children ..."

Luke 19:41—Jesus weeps over Jerusalem—His last heart-rending plea.

*For the Lord's imminent return, and all events preceding it
Jewish Evangelism—Church to be Jew and Gentile but **To the Jew First.**

Proof Jews are to be saved—Paul, Romans 9:1-2; 10:1 and 11:1.

First Church—All converts, Jews.

Jesus preached FIRST to the lost sheep of the House of Israel—Matthew 10:6.

—End of Message

SHALOM, JERUSALEM !

Although the name of Jerusalem itself incorporates the word "peace" ("City of Peace"), yet it is the one city in all the world which has been most often plundered. Historical records show that it has been besieged 47 times—completely brought to the ground 17 times. This, on the average, means that approximately once every 75 years it has been encompassed by enemy armies, and once every 200 years it has been left in ruins.

The greeting heard in the land of Israel today is "Shalom" which means "Peace." The natives and even the terrorists greet one another with this word, but it is a mockery there in that land; no word is so misused; for the Jew who knows not his Messiah has no true peace! There is no peace in Jerusalem, yet *God commands that we pray there shall be*! There is no security, no rest, no absence of fear in the heart of the Jew, yet we are exhorted by the Word of God to pray there shall be!

Prayers for the peace of Jerusalem will be answered when the Prince of Peace ("Sar Shalom") comes to earth. Prayers for peace to come to the heart of the Jew will be realized when he recognizes in Yeshua ha-Meshiach (Jesus, the Christ), his Prince of Peace, and accepts Him as the long-awaited Messiah of Israel and the Savior-Redeemer of mankind!

This peace which God desires for both Jew and Gentile was purchased at tremendous cost, even the precious life-blood of Messiah. Isaiah, the Jewish prophet, describes this:

> *"He* [Messiah] *was bruised for our iniquities, He was wounded for our transgression, the chastisement of our peace was upon him* [Messiah] *and by his bruises* [singular word in Hebrew] *was healing granted unto us"* (Isaiah 53:5, Hebrew text).

The Messiah of Israel was nailed to a "tree," shed His blood for the remission of sins, was bruised in His body for the healing of diseases and pains, and was "chastened" for our reconciliation, *peace* with God, according to prophecy written in the Tanakh, the Old Testament. He experienced separation from the Father on Golgotha's hill of sorrow that those believing in Him might have divine fellowship and communion. *Messiah made **peace** between us and our God by the blood of His Sacrifice on the Altar of Calvary* even as it was prophesied He would!

God has much to say concerning the Land of Israel (*Eretz Yisroel*) of which Jerusalem is the center. Prophecies of Israel begins far back in the time of Abraham in the opening verses of Genesis 12. God promises Abraham that He will give this land to his seed *forever*. There are nearly 100 references in the Pentateuch alone to the fact that God has given the Holy Land to His people Israel! The Bible prophetically describes its boundaries and also foretells its destruction and restoration. When restored, Israel shall cover an area of 300,000 square miles, or nearly twice and a half larger than England and Ireland together. The Land limits, according to prophecy, are from the "River of Egypt" to the Euphrates west to east, and from Hethlon to Kadesh, north to south. Many Jews believe that this territory will embrace the whole Peninsula of Arabia (see Genesis 15:18; Numbers 34:2-15; Ezekiel 48:1-35; Jeremiah 31:38-40).

This land was never to be sold to any other people:

*"The land shall not be sold for ever: **for the land is mine**; for ye are strangers and sojourners **with me** [the Lord]"* (Leviticus 25:23).

So, the land is God's and He gave it to the Jews. They are the *heirs* to the land of Israel. Through the prophet Moses, God tells the Jewish people:

*"And I will take you to me for a people, and I will be to you a God: and ye shall know that I am the LORD your God, which bringeth you out from under the burdens of the Egyptians. And I will **bring you in unto the land**, concerning the which I did swear to give it to Abraham, to Isaac, and to Jacob; and I will give it you for **an heritage**: I am the LORD"* (Exodus 6:7-8).

"Palestine became the *nerve center* of the earth in the days of Abraham. Later on, the country became the *truth center* because of Moses and the prophets. Ultimately it became the *salvation center* by the manifestation of Christ. His rejection led to its becoming the *storm center* as it has continued to be through many centuries. The Scriptures predict that it is to be the *peace center* under the Messianic Kingdom; and it will be the *glory center* in a new universe yet to be experienced. See Ezekiel 5:5."   —C.J. Rolls

"Zion" comes from a root which means a dry, barren place or arid wilderness. In this, its original condition, it is a type of the land and the people of Israel. But owing to the great power and skill of the Great Husbandman, the Messiah, this dry ground will be transformed into a fruitful garden and the spiritually barren people brought to full bloom!

*"Prophesy therefore concerning the land of Israel, and say unto the mountains, and to the hills, to the rivers, and to the valleys, Thus saith the Lord GOD; Behold, I have spoken in my jealousy and in my fury, because ye have borne the shame of the heathen: Therefore thus saith the Lord GOD; I have lifted up mine hand, Surely the heathen that are about you, they shall bear their shame. But ye, **O mountains of Israel**, ye shall shoot forth your branches, and yield your fruit to my people of Israel; for they are at hand to come. For, behold, I am for you, and I will turn unto you, and ye shall be tilled and sown: And I will multiply men upon you, all the house of Israel, even all of it: and the cities shall be inhabited, and the wastes shall be builded: And I will multiply upon you man and beast; and they shall increase and bring fruit: and I will settle you after your old estates, and will do better unto you than at your beginnings: and ye shall know that I am the LORD. Yea, I will cause men to walk upon you, even my people Israel; and they shall possess thee, and thou shalt be their inheritance, and thou shalt no more henceforth bereave them of men.*

Neither will I cause men to hear in thee the shame of the heathen any more, neither shalt thou bear the reproach of the people any more, neither shalt thou cause thy nations to fall any more, saith the Lord GOD.

And I will multiply the fruit of the tree, and the increase of the field, that ye shall receive no more reproach of famine among the heathen.

And the desolate land shall be tilled, whereas it lay desolate in the sight of all that passed by. And they shall say, This land that was desolate is become like the garden of Eden; and the waste and desolate and ruined cities are become fenced, and are inhabited" (Ezekiel 36:6-12, 15, 30, 34-35).

It has been doubtful to many peoples for thousands of years that Jews would ever return again to the Promised Land. It has been said that God was through with them and that they would never be nationally restored. Until May 14, 1948 there was a tendency on the part of some ministers of the gospel to preach against the return of the people of Israel and to spiritualize all the promises made to the natural seed of Abraham. But when the land of Palestine was declared the State of Israel and Jews from all over the world began to return as never before in history since the Exodus, these same ministers realized their interpretation had been wrong!

Moses wrote the words of God concerning the *scattering*[18] of Israel and the *desolation of the land*:

"And the LORD shall scatter thee among all people, from the one end of the earth even unto the other; and there thou shalt serve other gods, which neither thou nor thy fathers have known, even wood and stone. And among these nations shalt thou find no ease, neither shall the sole of thy foot have rest: but the LORD shall give thee there a trembling heart, and failing of eyes, and sorrow of mind: ..." (Deuteronomy 28:64-65).

"And I will bring the land into desolation: and your enemies which dwell therein shall be astonished at it. And I will scatter you among the heathen, and will draw out a sword after you: and your land shall be desolate, and your cities waste" (Leviticus 26: 32-33).

Even as every one of the prophecies concerning the *dispersion* of natural Israel were *literally* and are being *literally* fulfilled, just so the *regathering* and *restoration* of natural Israel must *literally* come to pass. As it was prophesied that a *literal* people were *literally* scattered among *literal* nations and suffered *literal* persecution and this was all *literally* fulfilled, just so these same prophets foretold

---

[18]"God scattered Israel in order that they should convert the Gentiles to Judaism." *Bab. Pes.* 87b.

that Israel would just as *literally* be preserved from extinction or assimilation, and would in the **end time**, just before the return of their Messiah Jesus, **be brought back again as a nation into their own land!**

> *"And yet for all that, when they be in the land of their enemies, I will not cast them away, neither will I abhor them, to destroy them utterly, and to break my covenant with them: for I am the LORD their God. But I will for their sakes **remember the covenant of their ancestors**, whom I brought forth out of the land of Egypt in the sight of the heathen, that I might be their God: I am the LORD"* (Leviticus 26:44-45).

God is gathering the Jews from the four corners of the earth even as He said He would! Israel *is* back in the Land! God has kept His Word **literally**!

> *"Therefore fear thou not, O my servant Jacob, saith the LORD; neither be dismayed, O Israel: for, lo, I will save thee from afar, and thy seed from the land of their captivity; and Jacob shall return, and shall be in rest, and be quiet, and none shall make him afraid. For I am with thee, saith the LORD, to save thee: though I make a full end of all nations whither I have scattered thee, **yet will I not make a full end of thee**: but I will correct thee in measure, and will not leave thee altogether unpunished"* (Jeremiah 30:10-11).

The Land of Israel has been passed from nation to nation. When it was in the hands of the Gentiles it remained undeveloped, untouched. Why? Because it is *not* Gentile property; because God decreed that under Him the *Jews* would do the restoring and renewing:

> *"And I will bring again the captivity of my people of Israel, and **they** shall build the waste cities, and inhabit them; and **they** shall plant vineyards, and drink the wine thereof; they shall also make gardens, and eat the fruit of them. And I will plant **them** upon **their land**, and **they** shall no more be pulled up out of **their land** which I have given them, saith the LORD thy God"* (Amos 9:14-15).

Genesis 15:18 tells that the land God promised to Israel in the Abrahamic Covenant is from the river of Egypt to the great river, the river Euphrates. This is usually estimated to be a territory of over 300,000 square miles.

In one of the prophecies of Isaiah there is an important notice to all the people of the world in the last days:

> *"All ye inhabitants of the world, and dwellers on the earth, see ye, when he lifteth up an ensign on the mountains; and when he **bloweth a trumpet**, hear ye"* (Isaiah 18:3; see also Isaiah 11:10-12).

In other words, when an ensign (flag) is lifted up in the mountains of Jerusalem and the ram's horn blown, let all the nations of the earth take notice. When the Allies granted the Palestine Mandate to England in 1920, and Sir Herbert Samuel, himself a Hebrew, became the first High Commissioner over Palestine in 2,000 years, the *Flag of Judah* was flown from the tower of David and Chief Rabbi Kook of Jerusalem blew the ***ram's horn*** (trumpet) which sounded out over the land!

The Lord is gathering the Jews back to *Eretz Israel* ("Land of Israel") for a specific purpose, not only to cultivate it, to cause "the desert to blossom as the rose," not only to have a homeland, *but God is bringing this dispersed and wandering people back **in readiness for the return of their Messiah**!*

> *"When the LORD shall build up Zion, he shall appear in his glory"* (Psalm 102:16).

There is an amazing prophecy concerning *Jerusalem* given by the Messiah Himself in His Olivet Discourse which was fulfilled in 1967! ***"Jerusalem shall be trodden down of the Gentiles until the times of the Gentiles be fulfilled"*** (Luke 21:24).

> "It is only during this first week of June, 1967, that the old city of Jerusalem to which Jesus is here referring has come into the hands of the Jews who are an independent nation, Israel. *THIS IS THE FIRST TIME JERUSALEM HAS BEEN IN THE HANDS OF AN INDEPENDENT ISRAEL SINCE 597 BC!"*[19]

DEATH AND RESURRECTION

Immediately after death, close relatives of the deceased perform the *keriah* custom by making a slight tear in their clothing as a sign of mourning (see Job 1:20 and 2:12). This act describes the severance of the living from the dead and is performed in moments of deepest grief. It is the mark on the clothing of a broken or *torn* heart.

Pious Jews direct that a little sack of Holy Land soil be placed in their coffin. It is written in the Jews' oral law (Talmud):

> "He that liveth in the Holy Land is as though he were without sin. He that inhabits the city one hour and dieth there is sure of the world to come."

My great-grandfather, Lipeh Saltzman, who was an ultra-orthodox *Hassidic* Rabbi, left Russia, the country of his birth and

---

[19]Wilbur M. Smith, *Israeli-Arab Conflict and the Bible,* (inside cover page, no number). Emphasis is mine.

ministry, to be in Jerusalem the last years of his life in keeping with this promise. Jews who have been denied the opportunity to live and die in the Land of Israel, yearn, at least, to be buried with a bit of the soil from the Holy Land. This also explains the custom of placing the body with the head to the east Zion-ward.

The burial shroud is made of white linen cloth and covers the undergarments. A prominent person may be buried with his *tallit* (Prayer Shawl) but the fringes (*tzitzith*) are removed or cut.

The grave is filled in, the first spadeful by family and friends, and the rest by members of the burial society. At the conclusion of the burial ceremony, the *kaddish* is recited by the sons of the deceased or by a close relative. As a five-year-old child I remember at the graveside of my Aunt's deceased mother when my grandfather led the relatives in saying the *kaddish*. And, though it was difficult for me to pronounce the Hebrew words, I joined them in this most solemn and sacred "prayer." (The word "kaddish" means "sanctification" and is a famous Jewish prayer which speaks of the greatness of God, of redemption from exile, and of everlasting peace in Messianic times.)

Upon returning home, a hard-boiled egg and a little ashes are placed before the mourners. The egg, being a symbol of life, reminds them that while death is inescapable, the living must face the future with faith and hope. Also the egg is a symbol of mourning. It has no opening or mouth, just as a mourner is struck dumb by his fate. The ashes, as a sign of mourning, date back to ancient times when ashes and earth were strewn on the head in times of misfortune. With this simple rite begins the period of *shivah* (seven), the seven days of mourning as it was in the days of Job (see Job 2:12-13). This custom is based on the fact that Joseph mourned for his father Jacob *seven* days (see Genesis 50:10).

Relatives and friends come to visit the mourners and to console them. The bereaved usually sit on low stools or boxes during this time. I followed this custom with relatives of the deceased when I was in Judaism. Throughout the seven days, the memorial lamp was kept lighted in memory of the dead. Naturally the mourners abstain from entertainment and pleasures on that day and for 30 days afterward it is unseemly for them to go to theaters, concerts or parties. In some families this custom is continued for 12 months. As another expression of grief, mirrors and other decorative objects in the house are usually covered up or put away. A large candle is lighted, which is renewed and kept burning for 30 days (except on the Sabbath) in reverence for the dead.

A year after the death, the relatives and friends come to pay their respects to the deceased. The "kaddish" is recited and one of the prayers is the famous Psalm: *"The Lord is my Shepherd"* (Psalm 23). Every year the anniversary of the death is observed at home and in the synagogue. At home a memorial *lamp* or a tallow *candle* (see Proverbs 20:27) within a glass is lit at sunset and allowed to burn until the next sunset. This ceremony is called *yahrzeit* (from the German meaning "anniversary"). On one occasion I asked my mother why the candle was lit at this time. She informed me that "the soul of the departed wandered and must have a light to guide it to its resting place!"

Yahrzeit

From the scriptural account, man was created to live forever and not to die. God's ultimate purpose is to have a world of perfect beings having eternal fellowship with Himself. And this eventually will come to pass even as God intended. But, in the meantime with our first parents in the Garden of Eden, the entrance of sin brought death, both physical and spiritual.

David testified to the fact that all men die:

"Remember how short my time is: wherefore hast thou made all men in vain? What man is he that liveth, and shall not see death? shall he deliver his soul from the hand of the grave? Selah" (Psalm 89:47-48).

Solomon, the wisest man that ever lived, also testifies to this truth:

"There is no man that hath power over the spirit to retain the spirit; neither hath he power in the day of death: ..." (Ecclesiastes 8:8)

"For that which befalleth the sons of men befalleth beasts; even one thing befalleth them: as the one dieth, so dieth the other; yea, they have all one breath; so that a man hath no preeminence above a beast: for all is vanity" (Ecclesiastes 3:19).

Death came as a tyrant because of sin and disobedience (Romans 5:12) and is an inescapable appointment (Hebrews 9:27). The moment Adam sinned he spiritually died and the seeds of physical death were sown in his body. The translation of the Hebrew text in Genesis 2:17, the last phrase: "thou shalt surely die," is literally: *"Dying [spiritually] thou shalt [eventually] die [physically]."* Adam lost the life of God and died spiritually (separation from God). From that moment he became mortal—that is, he continued in a dying state until he eventually died physically. From that time onward mankind was doomed to live in a land of the dead and dying. The whole earth groans because of this enemy which strikes quickly and without warning. Death is no respecter of persons but touches the homes of rich and poor, high and low, educated and ignorant alike. All must surrender to its power!

Many believe death is the end; that when a man dies, his body rots in the grave; that there is no life hereafter; that man lives a few span of years and then—"pouf," it is all over. We are told that the eagle lives 500 years and the turtle at least a century longer than human beings. Now would not this seem unfair on the part of God to give the eagle and the turtle such a long tenure of life and then after a brief span of years cut off the man whom He made in His own image? According to God's Word we are not so cut off for after this life there is another life!

The appearance of Moses and Elijah on the Mount of Transfiguration shows clearly that the souls of the departed are conscious (see Luke 9:30). Moses had been dead for *1,500 years*, and there he was back again on earth talking to the Messiah!

DEATH OF MOSES

"The *Gemara* describes the death of Moses in the last few verses of the Torah. The obvious question which comes to mind is how could Moses have recorded his own death? The Gemara's answer is that the whole Torah, which served as a blueprint for the creation of the world, was written by G-d in a jumbled form, one unintelligible to man, and that it was the task of Moses to rearrange the letters and unravel the words to render them intelligible to man. This he did with the exception of the last eight verses which were left to his successor, Joshua, to re-set in a comprehensible form, one which, as it transpired, recorded Moses' death."[20]

The foregoing quote is the *Jewish* interpretation of the death of Moses, but the Bible informs us that Moses possessed all the wisdom of Egypt. Beyond this earthly wisdom he was endowed with the wisdom of God. Also, being a *prophet* he could prophesy that which was to come. He could foresee his own death as the Spirit of God, which was upon him, directed his words and his very thoughts as he wrote the Torah. It is written that *all* Scripture, which includes the Torah, the Neviim, and the Ketuvim (T'nakh) was inspired by God (2 Timothy 3:16). Therefore, Moses was anointed by God to write even concerning his own death!

RESURRECTION AFTER DEATH

Concerning death and after this the resurrection there is an important question: Would God create the wonders of creation: the earth, the sun, the moon, and the stars, make provisions for the benefit of mankind and prepare all of these things for man if man is only to

---

[20]Rabbi M. Glazerson, *Sparks of the Holy Tongue*, p.1.

live a few years and then be no more forever? True, the earth is at present under a curse for man's sake, and man has been weakened and defiled by sin, but this is no reason for thinking that God will permit present conditions to continue indefinitely! Rather it is a reason for thinking that God has some *eternal* purpose for man, and that the time will come when He will have a new creation (physical and spiritual) where there will be no more evidences of sin and death.

If man was created in the image of God and is God's workmanship, then there must be a continuance of life or else God's work is eternally ruined. Creation is a failure if this present life is all there is for man. All is vanity and God made a mistake in ever making anything if nothing attains perfection here and now. But God's Word declares that man has an eternal existence whether he is a believer in Messiah Jesus or not. The wicked exist forever even though they do not have eternal Divine life.

All nature speaks loudly of *resurrection life.* In the fall, we witness the withering grass, the fading flower and the falling leaf, and soon the earth is in the grip of ice and snow. Death apparently is master! But as soon as spring comes, new life appears; the grass becomes green again, the barren trees put forth new buds, and the song birds are heard on every hand. All nature rejoices! That which was apparently dead is alive again!

In Judaism there is a belief in the resurrection as the 13th Article of Moses Maimon states. In the Talmud we read the following:

> "R. Eleazar stated, The dead outside the Land will not be resurrected; for it is said in Scripture, *And I will set glory in the land of the living,* (implying 'the dead of the land in which I have my desire') *will be resurrected."*   —*Kethuboth, Illa*

The *Tanakh* (the Hebrew Scriptures, the OT) declares life after death and the *resurrection.* We read that Isaac *"was gathered to his people"* (Genesis 25:8), as was Jacob (Genesis 49:33). To these patriarchs it meant that they were going to the region of *sheol*, "the place of departed spirits." Jacob contemplates joining his supposedly dead son, Joseph, in that region (cf. Genesis 37:35; 42:38 where the word *grave* is a wrong translation of the word *sheol*).

Job exclaimed:

> *"For I know that my redeemer liveth, and that he shall stand at the latter day upon the earth:* **And though after my skin worms destroy this body***, yet* **in my flesh** *shall I see God: Whom I shall see for myself, and mine eyes shall behold, and not another; ..."* (Job 19:25-27).

When one of his sons died, David exclaimed: *"I shall go to him, but he will not return to me"* (2 Samuel 12:23). And speaking to the Lord, he said: *"As for me, I shall be satisfied, when I shall awake with thy likeness"* (Psalm 17:15). David knew that he would be like the Lord at the *resurrection.* He, as a Jew, believed in the *resurrection from the dead* even as another fellow-Jew who lived after him (Paul) believed and wrote:

> *"For our conversation* [citizenship] *is in heaven; from whence also we look for the Saviour, the Lord Jesus Christ: **Who shall change our vile** [humble] **body** [the body of our humiliation], **that it may be fashioned like unto his glorious body**, according to the working whereby he is able even to subdue all things unto himself"* (Philippians 3:20-21).

When God appeared to Moses in the burning bush, He declared: *"I am the God of thy father, the God of Abraham, the God of Isaac, and the God of Jacob"* (Exodus 3:6) by which God meant that He was still their God, even though they no longer lived on earth, they continued to be *living personalities!*

The prophets of the Old Covenant Scriptures knew that ultimately there would be an end to the grave and that there would be a bodily *resurrection of the dead.* We see this in the following lesson: Psalm 17:15–*"I shall be satisfied when I **awake*** [*quwts, koots*]. Here the word for "awake" from the Hebrew is associated with resurrection (or an abruptness in starting from sleep). Isaiah 26:19—***Awake and sing, ye that dwell in the dust."*** Daniel 12:2, *"they that sleep in the dust shall **awake**."* Isaiah 26:19, *"... with my dead body shall they **arise** ..."* The Hebrew word for *arise (koom)* means "to get up," "to lift up," "to rise," "to rouse up," "to stir up," "(make to) stand," "to raise."

Continuing with this thought: See Job 14:12. As we examine the context of this verse we notice in verses 7-9 concerning the hope of a tree is that after it has *died* (or been cut down) the branch and the stock in the ground will *grow again* and bring forth boughs, etc. Then proceeding from this thought we come to verse 11 through 15 in which Job speaks of man's death and his patience until his "change" or his "resurrection" comes.

The prophets of the Hebrew Scriptures looked forward to the coming of the Messiah who would, by His vicarious death, provide the means of redemption from sin and death for those who would believe. Those who would accept God's free gift, would be free from eternal death and would participate with resurrection bodies in the glorious Messianic reign which will yet be seen on this earth. This era will be inaugurated at Messiah's second coming in power and glory. God's ultimate purpose of a world of perfect beings in fellowship with Himself forever, will then be fulfilled!

How may we receive the gift of eternal life with God? The Bible answers:

> "For God so loved the world, that he gave [as a sacrifice] his only begotten Son, that whosoever believeth in him should not perish, but have everlasting life" (John 3:16).

> "He that believeth on him [Messiah] is not condemned: ..." (John 3:18).

> "And this is the will of him that sent me, that every one which seeth the Son, and believeth on him, may have everlasting life: and I will raise him up at the last day [the resurrection]" (John 6:40).

Daniel, the Jewish prophet, spoke of this resurrection day:

> "And many of them that sleep in the dust of the earth **shall awake**, some to everlasting life, and some to shame and everlasting contempt" (Daniel 12:2).

How important it is that we experience the resurrection to "everlasting life," and that we not be among those scheduled for "shame and everlasting contempt." Those who refuse God's free gift of eternal life with Him, made possible in the Messiah, have nothing to look forward to but the ultimate resurrection to eternal separation from God, which is also called "hell." Why anyone would choose this, it is difficult to understand!

Yeshua (Jesus) took death and neutralized it, made it devoid of its power so that now it is unable to hurt those who believe in Him. His death on the Altar of Calvary was *the* death of "death"! He died that we might live; because He died, we will never die! He said at the tomb of Lazarus:

> "... I am the resurrection, and the life: he that believeth in me, though he were dead [before His return], yet shall he live: And whosoever liveth [at the time of His return] and believeth in me shall never die. Believest thou this?" (John 11:25-26).

> "Verily, verily, I say unto you, The hour is coming, and now is, when the dead shall hear the voice of the Son of God: and they that hear shall live. Marvel not at this: for the hour is coming, in the which all that are in the graves shall hear his voice, And shall come forth; they that have done good, unto the resurrection of life; and they that have done evil, unto the resurrection of damnation" (John 5:25, 28-29).

BRIT MILAH

"And God said unto Abraham, Thou shalt keep my covenant therefore, thou, and thy seed after thee in their generations. This is my covenant, which ye shall keep, between me and you and thy seed after thee; Every man child among you shall be circumcised. And ye shall circumcise the flesh of **your** *foreskin; and it shall be a token of the covenant betwixt me and you. And he that is eight days old shall be circumcised among you, every man child in your generations, he that is born in the house, or bought with money of any stranger, which is not of thy seed. He that is born in thy house, and he that is bought with thy money, must needs be circumcised: and my covenant shall be in your flesh for an everlasting covenant. And the uncircumcised man child whose flesh of his foreskin is not circumcised, that soul shall be cut off from his people; he hath broken my covenant"* (Genesis 17:9-14).

This Abrahamic Covenant which is the basis of Judaism and Christianity, is the most marvelous document in existence. Every Jewish boy today, when eight days old, is circumcised according to the commandment. This practice, which is 4,000 years old, is still held in high esteem by all Jews.

Covenant of Circumcision

"The root-meaning of the Hebrew word for covenant, *berith* [brit or bris], is not quite certain. By some it is supposed to contain the idea of *cutting*, and to refer to the division of the sacrificial victims which appears generally to have belonged to the ceremony of ratification (Genesis 15:9,10; Jeremiah 34:18,19). Now it is true that the verb which is commonly used of *making* (*karath*) a covenant means simply *to cut*, and seems to have reference to this rite. But probably the idea of the covenant is even older than this ancient ceremony, and *berith* is to be traced back to an Assyrian root *baru* which means *to bind*, whence is derived *biritu, a fetter*. Thus the ground-meaning of *berith* is that of *a bond* or *obligation*."[21]

"Brit Milah" is a great celebration which takes place in the home where relatives, friends, and neighbors have gathered. When the child is carried in for circumcision, he is greeted with the familiar Hebrew phrase: *Barukh habah* ("Blessed is he that cometh"). Attending the ceremony, according to custom, there is always the invisible guest, Elijah. The infant is placed upon "Elijah's Chair" just before the operation. This, the Jews believe, insures the child's health and promotes quick healing. At every circumcision, Elijah is supposed to be seated at the right hand of the *sandek*, the one who holds the infant during the operation, and the words: *Zeh Kisei Shel Eliyahu,* ("This

---

[21]C.F. Burney, *Outlines of O.T. Theology*, pp. 49-50.

is the Chair of Elijah") must be said in a loud voice (so as to disguise the cries of the infant?)!

The one who performs the operation of circumcision, called by the Hebrew term *Mohel*, is so expert in this operation that no surgeon can compete with him in his performance or in the safeguarding of the life and health of the baby.

From the human standpoint, the following explanation is given concerning the *time* for the circumcision, which is the eighth day:

> "Recent medical research has now discovered more fully all the elements that compose the blood. It was found that one element essential to the well-being of the human being is entirely absent at birth. This element is supposed to assert itself during the first *eight* days of life!"   —Dr. Justina Hill, *Microbes and Men*

Part of the ceremony is *naming the boy,* which is done immediately after the circumcision. The child is usually named after some near relative who has passed away. This is an Ashkenazic custom dating from around the Fifth or Fourth Century BCE (Before the Common Era). The Sephardic custom is to give the new child a name in honor of a *living* relative. But named after the deceased relative is intended to keep family memories alive. When the boy is named following the operation, he enters into the Covenant (*Brit*) and becomes an inheritor of everything connected with it.

When the "Child born" and the "Son given" of Isaiah's prophecy (Isaiah 9:6) was *eight days old*, Mary observed this ceremony for Him:

> *"And when eight days were accomplished for the circumcising of the child, his name was called JESUS* [Yeshua], *which was so named of the angel before he was conceived in the womb"* (Luke 2:21).

He, being a Jew "according to the flesh," (see Romans 1:3). was under subjection to every law and commandment of God given to Israel in order to "finish" or "fulfill" the Old Covenant and establish the New, for circumcision of the flesh is a type and shadow of a greater experience of the heart. The operation of circumcision signifies the cutting off of the *old* creation. The eighth day is the "morrow after the Sabbath," the day of the Resurrection, the day of the *new* creation!

God does not establish the fact of a person's Jewishness from the outward manifestation, but He recognizes the *true* Jew from the condition of the *inner* man! He commanded the Israelites: *"Circumcise therefore the foreskin of your **heart**, and be no more stiffnecked"* (Deuteronomy 10:16).

When Nicodemus, a religious leader of the Jews, a Pharisee, came to the Messiah by night to inquire concerning the way to heaven, the Messiah answered: *"Ye must be born again."* The Old Covenant was sealed with circumcision of the *flesh*; the New Covenant is sealed with the new birth or circumcision of the *heart*. (Here, circumcision was inferred to be the "mark of death" upon the Adam life.) With the natural man there is no power to love God with all the heart, soul, and strength, but the Lord promised a spiritual birth which would make this possible:

> *"And the LORD thy God will circumcise thine heart, and the heart of thy seed, to love the LORD thy God with all thine heart, and with all thy soul, that thou mayest live"* (Deuteronomy 30:6).

The new birth takes place when "with the heart man believeth unto righteousness and with the mouth confession is made unto salvation," when an individual makes a *turn-about-face* to forsake his sins and accept the righteousness of God in Yeshua (Jesus) ha-Meshiach (the Christ). The heart is circumcised, the old law is cut away, and a new law takes its place. The ordinances, rituals, ceremonies, sacrifices *under the Old Covenant* are fulfilled, finished by the Holy One of Israel, the Deliverer who has come out of Zion–Jesus of Nazareth, the Son of the Living God. (However, these animal sacrifices will be renewed during the Millennium, the future Kingdom.)[22]

> *"And ye are complete in him, which is the head of all principality and power: In whom also ye are circumcised with the circumcision made without hands, in putting off the body of the sins of the flesh by the circumcision of Christ* [Messiah's death]:*"* (Colossians 2:10-11).

Jewish person, do you pride yourself that you are a Jew and that you have obeyed the commandment of God under the Old Covenant? Listen to the words of Jeremiah, your own Jewish prophet, who wrote by the inspiration of the Spirit of God:

> *"Behold, the days come, saith the LORD, that I will punish all them **which are circumcised** with the **uncircumcised**; Egypt, and Judah, and Edom, and the children of Ammon, and Moab, and all that are in the utmost corners, that dwell in the wilderness: for all these nations are **uncircumcised**, and all the house of Israel are **uncircumcised in the heart**"* (Jeremiah 9:25-26).

---

[22]See Isaiah 56:7; 66:20-23; Jeremiah 33:18; Zechariah 14:16-21. Ezekiel Chapters 40-46 tells of the coming restoration of Levitical worship in a new temple in Jerusalem, the sacrifices to be slain and washed on 8 tables, etc.

God regards the new birth above circumcision of the flesh. Jew and Gentile alike are commanded to obey *"Ye must be born again"*! Jews *and* Gentiles need an operation to cut away the foreskin of their heart in order to enter into the kingdom of God. It does not matter if one is born a natural Jew; he does not merit heaven by that fact; he is not even known as a **true** Jew by God Himself until his heart is changed, until he repents of his sins and accepts as his Messiah the Lord Jesus Christ.

The Bible instructs that not only the Jew but *everyone* must repent of his sins. Repentance is associated with *conversion.* The unbeliever becomes a *convert* when he repents and turns to God. Abraham was not a Jewish person. His father was an idolater therefore a Gentile. In the Bible, the title, Gentile, means that person or persons were heathen. Of course, in our day a Gentile is simply not a Jew. According to the Jewish religion Abraham, a *Gentile*, became the first **convert**! The blessing that is recited in the synagogue for Gentiles who accept Judaism is: "May he who blessed our ancestor, Abraham *the first convert,* and said unto him: 'Go thou before Me and be righteous,' bless and give courage to this convert who enters the fold." According to Jewish law this is the last reference ever made to this person's conversion.

God regards circumcision of the heart (a new creature) above circumcision of the flesh:

> *"For in Christ Jesus neither circumcision availeth any thing, nor uncircumcision, but a new creature* [creation]*"* (Galatians 6:15).

> *"For he is not a Jew, which is one outwardly; neither is that circumcision, which is outward in the flesh: But he is a Jew, which is one inwardly; and circumcision is that of the heart, in the spirit, and not in the letter; whose praise is not of men, but of God"* (Romans 2:28-29).

SUPPLEMENTAL NOTE ON CIRCUMCISION

> *"Ye shall not make any cuttings in your flesh **for the dead**, nor print any marks upon you: I am the LORD"* (Leviticus 19:28).

The heathen had a custom whereby, upon the death of a relative, they cut themselves as a sign of deep sorrow. But because of this commandment of God, the children of Israel cut their *garments* instead of their flesh at the passing of a loved one or at times of greatest grief. (This is practiced today among most Jews.) Such a custom was later condemned, however, when it came to be observed as a ritual to the exclusion of the Lord. God said: *"rend your **heart**, and not your garments"* (Joel 2:13). The condition of the soul toward the Lord is more important than an outward show toward man. It is interesting to note that, in obedience to this law, the heart of Messiah was torn, but not His garments (see John 19:23-24)!

According to the great Hebrew scholar and teacher, Rashi, "*nor print* any marks" is to be translated "*nor imprint* any marks"; i.e., tattooing with a needle. God's own people at that time should not have any mark in their flesh other than "the sign of the covenant," or *circumcision* (Genesis 17:9-14)! This physical mark was also fulfilled in Messiah Jesus (Luke 2:21). He "finished" the Old Covenant in order to establish the New. (The spiritual "Circumcision of Christ" intimates His death; see Colossians 2:11-12.)

It was on the *eighth* day of their birth that all Jewish males were to be "cut in their foreskin." This was a type and shadow of a greater experience to come. The operation of circumcision signifies the cutting off of the Old creation, the *eighth* day is the "morrow after the sabbath," the day of the resurrection of Messiah and of the *new* creation! The Old Covenant was sealed with circumcision of the flesh; the New Covenant is sealed with the *new birth* or *circumcision of the heart.* For He had promised:

> "And the LORD thy God will circumcise thine **heart**, and the **heart** of thy seed, to love the LORD thy God with all thine **heart**, and with all thy **soul**, that thou mayest live" (Deuteronomy 30:6).

When the heart is circumcised, the old law is cut away and a new law takes its place. The ordinances, rituals, ceremonies, sacrifices under the Old Covenant are fulfilled, "finished" in the Holy One of Israel, the Deliverer who has come out of Zion, Jesus of Nazareth, the Son of the Living God!

By cutting or imprinting marks upon their flesh outside of the covenant of circumcision the Israelites would be defying and rejecting the prophecy and its fulfillment. They would be "breaking" the type in which God is instructing them concerning the new birth which only He Himself could perform. They would be making their own way of religion which would come to heathen institutions and end in idolatry!

✡ ✡ ✡ ✡ ✡ ✡ ✡

PIDYON HA-BEN (Redemption of the Son)

The child has been considered by Jews, even since olden times, as the greatest of human treasures. To beget and raise children is a religious commandment and is the cause for rejoicing in the home. However, when a *son* is born, there is special joy, for the parents trust that he will carry on the family name with honor. Jewish women consider it a great blessing from God to bear a son. It is natural that the first child should be received with special attention by the new parents. The oldest son has always taken first rank in the Jewish family. In case of the father's death, he usually becomes the head, to whom the younger brothers and sisters look for advice and help. He inherits a larger share of the family's possessions than any of the other children. In my family, my brother Hyman, though he was the *youngest*, became *the head of the family* when our father died, and it was the custom for my sister and I, and sometimes even my mother, to receive advise from him on some occasions!

Ever since the first promise of redemption, Jewish women (who are very devout) have hoped to be the mother of the Redeemer. Deeply imbedded in the Jewish soul there is the hope of the coming Messiah and "Who knows?" perhaps their little boy will grow up to be the Deliverer of Israel! Eve, when she gave birth to Cain, believed it was He for whom she waited to save her from her sins. She exclaimed: *"I have acquired a man-child from the Lord!"* (Genesis 4:1). The word translated as *from* is simply the *first* and *last* letters of the Hebrew alphabet, (אֵת) Aleph-Tav, which represents Him who is the First and the Last, the Beginning and the Ending, who *is*, who *was*, and who *ever shall be*! So what Eve exclaimed was that the One who was born of her was, indeed, the Messiah-Lord, the Aleph-Tav! (See *More Things Jewish*, "Aleph-Tav," pp. 331-333.) What a disappointment to Eve that Cain turned out to be–not the Deliverer–but the first murderer; not the Life-giver, but the Life-taker!

One glorious day in the city of David, an event took place of which Isaiah wrote: *"Unto us a child is born, unto us a son is given"* (Isaiah 9:6). This was a Child the like of no other child before Him or after, who was the greatest of heaven's treasures; He is the Son who far surpasses all the sons of earth; His was a birth at which all the hosts of heaven rejoiced; Mary (Miriam), who gave birth to this Son, truly could declare in reality: *"I have acquired a man-child, the Lord"* for the Messiah had come!

The birth of the Savior in the city of David caused all heaven "and the morning stars to sing together," but one writer has expressed a significant fact: "Though Christ a thousand times in Bethlehem be born, and not within thy heart, thy soul will be forlorn." When He, the Messiah, the Son, is born in the heart, what rejoicing in heaven! By faith we who are sons of men, become sons of God through the new birth. Because He came into our humanity, we can become partakers of His divinity. He, who was born the son of Abraham, the son of David (Matthew 1:1), brings us into the family of God and we also are sons of David, sons of Abraham, of the heavenly family by faith.

*"He came unto his own, and his own received him not. **But as many as received him**, to them gave he power to become **the sons of God**, even to them that believe on his name:"* (John 1:11-12).

Jewish people redeem their firstborn son according to God's commandment: *"and all the firstborn of **man** among thy children shalt thou redeem"* (Exodus 13:13). The first part of this verse states that even an unclean animal was to be redeemed and that redemption was to be done for a *lamb*. We understand by this that redemption of the son was also to be with a lamb! Oh, what a Redeemer is our Messiah Jesus who is the *Lamb of God* who takes away the sin of the world!

On the 31st day after the Jewish boy's birth, a home gathering is arranged to which relatives and friends are invited. Among the guests is a *Kohen* (Priest) who is thought to be a descendant of Aaron. The ceremony consists of giving the Kohen the sum of five *shekalim* ($2.50), or the more popular sum of five silver dollars, and reciting appropriate prayers. The boy is then pronounced redeemed or freed from the service commanded for all firstborn males. (Unless the Kohen is very poor, he returns the money to the parents who give it to a worthy Jewish cause.) Most Jews do not practice this custom today, but among the very orthodox Jews, the firstborn is always redeemed, not with a lamb as in the commandment, but as stated above, with five silver dollars. This custom is kept in remembrance of the salvation of the firstborn in Egypt when God commanded the Israelites to substitute a lamb for their deliverance from death. The redemption ceremony is followed by a party as an expression of thanksgiving for this privilege.

It is written concerning the firstborn Son of Mary (Miriam):

"... they [Joseph and Miriam] brought him to Jerusalem, to present him to the Lord; (As it is written in the law of the Lord, Every male that openeth the womb shall be called holy to the Lord;)" (Luke 2:22-23).

*"And, behold, there was a man in Jerusalem, whose name was Simeon; and the same man was just and devout, waiting for the **consolation of Israel**: and the Holy Ghost was upon him. And it was revealed unto him by the Holy Ghost, that he should not see death, before he had seen the Lord's Christ [Messiah]. And he came by the Spirit into the temple: and when the parents brought in the child Jesus, to do for him **after the custom of the law**, Then*

*took he him up in his arms, and blessed God, and said, Lord, now
lettest thou thy servant depart in peace, according to thy word:
For mine eyes have seen **thy salvation**, Which thou hast prepared
before the face of all people; A light to lighten the Gentiles, and
the **glory** of thy people Israel"* (Luke 2:25-32).

Simeon, who perhaps had held many boy babies in his arms in
the Temple at the Redemption Ceremony (*Brit Milah*), was led of the
Spirit of God on this special occasion to see and recognize the
promised Messiah. This Son needed not to be redeemed, for He came
to redeem all those who put their trust in Him. Everyone has the same
privilege as Simeon to see and recognize in Jesus (*Yeshua*) the
Redeemer and Savior of the world! He *has* redeemed us not with
corruptible things but with His own blood! He is the Substitute, the
Antitype of the lamb which redeemed the firstborn of Israel. We,
who know Him, can exclaim with Simeon: *"Lord, we have seen **Thy
Salvation**!"*

MIKVAH

(Ritual Bath) Purifying of the Mother

*"And the LORD spake unto Moses, saying, Speak unto the children
of Israel, saying, If a woman have conceived seed, and born a
man child: then she shall be unclean seven days; according to the
days of the separation for her infirmity shall she be unclean. And
she shall then continue in the blood of her purifying three and
thirty days; she shall touch no hallowed thing, nor come into the
sanctuary, until the days of her purifying be fulfilled. And when
the days of her purifying are fulfilled, for a son, or for a daughter,
she shall bring a lamb of the first year for a burnt offering, and a
young pigeon, or a turtledove, for a sin offering, unto the door of
the tabernacle of the congregation, unto the priest: Who shall
offer it before the LORD, and make an atonement for her; and she
shall be cleansed from the issue of her blood. This is the law for
her that hath born a male or a female. And if she be not able to
bring a lamb, then she shall bring two turtles, or two young
pigeons; the one for the burnt offering, and the other for a sin
offering: and the priest shall make an atonement for her, and she
shall be clean"* (Leviticus 12:1, 2, 4, 6-8).

The statement of David that "in *sin* did my mother conceive me"
(Psalm 51:5) requires her purification in the *Mikvah*. The *woman*
was in the transgression (1 Timothy 2:14). According to the Hebrew
Scriptures the woman must be purified since she brought sin into the
world and the children she bears are "shapen in iniquity, conceived
in sin." This pronouncement was not applied to *David's* mother **only**
but to **all** mothers and their offspring for **all** have sinned and must be
cleansed (see Psalm 14:1-3 with Romans 3:10-12)!

Forty days after the birth of a child, the mother was "purified by a ceremony in the Temple. She was said to be unclean for seven days after the birth and then 33 days later she would keep her appointment for her purification. But though the woman brought sin into the world, God in His infinite love and grace allowed her to bear the Remedy for it! (Genesis 3:15; Galatians 3:13)

> "The washing of the body inculcated for purity figured prominently in the service of God in the Sanctuary where the sacred vessels were also washed. Later it became a symbol of regeneration, and all proselytes to Judaism underwent baptism as a new birth into the family of God. Frequently accompanied by confession of sin baptism was administered to Jews by various Jewish groups such as the Essenes and Baptists, and some made a religious duty of daily bathing. Among the orthodox the ritual bath (mikvah) is taken by women before marriage and after menstruation and childbirth. 'Ye shall be clean' is one of the holy laws of Judaism."[23]

In this purification ceremony for the Jewish mother we notice a form of *baptism* which, of course, is Jewish in origin. There were other baptisms for cleansing in the ritual bath (*Mikvah*) that are recorded in the Hebrew Scriptures (see Numbers 19:16-20). The many *washings* are called *baptisms* and this cleansing is implied by the Lord in the following Scripture verse:

> *"Then will I sprinkle clean water upon you, and ye shall be clean: from all your filthiness, and from all your idols, will I cleanse you"* (Ezekiel 36:25).

> "According to Rabbinical teachings, which dominated even during the existence of the temple (*Pes.* 8:8), baptism, next to circumcision and sacrifice, was an absolutely necessary condition to be fulfilled by a proselyte to Judaism." (*Meb.* 46b, 47b, etc.) "... to receive the Spirit of God, or to be permitted to stand in the presence of God (His Shekinah) man must undergo baptism (*Tan. Mezora*, 6, *Ed. Buber*, p.46)." [24]

Mikvah (Mikpha)—a collection of water. Ritual baths or *miqva'ot* stood just outside Jerusalem's wall, in accordance with Biblical law: "If anyone among you has been rendered unclean by a nocturnal emission, he must leave the camp ... Toward evening he shall bathe in water, and at sundown he may re-enter the camp" (Deuteronomy 23:11-12). (The Essenes regarded Jerusalem as equivalent to the camp.)

Today, Jews go to bathe at certain times in the Mikvah and as there is no administrator to assist them, it is necessarily deeper than

---

[23]Hugh Schonfield, *A Popular Dictionary of Judaism*, pp.31-32 under article "Baptism."
[24]*Jewish Encyclopedia*, Volume 2, p. 499, Article on the Talmud.

our baptisteries. The man or the woman, as the case may be, goes down into the water to a certain depth, when he will dive his head, and thus he is immersed even while standing. This done, he comes up out of the water and the performance is over. (See *immersion* as *burial* in Romans 6:3-5, *buried in baptism,* Colossians 2:12.)

In the case of the mother's purification according to *Talmudic Judaism*, the "water" of the *mikvah* corresponds to the original living water, the womb of the world, from which all life comes. The unborn child, as it were, is rocked in the womb where is the "living water." To be reborn, one must re-enter this womb and "drown" in the "living water." Not only mothers but also Jewish *men*, for their purification, enter the "living waters" and are submerged entirely until the water covers the head. (See Paul's purification in the Mikvah with 4 other Jewish men, Acts 21:26.) It is also considered by the Rabbis according to the Talmud that a Gentile who is a convert to Judaism does the same, reemerging from immersion in the Mikvah as a final step, the rebirth of a Gentile "as a Jew"! (However, according to the Holy Scriptures, a Gentile remains a Gentile until death and a Jew remains a Jew until death.)

In the mother's purification, a lamb was to be brought as the mother's sacrifice-offering if she could afford one. If she was too poor to bring a lamb, provision was made for her to bring instead, two turtle-doves or two young pigeons. Blood must be shed, however, in each case.

Mary, the mother of Jesus (Yeshua), observed this law:

*"And when the days of her purification **according to the law of Moses** were accomplished, they brought him to Jerusalem, to present him to the Lord; And to offer a sacrifice according to that which is said in the law of the Lord, A **pair of turtledoves,** or **two young pigeons**"* (Luke 2:22, 24).

She was poor: she could not afford a lamb, therefore she brought the pigeons. But in reality she brought forth the only *true **Lamb*** who was the Sacrifice for the entire world! A lamb is innocent and unresisting which speaks of The Lamb of God who is pure, without blemish. He did not resist but perfectly obeyed God's commandment for the giving up of His life in sacrifice and in so doing fully satisfied the Father's heart. Our Lord, the Maker of the Universe, did not make His appearance here among the rich and noble of earth. He became poor; He was born in a stable, with a manger (an animal feeding-trough) for His crib!

BAR MITZVAH

The Jewish boy looks forward to his 13th birthday as one of the most important events in his life. It symbolizes the beginning of maturity for him. When the boy reaches *Bar Mitzvah* age, he is not only old enough to enjoy the ceremony but also to appreciate its importance to himself, to his family and friends, and to his people.

It is believed by religious Jews that up to the thirteenth year, the father bears the sins of his son. After that, the boy must account for his good or

"Son of Commandment," *Bar Mitzvah*

evil actions. The father therefore, recites the following benediction at the Bar Mitzvah ceremony: "Blessed be Thou, O Lord, our God, King of the Universe, who has relieved me from punishment for this one (the son)."

Many months before this great occasion, the son is taught at the synagogue how to wear the phylacteries and prayer shawl. He is taught his various prayers in Hebrew, his religious duties, the Haftorah and blessings, and how to write and memorize a speech in Hebrew. He is accepted as one of ten necessary for a *minyan* (ten adult men without whom services cannot be conducted in the synagogue). He is also entitled to be called on to read the Torah (Scriptures) in the public services.

The Bar Mitzvah ceremony is celebrated in the synagogue and in the home. Relatives and friends come to the synagogue to hear the boy chant the *haftorah* and deliver the oration. The term, "haftorah," means "conclusion" and is applied to the passages from the books of the Prophets read on Sabbaths and festivals after the reading from the books of Moses. To be called up to read the Haftorah is an honor. A different intonation is used in reading the Haftorah than the intonation used in reading the Torah.

At the Bar Mitzvah celebration the Rabbi talks to the boy and blesses him. After the service, the entire congregation is invited by the family to the vestry rooms for refreshments. The boy receives gifts and congratulations from everyone. He is now considered a man who is responsible for his own sins.

"The following prayer is in use in English Sephardi Congregations on the occasion of a lad reaching the age of thirteen-his religious majority:

'O my God, and God of my Fathers, on this solemn and sacred day, which marketh my passage from boyhood to manhood, I humbly raise my eyes unto Thee, and declare with sincerity and truth that henceforth I will observe all Thy commandments, and undertake to bear the responsibility of all mine actions towards Thee. In my earliest infancy I was brought within Thy sacred covenant with Israel, and today I again enter as an active responsible member the pale of Thine elect congregation, in the midst of which I will never cease to glorify Thy holy name in the face of all nations.

'Do Thou, O Heavenly Father, hearken unto this my humble prayer, and bestow upon me Thy gracious blessings, so that my earthly life may be sustained and made happy by Thine ineffable mercies. Teach me the way of Thy statutes, that I may obey them, and faithfully carry out Thy ordinances. Dispose my heart to love Thee and to fear Thy holy name, and grant me Thy support and the strength necessary to avoid the worldly dangers which beset the path lying before me. Save me from temptation, so that I may observe Thy holy Law and those precepts on which human happiness and eternal life depend. Thus I will every day of my life trustfully and gladly proclaim: Hear, O Israel, the Lord is our God, the Lord is one!' —Benjamin Artom, 1868

An interesting item printed in the Jerusalem Post declared 1961 **Bar Mitzvah Day** in Israel. It was the **Thirteenth** Independence Day celebration. This was because of the number "Thirteen." It is at age 13 the boy is called *Bar Mitzvah* or "Son of the Law." According to Jewish authorities, the reason for "13" is because that is the number of God's attributes listed in Exodus 34:6-7.

Isaiah the Jewish prophet speaks of One upon whose shoulder is the government, the law (the Torah), the blessing, whose name is called *"Wonderful Counsellor of the Mighty God, of the Everlasting Father, Prince of Peace"* (Isaiah 9:5, Hebrew translation). We find Him in the Temple at the age of 12, astounding the doctors of the law with His perfect knowledge, His wisdom, His authority in the Scriptures (Luke 2:46-48). He needed not a ceremony; He needed not a ritual; He needed not a celebration! He fulfilled not only the law, but the tradition of the Jews as well. He had no sins for which Joseph was responsible before He was twelve, but it was for *our* iniquities He was bruised, for *our* transgression He was wounded (Isaiah 53:5). Surely this *Son* did not suffer for Himself as He hung on that Altar on Golgotha; He did not bear the punishment of His own sins, but surely, surely He bore *our* diseases and carried *our* pains! The chastisement for *our* peace was upon Him and through His bruise (*blow-mark*; i.e., of the Cross) was healing granted to us! Blessed be His wonderful Name forever!

It is interesting to note that Jews use two words for "son" (and so it is in the Scriptures; see Proverbs 30:4; 31:2, Hebrew text). The one is *ben* which is a general term applied to each male child in a Jewish family. The other is *bar* which has a larger meaning, the term used of a son who has reached maturity; one who has attained to the age of religious duty and responsibility. In other words, he is a *full-fledged Jew*! (*Bar* is Aramaic, a dialect of Hebrew. Examples: *Bar*-Kokhba, "Son of a Star," AD 132-135, *Bar*-Abbas, "Son of Abbas," *Bar*-Jonah, "Son of Jonah".)

The Holy Spirit, through the Second Psalm, which is considered Messianic, declares to the people of Israel (and "the nations") that the One who is "Anointed" ("Meshiach") is the *Son* of God. In verse 7 He is called by the term, *ben*. Then in verse 12 Israel is admonished to do homage to Him ("Kiss the *Son*") and they are *"blessed who put their trust in **Him**."* In this instance the term *bar* is used for *Son*. But Jewish translators do not agree on the meaning of the words *nashku bar* in this Psalm. They hide the word "son" in connection with God's *Anointed One*. The Soncino Chumash (editor, A. Cohen) translates it as "Do homage in purity" or "Do homage to the purified." Alexander Harkavy gives it as "Arm yourselves in purity." *The Jewish Bible According to the Masoretic Text*, published in Tel Aviv, Israel by "Sinai Publishing Co." gives the translation of "nashku bar" as "worship him in purity" [*him* is in italics]. Yet this same word, "bar" is used today to indicate the Jewish boy who has reached his religious majority at age 13! I feel that one of the reasons our beloved Jewish people translate this as "Do homage to the purified," etc., is because they do not want to acknowledge the divine Son! However, in Proverbs 30:4 it is written that Israel's Messiah *is* the **Son** of God! Jesus (Yeshua) is not only *Ben Elohim*, Son of God, but He is *Bar Mitzvah*, Son of the Law, as well!

THE JEWISH WEDDING

"Wedding Canopy"

The orthodox Jew realizes from God's Word that he is to be holy and different from other peoples (Leviticus 20:26), that he is not to be yoked with unbelievers. (To the Jew, Gentiles and unbelievers are synonymous.) God warns the Jewish people against intermarriage and this the *orthodox* Jews faithfully try to obey even in these present days. Underlying their separation from other peoples and ingrained on their hearts from ancient times, though they do not realize it, is the hope of the coming Messiah. If intermarriage is permitted, the birth of the Deliverer of Israel

Hupah

through them would be impossible, because of the broken Jewish line. Therefore, *religious* Jews are very careful to see that this does not occur. Knowing that the Jewish faith is not understood by Gentiles and therefore would cause embarrassment and heartache if Jews married those outside of it, Jewish parents drill the thought of separation (in marriage) from Gentiles into the hearts of their children. My orthodox Jewish mother was careful to teach this very vital "law of God" to us in our childhood.

The commandment of God is given to all who believe upon Him that there is to be no affiliation with the worldly system. Believers in Yeshua-Messiah are to be a separated, peculiar people to God, touching not the unclean thing. They are to be united only with believers in the Lord Jesus. The world does not understand the teachings of Messiah concerning the laws of holiness, and therefore a believer yoked with an unbeliever would cause embarrassment, heartache, and shame, for it is against the commandment of God and invites His displeasure.

The children of Abraham in the flesh know that *marriage* is a sacred institution made by God in the very beginning. Since they consider it a commandment of God and a holy union, there is very seldom a divorce among devout Jews.

THE FIRST MARRIAGE

In the very beginning, God created man and placed him in the Garden of Eden to take care of it, but He saw that it was not good for man to be alone. This signifies a deeper spiritual truth for all. That which occurred physically in the first creation prefigured the spiritual in the new creation. God not only looked upon the first Adam in this relationship but also He looked upon the Last Adam (Messiah) and saw it was not good for HIM to be alone. The Talmud's statement agrees with this: "He who abides without a wife abides without goodness, help, joy, blessing, and atonement."

God put the First Adam to sleep on the dust of the ground and while he was asleep, the Great Creator performed an operation. From his "side parts" was taken a bride to be called by his name. "God was the Author of marriage and the first Father to give away a Bride!"

Just so, God put to sleep the Last Adam (Jesus, the Messiah) upon Calvary's Altar (a tree which came from the dust of the ground), and while He was asleep, God performed an operation. From Messiah's side there flowed a stream of blood (life) which made it possible for a bride to be brought to Him to be called by His Name!

When the woman was presented to the first Adam, he declared: *"This is now bone of my bone and flesh of my flesh"* (Genesis 2:23). And too, those who are presented to Christ as His Bride, His own, are a very vital part of Him, members of His body, flesh of His flesh and bone of His bone (Ephesians 5:30).

THE SHADCHAN (*Shadkhan*)

In some Jewish communities there is a person (man or woman) hired by the parents to make a match for their son or daughter. This person is called a *Shadchan*, a term derived from the Talmudic Hebrew verb *shedakh*, "to persuade," "to influence," with particular reference to marriage contracts. The business of the Shadchan is to influence young couples to fall in love and marry!

No doubt the Oriental seclusion of women gave rise to this profession of *marriage broker*, which is still practiced today.

> "In Eastern Europe, the parental negotiations are preceded by the activity of a matrimonial agent...a prized visitor in the home of every marriageable girl."[25]

An association of Shadchans was incorporated in New York City in 1929. These matchmakers consider their business not merely as a source of income, but also a pious task desired by God and thus are very prayerful and cautious in their work. After being hired by the parents, the "Shadchan" studies the couple, sometimes for years, and then seeks to influence each as to the character and possessions of the other. He is paid a handsome sum for his services and because "he knows his business," very seldom does the marriage end in failure. The Shadchan's "right to compensation was dealt with in the *'Or Zarua'* and the *'Mordekai,'* and in the ordinances of the Council of the Four Lands."[26]

> Explanation: The "Council of the Four Lands" is a community of Jews within a community. This community of Jews have a self-government which remains under the firm control of the "host" Gentile Society. The name (above) began in the fourth century BC after Alexander the Great had made himself master of the Jewish destiny. At that time, though in the midst of the Gentiles, this Jewish community had a separate religious life, language, culture and its own Institutions. Even in the ghettos where their enemies isolated them from the rest of society they were self-governing and the enemies of the Jews actually helped to preserve the Jews as *Jews*. Originally, the *Four Lands* were Great Poland, Little Poland, Galacia and Volhynia. The *Council* acted as the *Sanhedrin of Poland.* Today there are these Jewish self-governing communities within Gentile communities all over the world.

> *"And Abraham said unto his eldest servant of his house, that ruled over all that he had, Put, I pray thee, thy hand under my thigh: And I will make thee swear by the LORD, the God of heaven, and the God of the earth, that thou shalt **not** take a wife unto my son of the*

---

[25]Cohen, *Jewish Life in Modern Times*, 1914.
[26]*Encyclopedia of Jewish Knowledge*, p. 509.

daughters of the Canaanites, among whom I dwell: But thou shalt go unto my country, and to my kindred, and take a wife unto my son Isaac" (Genesis 24:2-4).

The eldest servant of Father Abraham was a *Shadchan* (matchmaker) who was sent to find a bride for Isaac. He is unnamed in this instance and this is so fitting—for he will not be speaking of himself but of the excellencies of Isaac. Bible Chronology gives the date when Abraham spoke of Eliezer becoming his heir as 1913 BC, whereas the eldest servant mentioned in this case (Genesis 24:2) the time is 1857 BC, 56 years later. It is probable, therefore, that Eliezar had passed away, and that another had been chosen to take his place. This being so, the present steward of Abraham's house may rightly be called "the *unnamed* servant."

This "unnamed servant" considered it a sacred trust of the Lord for he prayed concerning God's choice. When he saw Rebecca and knew this was the one whom God, had chosen (by a sign), he "influenced" her by describing the beauty and the possessions of his employer's son in such a manner that when the invitation was given, she could not resist. Rebecca fell in love with Isaac though she had never seen him. She left all she held dear to her life and rode in a camel train to a far country where she had never been to become the bride of this man she had never met! On the way, surely she inquired concerning her bridegroom and the more he was described to her the more her heart pounded with love for him. She could hardly wait to see him face to face! At the end of her long journey, she dismounted her camel and ran to meet her Isaac whom she had learned to love because of the Shadchan's faithful description. When the marriage ceremony was performed, that was a holy consummation, a glorious jubilee, a wonderful wedding day!

There is a "Shadchan" sent from God, the Father, who is seeking a Bride for the Heavenly Isaac. He is called the Holy Spirit. However, He is more than a servant to the Father God. He is equal with God. He *is* God, the third Person of the Godhead. He does not speak of Himself, but glorifies the Heavenly Isaac, the Messiah Lord! The Holy Spirit has presented and described to us the Altogether Lovely One, the Fairest of Ten Thousand, the Lily of the Valley, our Matchless Bridegroom! At the invitation, we could not resist Him. Though we have never seen Him as He really is, we fell in love with Him; we left all to follow the Lover of our soul and we are now on a long camel journey as pilgrims and strangers in this world, to go to a Land where we have never been, to become the "Bride" of this One we have never seen face to face. As we travel on our way to our Heavenly Home, the Heavenly Shadchan describes our Heavenly Isaac more and more to us and our love grows stronger and stronger. Some day we shall light from off our camels (leave this world behind); we shall know Him whom our soul loveth; we shall see our Heavenly Bridegroom face to face! We who are His, with our hearts full of yearning toward Him, cry with the voice of the Bride: *"Oh Lord, speed the day when the spiritual Shadchan's work will be consummated in the **marriage supper of the Lamb!***

✡ ✡ ✡ ✡ ✡ ✡ ✡

THE BRIDE

*"... and he took one of his **ribs**, ...* [Hebrew: "He took one from his **side parts**]*"* (Genesis 2:21).

*"And the **rib**, which the LORD God had taken from man, made he a woman, ...* [Hebrew: And the **side portion** which God had taken from man, builded he a woman]*"* (Genesis 2:22).

*"**And Adam said,** This is now **bone** of my **bones**, and **flesh** of my flesh: she shall be called Woman* [Isha], *because she was taken out of Man* [Ish]*"* (Genesis 2:23).

"Adam was first formed, and then Eve. She was taken out of the man and builded for the man as a helper, guide, philosopher, and friend. As the last created, the woman was the best and most honored of all. She was not made directly from the dust of the ground, but builded from a living, warm portion of man's body. Man was created from the cold, soul-less dust.

"The woman was one step farther removed from the earth than the man, and was intended to pull man upward and heavenward. The word *Isha* means a she-man, differing from man, not in nature or equality, but only in sex. The Hebrew word translated *Ish* signifies man, and the word used to express what we term woman is exactly the same with a feminine termination and literally means a she-man *(Isha)*.

"The word woman is not compounded of *wo* and *man* as though she were man's woe. She was intended to be man's help, and every true she-man is man's help-meet. Because of disobedience, woman has become instead of a queen, a chattel, a toy, a slave, and a cipher.

"It was not until after the curse had been pronounced and punishment meted out to the offenders that Adam (not God) called his wife's name 'Chavah,' at the same time giving his reasons for doing so: 'because she was the mother of all living.' The word 'chavah' means 'living' and points to our Lord Jesus Christ as the Living One. 'And Adam called his wife's name Chavah [Eve,] because she was [to be] the mother of the Living One.

"Thus the woman who brought death would also bring life, even the Living One. 'Adam called his wife's name life, because she was to be the mother of the living one.' The eye of Adam was on the seed of the woman, the coming Redeemer. In this hope he lived and trusted, and in this hope he triumphed. By divine appointment, and as one more irrefutable proof of the Divine inspiration of the Bible, the woman was to be more than the soil: she was to bear the seed! 'Her seed' was a truth that uninspired, egotistical, self-conceited man would never have allowed. 'Her seed' reveals a wonderful biological secret given to Moses by inspiration."

—W.G. Heslop, *Seed Thoughts*

THE WEDDING GARMENTS

In days past, the Jewish wedding dress always had blue in the bosom, and often a blue shawl was draped over the head of the bride. This represented the faithfulness of the bride to her vows of marriage and also her faithfulness to the law of God concerning these vows. From God's commandment that Israel wear a blue ribbon (or thread) with the fringes in the corners of their garments as in Numbers 15:38, comes the custom for "something old, something new, something borrowed and something blue."

> *"I will greatly rejoice in the LORD, my soul shall be joyful in my God; for he hath clothed me with the garments of salvation, he hath covered me with the robe of righteousness, as a bridegroom decketh himself with ornaments, and as a bride adorneth herself with her jewels"* (Isaiah 61:10).

Among orthodox Jews the bridegroom still wears the prayer cloak called *tallit* (tallis) at his wedding. This is a type of the priest's garment of righteousness (white) and the king's robe of majesty and power (blue). The Jewish husband is king and priest in his own household. A Sephardic custom is for the bride and groom to be enwrapped together by a single tallit at their marriage ceremony.

> "Not only does the white show forth the spotlessness of the Bridegroom, but we are told in Revelation 19:8 that it has been given to the wife of the Lamb, 'That she should array herself in fine linen, bright and pure, for the fine linen is the righteous acts of the saints.' The literal meaning of 'bright and pure' is '*radiant* and pure.' The word translated 'bright' is from a word meaning 'flaming torch.' This is the wedding garment that has been prepared for the Lamb's wife. It is not only pure and holy, it is *glorious, shining, radiant!*"[27]

---

[27]Cora Harris MacIlravy, *Christ and His Bride*, p. 52.

As the white dress suggests the purity and righteousness of Messiah, so the blue suggests our faithfulness to His Word and to our vows which we made before Him when accepting His righteousness!

> *"And Jesus* [Yeshua] *answered and spake unto them again by parables, and said, The kingdom of heaven is like unto a certain king, which* **made a marriage for his son,** *And when the king came in to see the guests, he saw there a man which had not on a* **wedding garment:** *And he saith unto him, Friend, how camest thou in hither not having* **a wedding garment?** *And he was speechless. Then said the king to the servants, Bind him hand and foot, and take him away, and cast him into outer darkness; there shall be weeping and gnashing of teeth"* (Matthew 22:1-2, 11-13).

Everyone who accepts the Lord Yeshua into his heart is immediately clothed with an "earnest" of the wedding garment, is ordained a king and a priest to God, is made ready for the Marriage Supper of the Lamb. But woe to those who have refused the Lover of their soul; they do not possess the promise of the wedding apparel; they shall be cast out from the presence of God; they shall not participate in the Wedding of all weddings because they are not properly dressed for the occasion! Dear reader, be sure the following verse is true of you: "This old world can never hold me, Any moment I'll be gone—For I've made my consecration, And I *have* my wedding garments on!"

The word "trousseau" is from "trusse," which means "a little bundle." In ancient days it was in the form of a dowry, and was the indirect means of compensating a bridegroom for the money and goods he paid out to the girl's father. As a natural bride is very careful over her trousseau, so we now find it necessary to consider the care we are to exercise over our spiritual trousseau. (See above Scripture verse, also Revelation 7:13, *robes of white*, Revelation 19:8, *fine linen clean and bright*, Revelation 3:4-5, *white garments*, Revelation 16:15, keepeth his garments, *white raiment*.)

Blue. As the *white* dress suggests the purity and righteousness of Christ, so the blue suggests our faithfulness to His Word and to our vows which we made before Him when accepting His righteousness.

In the story of Rebekah and Isaac, the servant of Abraham *"brought forth jewels of silver, and jewels of gold, and raiment, and gave them to Rebekah, he gave also to her brother and to her mother precious things"* (Genesis 24:53). When Isaac saw *his own jewels* on Rebekah, he recognized in her his bride who was chosen for him! These jewels were the token; the earnest of the glory that was to come.

Notice that the servant did not speak of himself; he testified of Isaac and carried out the plans of the father Abraham. The bride did not search for her groom but the servant sought for her to present to her the gifts of Isaac which she accepted. The true Church or Congregation of the Lord is the Bride. The servant is the Holy Spirit of God who did not speak concerning Himself but testified of the Messiah, the Heavenly Bridegroom. We, as the Bride, did not search after our Messiah; the Holy Spirit sought us out and presented to us the gifts of salvation which we accepted. We are now wearing these "jewels" and are recognized by our Heavenly Isaac as His Bride by *his own ornaments* which He has lavished upon us:

> *"I decked thee also with ornaments, and I put bracelets upon thy hands, and a chain on thy neck. And I put a jewel on thy forehead, and earrings in thine ears, and a beautiful crown upon thine head. Thus wast thou decked with gold and silver; and thy raiment was of fine linen, and silk, and broidered work; thou didst eat fine flour, and honey, and oil: and thou wast exceeding beautiful, and thou didst prosper into a kingdom. And thy renown went forth among the heathen for thy beauty: for it was perfect through **my comeliness, which I had put upon thee,** saith the Lord GOD"* (Ezekiel 16:11-14).

When we are betrothed to the Lover of our soul, we become partakers of His own Divine nature, and begin to wear and express forth the *jewels* (His nature) by the power of the Holy Spirit! We are spiritually made beautiful by His own beauty which He does put upon us. Praise His Name!

HUPAH (Wedding Canopy)

"Hupah" ("Chupah") literally means "a covering." It is a canopy of equal length and width used in the marriage ceremony of the Jewish people. Sometimes this canopy is made of either silk or satin (some prefer velvet) and is supported by four poles (one on each corner) which four guests carry. Some, especially in Israel, use the "tallit" as the canopy covering. Sometimes the canopy is made of fresh flower arrangements. Over each of the poles on the cloth canopy there is printed or

Seen on two sides of the *Hupa* are the two phrases in Hebrew: *Kol Hatan* (Voice of the Groom) and *Kol Chalee* (Voice of the Bride).

embroidered one of the following phrases in Hebrew: "The Voice of the Bride," "The Voice of the Groom," "The Sound of Gladness," "The Sound of Joy" (see Jeremiah 33:11).

The *Hupah* reminds the Jew of the litter in which the bride was carried in the processions of long ago. It also brings to remembrance the ancient tent life of Israel especially referring to the time when Isaac took Rebecca to live in his tent home when they had been joined together in marriage. This "canopy" stands as a picture of the future home of the couple. The groom (*Hazan*) enters beneath the canopy first, escorted by his father and mother. Then the bride (*Cholee*) enters, escorted by her parents.

As the people of God (both Jew and Gentile who believe in Messiah Yeshua) look upon the canopy of Jewish custom, they can see the future home of the Bride and the Heavenly Bridegroom:

> *"And the city lieth **foursquare**, and the length is as large as the breadth: ... The length and the breadth and the height of it are equal"* (Revelation 21:16).

Silk, satin or velvet can hardly compare to the materials of which that city is made, for "the building of the wall of it is of jasper: and the city is pure gold, like unto clear glass. And the foundations of the wall of the city are garnished with all manner of precious stones" (Revelation 21:18-19).

> *"And the twelve gates were twelve pearls: every several gate was of one pearl: and the street of the city was pure gold, as it were transparent glass"* (Revelation 21:21).

The number "four" suggests the world: *"And the **nations** of them which are saved shall walk in the light of it"* (Revelation 21:24). From the *four* corners of the globe, from the east, and from the west, from the north, and from the south the company of the redeemed shall come and shall enter the New Jerusalem, that city that lieth ***foursquare***.

The Heavenly Bridegroom went first under the Canopy, but before He went away He encouraged His disciples who were then living, and all those who would believe in Him through their word:

> *"Let not your heart be troubled: ... **I go to prepare a place for you**. ... **I will come again**, and receive you unto myself; that where I am, there ye may be also"* (John 14:1-3).

Some day, in fulfillment of prophecy, there will be heard *the voice of the Bride, the voice of the* (Heavenly) *Bridegroom, the sound of gladness, the sound of joy*! and we who have made ourselves ready shall go to be with Him forevermore. He who is our Lord and King has captured our hearts! Halleluia!

THE CEREMONY

The orthodox Jewish wedding lasts for seven days of singing, dancing, eating and drinking. Rabbis say the period of *seven* in celebrating the wedding refers to the story of Jacob and Laban where Laban tells Jacob to fill out the seven (years) after Jacob married Leah. Also it refers to the story of Samson who journeyed to the land of the Philistines and after he had taken a bride there he celebrated for *seven* days. Sometimes the ceremony is performed in the Rabbi's study, sometimes in the synagogue, or in a community hall. But the favorite place is in the *home of the bride* (if it is large enough to accommodate all the guests). The month best suited for this union falls in June after Pentecost ("Shavuot").

Those of us who know the Heavenly Bridegroom are waiting for the great consummation in the *Home of the Bride* (heaven), in the month of months, the day of days, the holiest moment of all. This will last a perfect number of years with music, singing, dancing, drinking of the *new wine,* and eating of the rich things which God has prepared for those who love Him, at the Marriage Supper of the Lamb (see Revelation 19:7-9)!

At orthodox weddings the bridegroom lifts the Veil of his bride before the ceremony. This custom assures him that the bride is the girl promised him and recalls the experience of Jacob and Leah (Genesis 29:20-25; see also the use of the Veil in Genesis 24:65).

> "The custom of dressing the virgin bride with a veil is mentioned in the Mishnah: covered with a veil (*'hinuma'*) and seated on a litter, she was carried in the wedding-procession from her father's house to the nuptial ceremony (*Ket*.ii.l). In modern times the bride is 'covered' with a veil in her chamber in the presence of the groom, just before they are led under the canopy. In some countries the groom, and in others the Rabbi, performs the ceremony of covering the bride." [28]

In Israel, among the very Orthodox, the bride's face is covered. At the wedding ceremony, the high point is when the bridegroom, after walking around the bride three times, removes the veil covering from her face and throws it over his shoulder. By this, he is saying to those gathered together at the wedding that the government of his bride now rests upon him!

The Rabbi welcomes the couple with the words: "Blessed is he who cometh in the name of the Lord." In many of the ceremonies of the Jews this expression is prominent, but they refuse to say this of

---

[28] *Jewish Encyclopedia.* Taken from a summary on *Ketubot*, the second Tractate of the *Seder Nashim* of the Talmud.

the Messiah Jesus to whom it really refers, for He said to (the Jews) of Jerusalem *("... Ye shall not see* **me** *henceforth, till ye shall say [of* **me**]: *'Blessed is he that cometh in the Name of the Lord"* (Matthew 23:39).

Oh, that these dear people would acknowledge the One who was promised of God; the One who came to His own (things) and His own (people, the Jews) received Him not; the One who wept over Jerusalem because they did not know their God when He visited them; the One who longs to take them in His arms of love and fold them to His bosom; the One who yearns over them with compassion; the One who is their Messiah, their Shiloh, their King!

The Rabbi's greeting ends with the words: "Serve the Lord with joy, come before Him with shouting." The young couple are admonished to be joyful as *they serve God together.* One Rabbi observed that when the letter ' (*yod*) is removed from the Hebrew word for "man," the remaining letters spell the Hebrew word for "fire." Similarly, remove the letter ה (*heh*) from the Hebrew word for "woman" and the remainder also spells the Hebrew word for "fire." But ' (*yod*) and ה (*heh*) together spell a Hebrew word for God (*Yah*; i.e., *yod-heh,* יה). This implies, said the Rabbi, that when God departs from the marriage, nothing but the fire of contention remains!

Those who know the Heavenly Bridegroom can truly serve Him with rejoicing, can truly come before Him with shouting, for "in His presence is fullness of joy and at His right hand there are pleasures forevermore!" (Psalm 16:11).

After the greeting the Rabbi speaks to the man and woman concerning the sacredness of marriage and the ideals to guide them in their union. He then blesses two goblets of wine from which the bride and groom drink. These two cups represent joy and sorrow. Therefore, when the couple partake of them, it is as though they are vowing that they will share the joys and sorrows of life together. At the first cup the betrothal benediction is given: "As together you now drink from this cup, so may you under God's guidance, In perfect union and devotion to each other, Draw contentment, comfort, and felicity From the cup of life; Thereby may you find life's joys doubly gladdening. Its bitterness sweetened, And all things hallowed By true companionship and love." (The betrothal, up to the 11th or 12th Century, took place months earlier.)

The Heavenly Bridegroom has partaken all of the "Cup of Sorrow" (the bitter cup) that His Bride might drink all of the "Cup of Joy" (Salvation)! He not only *shares* our burdens but He carries the heavy end of the Cross! He is the Burden-Bearer!

THE RING

In orthodox weddings the use of precious stones in a wedding ring is prohibited. The custom is to use a plain ring for it is not to be assumed by the bride as of higher value than it is. The minimum requirement for the ring is that it be worth more than a penny!

After drinking of the first cup of wine just blessed, the groom places the unadorned ring on the forefinger of his bride's right hand (the most visible) declaring: "Be thou sanctified unto me in accordance with the law of Moses and Israel." Or it is said: "Behold, thou art consecrated unto me by means of this ring, according to the law of Moses and Israel." At a later time, the groom places the ring on the traditional ring finger, from it is believed, a vein runs straight to the heart.

The index finger is chosen because it is used for *pointing* and can easily be shown to the witnesses! The moment anyone has accepted Jesus-Messiah as his personal Saviour, that moment he becomes "betrothed" to the Lover of his soul, that moment a Ring or Seal of His approval is put upon him and one can almost hear the Bridegroom's voice saying: "Behold, thou art consecrated to Me by means of the *Holy Spirit* according to the laws of God and His Kingdom!" And the Ring (the Holy Spirit) on the "pointer-finger," so to speak, makes the believer a Witness for Him!

THE SEVEN BENEDICTIONS

After the *Kiddushin* (*Sanctification* prayer of the groom) is done, the marriage contract (the *Ketubah*) is read and given to the Bride. The "Ketubah" or marriage contract (written in Aramaic) tells what are the obligations of man to woman in married life. (Reform Judaism omits the *Ketubah*.) The clergyman then recites the following *Seven Benedictions* (**Bruchot Nessuin** or **Sheva Berachot**) as he lifts up the *second* goblet of wine: (The blessing over the wine is first.)

1. Praised art Thou O Lord, our God, King of the Universe, Who creates the fruit of the vine.
2. Praised art Thou O Lord, our God, King of the Universe, Who creates all things for His Glory.
3. Praised art Thou, O Lord, our God, King of the Universe, Creator of man.
4. Praised art Thou O Lord, our God, King of the Universe, Who made man in his image, according to his likeness, and prepared for him out of his own being, an *everlasting fabric*. Praised art Thou O Lord, Creator of Man. May she who was barren; i.e., Zion, be

exceedingly glad and exult when her children are gathered within her in joy.

5.   Praised art Thou O Lord, our God, King of the Universe Who makes Zion glad because of her children. Cause the loved companions to rejoice, even as Thou didst in days of old gladden Thy creatures in the Garden of Eden. Praised art Thou O Lord, Who causes the bridegroom and the bride to rejoice.

6.   Praised art Thou O Lord, our God, King of the Universe, Who created joy and gladness, bridegroom and bride, mirth and exultation, pleasure and delight, love and brotherhood, peace and fellowship. May there be heard soon in the cities of Judah and in the streets of Jerusalem the voice of joy and gladness, the voice of the bridegroom and the voice of the bride, the jubilant voice of the bridegrooms from their canopies and of youths from their feasts of song.

7.   Praised art Thou O Lord, Who causes the bridegroom to rejoice with the bride."

At Orthodox Jewish weddings, the bride is led around the groom *seven* times before these benedictions are chanted. It is felt that this "circling of the groom" is to observe Jeremiah 31:22 *"A woman shall compass* (go around) *a man."* With both sets of parents at her side the Bride (Kallah) circles the Groom (Hazan) *seven* times (to correspond to the seven verses in the Bible that state *"when a man takes a wife"*). This number (seven) of circles stand for her *purity* and tells that she is a *perfect* bride for the bridegroom. To attain purity, both the bride and groom *fast* on the day before the ceremony. They read the Book of Psalms and also ask forgiveness for past wrongs. When the Bride circles her Groom she is saying by this to all those gathered at the wedding that she is a perfect, pure Bride for the Bridegroom!

What a picture of the Bride of Christ (the Church) who is described as without spot, holy, and blameless, and some day to be declared *perfect* in Him before a countless number in attendance at the greatest of all weddings (see Revelation 19:7-9)!

BREAKING THE GLASS

After the Seven Nuptial Blessings the couple drink from the second cup of wine and following this a very interesting part of the ceremony takes place:

The groom wraps an empty goblet or glass in a napkin or in his own handkerchief, places it on the floor and with one stamp of his foot, breaks it to pieces. It is considered an ill omen if the glass is not broken under the first stamp of his foot! This denotes the severing of the ties of the past, the destruction of evil threatening the home, but most important of all, it signifies mourning for the Temple and the glory which has departed from Israel.

A Jewish description of "breaking the glass" follows:

"After the wedding ceremony, the bridegroom is handed a small glass which he places under his heel. He stamps upon it so that it breaks into splinters. There are several reasons for this custom. First of all, it reminds us of the destruction of the Temple. We have been enjoined by the Sages to remember our dire loss even in the midst of our supreme rejoicing. In other words, no matter how happy we may be, we must bear in mind the fact that the Holy Temple, the House of God built by man, was destroyed because of our sins.

"There is another, more spiritual, meaning for the observance of this custom. The bride and groom should remember that life is transitory, and that it is furthermore beset by all sorts of problems and difficulties. And, just as the fragile glass can be broken by a hard blow, so can connubial bliss be disrupted by lack of harmony, lack of sympathy with each other, lack of tolerance.

"The third reason for breaking the glass is that the glass vessel typifies the body of man. Just as the glass is fashioned from sand and blown into shape, so is the body of man created from dust, fashioned into shape and imbued with the breath or spirit of God. And, just as any flaw in the glass will cause it to split so will any flaw in the character of the individual cause his downfall. And, just as a glass which becomes polluted must be broken, so must man's hauteur and pride be broken by repentance if his mind becomes sullied by sin." (Ruth Jacobs, *The Jewish Wedding*, a small pamphlet.)

"The Rabbis teach there are three that have a share in a man: God, and his mother and father. The father's part consists of all that is *white* in him–the bones, the veins, the nails, the brain and the white of the eye. The mother's part consists of all the *red* in him– the skin, the flesh, the hair and the black of the eye. God's part consists of the breath and the soul, the physiognomy, sight and hearing, speech, motive power, knowledge, understanding and wisdom. And when the time comes that the man should depart from the world, God takes away His part, and leaves those that belong to the father and mother. Reverend Pappa says, This is the meaning of the proverb, 'shake off the salt and throw the flesh to the dogs' (*Niddah*, fol. 31, col.1)."[29]

The couple who have just been united in holy wedlock are to leave all their activities, pleasures, all their friends and relatives in their past life in order that they might be able to cling to each other first of all.

---

[29]David Goldstein, *Jewish Panorama*, p.137.

When believers in Messiah Jesus accept Him, the greatest Beloved, all ties are severed with loved ones (in a sense), and it is He to whom their hearts cling forever!

The bridegroom, in stamping the glass to fragments, is promising by his action, that he will stamp out all evils that ever threaten to come into the home. From the Talmud the husband is commanded: "Love thy wife as thyself and honor her more than thyself." When we give ourselves to the keeping of our Heavenly Bridegroom He will not allow us to fall into temptation, but will deliver us from evil, and what is more, will give His bride that same power to *"tread upon serpents and upon scorpions and over all the power of the enemy, and nothing shall by any means hurt* [her]" (Luke 10:19).

To the Jewish people the destruction of the Temple in Jerusalem was the saddest event in their history. The glory of Israel then departed, but that ancient "glory" at the height of their greatest joy (which is the wedding) is never to be forgotten. The following Scripture verses are recited at Sephardic Jewish Weddings:

> *"If I forget thee, O Jerusalem, let my right hand forget her cunning. If I do not remember thee, let my tongue cleave to the roof of my mouth; if I prefer not Jerusalem above my chief joy"* (Psalm 137:5-6).

The actual Temple was destroyed, the sacrifices ceased to be practiced, and the glory departed, but the spiritual temple, sacrifice and glory is still with us! Messiah Jesus spoke of Himself when He said: *"Destroy this temple and in three days I will raise it up"* (John 2:19). HE is the Temple of God. HE is the Sacrifice for sin. HE is the Glory of Israel. The Jew need not mourn but be glad and rejoice in his Messiah-Jesus, the Son of the Living God!

CONCLUSION OF THE WEDDING

In some instances the groom places a crown upon the head and a robe (his prayer shawl-*tallit*) about the shoulders of his bride after they are pronounced husband and wife. Then he leads her to a throne where they preside over the merrymaking of the guests. They reign there as King and Queen.

The Heavenly Bridegroom has promised that some glorious day He would give us, His Bride, a *crown* of Life (James 1:12) and to *"him that overcometh will I grant to **sit with me in my throne***" (Revelation 3:21).

After the three-fold priestly benediction, everyone greets the couple saying: "Mazal Tov!" ("Good Luck," "Congratulations"). The words "Mazal Tov" are used in the Ashkenazi custom. *Be-siman tov* is the Sephardi custom. Some use "Lo Tov," meaning "not good" which refers to the biblical statement that "it is not good for man to be alone."

> "Modern Judaism rejects astrology and the popular greeting 'mazal tov,' 'good luck,' is never used in the sense of its astrological origin. The term is originally derived from the Hebrew word meaning constellation, planet; i.e., man's destiny is dependent upon the planets according to the month and day of one's birth. Such astrological concepts are foreign to the basic principles of Judaism, which maintains that all we are and all we have is due to God's rule in the universe."[30]

DANCING

The oldest guest at the wedding leads others in a dance, a little jig called *Katzotske*. Everyone dances and sings, and all are very happy. "There are many Jewish wedding dances, the *'Shereleh'* and the *'Brogez Tanz'* being the best known, danced to tuneful Jewish music. In recent years, the Palestinian *Horah* dance has become popular at weddings."[31]

> "It is a common sight today, in the 'changeless East,' in any procession, to see a man dancing with strange attitudes to do honour to the bridegroom or other hero of the day, and the more grotesque his attitudes the more honour is done. The man dances backwards, and with his dress girded to give free play to his limbs, as the common peasants gird themselves for active work. Thus, no doubt, David danced to do honour to God's Ark!" (Rev. James Neil, *Pictured Palestine.*)

> "The Hebrews, in common with other nations, had their sacred dances, which were performed on solemn anniversaries, and other occasions of commemorating some special token of Divine goodness and favor. The performers were usually bands of females, who, in cases of public rejoicing, volunteered their services to God (Exodus 15:20); and who in case of religious observances, composed the regular chorus of the temple. Psalm 149:3; 150:4. Men also joined in the dancing. David did not consider it hurtful to his dignity as King to dance before the Ark of God.

> The conduct of David was imitated by later Jews and the dance was incorporated in the ceremonies of the Feast of Tabernacles. There is dancing in the old synagogue during the Feast of Pentecost which is in joyful commemoration of the giving of the Law. In certain parts of Russia and in Poland there is a 'holiness sect' among the

---

[30]Abraham Heller, *Vocabulary of Jewish Life*, p. 139.
[31]Ben M. Edidin, *Jewish Customs and Ceremonies*, p. 71.

Jews known as the Hasidim, who engage in ecstatic dancing during their religious services.

The Jewish dances were performed by the sexes separately. In the sacred dances, although both sexes seem to have frequently borne a part in the procession or chorus, they remained distinct and separate companies. When the Hebrews practiced pagan rites, as in the worship of the Golden Calf, the case was different. Then all standards of modesty were lost sight of."

–Meyer Pearlman in *The Pentecostal Evangel*

No sadness, no tears are allowed at a Jewish wedding. (I remember my grandmother leaving the party to go to another room in the house where she could cry. She could not do so in the room where a wedding was in progress.) There is to be rejoicing in the happiness of the bride and groom. This forecasts another Wedding for there are no tears in heaven; no sorrows, no sickness, no death there. *"Let us be glad and rejoice and give honour to him: for the **marriage of the lamb** is come and his wife hath made herself ready"* (Revelation 19:7).

At the wedding there is feasting such as at no other gathering. A table is spread with good food and wine. The bride and groom sit at the head of this table and the guests are seated with them. There is laughter and song; much happiness and much rejoicing, wine adding to the exhilaration of all at the marriage.

The Word of God tells that at the union of Messiah and His own blood-bought Church, His Bride, there will be a great *feast*. The believers in Messiah-Jesus will sit down with Him and with Abraham, Isaac, Jacob, Isaiah, Sarah, Rachel, Esther, etc. They will eat the food, and drink the "wine," the pure juice of the grape. (At the last Passover Seder of Messiah He promised that one day we will all partake of the "fruit of the vine" with Him; see Matthew 26:29.)

We, who are believers, will be happy, rejoicing in the Beloved Master and Lover of our souls! What a holy consummation! What a glorious Jubilee! What a wonderful Wedding Day that will be (see Revelation 19:9)!

LOUIS AND ANNA SPECTER
(Author's Parents)

CHAPTER THREE

JEWISH HOLY DAYS

SHABBAT (Sabbath)[32]

"Thus the heavens and the earth were finished, and all the host of them. And on the seventh day God ended his work which he had made; and he rested on the seventh day from all his work which he had made. And God blessed the seventh day, and sanctified it: because that in it he had rested from all his work which God created and made" (Genesis 2:1-3).

It is interesting to note that there are three words for God's Holy Sabbath: the first is *shabbat* which means *to rest, to cease* (from work), *to repose, to complete*. God "sabbathed," reposed, ceased, from His work of creation. In other words, God could have *sabbath* because the (first) Creation was *completed*. The second word is *nuach*, or rested, to be comforted, consoled, to settle down (from Exodus 20:11). God could have *sabbath* because He was *contented* or *satisfied* with the work He had done. The third word is *shabbat-*

Woman in Sabbath Prayer

naphash, which is translated as rested-refreshed, resouled, restored ("caught his breath"). This word is found in Exodus 31:17. God could have **sabbath** because He was *refreshed* in the perfect work of His Creation!

All the foregoing is concerning ***God's*** Sabbath. There is no command of God in this Genesis passage for *man* to keep *this* Sabbath! The Sabbath which was for *man* is not given until after the Exodus, 2,513 years after the record in Genesis 2:2 where God is the One who "rested"! Not one word is said about the seventh day having been commanded or ordained, until it was given to Israel.

*"And he said unto them, This is that which the LORD hath said, To morrow is the **rest** of the holy **sabbath** unto the LORD: bake that which ye will bake to day, and seethe that ye will seethe; and that which remaineth over lay up for you to be kept until the morning. And they laid it up till the morning, as Moses bade: and it did not stink, neither was there any worm therein. And Moses said, Eat that to day; for **to day** is a sabbath unto the LORD: to*

---

[32]Portions of this writing on the Sabbath is also in my *God's Calendar of Prophetic Events*, Appendix II, p. 65.

*day ye shall not find it in the field. Six days ye shall gather it; but on the seventh day, **which is the sabbath**, in it there shall be none"* (Exodus 16:23-26).

No mention is made of the Sabbath during the entire period preceding Israel's Exodus from Egypt and then when it is mentioned we are told that it was *ordained for **that** nation* as a *memorial of their deliverance.* (It is said by Ahad Haam, the Hebrew Essayist: "More than Israel has kept the Sabbath, it is the Sabbath that has kept Israel.")

*"But the seventh day is the sabbath of the LORD thy God: in it thou shalt not do any work, thou, nor thy son, nor thy daughter, nor thy manservant, nor thy maidservant, nor thine ox, nor thine ass, nor any of thy cattle, nor thy stranger that is within thy gates; that thy manservant and thy maidservant may **rest** as well as thou. And **remember** that thou wast a servant in the land of Egypt, and that the LORD thy God brought thee out thence through a mighty hand and by a stretched out arm: **therefore** the LORD thy God commanded thee to **keep the sabbath day**"* (Deuteronomy 5:14-15).

So that they would not fail to remember, God commanded Israel to set apart the seventh day *to commemorate their deliverance from bondage.* They left Egypt on the Passover Sabbath! (In the Bible, weekly Sabbaths for the year always began with the Passover Sabbath!)

*"And they departed from Rameses in the first month, on the fifteenth day of the first month; on the **morrow after the passover** the children of Israel went out with an high hand in the sight of all the Egyptians"* (Numbers 33:3).

In Exodus 16:23-30 we see that the Sabbath was something *new* (*before* the Law was given on Sinai) and since it was new, it is being explained to them. It had not been known among them or their fathers. In Genesis 2:2 and in Exodus 16:30 there are two outstanding differences. We notice that in Genesis 2:2 it was **God** who "rested." He *ceased* from His work of creation. In Exodus 16:30 it is the **people of God** who "rested." They had been delivered from bondage and death and could now rest!

In Genesis 2:2 we learn that GOD **rested** or "stopped" ("sabbath-ed") because His work of creation was finished, but (we repeat): we do not read in all the Genesis account that God *commanded **man*** to observe that Sabbath with Him! After all man was created on the sixth day and had not worked for six days as yet in order to "rest" or "stop" as God did! As far as we know from the Scriptures, there were only 3 commandments which God gave in the Garden of Eden: (1) Be fruitful and multiply, (2) Subdue the earth (Genesis 1:28) and 3) Do not eat from the tree of the knowledge of good and evil (Genesis 2:16, 17).

The question is concerning the *time* that the Sabbath commandment was first given. First of all, we must understand that every one of the commandments of the Lord are included in His law, His judgments, His statutes and in His Covenants as Moses declared to Israel:

*"And he [God] declared unto you **his covenant**, which he commanded you to perform, even **ten commandments** [ten words]; and he wrote them upon two tables of stone. And the LORD commanded me **at that time** to teach you **statutes** and **judgments**, that ye might do them in the land whither ye go over to possess it"* (Deuteronomy 4:13-14).

*"And this is the **law** which Moses set before the children of Israel: These are the testimonies, and the statutes, and the judgments, which Moses spake unto the children of Israel, after they came forth out of Egypt,"* (Deuteronomy 4:44-45).

The Scriptures answers the question as to *when* the Sabbath law was first given: The Law, the Covenant (which included the Ten Commandments) were given *after* Israel left Egypt. The Law Covenant was in force from the time Israel left the land of bondage. It is continually referred to as dating from that time (see Hebrews 8:9; Jeremiah 31:32; Ezekiel 20:5-6).

Let us pin-point the time of Israel's *first Sabbath*. In the first verse of Exodus 16 we learn that it was the 2nd month, the 15th day after Israel left Egypt. Reading further in this chapter we find that the Israelites were instructed to gather twice as much manna on the sixth day than they had gathered the other five days. There was *no reason given* at this time for the command, only that God was going to prove them whether or not they would obey Him without question (see verse 4). The bread had not come down as yet and when it did they knew not what it was. Moses explained to them that it was the bread which God had given to them to eat (verse 15).

In the 16th verse now Moses begins to tell the Israelites of the command which God gave him concerning the Sabbath. For each of the six days they were to gather the manna, not to leave any over for the next day. Some did not understand (for this was something new to them). They left it over for the next morning which caused it to breed worms and to stink. Moses was angry with them because they were to obey God *even though they did not understand*; they were to give God their *unquestionable obedience*. Moses explained further and on the sixth day (now the 21st of the 2nd month), they gathered twice as much bread according to God's commandment. They were now obeying Him, not knowing *why* they were to have twice as much on the 6th day as they had gathered on the other days.

Then Moses explained to them the reason: *It was the holy Sabbath unto the Lord* and they were to cease from the work of gathering the manna *to remember GOD's Sabbath* when He ceased from His work of Creation. Even after this explanation by Moses concerning something new to them, there were some who still did not understand (verse 27) and Moses continued to explain (verse 29). Finally, after all this, we read in the 30th verse:

*"SO the people **rested** on the seventh day."* This would now be the 22nd day of the month *Iyar* when the Israelites observed their *first* Sabbath day. **This is the FIRST mention of the Sabbath observance by Israel in Scripture since Genesis 2:2 when God was the One who "rested."**

> *"**Remember** the sabbath day, to keep it holy. Six days shalt thou labour, and do all thy work: But the seventh day is the **sabbath of the LORD thy God**: in it thou shalt not do any work, thou, nor thy son, nor thy daughter, thy manservant, nor thy maidservant, nor thy cattle, nor thy stranger that is within thy gates: For in six days the LORD made heaven and earth, the sea, and all that in them is, and rested the seventh day: wherefore the LORD blessed the sabbath day, and hallowed it"* (Exodus 20:8-11).

The Hebrew word for *remember* here is *zakar* which means *to mark in the mind, bring to remembrance, think on*. This, then, is *not* the original *Sabbath commandment* but an exhortation to *recall* to their memory the law of the Sabbath which had *already been given*! The people of Israel were to *remember* God's rest in His creation and *remember* the Sabbath commandment given to them *after* they left Egypt. (See Exodus 16:23, 30—the first Sabbath commandment.)

> *"And Moses said unto the people, **Remember** this day, **in which ye came out from Egypt**, out of the house of bondage; for by strength of hand the LORD brought you out from this place: there shall no leavened bread be eaten. This day came ye out in the month Abib"* (Exodus 13:3-4).[33]

The Lord commanded Israel to have a Sabbath on the seventh day of the week, when they would *cease from their labor* and have a time of relaxation to take its place. God made the sabbath to be a delight, a day of joy, gladness and help for His people. It was not His intention that this day be one filled with rules which were difficult to observe so that they might obtain His favor. He not only made it for their own health's sake, but, most important, *to remind* them of that typical day when He Himself rested (or ceased) from all His mighty

---

[33]Compare with Numbers 33:3 and see *Abib* in Exodus 13:4; 23:15, 34:18, Deuteronomy 16:1. After the captivity, this month was called *Nisan*, a Babylonian word. Nehemiah 2:1; Esther 3:7.

acts of creation and also to remind them that now they can rest because they had been *delivered from bondage!* On that day it was the joy of the Lord to have His people gather together to worship Him.

To *whom* was the Sabbath commandment given? We discover the answer to this question in the Scripture following where God commands Moses:

> *"Speak thou also unto **the children of Israel**, saying, Verily my sabbaths ye shall keep: **for it is a sign** between me and you throughout your generations; that ye may know that I am the LORD that doth sanctify you"* (Exodus 31:13).

Here we see that it was to the *Israelites* that the law of the Sabbath was given as a *sign* between them and God. The commandment for observing the Sabbath was not given to the heathen nations. Rest could not be enjoyed apart from redemption and Israel alone was redeemed. This Law was not given before to any people:

> *"The LORD made **not** this covenant with our fathers, but with **us**, even **us**, who are all of us here alive this this day"* (Deuteronomy 5:3).

The "us" in the foregoing verse of Scripture refers to those who left the land of bondage through God's deliverance. The Sabbath commandment was given particularly to *Israel* as a sign between God and His people. He was dealing with Israel, and when He ceased having Israel as His people, then the Sabbath also ceased. Again, when He deals with them as His *earthly* people once more, the Sabbath will be renewed:

> *"And it shall come to pass* [in that Kingdom age when Israel is restored] *that from one new moon to another, and from one sabbath to another, shall all **flesh** come to worship before me, saith the LORD"* (Isaiah 66:23). [Notice "all *flesh*" meaning the *earthly* people. Believers in Messiah are the *heavenly* people!]

It is interesting to note that in post-Biblical and in later Hebrew literature *Friday* is known as "Ereb Shabbat" ("Sabbath evening," i.e., the day before the Sabbath). In Modern Greek and Ecclesiastical Latin, "Parasceve," translated as "the Preparation," the sixth day of the week, is the word for *Friday!* (See Mark 15:42; John 19:31, 19:14; Luke 23:54.)

The Sabbath was to be observed by Israel *in her land.* Only in that land were all God's laws to be observed. The day began at sunset (usually) and ended the following sunset. It would be very difficult for people in other parts of the world to observe the Old Testament Sabbath because of the time element.

God did not command that the Sabbath should be kept on Sunday, neither did He command it to be observed on Saturday. What He did command them was that after they had *worked for six days*, then they should "stop and rest." He did not say that their work should begin on a certain day, only that they were to work for six days, then cease from work on the seventh day (of their work). There were no names given to days in the Bible such as Sunday, Monday, Tuesday, Wednesday, Thursday, Friday and Saturday. These names were given in honor of Greek gods. In the Bible the days were designated by ordinal numerals according to the creation story: First, Second, Third, etc.

Since it is impossible for the Jew to keep the Biblical Sabbath in all its original setting, today they observe only the Seventh Day according to the Rabbinical interpretation of it found in the Talmud.

The religious Jew observes *Shabbat* (Shabbos, Sabbath) and holidays from evening to evening for it is often repeated in the Biblical creation story: *"It was evening and it was morning,"* the evening always preceding the morning in the mention of the day. Every Friday evening before sunset, therefore, the Jewish housewife, and in her absence or inability, the husband, kindles at least two candles. (My orthodox Jewish grandmother observed this custom.) They represent the two versions of the commandment regarding the Sabbath: "to remember" and "to observe." A special blessing is recited immediately after the lighting as it is recommended by the Talmud.

There is a special prohibition contained in Exodus 35:3: *"You shall kindle no fire throughout your habitations upon the Sabbath day."* Light is therefore provided beforehand. If it becomes necessary to light the fires or do any work forbidden to the Jews on the Sabbath, a Gentile (called *Shabbos-Goy*, "Sabbath-Gentile") is engaged for this purpose.

Added laws concerning fire on the Sabbath were given in the *Mishnah* (part I of the Talmud), the following is one of them:

> "Although it has been pronounced lawful to kindle fire on the holy day, even where not absolutely necessary, yet it is unlawful to extinguish fire, even though it had been kindled for the preparation of food; for the extinguishing of fire is work, and is not at all necessary for the dressing of food. And as fire is not to be extinguished, so neither is a candle to be extinguished, and whosoever extinguishes is to be flogged, just as he that weaves or builds. ... Fire is not to be extinguished in order to save property on a holy day, no more than on the Sabbath. On the contrary, one lets it burn and goes away"
>
> —*Hilchoth Yom Tov*, c.iv. 2, 4)

The Messiah said (referring to the Mishnah):

"For they [the scribes and Pharisees] *bind **heavy burdens** and grievous to be borne, and lay them on men's shoulders; ..."* (Matthew 23:4).

"Today, Jews observe Sabbath in different ways. Orthodox Jews will not ride on the Sabbath, nor will they kindle a light. Work, the exchange of money, financial activity of any kind is forbidden. Conservative and Reform Jews, who interpret the traditional injunctions more liberally, do not limit their activities to the same degree. But for all Jews, the inner meaning of Sabbath is the same: it is the time for physical relaxation and spiritual renewal. In the words of the Talmud:

"The Holy One, Blessed Be He, said unto Moses, 'I have a precious gift in my treasure house and Sabbath is its name. I wish to present it to Israel. Go and bring them the good tidings'."[34]

The longest distance a Jew may walk from the outskirts of the city on his Sabbath as prescribed by the *Talmud Berachoth* is 3,675 feet and 9 inches or about a little over 3/4 of a mile. It is the Hebrew *T'chum Shabbos*, meaning *"the limit of the Sabbath"* (Exodus 16:29). A Sabbath Day's journey is mentioned in Acts 1:12. It was the supposed distance between the camp and the Tabernacle (*ark*), 2,000 cubits–3,000 ft. See Joshua 3:4.

No business is transacted by orthodox Jews on their Sabbath, for this is considered as labor, and it is very definitely a command of God to cease from all manner of work on that day. The Jewish people held so tenaciously to the Sabbath that when Titus made his attack upon the city of Jerusalem in 70 AD, he chose the seventh day because he knew the Jews would not fight on that day! As a result, approximately a million of them were slain, and the gutters of the streets filled with their blood. An interesting note along these lines but from the opposite viewpoint, relates that in June, 1967, a battle involving Jews and Egyptians in the mid-East (known as "The Six-Day War") began on a Sunday and ended in time for the Jews to keep their Holy Sabbath!

In order for Jews to keep from desecrating the Sabbath various inventions have been introduced in Israel such as the following:

Shabbat telefon (Sabbath telephone). The switch and the signal functions are indirect and *does no work* nor lights any lights!

An item in the *Jerusalem Post* was headed by the title: **Electronic Brain Saves Jews From Violating Sabbath**. JERUSALEM—Strict

---

[34]*ADL The Christian Friends Bulletin*, Vol. 16, Number 2.

Orthodox Jews in Israel apply the Mosaic prohibition against kindling fires on the Sabbath to turning on electricity. They have found, however, two remedies to the problem for security purposes.

"One is a flashlight system operated by a small electronic 'brain' for use by Orthodox members of the Civil Guard. The other is a fully automated 'Sabbath Jeep' with rotating searchlights. It travels along a predetermined course in agricultural settlements. *Perception* newsletter said the jeep serves as an electronic 'scarecrow' against thieves who try to steal farm produce on Sabbath eves in unpatrolled religious settlements throughout the country (May 20, 1979).

The Jewish Sabbath is dedicated by reciting *Kiddush* ("Sanctification") over wine, besides the lighting of the candles. "The *Kiddush* is a prayer by which the *holiness of the Sabbath* is proclaimed." "Jewish prayers have a beautiful characteristic. At meals the non-Jew will frequently thank God for his food. This is good, but the *kiddush,* like most Jewish prayers, is a *benediction upon God Himself.*"

Jewish people conclude the Sabbath in the synagogue and home service by making the *Havdalah* (separation) benediction. The family gathers around the father, one child holding a twisted candle, while another holds the *Besamim* or spice box. The father places his hands upon the heads of his children and blesses them; he sings a hymn of praise to his faithful wife (Proverbs 31). Even as the priest ministered in the Holy Place, so does the Jewish father minister in his home. He raises the goblet of wine to proclaim the holiness of the Sabbath. He thanks God for this holy day and for the days of work, and asks for light and joy; gladness and honor. He inhales the fragrance of the spices and recites a blessing for the good things of life. He brings his hands close to the light, bending his fingers to make a shadow, so as to distinguish between light and darkness, and he offers thanks to God for creating light. With the greeting *Gut Woch* ("Happy" or "Good Week"), he concludes the ceremony. But the Sabbath spirit lingers on as the family sing several melodies, the favorite song being about Elijah and the Messiah.

The Havdalah ceremony observed in the home has spiritual significance: The cup of *wine* (which is allowed to overflow into a saucer) represents the unbounded *grace* of God. The *spices* indicate the *pleasure* in the Sabbath and are a substitute for the incense used in the ancient Temple at the time of prayer, while the *light* is a reminder of *God's creation on the first day*, to which the approaching days of the week correspond. The placing of the hands over the candles by the father, when he reaches the words "between light and darkness" is simply to illustrate the words by showing the light inside the hands and the shadow outside them.

To the believer in Messiah Yeshua, the *light* is symbolical of the One who does separate us from the darkness of sin and translates us into the Kingdom of the Sun (Son) who is the Light! The *wine* pictures the *grace of God* through the "blood of the Everlasting Covenant" which belongs to all who believe. The *incense* expresses the words of the Psalmist: *"In thy presence is **fullness of joy** and at thy right hand are **pleasures forevermore"*** (Psalm 16:11).

OPENING SONG FOR SABBATH

The opening song for the Sabbath service in the Synagogue is taken from Psalm 133:1 as follows:

"Behold, how good and pleasant it is for brethren to dwell together in unity."

OPENING SONG: HINE MA TOV

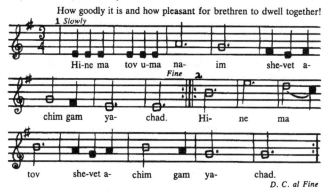

It is customary to read a portion from the Pentateuch and the prophets each Sabbath. This portion may be read by a member of the congregation after which the Rabbi will comment and interpret.

While the head of the family is at the synagogue, the wife and mother or oldest female member of his house covers the table in the dining room with a white cloth and places upon it two candlesticks holding the candles which she has already kindled and prayed over just before sundown. She also places upon the table, two loaves (hallot) of bread called *berches*, a Jewish corruption of the Hebrew *berachoth* meaning *blessings*, directly in front of the seat occupied by the head of the family during the evening meal.

Jewish women bake the *challah* (hallah) with a braid of dough upon it which represents the "ladder" to heaven. When the housewife bakes these loaves of bread she takes from the dough a portion corresponding to the first part of the dough to be given to the Lord (Numbers 15:17-21), and places it in the stove to be burnt. What a picture of the Messiah who, at His first coming (the *Challah*) was born in the city of *Bethlehem* ("House of Bread") and burnt in the oven of God's wrath for the sin of the world! These loaves of bread are a specially prepared white bread for use on the Sabbath. For centuries, Jews have, as a rule, eaten no other bread on Sabbath days.

The two *hallot* reflect the double portion of manna which fell on the sixth day to provide for that Sabbath when no manna fell. See Exodus 16:20. According to the Talmud: *"R. Abba[35] saith, ... A man is bound on the sqbbath day to break upon two loaves, because it is written* לחם משנה *double bread, Exodus xvi.22."[36]* Also the bread represents the continuation of the ancient Temple custom when the twelve loaves of "shewbread" *Lehem ha-Panim* ("Bread of Faces," [God's] "Presence Bread") on the altar were renewed in honor of the Sabbath. (The word *berachah* applied to these two *hallot* means *blessing* or *praise*-from the Hebrew word "knee" or "to kneel.") Today the position of Jews in prayer is "standing," or sitting, but we notice that the *kneeling* position was used of Daniel (6:10) and mentioned by David in Psalm 95:6.

At the conclusion of the Shabbat ceremonies in the Synagogue the following recitation is made:

> "Shake off the dust;
> Arise, O my People!
> And adorn thyself with
> Thy beautiful attire,
> By the hand of Jesse's Son,
> The Bethlehemite, draw
> Nigh to my soul, redeem it.
> Awake, awake, arise and shine,
> For thy Light has come.
> Awake, awake, utter a song;
> For the Glory of Jehovah
> Upon thee is revealed.
> To right and to left thou wilt extend,
> And Jehovah thou wilt magnify.
> By the hand of the Man, the Son of Perez,
> We shall rejoice and be glad."[37]

---

[35]*Schabb.* fol. 117. 2.
[36]John Lightfoot, *A Commentary on the New Testament From the Talmud and Hebraica,* Vol. 4, p. 36.
[37]*Singer* p. 112—Quoted in *American Hebrew Christian* Magazine.

THE SABBATH COMMANDMENT

The Old Testament Sabbath Commandment belongs to the Ceremonial Law and was not given to the Gentiles or the Christians, but to *Israel*, for a definite purpose. The Lord commanded Moses:

> *"Speak thou also unto the children of Israel, saying Verily my sabbaths ye shall keep:* **for it is a sign between me and you** *throughout your generations; that ye may know that I am the LORD that doth sanctify you"* (Exodus 31:13).

This Commandment to keep the Sabbath is nowhere mentioned in the New Testament. All the other commandments of the Decalog are repeated in the New Testament but never the commandment: *"Remember the Sabbath day to keep it holy."* There is a reason for this. The other commandments of the two tables of the Law mentioned in the New Testament, are connected with the *law of love*. Love is the fulfilling of all the law and the prophets (Romans 13:8-10; Matthew 22:37-40). But the commandment to observe the Sabbath is not connected with the law of love.

In the New Testament every moral principle contained in the "Ten Commandments" (in essence) has been stated in the form of an exhortation with the exception of the commandment to keep the Sabbath!

1st	One God	1 Timothy 2:5
2nd	No idolaters	1 Corinthians 10:7
3rd	Swear not	James 5:12
The fourth is nowhere in the NT		
5th	Honor parents	Ephesians 6:2
6th	No murderer	1 John 3:15
7th	No adulterer	Hebrews 13:4
8th	Steal no more	Ephesians 4:28
9th	Lie not	Colossians 3:9
10th	Covet not	Ephesians 5:3

OBSERVING THE BIBLICAL SABBATH

To observe the Biblical Sabbath we would follow these conditions:

1. We would be Jews, a part of the nation of Israel.
2. We would be in the Holy Land.
3. We would work for *six* days and then keep the Sabbath or "stop," "cease" from working to observe "rest" on the *seventh* day. (The beginning of our work could be on the second, fourth, etc. day which would determine what the seventh day would be.)
4. We would not lift any burden or carry any burden out of our house on the Sabbath day (Jeremiah 17:21, 22).

5. We would begin the Sabbath day at sunset of the preceding day.

6. We would not go out of our houses—even to go to church on that day. (See Exodus 16: 29 *"... Let no man go out of his place on the seventh day."*)

7. We would not light a fire (Exodus 35:23; Numbers 15:32-36).

8. We would not work at our regular employment or do any unnecessary work on that day, etc.

THE EIGHTH DAY

There is a *New Day*, the **Lord's** *Day*, the *eighth day* which was a prophecy of *better things*. The Seventh-Day Sabbath was a memorial of the Old Creation. There is a New Creation, a New Beginning which is on the *eighth day* of the week as the Scriptures tell us: The *First Day of the Week* (the *eighth* day) is emphasized in the "keeping of a holiday," not the seventh!

1. Circumcision was to be on the **8th day** after birth and speaks of a NEW beginning, a NEW Life, the NEW BIRTH.

2. The Typology of Leviticus 23 and the Old Covenant makes the **first day of the week** prominent.

   (a) The offering of First-Fruits always fell on the *first day* of the week prophesying of the resurrection of Jesus, "the Firstfruits." If the law of the Sabbath had been perfect, Christ would have arisen on the *seventh* day of the week!

   (b) The Last Sabbath of the Seven Feasts of the Lord fell on the **8th day** or the *first day* of the week.

3. The Day of Pentecost fell on the *first day* of the week, and its fulfillment (the outpouring of the Holy Spirit) came upon the waiting disciples on that day (Acts 2:1).

4. The Feast of the Great Hosannah (or Vintage), the last day of the Feast of Tabernacles, always occurred on the *first day* of the week and it speaks of the great Ingathering of the spiritual fruit of the earth.

5. God honored the *first day* by giving the Law on that day (Exodus 19:1, 3, 11; Leviticus 23:5-6 with Exodus 12:2-18).

6. God honored the *first day* by giving the *Book of the Revelation* on that day (Revelation 1:10).

7. The first Gospel sermon after the Ascension was on the *first day* and the first conversions (about 3,000 Jews) took place on the *first day* (Acts 2:1-42).

8. Christ's special manifestations to His disciples after the resurrection were on the *first day* of the week (Matthew 28; Mark 16; Luke 23-24; John 20:19, 26).

Furthermore, Law and Sabbath-keeping were not required by the Apostles (Acts 15:5-29; Romans 14:4,5; Galatians 4:9-11; Colossians 2:14-17).

It is also amazing to know that the second part of the Bible (the New Covenant or Testament) tells that *after* the resurrection of Messiah Jesus He never once met with the disciples or any other group on the Sabbath Day! He did not regard the seventh day after He had risen from the dead! *Before* this, Messiah Jesus *did* observe the seventh-day Sabbath (and all other commandments God gave to the Jewish people) for He was the fulfillment of the entire law of God! But now since He had kept them perfectly under the Old Covenant–establishing a New Covenant–and was resurrected as was prophesied in the Hebrew Scriptures, He did not once refer to the seventh-day Sabbath!

When Messiah Jesus met with His disciples *after* His resurrection and the *day* is mentioned, it is *always the first day of the week*! He met Mary and the women on the *first day* of the resurrection which was the *first day of the week*. He met with His disciples and broke bread with them at Emmaus on the *first day*. He was with His disciples in the Upper Room on the *first day* of the week (Luke 24:1) and a week later He met these same disciples on the *first day* of the week (John 20:19 and John 20:26). In the apostles' day, one day was set aside for gathering of the people (see 1 Corinthians 16:1,2; John 20:19-23, 26; Acts 20:7).

Paul, under the inspiration of the Holy Spirit, wrote:

*"Let no man therefore judge you in meat, or in drink, or in respect of an holyday, or of the new moon, or of **the sabbath days**: Which are **a shadow of things to come**; but the body is of Christ"* (Colossians 2:16-17).

In the Old Testament, God had given to Israel many ceremonial laws, such as those governing circumcision, the Day of Atonement, the various sacrifices, and others, which prophesied of the work of the Messiah and was to arouse in the hearts of the Israelites a deep longing for His coming to redeem them *from* the Law. In the passage of Colossians just quoted, Paul mentions some of these laws, pertaining to food, drink, holy days, the new moon, and **sabbath days**, saying of them that *they were shadows of the things to come,* which means that when the Messiah would appear then all these ceremonial laws would be ended!

When the Messianic believers in Galatia were being re-introduced to the ceremonial laws by heretical teachers, the Apostle wrote:

*"Stand fast therefore in the liberty wherewith Christ hath made us free, and be not entangled **again** with the yoke of bondage"* (Galatians 5:1).

*"But now, after that ye have known God, or rather are known of God, how turn ye **again** to the **weak and beggarly elements**, whereunto ye desire **again to be in bondage? Ye observe days**, and months, and times, and years. I am afraid of you, lest I have bestowed upon you labour in vain"* (Galatians 4:9-11).

As mentioned before, the Sabbath was *a shadow of things to come.* What a wealth of meaning the Day of Rest has for those who have entered into the New Covenant, who have found their freedom, their delight, their rest in the Lord of the Sabbath, who have ceased from their own labors for salvation and now are leaning upon the "everlasting arms"!

God ceased from His work of creation on the seventh day. He did not rest as though He was tired, for God is incapable of such a human characteristic, but He rested in the sense that it was *finished.* He now commands His own people to share that rest, to cease from their own labors in the *spiritual* for they cannot add to His salvation! The believer in Yeshua must trust in the finished work of Calvary, to rest in Him, to express absolute confidence and faith in the Holy One of Israel and thus keep His Sabbath holy!

Israel was to commemorate their deliverance from bondage by observing the Sabbath. We have been delivered from bondage. We have found our *sabbath* in Messiah Jesus. We rest in Him *every day.* We come together as His people on the first day of the week because we remember He arose on the first day of the week. He fulfilled the Old Covenant Sabbath and established Himself as the New Covenant Sabbath for His people. We trust in the work *already* done. We rest in the finished work of Calvary's Altar which fulfilled the First Covenant Scriptures!

The Jewish people were laboring under the bondage of the Law upon whom their religious leaders had heaped laws and ordinances which were not God-given (see Matthew 23:4). The Messiah offered His Rest to them when He said:

"Come unto me, all ye that labour [under bondage] *and are heavy laden* [with rules and man-made regulations], *and I will give you rest* [Sabbath]. *Take my yoke upon you, and learn of me; for I am meek and lowly in heart: and ye shall find **rest unto your souls**"* (Matthew 11:28-29).

*"**For we which have believed do enter into rest**, as he said, As I have sworn in my wrath, if they shall enter into my rest: although the works were finished from the foundation of the world. For he spake in a certain place of the seventh day on this wise, And **God did rest** the seventh day from all his works"* (Hebrews 4:3-4).

> *"There remaineth therefore a rest to the people of God. For he that is entered into **his** [God's] **rest**, he also **hath ceased from his own works**, as God did from his"* (Hebrews 4:9-10).

> *"Wherefore the children of Israel shall keep the sabbath, to observe the sabbath throughout their generations, for a **perpetual covenant**"* (Exodus 31:16).

The Sabbath was to be *perpetual* and to be observed by Israel, the *natural* people of God. The sacrifices of the Old Covenant were also to be observed *perpetually* (Leviticus 3:17). It was to *natural* Israel that this Sabbath law was given and therefore must be fulfilled *perpetually* and forever by these *natural* (earthly) people of God. When can this be? According to the Scriptures we find that it will be during the Millennium by the *earthly* people of God, but to the eternal *heavenly* people of God this Sabbath law will be fulfilled in Messiah Jesus in whom they will *rest* forever (Hebrews 9:8-10)!

In conclusion: The Sabbath was a ***prophecy*** "a shadow of things to come." It was to be observed "forever" at God's commandment. But since Israel, to whom the commandment was given, broke God's Covenant thereby breaking His Sabbath Law–how can it be that the Sabbath will be observed ***forever***? This seems to be a contradiction. However, God keeps His Word; His promises and commandments will be observed by His people Israel as He said. When the Lord deals again with Israel as His *earthly* people the Sabbath will be renewed.

> *"And it shall come to pass* [These words imply something in the future, in the Kingdom age, the Millennium when Israel is restored], *that from one new moon to another, and from one **sabbath to another**, shall all flesh* [**earthly** people. Believers in Messiah Jesus are the **heavenly** people of God] *come to worship before me, saith the LORD"* (Isaiah 66:23).

THE LORD'S SABBATH

Following is an excerpt from Eilet J. Waggoner's article "Three Sabbaths." He was trained as a physician at Battle Creek College and obtained a medical degree from the Bellevue Medical College in New York City. Because his heart was in evangelism, he entered the ministry. He spent the last six years of his life teaching at Dr. John Harvey Kellogg's Battle Creek College in Battle Creek, Michigan.

> The word "Sabbath" means "rest." It is a Hebrew word transferred into the English language. When the Hebrews used the word, "Sabbath," it conveyed the same idea to them that the word "rest" does to us. ... We must not make the mistake of judging the Lord's

rest from what men are accustomed to call rest. God is not a man. We should rather learn from God's rest what rest really is. God's rest is not mere physical rest from weariness. This we know from two facts: first, "God is spirit" (John 4:24). Not "a spirit," as though He were one of many; but He is Spirit, as it is rendered in the margin of the Revised Version. Second, "The everlasting God, the Lord, the Creator of the ends of the earth, fainteth not, neither is weary" (Isaiah 40:28). The Lord therefore did not rest because He was tired, and His rest is not physical, but *spiritual* [emphasis, mine], since He is Spirit. "They that worship him must worship him in Spirit and in truth" (John 4:24).

... [God's rest] is gained by faith. "We which believe do enter into rest." How so?—Because by faith we have the finished, perfect work of the Lord as our own. "This is the work of God, that ye believe on him whom he hath sent" (John 6:29). Believing Him means receiving Him; and since in Him the works of God are complete, it follows that by believing on Him we find the rest. ...

The rest that Jesus gives is rest from sin. The heavy-laden whom He calls to Him are those who are burdened with the weight of their sins. All men are thus burdened, "for all have sinned." Our best works are utterly worthless. Christ will have a people who are "zealous of good works" (Titus 2:14-15); but the good works must be those which God Himself has wrought for us in Christ. Only His work is enduring. "His work is honourable and glorious; and his righteousness endureth forever." Psalm 111:3. Therefore, "by grace are ye saved through faith; and that not of yourselves; it is the gift of God; not of works, lest any man should boast. For we are his workmanship, created in Christ Jesus unto good works, which God hath before prepared that we should walk in them" (Ephesians 2:8-10).

–E.J. Waggoner (1855-1916)

PESACH (Passover)

The Passover Feast is mentioned more times in the Old Testament than any other Feast, a total of about 48 times. Likewise, Passover is referred to more often in the New Testament than any other Feast (28 times as Passover and one time translated from *Pesach* as Easter, Acts 12:4). This brings the total to 77 that this Feast is cited in the Word of God. The Feast of Pentecost is written three times; the Feast of Unleavened Bread, nine times; the Feast of Tabernacles, twice (John 7:2, 37).

"The idea of liberty in Western thought owes much to the Passover holiday...What is universal is the exodus from Egypt, one of the great symbols of Western civilization. Many of the revolutions, including the American revolution, patterned themselves after the exodus. At one time, it was proposed that the seal of the U. S. show Jews passing through the Red Sea and the Egyptians being engulfed by the waters."[38]

The First Passover

Different names in either the Bible or in later Jewish traditional literature is given to The Passover Feast; i.e., "Festival of Pesach," (Exodus 34:25); "The Festival of Matzot" (Exodus 23:15 & 34:18); "The Time of Freedom and Redemption" (*Mishnah Pesachim* 10:5); and the "Festival of Spring" (Deuteronomy 16:1). The first night of Passover is also called the "Night of Vigil" or the "Night of Seder." (The first [order] Seder of service for the Haggadah was written around 300 AD.) We are told that the *Seder* is in recognition of the fact that when the children of Israel fled Egypt-though in great haste-they did so with a sense of order rather than of chaos.

"In the fourteenth day of the first month at even is the LORD's passover" (Leviticus 23:5; see with Exodus 12:2, 14).

According to God's commandment, the first month of the Jewish calendar should be *Nisan* or *Abib* which occurs in the Spring and begins in either March or April. Those who could not observe Passover on the 14th of Nisan were allowed to do so on the 14th of *Iyar* (called the *Second Passover*; see Numbers 9:9-14).

The Passover, observed continuously for 3,000 years, remains one of the three great festivals in the calendar year of orthodox Jews and the favorite holiday in their homes. It is a joyous feast to them, recalling their emancipation from slavery to Pharoah. In the synagogue psalms of thanksgiving and glorification are read including the biblical scroll "Song of Songs" which Rabbis say, teaches the espousal of Israel, the beloved, and God, the Lover, which took place at the time of the first Passover!

The Jewish people today recognize the seventh month as the beginning of their Agricultural or Civil Year. The date of the Passover is governed by four changes of the moon after December 21st of the preceding year. Easter Sunday is always the first Sunday after the full moon, on, or the next after the vernal equinox, March 21. The

---

[38]Friday, April 8, 1985 *U.S.A. Today*—Rabbi Mordecai Waxman, Synagogue Council of America, N.Y., N.Y.

Passover Feast is celebrated in the same general procedure in Jewish homes today but in a slightly different manner in certain parts of the world. (For more of the ritual and songs of the Passover Seder see my book *New Covenant Passover Haggadah*, p. 122.)

The "beginning of months" to those of us who are of the family of God began on that memorable day when we accepted our purchased deliverance from a bondage worse than that of Egypt and a slavery more terrible than that of Pharoah! It was then we began to really live when we recognized the Messiah (Christ) as our Passover who saved us from the bondage and slavery of the Evil One. How we can rejoice now in song and testimony not only in the house of the Lord once a year, but in all places at all times when we remember that we are the espoused Bride of the Heavenly Bridegroom who is coming some day to take us to be with Him forever!

"Feast," rather "Festival" is translated from the Hebrew word "Hag" or *Chag,* the root meaning "to move in a circle," "celebrate," "dance," "to be joyous," "reel to and fro," "to be giddy," "to march in a sacred procession." "Hag" is applied exclusively to the great annual Feasts *Pesach, Shavuot,* and *Succot* (Passover, Weeks or Pentecost, and Tabernacles).

Of all the Feasts of the Jews, the Feast of the Passover emphasized the separation between Israel and every other people in the world, for no outsider could take any part in it whatsoever. Only the children of Israel could enjoy the privileges of the Paschal Feast for it was the *Lord's* Passover and only those who knew Him, obeyed His commandments, and kept His Covenants, were permitted in its celebration.

However, some writings tell of hospitality at Passover. Though the Talmud forbids the stranger it is written that at Passover the Jew does extend hospitality. This custom is traced back to Abraham who opened his tent to all in the hope that they would be brought closer to God. There are those who feel that it developed because of the belief that any visitor might be the *Messiah* in disguise and that turning him away would be a sin too great to bear! On Pesach, as on Shabbat, it is considered a *mitzvah* (good deed) to feed the hungry or the stranger.

One thing alone could enable *even* a Jew to share in this feast: He must be *circumcised*!

"... There shall no stranger eat thereof: But every man's servant that is bought for money, when thou hast circumcised him, then shall he eat thereof. ... no uncircumcised person shall eat thereof. One law shall be to him that is homeborn, and unto the stranger that sojourneth among you" (Exodus 12:43-44, 48-49).

If an alien or a stranger (that is, one who was not an Israelite) wished to be considered worthy to eat of the Feast, he must become *circumcised* as were the children of God, thereby making himself also a child of God to be a part of the commandments and covenants of the Almighty!

According to the Talmudic and Rabbinical laws, no Gentile may sit at the Passover table. Messiah Jesus broke down this middle wall of partition (Ephesians 2:14) and Jews and Gentiles are made one in Him (Galatians 3:28). Only those who have been born-again or *circumcised in heart*, changed from worldly citizens to citizens of heaven) who believe in the great Passover Sacrifice, can participate in the great Marriage Supper of the Lamb!

The Hebrew word for this holiday is "Pesach" and has been pointed out to be a feminine word, the English equivalent to "pause over to protect" as a hen would pause over her chicks to protect them from harm and danger. This is exactly what God did in that ancient time. When He saw the blood upon the door, He "paused over" to protect them from the decree of death which was pronounced upon all unbelievers.

The word "Pesach" is taken from another Hebrew word which means "to hop"; i.e. (fig.), "skip over" (or "spare"); by implication "to hesitate"; also (lit.) "to limp," "to dance," "to leap," "to pause over" or "pass-over." When God saw the blood of the lamb on the doorposts He hesitated there, leaped with joy at the obedience of His people in offering the perfect, sacrificial lamb for their deliverance!

THE HAGGADAH

The Emancipation Story is read from the *Haggadah* at the first night's (and sometimes the second night's) service called *Seder*. The word *Haggadah* literally means the "telling" or "showing forth." This book is used in every pious Jewish home on the first and second evenings of the Feast in obedience to the commandment found in Exodus 13:8 and Exodus 12:26, 27. The Haggadah is the ritual or the order for the established ceremony on the first nights of Passover week. The oldest passage in the Haggadah, which was developed during the years following the destruction of the Temple, is thought to be that which calls the *Matzah* "the bread of affliction," probably dating from the Sixth Century, BCE. There are over 3,500 editions of the Haggadah today!

An illuminated page from the renowned *Sarajevo Haggadah*. At the beginning of the Haggadah, one recites the Aramaic passage *Ha-Lahma Anya* הָא לַחְמָא עַנְיָא, "This is [like] the Bread of Affliction," followed by an invitation for all who are needy to join in the meal.

One copy of the Haggadah is placed on the table for each person, or one for every two. "Both in the arrangement of the table and in the psalms, benedictions, and other recited matter the Seder of the present day agrees substantially with the program laid down in the *Mishnah*."

Haggadah shel Pesach —*The Jewish Encyclopedia*

The greatest story ever told is of a greater Deliverer than Moses. Yeshua ha-Meshiah (Jesus, the Christ) is the Great Emancipator of all time, and the great deliverance He performed should never be forgotten. Always at the Feast (the Communion), the Redeemed of the Lord should *"remember His death 'til He come"* and not only at the Communion Table, but every moment of their lives should the story of love be recounted and the Lover of souls remembered. Like as the Israelites were commanded to keep the Passover in remembrance of their escape from Egyptian bondage, so are believers in Messiah Jesus required to keep the Sacrament of the Lord's Supper in memory of their deliverance from the yoke of sin.

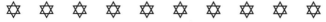

THE JEWISH WOMAN

In the ceremony called *bentsh licht* (benediction over light) the woman mimics the original act of creation, "Let there be light." After lighting at least two candles, she draws the light toward herself three times, like drawing water from a pool, covers her eyes on the third drawing of the hands toward her, then uncovers them. I saw my *bubbe* (grand-mother) doing this at the beginning of *Shabbat* (Sabbath) and *Pesach* (Passover). She would then cover her head with a white napkin or towel. She would pray that God would remove the darkness and return the light that went out when Eve broke His commandment.

The Orthodox Jewish woman performs only two religious duties in the home. She does not have the same privileges as the man has concerning the ceremonies and rituals of Judaism. She is taught (through the Rabbis) to be in subjection to him and looks to him for leadership. Her place in Judaism is beneath that of her husband, father, or brother. She was ignorant concerning Judaism but a change has been introduced in recent years. In Conservative and Reformed Judaism she is now being educated in Judaism and given privileges to participate in the Jewish ceremonies not only in the home but in the synagogue as well.

Jews believe that it is the wife who brings success or failure to her husband. She is loved and respected by all the family. Her religious duty at Passover is to *light the candles and pray over them* at sunset before the first service begins. A strict Rabbinical law commands that only the woman must light the candles, for it was a woman who put out the lights in the first place and she only can put them on again! We realize that it *was* a woman who "put out the lights" in the Garden of Eden, but we also remember that it is a woman through whom the Light returned! It is true, a woman brought darkness, but she also brought the One who lights every man that comes to Him (John 1:9).

How gracious of our Lord (who is no respecter of persons) to make no distinction between the sexes when it pertains to salvation and the privileges in the gospel! *All* are *one*. *All* are equal in Him. Not one is lower, not one is higher in His estimation. Each one in Messiah Jesus is granted the riches of His grace, the greatness of His love, the glory of His presence, and the power of His gospel. Praise the Lord, He included even me, a Jewish *woman*!

SEVEN-BRANCH LIGHT

In many orthodox Jewish homes, on the Passover night, the table is adorned with a seven-branched *Menorah* ("a place of light"). The candle in the center of the candelabrum usually is taller than the rest. To the Jew this represents the hope of the coming Messiah. After all the other six candles are extinguished, the middle one, or the seventh, is still found burning, signifying that although other lights and teachings may fade, the hope in the coming of the long-looked-for Messiah will still be burning in the heart of the devout Jew.

To followers of Messiah Yeshua, the Seventh Light can never be extinguished, for He is the First and the Last, the Beginning, and the Ending, the *Alpha* and the *Omega*, the *Aleph* and the *Tav*, the A and the Z, who was, and is, and ever shall be!

HAMETZ (Leaven)

"Seven days shall ye eat unleavened bread; even the first day ye shall put away leaven out of your houses: for whosoever eateth leavened bread from the first day until the seventh day, that soul shall be cut off from Israel" (Exodus 12:15).

Leaven represents sin and unrighteousness. We see this in the baking of bread. Leaven puffs up and swells the substance that it permeates to unnatural proportions. Actual material leaven consists of microscopic vegetable ferment, which we would call "mold," characterized chiefly by rapidity of growth and diffusiveness, so that it permeates the whole lump into which it is put—a picture of corruption and nothing is able to stop its growth except *fire*!

Since leaven represented sin to the Jew he was to put away leaven from his household the moment the lamb was slain. Nothing was to contaminate the pure, unblemished lamb. In Jewish homes today there is a great preparation before Passover, sometimes a month in advance, in order to obey this commandment to remove all leaven. I remember how for weeks preceding the first night of the Passover celebration (called Seder) in the home, my mother would wash and iron linens, curtains, towels, all the clothes, etc. She would scrub floors and walls and ceilings. We would help her turn pockets of the clothing inside out to empty them of crumbs of leaven, strings which might have been caught in them from the last washing, or articles which had been used before "Pesach." She would give our residence what could be called a "good spring house cleaning" but it was more than that, for it was a religious duty. She would take the dishes, cooking utensils, silverware, pots and pans, which had been used during the year (all these called "hometz" or "unclean) and place them out in the garage. Then she would take from the "sacred" place, dishes, utensils, pots, and pans, and silverware which would only be used for the Passover.

It has been known in some homes that the wall paper is torn down and the walls painted because it is feared there is leaven in the mixture of the paste. In some communities a Jewish man who owns a business wherein leaven is contained, sells that business to some trusted Gentile friend for a dollar (or some small fee). In the days of my grandfather the fee was small, but the prices are higher today. Not only leavened bread but anything in the home or business which is not permitted during the Passover of eight days is considered as *hametz* and must be "sold" in order to "remove all leaven" according to the commandment. The Jew feels that by observing this he is no longer in possession of the sin (leaven) but the sin now is in the possession of the Gentile!

Mekihirat Hametz (Sale of Leaven)

"To conform with Biblical law which prohibits the possession of all leaven during the Passover season, a legal sale, transferring title to a non-Jew but retaining possession, has been contrived, assuring the recovery of title and goods after Passover. Therefore, the traditional Jew, in order not to violate the injunction against the personal possession of any leaven, goes through the legal ceremony of the 'sale' before Passover. Since the transaction is a legal procedure, the execution of the 'sale' is conducted with the aid of the community Rabbi or some other person designated by the Rabbi."[39]

---

[39]Abraham Mayer Heller, *The Vocabulary of Jewish Life*, p. 94.

When the seven days are finished, this Jewish man buys this same business back from this same Gentile for the same amount of money. The business containing the leaven is no longer owned by the Gentile but is returned to the Jew! What a description of the individual who sits in the seat of judgment and condemns another for a sin of which he feels he is not guilty! For even as the Jew still owns the leaven (though a transaction has taken place to excuse him from it) so also does he that is a judge over his brother; he is as guilty of sins as that one he condemns! The Messiah said:

> *"Judge not, that ye be not judged. For with what judgment ye judge, **ye** shall **be judged**: and with what measure ye mete, it shall be measured to you again"* (Matthew 7:1-2).

After all is done to make sure the leaven is absolutely out of the home, the man of the house performs a ceremony on the night before the Feast which is called *Searching Out the Leaven*. He holds a feather and a wooden spoon while one of the family carries a candle and a paper bag. They enter each room in the house, looking into every corner for leaven. They search from the basement to the attic. The mother has already purposely placed pieces of leavened bread on the window sills and in the corners of the rooms. According to the Talmud at least ten pieces of leavened bread should be placed in different parts of the house. The family join in the search and when there is discovery of a piece or pieces which have been scattered, the father is informed so that he can approach it and with the feather sweeps it into the paper bag. This performance is carried out with each piece of leavened bread that is found. The father uses the feather instead of his hand to touch the leaven for God commanded: *"Touch not the unclean thing."* The next morning he takes the leaven in the paper bag out to the back yard where he burns it reciting a prayer to God at the conclusion: "All leaven and sourdough which is in my possession, and I have not seen it, not removed it, not known of it, shall be valueless as the dust of the earth." This ceremony is called *Bi'er Hametz*—"the burning of the leaven."

As the leaven represents sin to the Jew, he earnestly feels that by cleansing his home, clothing, closets and putting even the thought of leaven out of his mind, he is observing God's commandment and is free from all sin!

When the Great Purifier comes into the heart, He removes all leaven from His dwelling place. Yes, He searches through every room in every corner of our being and He cleanses from sin. He separates us from all unrighteousness to Himself who is holy. We no longer touch the unclean thing; we no longer love the world or the things that are in the world, but we cling to Him who is our righteousness, who has cleansed us from our sins by giving His own precious "blood" on the Altar of Calvary.

As we look upon the various objects used in the ceremony of "Searching Out the Leaven," we are again reminded of the Great Salvation Story. We can see that the *candle* represents the Light of the World; the *feather* is the Holy Dove, the Holy Spirit; the *leaven* symbolizes the Messiah *made sin* for us; the *wooden spoon* is significant of the Altar of Calvary; the *paper bag*, the grave where it was prophesied that Messiah would be laid; the *burning of fire* tells of the wrath or judgment of God for sin. The Feather of God, the Holy Dove, the blessed Holy Spirit, led Messiah to the Altar (wooden spoon) to be made sin (leaven) to receive the judgment, the fire of God's wrath upon Him for our sin; He was laid in the grave (paper bag) but the grave was just like the flimsy paper bag; it could not hold Him! He broke the bars away. He arose! Halleluia!

MATZAH (Unleavened Bread)

"Matstsah" prop. "sweetness"; concr. "sweet" (i.e., not soured or bittered with yeast) spec. an *unfermented cake* or *loaf*. "Azumos" (Greek) "unleavened," i.e., (fig.) "uncorrupted." Restrictions concerning the Matzot:

> "Eighteen minutes are allowed to pass from the time the water touches the flour until the finished product comes from the oven. This is to ensure that even in the most humid of climates there will be no possibility for any fermentation or leavening to occur."
> —*Encyclopaedia Judaica*, article on "Matzah"

The mystical Kabbalah attaches profound meaning to the symbols of the Passover. *Hametz*, which Jews traditionally do their best to be rid of before the Seder, is symbolic of man's evil inclinations. The *Matzot*, on the other hand, symbolizes man's positive inclinations. Since Scripture forbids the eating or even the possession of *leaven* (*hametz*) for seven days, the Jewish homemaker must exert a great deal of extra effort and ingenuity to produce palatable holiday meals in accordance with Jewish law.

> "Beside the obvious leavening agents such as yeast, baking powder, and baking soda, also forbidden are those substances that ferment. On the other hand, Ashkenazi (Eastern European) Rabbinic authorities forbid rice, beans, peas, maize, and peanuts along with the other grains. They base this edict on the grounds that use of those non-fermenting foods might confuse some Jews, who might then err by using the same methods of preparation with other foods that do have the potential of fermenting."

Instead of the leavened, the Jewish people eat unleavened bread (along with other permitted foods) for the seven days of the Feast. God not only commanded the Israelites to put away leaven, but He also commanded that they partake of unleavened bread in its place. Also, Israel remembered that when they left Egypt it was in haste so they could not leaven the bread but carried the unleavened dough wrapped in a napkin, carried in their clothes on their shoulders. God intended by this that there was to be no leaven (sin) in connection with the Passover Lamb! As leaven represents sin, unleavened bread represents righteousness. After we have had leaven (sin) removed by the blood (life) of the Lamb, we are to partake of the bread that is unleavened (His righteousness).

> *"Purge out therefore the old leaven, that ye may be a new lump, as ye are unleavened. For even Christ [Messiah] our passover is sacrificed for us: Therefore let us keep the feast, not with old leaven, neither with the leaven of malice and wickedness; but with the unleavened bread of sincerity and truth"* (1 Corinthians 5:7-8).

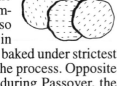

Matzah-baking machine in 1875 made the matzot round. The Rabbis claimed that the trimming took extra time and caused *fermentation* so they were made *square*. This is the type sold in stores of most Jewish areas today. The Matzot is baked under strictest supervision to insure that it will not *ferment* in the process. Opposite to the prohibition of wheat or wheat products during Passover, the *Matzot itself must be made from a grain which does have the capability of fermentation*, and traditionally this grain is wheat. The stark Matzah formula for the seder meal consists of flour and cool water, with not even a trace of salt. The entire baking process, from kneading to oven, must not take longer than *eighteen minutes*, as it is thought that this would be the maximum time before flour mixed with water would begin to *ferment* under normal conditions.

To allow for *quick* baking and to prevent the Matzot from rising and swelling, it was perforated after being rolled into shape by the use of a *riedel* or wheel provided with sharp teeth and attached to a handle.

> "The perforator, usually a youth, would run his *riedel* through the Matzah in lines crossed at right angles, and about one inch apart. The *Matzot-machine* has an automatic perforator that makes lines at intervals of a half inch."[40]

The Matzot can be purchased all year long, but for the Passover celebration it is specially prepared and examined. It is baked in ovens where nothing leavened may touch the pure spring water and the pure white flour with which it is baked. Every year around March or April, the Rabbis ceremonially inspect these mills where it is threshed,

---

[40]*Jewish Encyclopedia*, Vol. VIII, pp. 393-396 (MAZZAH).

heaped, stored, and certified. On the boxes containing the Matzot for the Passover celebration are printed the words: "For Passover Use Only," or just "Passover Matzot." Also, usually printed are the words: "Prepared for Passover under strict, orthodox Rabbinical supervision of the Union of Orthodox Jewish Congregations of America." And if there is question as to the Matzot being Kosher for Passover, the boxes are printed with the statement: "Certificate on request."

Jewish humor is found in the following item which I read in one of the Haggadahs during my research:

> "Why is *Matzah* called 'Matzah'? Because it has the shape of *Matzah*; it has small holes like *Matzah;* it is dry like *Matzah*; it tastes like *Matzah*. What else can you call it but *Matzah*?"

Following is an interesting item printed in *The Jerusalem Post* concerning the Matzah:

> "We are what we eat, especially on Pessah. Symbolic foods adorn the seder plate and traditional favourites comprise meals and snacks for eight days. We have Matzah with everything, and everything with Matzah. We're scrupulously careful of what foods we allow into the house, and all the human beings of a Jewish household are well aware of what we can, and cannot, eat. But what about the others? Furry, finny and feathered friends of a family certainly have to abide by the stringent rules of the holiday. No more peanut butter sandwiches for Fido. If old Puss is going to rummage through garbage cans, she'd better not bring home any *hametz* booty. Rabbits, mice and hamsters can make do with veggies, and fish can get by on a shaving of Matzah for a few days. Of course, you've got no problems if your pet is a camel: feed him at Purim, and then again at Hanukka."

There is nothing added to the pure flour and water of the ritual Matzah to make it rise. Oh, what a beautiful picture of the Messiah who is described as the Bread from Heaven, the Bread of which we eat that we might never hunger again. He is pure and undefiled. There need not anything be added to His wonderful salvation to make it "rise" for it is a complete and perfect work. The work was "finished" (completed, fulfilled) on Calvary! As the Matzah, Messiah was whipped, striped, pierced, then baked in the oven of God's wrath for sin. He, who was unleavened, came to "bring many sons to glory," that they, too, might become unleavened (righteous). Messiah came that we might no longer partake of the leaven (sin), but be nourished by the Pure Staff of Life, that Unleavened Living Bread! Oh let us, who have put away the leaven, evermore eat of that Bread which came down from heaven!

THE JEWISH MAN

In a Jewish home, the man is the leader, the head, the Rabbi or minister (priest), the teacher of his household. His word is law; he is respected above the rest of the family, and he it is to whom they look for advice. But at the Passover service, he is given even a higher position. Now he is the one who sits in a "King's Chair" and is *Lord* over those who are seated at his table. How we did admire and respect our grandfather (who took the place of our father who had passed away) all year long but it seemed to be a very special time of admiration, honor and love at the first two nights of the Passover! How our family appreciated the fact that he was not so much elevated above us that he did not permit us to sit with him; we enjoyed his presence and he enjoyed ours; we conversed with him (and with one another of the family) after the service during the meal and there was sweet fellowship together more than at any other time of the year.

Also, at the table, the father or husband who presides over the ceremony, sometimes wears a white satin priest's hat and a white robe called *Kittel* (or the *Tallit* prayer shawl usually a *white* one: white, denoting righteousness). This *kittel* is a long wide tunic and wide sleeves in white linen, trimmed with lace or gold, according to his means. It is the garment of Israel's ancient High Priest. The Jewish people remember that God has promised to them that they will be priests and kings in Jerusalem when Messiah comes. Now as the Master of the household sits before the family, he is a king and a priest in anticipation of that promise.

There is One whom we believers in Yeshua know who is the Leader over every leader, the Teacher over every teacher, the Head over all, the Rabbi who is over every Rabbi, the Master of masters, the King of kings and the Lord of lords, who is elevated far above us. He is the Highest. His thoughts are far above our thoughts; His ways are high above our ways. But, thank God! He is not too high above us that He does not sit *with us* in heavenly places! Oh, this Head of the Church has condescended to come down and dwell with His people, to walk and talk with us, to show Himself a Friend who is closer to us than a brother. We can enjoy His presence and He can enjoy ours; we can have fellowship with Him and sweet communion! We who know this King and Priest don't have to wait to arrive in heaven to realize this, but we acknowledge with Him *now* that we are His people (both Jew and Gentile) and look forward to the coming of God's kingdom on earth when we shall rule and reign with Him forever, according to His promise!

The Youngest

At the right of the Leader, there is a place set for the youngest of the family. He has the privilege of sitting next to the Master. During the ceremonial service he asks four questions from the Haggadah which are answered by the one presiding over the service. *"Why Matzot? Why Maror* (bitters)*? Why dip twice? Why recline?"* This practice is taken from the instructions given in Deuteronomy 6:20-24.

We who are the children of the King have the wonderful privilege of sitting very near to Him by the power of the Holy Spirit, questioning Him and receiving counsel from Him, for He is the Mighty Counselor, praise His Name!

Leaning

At Pesach on the first night's service, at each drinking of the wine, the family lean left toward one another around the table. This reclining position indicates rest, safety, and liberty. When the Israelites were slaves under Pharoah, they could not sit down or relax in the presence of the Egyptians. Being slaves at that time they must serve their enemies and constantly be at attention to their demands. Also in God's deliverance from Egypt, the Israelites left in haste after eating the Passover; they were instructed to do so, to stand as they ate, with loins girded, feet shod, and staff in hand. Now they feel they are no longer slaves in Egypt's bondage; they need not hurry, but they can take their ease; they can relax; so they lean toward one another (or upon pillows) as significant of their freedom.

We remember the New Testament account of the Passover (Last Supper) when John, the youngest of the disciples, was at the right of Messiah Jesus and leaned upon His bosom. At their meals they reclined on couches at that time. (See *Passover Seating Arrangement in Bible Days* Diagram pictured on page 136.)

"Abraham's Bosom" is a term derived from this custom of leaning upon the bosom of his neighbor at the banquets of the time (see John 13:23). This was regarded as a sign of great love and friendship. It was not that Jesus loved John more than the other disciples. No, He loved them (and He loves us) all the same. But it was the custom that next to the Master was the youngest and that he was to lean toward him or lean upon his chest (bosom).

In a spiritual sense, the Jewish people are yet in bondage as in Egypt's land and have no reality in the significance of their freedom, but we who have received Yeshua (Jesus) as our Messiah have been delivered from the enemy of our souls. *"If the Son therefore shall make you free, ye shall be free indeed"* (John 8:36). Now we can draw near to God and He will draw near to us; we can place our lives

upon the bosom of the Father in the Name of His only begotten Son.
How glorious is this personal experience with the Almighty God!

> Like John of old who laid his head
> Upon the Master's breast,
> Can we recline and find sweet peace,
> Content and perfect rest?
> If we but dare to trust in God,
> And on His bosom lie,
> We can but look into His face-
> He will us not deny;
> And when we, like John of old,
> Upon God's bosom lean,
> We find sweet peace and perfect joy
> If we but there remain!
> Bosom of God—Oh, the bliss!
> To end all care and strife;
> There rest my head in sweet repose
> Throughout this earthly life!
>
> —*Ruth Specter Lascelle*

THE SPECIAL GUEST

At the left-hand side of the Leader is the place of chief honor
next to that of the Master. There is set for a special guest (who is
expected to come as a forerunner of the Messiah) a goblet of wine
called *Koso Shel Eliyahu* ("Cup of Elijah" or "Elijah's Cup").
Sometimes "Elijah's Cup" is placed in the center of the table for
convenience.

Also with the Cup or Goblet in the place setting is a dish, silverware in place, and an empty chair at the table, for the Jewish people
read in their Jewish Bible this promise of God:

> *"Behold, I will send **my messenger**, and he shall prepare the way
> before me: and the Lord, whom ye seek, shall suddenly come to
> his temple, even the messenger of the covenant, whom ye delight
> in: behold, he shall come, saith the LORD of hosts"* (Malachi
> 3:1).

> *"Behold, I will send you **Elijah the prophet** before the coming of
> the great and dreadful day of the LORD:"* (Malachi 4:5).

It is before the drinking of the third cup of wine during the praise
that the following words are recited from the Haggadah:

> "May He, who is most merciful, send us abundant blessings in
> this house, and on this table, on which we have eaten. May he who

is most merciful, send us *Elijah the prophet, of blessed memory, to bring us the good tidings of salvation and consolation."*

The service continues until its conclusion, usually at the midnight hour, since the Haggadah tells "The eating should not continue longer than 12 o'clock, for during the time the holy temple stood the paschal lamb was eaten only until midnight."

My dear Jewish people continue in their service expecting Elijah to come at midnight to announce that their Messiah has come-but He does not come. How sad, how hopeless, how blind is Israel! Oh that they would know that the Spirit of Elijah was on John the Baptist who was the special messenger preparing the way of the Lord! When John saw the Messiah Jesus, he exclaimed to the Jewish people who had gathered there: *"Behold the Lamb of God that taketh away the sin of the world"* (John 1:29). He brought tidings of "salvation" and "consolation" for which Jewish people pray at Passover!

Messiah said of John the Baptist: *"This is Elias* [Elijah] *which was to come"* (Matthew 11:14, cf. 17:10-13 with Luke 1:17). A Folk Song sung at Passover is about Elijah:

"We await the coming of the prophet Elijah. May he appear, bring Messiah with him." (*Eliyahu hanavi, Eliyahu hatishbi, Eliyahu, Eliyahu, Eliyahu habiladi, Bimhera v'yamenu yavo eleynu, im Mashiach ben David, im Mashiach ben David.*)

We who know this precious Lamb, who was announced by the prophet, have opened the door of our hearts to Him. He has sat down at our table. We are supping with Him and He with us. We are sitting together with Him and feasting on the good things He has prepared for all those who love Him. We do not wait for Him to come the first time. *He has already come!* But we wait expectantly for Him to come the *second* time to take us to Himself that where He is, there we may be also.

It is remembered that at the Last Supper, Judas occupied the position as chief guest at the table. The Passover ritual of "dipping the sop" began with Judas and did not excite any question among the disciples for it was the custom for the one to the left of the Master to be served first. The heart of man is nearer the left side, therefore this was a place of affection and trust. Judas was the "trusted" treasurer of the group and the Lord described him in the Psalms: *"Yea, mine own familiar friend in whom I trusted, which did eat of my bread, hath lifted up his heel against me"* (Psalm 41:9). Yes, Judas occupied a place of high honor next to the Master but he betrayed his Lord with a kiss, and sold Him for 30 pieces of silver according to the prophecy in the *T'nakh* (Old Testament).

SEATING ARRANGEMENT
(in Bible Days)

The Passover Table, as was used by the Jews in Bible Days was always constructed in the shape of a parallelogram, with one side left open. This arrangement gave the table three sides, one long side, a short side, starting from left to right, and then on the other side, a long side. In other words it was U-shaped (see diagram below). In this way the servants who brought in the food could enter through the opening space of the "U," and serve the guests from that vantage point. They could serve the guests in all directions from their central position. Those who would come to the Passover would be "seated" on the floor at the outside rim of the table, the table being about 9 or 10 inches high.

> "From Jewish authorities we know that the average dining apartment was computed at fifteen feet square; the expression 'furnished' no doubt refers to the arrangement of couches all around the table, except at its end, since it was a canon [law] that the very poorest must take of that supper in a reclining attitude, to indicate rest, safety and liberty."[41]

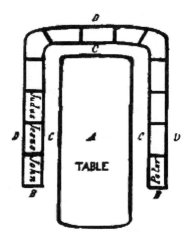

> "Here (A) represents the table, (B) respectively the ends of the two rows of single divans on which each guest reclines on his left side, with his head (C) nearest the table, and his feet (D) stretching back towards the ground.
>
> Jewish documents are equally explicit as to that of the guests. It seems to have been quite an established rule that, in a company of more than two, say of three, the chief personage or Head, in this

---

[41]Alfred Edersheim, *The Life and Times of Jesus the Messiah*, Vol. 2, p. 494.

instance, of course, Christ, reclined on the middle divan. We know from the Gospel narrative that John occupied the place on His right, at that end of the divan, as we may call it, at the head of the table.

But the chief place next to the Master would be that to His left, or above Him. In the strife of the disciples, which should be accounted the greatest, this had been claimed, and we believe it to have been actually occupied, by Judas. This explains how, when Christ whispered to John by what sign to recognize the traitor, none of the other disciples heard it. It also explains, how Christ would first hand to Judas the sop, which formed part of the Paschal ritual beginning with him as the chief guest at the table, without thereby exciting special notice.

Lastly, it accounts for the circumstance that, when Judas, desirous of ascertaining whether his treachery was known, dared to ask whether it was he, and received the affirmative answer, no one at the table knew what had passed. But this could not have been the case, unless Judas had occupied the place next to Christ; in this case, necessarily that at His left, or the post of chief honour. As regards Peter, we can quite understand how, when the Lord with such loving words rebuked their self-seeking and taught them of the greatness of Christian humility, he should, in his impetuosity of shame, have rushed to take the lowest place at the other end of the table. Finally, we can now understand how Peter could beckon to John, who sat at the opposite end of the table, over against him, and ask him across the table, who the traitor was. The rest of the disciples would occupy such places as were most convenient, or suited their fellowship with one another."[42]

The couches were very low, almost like mattresses, upon which the guests at the Passover would recline to make themselves comfortable. It was the custom to recline at the table, lying on the left side and leaning on the left hand, the feet stretching back towards the ground and each guest occupying a separate divan or pillow.

THE FOUR CUPS

Each participant in the Seder is expected to drink four cups of wine. The number is determined by the four divine promises of redemption made to Israel in Exodus 6:6-7. The first cup serves for

[42]Edersheim, *ibid.*, (includes Diagram), Vol. 2, p. 494.

Kiddush meaning *Sanctification*, the second is taken at the conclusion of the first part of the Seder; the third follows the grace after the meal, and the last comes at the end of the second part of the Seder. All the participants partake of the wine leaning toward the left. Rabbinical law commands every member of the family to drink four cups of wine especially prepared for the Passover (or take four sips from the wine in one cup). The wine is generally non-intoxicating and sparingly used. Unfermented raisin wine may be substituted for sweet wine at Pesach. according to the *Shulkan Arukh.*

> "During the Seder the drinking of four cups of wine is obligatory,
> the wine being often NON-ALCOHOLIC made for the occasion
> from the strained juice of raisins."[43]

The wine reminded the Jews of the blood struck on the Israelites' doorposts in Egypt's land which delivered them from the destroying angel. The Jewish people feel that the four cups of the Feast correspond to the four expressions of redemption used in the Bible in connection with the story of Israel's liberation. These four expressions found in Exodus 6:6-7 are: *"I will **free** you," "I will **deliver** you," "I will **redeem** you," "I will **take** you* [to be my people]."

The four cups are called in Hebrew: *V'hotzesi, V'hitzalti, V'goalti,* and *V'lokahti.* The first cup *(Kiddush)* at the beginning, the second is taken at the conclusion of the first part of the Seder; the third follows the grace after the meal, and the last comes at the end of the second part of the Seder. The *fifth* cup is *V'hevesi,* the fifth promise of God after the four promises of redemption was to bring Israel into Canaan. This cup came to be known as *"The Cup of Elijah."*

Wine

The Mishnah of the Jews (used in the days of Messiah's sojourn on earth) contains many laws for the Passover in the section named *Pesahim.* It states that all food (or drink) containing *leaven* is forbidden since there is a possibility for *fermentation.* This law is taken from Exodus 12:19 which forbids "hametz" ("leaven") throughout the seven days (15th-21st of Nisan or Abib) of the Passover observance.

Also the Mishnah (*Kitto*, volume 2, page 477) tells that the Jews used *boiled* wine. According to ancient documents, it is recorded that in order to keep the juice of the grape from fermenting, (which would then be prohibited as *"hametz"* or "leaven" for the Passover), the juice was boiled until it became thick like a syrup. This syrup then was stored in bottles (of lamb or goat skin) and diluted with water

---

[43]Hugh Schonfield, *A Popular Dictionary of Judaism*, p. 129. Emphasis is mine.

when a wine was required. Sometimes the syrup was thick enough to be a *jam* to be spread on bread if desired. In other words, the juice of the grape could become either a drink or food whatever was preferred or needed. According to the Mishnah the "wine" used during *Passover* was mixed in a ratio of three parts water to one part wine. The Talmud (combination of Mishnah and Gemara), the section *Pesahim* 7:13 refers to the kettle "in which the water is warmed for mixing with the wine (syrup)."

The word for "wine" in Hebrew is *yayin*. The Hebrew word for "strong drink" is *shekar*, "to be or become drunk." See Genesis 9:21, Isaiah 29:9, Jeremiah 25:27, etc. In Greek it is *sikera*, probably from the same root as "sugar," "saccharine." "Strong drink" is coupled with "wine" in the Bible, with one exception, Numbers 28:7.

The Bible does not specifically state of what *"shekar"* (*"strong* drink") is made, but does intimate it as *intoxicating* from the word itself. Only in one place is this drink referred to as from the pomegranate (Song of Solomon 8:2, "the juice of my pomegranate," RV "sweet *wine* of my pomegranate"); but it is inferred that other kinds of "shekar" besides that obtained from pomegranates were in use, such as drinks made from dates, honey, raisins, barley, apples, etc.

According to Jerome (c.400 AD), "*Sikera* in the Hebrew tongue means every kind of drink which can *intoxicate*, whether made from the juice of apples, or when honey combs are boiled down into a sweet and strange drink, or the fruit of palm oppressed into liquor, and when water is coloured and thickened from boiled herbs." In short, *shekar* ("strong drink") is a comprehensive term for *all* kinds of *fermented* drinks, *excluding* wine ("yayin").

Ministering priests of the Tabernacle were prohibited from "strong drink" or "shekar" (see Leviticus 10:9); Nazirites, "separated ones" unto God, also could not partake of this "strong drink" (see Numbers 6:3; Judges 13:4, 7, 14; cf. Luke 1:15).

Many different Greek, Hebrew and Chaldee words and vocables used in the Bible have *all* been indiscriminately translated as "wine" or "strong drink." In other words, in some cases, the word "wine" in the Bible means a *non*-intoxicant or a *food*! Fresh grape-juice, to make it keep without fermentation, was boiled until it became thick, like molasses, and in that form was stored away in *new* wine skins or large jars to prevent fermentation. This wine was referred to as **new wine** and it was to be eaten spread upon bread, or mixed and stirred up in water to make a drink.

*"And saith unto him, Every man at the beginning doth set forth **good** wine; and when men have well drunk, then that which is worse: but thou hast kept the **good** wine until now"* (John 2:10).

The Roman writer, Pliny, records that when grapejuice was *boiled* down to one-third of its bulk to secure the *finest flavor*, it is called *"Sapa,"* (the *best **wine***). Jesus produced a ***non**intoxicating, unfermented "wine"*!

Due to ignorance of the different meanings of the English word "wine" in the Bible, much confusion has resulted. But our Lord himself did not even use intoxicating wine (strong drink), since He was under the authority of the Law which prohibits it. In the four passages (Matthew 26:26-29; Mark 14:22-25; Luke 22:15-20 and 1 Corinthians 11:23-26) in which is given the account of the institution of the Lord's Supper (*The Passover Feast*), there is no mention of this word *"oinos"* or wine but the drink is called *fruit of the vine!*

We must determine what the word "wine" means by the *context*. At the wedding in Cana, the miracle of water turned to wine was a sign to show Christ as *Creator*. Alcohol is the product of breakdown and decay. It is an end product of digestion, like urine or manure. Jesus would hardly have created a poisonous decay product to show Himself the Creator! "Good wine" (John 2:10) refers to the ***flavor***, not the ***kick***! Otherwise, Jesus would have been guilty of encouraging drunkenness.

> "Not all wine is alcoholic any more than all cider is hard. It is inconceivable to me that our blessed Lord would ever produce an intoxicant, or that He used fermented wine at Passover as the symbol of His own shed blood.
>
> Fermented wine is decayed wine. Can that be the symbol of the new life in the Spirit? His holy flesh never saw decay or corruption. The cup of the Lord and the cup of the devil are two entirely different things. Jesus also miraculously created bread to feed the five thousand, but it was not moldy bread. Nor did He create rotten fish. Christ is the Creator of life, not death!"
> —David Wilkerson, *Sipping Saints*

A key passage is Ephesians 5:18, which ***does*** deal with *fermented* wine: *"Be not drunk with wine, wherein is excess* (the word "excess" here does not mean an over-amount but means debauchery, dissipation, profligacy, wildly extravagant, these sins are found in *fermented* wine. In other words, drinking fermented wine continually will lead to these sins); *but be filled* [keep on being filled] *with the Spirit."* The Spirit-filled believer does not need the *false stimulants* used by the world!

"Less than a decade ago at least 80 percent of wine produced, sold, and consumed in Israel was what could be called **kiddush wine**, red, *sweet* wine used for ceremonial purposes, such as *Kiddush* [i.e., sanctification prayer] or **seder** [of Passover]. Today this is not the case!" —*The Jerusalem Post*

It is true that most all Bible Commentaries (not by *Jewish* writers), suggest that the wine referred to in both the Old and New Testaments was *fermented*. This is an unfortunate interpretation which has caused much confusion and misunderstanding. It is inconceivable that our Lord who created man on the sixth day and on that day declared him to be "very good" would create or sanction something rotten or fermented for this man to consume!

At the Last Supper (Passover) Messiah said that the wine (fruit of the vine) represented His blood shed for redemption. It could not be fermented grape juice because this properly did not represent the blood of the sinless One and God had commanded Israel to put away **all leaven** for the observance of the Passover!

"Wine was a common drink in Bible times. It was the juice squeezed from the grape. Almost always it was diluted with water, as indicated in the contrast drawn in the Scriptures between 'wine' and 'strong drink' (See Leviticus 10:8-9; Numbers 6:3; Deuteronomy 14:26; 29:6; Judges 13:4,7,14; 1 Samuel 1:15; Proverbs 20:1; 31:4,6; Isaiah 5:11, 22; 28:7; 29:9; 56:12; Micah 2:11.)

"'Strong drink' was generally a mixture of equal parts of water and wine. The wine used during Passover was mixed in a ration of three parts water to one part wine, according to the Talmud.

Paul's instruction to Timothy to use a little wine for his stomach's sake must be interpreted in the light of the background (1 Timothy 5:23). This was an admonition to a specific individual in a specific situation, and should not be applied universally. Evidently Timothy was continually sick, and by the negative admonition to 'drink no longer water' it is clear the water was not fit to drink.

Isaiah said, 'Woe unto them that are mighty to drink wine, and men of strength to mingle strong drink' (Isaiah 5:22).

Joel said, 'Awake, ye drunkards, and weep: and howl, all ye drinkers of wine, because of the new wine; for it is cut off from your mouth' (Joel 1:5)."[44]

---

[44] Joseph R. Flower, Pentecostal Evangel, January 13, 1980, Article: *The Christians' Attitude Toward Intoxicating Drinks.*

The First Cup

Over the first cup filled with wine, the "Kiddush" or "Sanctification" prayer is recited:

"Blessed art Thou, Jehovah our God, who hast created the fruit of the vine! Blessed art Thou, Jehovah [Adonai] our King, King of the Universe, who hast chosen us from among all people and exalted us among all languages and sanctified us with Thy commandments. And Thou hast given us, O Jehovah [Adonai] our God, in love, the solemn days for joy, and the festivals and appointed seasons for gladness; and this the day of the feast of unleavened bread, the season of our freedom, a holy convocation, the memorial of our departure from Egypt. For us Thou hast chosen; and us hast Thou sanctified from all nations, and Thy holy festivals to inherit. Blessed art Thou, O Jehovah [Adonai], who sanctifiest Israel and the appointed seasons. Blessed art Thou, Jehovah [Adonai], King of the Universe, who hast preserved us alive and sustained us and brought us to this season."

This divides all the days gone before from the seven days of Passover, separates the family, even the houses and all contained therein to holiness, purity, and righteousness. All in the past is washed and scrubbed away; all memory of the unclean is burned; all sin is removed.

Praise God, those of us who know the Messiah have drunk of that Kiddush cup! For He is our Sanctification, our Separator from all that defiles. He has cleansed away all our sins by His precious blood which was shed on Calvary; He has blotted out all our transgressions; He has removed all our wickedness of the past; He has washed us and made us "whiter than the snow," He has put away our iniquities and has separated us to His holiness, His purity, and His righteousness. Praise His dear Name forever!

After the first cup of wine is drunk, each person washes his hands saying: "Blessed art Thou, Jehovah, our God, who has sanctified us with Thy commandments, and has enjoined us concerning the washing of our hands." It might have been at this time that the Saviour Yeshua in His self-humiliation proceeded also to wash His disciples' feet. Yes, and when we receive Christ into our hearts, He washes not only our hands and feet but all, body, soul, and spirit, that we might be pure as He is pure!

The Second Cup (Judgment)

The cup is filled the second time and many scholars have named it the "Cup of Judgment," because at this point the punishments that fell upon Pharaoh and the Egyptians are recited. The Head of the family demonstrates the following ritual:

"These are the ten plagues, which the Most Holy, blessed be He, brought on the Egyptians in Egypt, viz., (Drop of wine out of the cup onto the saucer below while uttering each of the ten words): *Blood, Frogs, Lice, Flies, Murrain, Boils, Hail, Locusts, Darkness, Death of the First-Born.*"

These ten plagues befell the Egyptians as the judgment of God. *Ten* is the number suggesting the perfection of divine order. The whole cycle is complete; nothing is wanting. In the ten plagues we have the perfection of God's judgments against the gods of Egypt.

"These plagues are all significant, proving the power of God, and rebuking idolatry:

1. The Nile, blood: an object of worship turned into an object of abhorrence.
2. The sacred frog itself their plague.
3. Lice, which the Egyptians deemed so polluting that to enter a temple with them was a profanation, cover the country like dust.
4. The gad-flies (Zebub), an object of Egyptian worship, fall dead before their worshipers.
5. Murrain—a blow against Hathor, the cow goddess and Apis, the bull god.
6. The ashes, which the priests scattered as signs of blessing, become boils.
7. Isis and Osiris, the deities of water and fire, are unable to protect Egypt even at a season when storms and rains are unknown, from the fire and hail of God.
8. Isis and Serapis were supposed to protect the country from locusts. West winds might bring these enemies; but an east wind the Egyptian never feared, for the Red Sea defended him. But now Isis fails; and the very east wind he reverenced becomes his destruction.
9. The heavenly hosts, the objects of worship, are themselves shown to be under Divine control.
10. The last plague explains the whole. God's firstborn, Egypt had oppressed; and now the firstborn of Egypt are all destroyed. The first two plagues, it will be noticed, were foretold by Moses, and imitated by the Egyptians. The rest they failed to copy, and confessed that they were wrought by the finger of God."

—*Gray and Adam's Bible Commentary*

Nine plagues came into the land of long ago and the Israelites were yet in bondage, enslaved to Pharoah, held captive by their enemies in a land of death and darkness. But at the *tenth plague* they were set free; they were delivered; they were redeemed! For it was at the 10th plague there was *the shedding of sacrificial blood. A lamb was slain, a Substitute died, a Life was given.*

It is claimed that it was after drinking of this "Cup of Judgment" and *having received the sop*, Judas went out to betray his Lord. Judas drank of the cup of judgment and remained no longer to partake of the Passover meal; he did not partake of the Cup of Blessing and the Cup of Praise. The Lamb, the Bread, the Fruit of the Vine, the King of the Kingdom, is not promised to those who betray Him or for those who reject Him. They will never partake of the Great Marriage Supper of the Lamb!

The Third Cup (Kingdom Blessing)

The cup is filled the third time and this has been called the "Cup of the Kingdom" or the "Cup of Blessing." It is believed Paul was speaking concerning this cup when he said: *"The cup of blessing which we bless, is it not the communion of the blood of Christ (Messiah)?"* (1 Corinthians 10:16). Prayers are read which plead with God for the rebuilding of Jerusalem and the Holy Temple, for restoration of the Jewish people to "Eretz Yisroel" ("Land of Israel"), and most important of all, for the speedy coming of the Messiah! Following is one of the prayers:

> "O Lord our God! we beseech Thee, have compassion on thy people Israel, on Jerusalem, the city, on Zion, the residence of thy glory, and on the great and holy house, which is called by thy name. Thou art our God, Father, Pastor, and Feeder, our Maintainer, Supporter, and Enlarger. Enlarge us speedily from all our troubles; and suffer us not, O Lord, our God! to stand in need of the gifts of mankind, nor their loan; but let us depend on Thy full open, holy and ample hand; so that we may not be put to shame, nor even be confounded."

It is thought that it was at the time when the Lord Messiah took this cup that He made His blessed and prophetic announcement: *"I will not drink henceforth of this fruit of the vine, until that day when I drink it new with you in my Father's Kingdom!"* (Matthew 26:29). This "new wine" represents the New Covenant in His blood which He was to shed for the remission of sins. (Both the Old Covenant and the New Covenant were sealed with the blood of the Passover Lamb. See Jeremiah 31:31-34 with Hebrews 8:6-13; 9:12, 18-22.) He gave His blood for the life of the world and this would be the *new and living way* into the Holy of Holies, into the very throne room of Almighty God! For did not God promise throughout the Jewish Scriptures that He would do this? One outstanding promise is found in Leviticus the 17th chapter, the 11th verse:

> *"For the life of the flesh is in the **blood**: and I have given it to you upon the altar to make an atonement for your souls: for it is the **blood** that maketh an atonement for the soul."*

The Fourth Cup (Praise)

The cup is filled the fourth time and at the drinking of this "Cup of Praise," there is chanted or sung the last part of the great *Hallel* (Praise) which includes Psalm 115 to Psalm 118. These six Psalms (113-118) formed the special praise, sung in the Temple courts in circumstances of great joy and solemnity on the three great "Feasts of the Lord": *Passover, Pentecost,* and *Tabernacles.* This forms the chief feature in the *Haggadah* and was sung in the time of the Temple when the lambs were being slain by the Levites for the Passover. It is said that it was at this cup the Lord took after supper and proclaimed: *"This is my blood of the new testament* [covenant] *which is shed for many"* (Mark 14:24). We read further in this account of the Last Supper that *after* Messiah Jesus had eaten with His disciples and declared that blessed truth of His blood, they sang a hymn (*Hallel*) and went out (Mark 14:26). The first portion of the hymn comprising Psalms 113 and 114 was sung in the early part of the meal, and the second part after the 4th cup of wine. No wonder a *song of praise* ascended from their hearts! How can we help but praise Him when we remember the significance of the wine in relation to His blood given for the life of the world! Wonderful Redeemer! Wonderful is His redemption through His blood shed for the remission of our sins!

ANCIENT HEBREW MUSIC

The *early* Hebrew Scriptures contain musical notes which are found in tiny symbols above and below the Hebrew words. Jewish melodies of 2,000 years ago have been preserved through a system of notes called *trope* which was applied to the cantillation of Scripture. This system existed long before the present system of writing musical notes on a five-line bar. Since the marks with certain musical value in the Hebrew text are *fixed,* the tunes of the Biblical and prophetic portions containing them have been transmitted from generation to generation.[45]

Psalms 114-118 are sung as the last part of the Passover service. A portion of it is as follows:

> *"I will praise thee: for thou hast heard me, and art become my salvation. **The stone which the builders refused is become the head stone of the corner"*** (Psalm 118:22). [Compare with Acts 4:1-12.] *This is the LORD'S doing; it is marvelous in our eyes. This is the day which the LORD hath made; we will rejoice and be glad in it."*

---

[45]Excerpts from *Your Neighbor Celebrates* by Arthur and Oscar Tarcov, p. 86. Also see my *New Covenant Passover Haggadah*, Section Seven, "Sound of the Temple Restored," p.122.

Over and over again, at the conclusion of the Passover Seder, my Jewish people recite the words concerning the rejection of their Messiah who has already come and He has become the Headstone of the Corner. They acknowledge that this is the Lord's doing and they will rejoice in it! But they do this in darkness, not realizing that their Messiah, their Passover, is the Lord Himself!

✡ ✡ ✡ ✡ ✡ ✡ ✡

The Fifth Cup (Cup of Elijah)

The fifth promise of God to bring Israel into Canaan, which follows the four promises of redemption, gave the need of this fifth cup of wine in the Seder which is a late custom dating probably from the 18th Century. This is usually a tall goblet which is placed in the center of the table. It is filled *midway* through the Seder. After the third cup of wine this fifth cup is filled and the door of the house is opened.

הסדר—*The Seder;* Illustration pictured in my grandfather's Haggadah. **"A Door is Opened for the Prophet"**

The company then rise to greet the prophet *Elijah* saying *Baruch habah,* "Blessed be he that cometh." *Elijah,* the forerunner of the Messiah, was to come to announce the good tidings of peace and salvation. "Blessed be he who cometh in the name of the Lord. O Lord! save us now, we beseech thee!"

After drinking from the fourth cup, final grace is recited ending with: *"Coming year in Jerusalem!"*

Over 35 years ago I received an interesting letter which I would like to share at this time. A short excerpt follows:

"The reading of your book, 'The Passover Feast,' prompts me to tell you of a revelation concerning the 'CUP' the Lord Jesus drank for you and for me when He went to the Cross.

"I realized that before man was created, God placed the symbol of that CUP in the heavens for all men to see, the most conspicuous of all constellations in the North (in *Ur'sa Major*) commonly known as 'The Big Dipper.'[46]

---

[46]See illustration on p. 320 with article "God Wrote a Book" showing a scroll and feather. In the background of stars find "The Big Dipper."

"I am a retired Forest Ranger and I have spent many nights out under the stars. A few years ago, as I was meditating on the Lord one evening, I was impressed with the fact that this great *cup* in the sky was the symbol of the Cup which our Lord Jesus emptied for us at Calvary. Also, I noticed that this great constellation rotated about the *North Star*. I was curious to know just *when* this great Cup was completely inverted or 'emptied.' I wrote to the Dean of Astronomy at the University of Washington and learned that this great Cup emptied once each year at about March 15 (at that time), the Passover!" (Lee F. Chartrand, Kennewick, Washington, October 2, 1956.)

Another Prayer at Passover:

"Oh, may He who is mighty, soon rebuild His house, speedily, speedily, soon in our days; O God! rebuild it, O God! rebuild it, build Thine house betimes. Oh, may He who is the Chosen One, who is great and exalted soon rebuild, etc. Oh, may He who is all-honored, all-worthy, most immaculate, soon rebuild, etc. Oh, may He who is all-powerful, the all-knowing and all-ruling, soon rebuild, etc. Oh, may He who is most revered and elevated, the God of strength, soon rebuild, etc. Oh, may He who is the Redeemer, the all-righteous, the most Holy, soon rebuild, etc. Oh, may He who is the most compassionate, the Almighty, all potent, soon rebuild His house, speedily, speedily, soon in our days. O God! rebuild it, O God! rebuild it, rebuild thine house betimes."

ĶĄ'ĄŖĄĦ (Seder Dish)

Placed before the "Head of the House" is either a golden or silver platter (called *Ka'arah*) upon which are some bitter herbs; greens or parsley, roasted egg, a mixture of apples, nuts and raisins called *Haroseth*, grated or a whole horseradish (sometimes an onion) and a shankbone or shoulder bone of a lamb. The lamb is present by proxy in the form of the roasted shankbone.

The *Ka'arah*[47]

This is the only reminder of the lamb of the Exodus. The Feast emphasizes the unleavened bread. But without the *Lamb* there would have been no deliverance for Israel. Without the *Lamb* Israel would have no life or freedom, no redemption, no people of God! Everything revolves around the *Lamb,* Messiah Yeshua.

Here is an interesting fact about the shankbone of the lamb: The sheep bone is distinct from that of (some) other animals in that it is *impregnated with a natural oil*, which does *not* readily *bleach out!* This is asserted by *zoologists*. The shankbone of a lamb, which I

---

[47]Sketch by artist Howard Morlock, copyright © by *Bedrock Publishing*, 1997.

used in my demonstrations of the Passover Feast over 45 years, shows a polished, oily exterior though it has not once been oiled or shined! It is clearly *oily still!*

> "If this is a biological distinctive of sheep, it beautifully portrays our Christ, God's *Lamb*, for He was filled with the *oil* [The Holy Spirit] without measure! He began His ministry only after the symbolic dove, the Holy Spirit, lighted upon Him. He commanded His disciples that they, too, would receive the *oil*, the enduement of power at Pentecost. They would have power as they knew the permeating Oil of Holy Ghost authority. As lambs among wolves, they would be invincible." (Joseph Conley, *Regions Beyond Missionary Union*, 1979.)

The Lord commanded that the Passover was to be eaten with bitters (bitter herbs). This reminds the Jews of the bitterness which their forefathers suffered as slaves in Egypt. It is believed that these bitter herbs were the "sop" which the Lord Jesus gave to Judas after He had dipped his hand into it. It was after this that Judas went out to sell Him for thirty pieces of silver. (John 13:26) This should remind us of the bitter cup Messiah drank to the very last drop that we might not have to endure bitterness but that we may have the sweetness of His salvation!

Messiah prayed in the Garden of Gethsemane: *"O my Father, if it be possible, let this **cup** pass from me: nevertheless not as I will, but as thou wilt"* (Matthew 26:39). Thank God, He obeyed the will of the Father and drank that bitter cup for you and me that we might be able to drink of the Cup of Blessing!

The parsley, or greens, represented the hyssop which was dipped in the blood of the lamb in that ancient time and struck upon the side posts and upper doorposts on the houses of the Israelites. (Hyssop, the Egyptian *marjoram*, a member of the mint family, was used because of its hairy sponge-like stem and branching to hold liquid. Also, it was very common and easily obtained, even growing near the doors of the Israelites.)

> "Hyssop figures prominently in the later Biblical, and in the Talmudic literature, usually in conjunction with the cedar. The two flora are regarded by both as representing the two extremes–majesty and haughtiness on the one hand–and humility and lowliness on the other. Many and beautiful are the Rabbinical homilies on the subject, whose purpose is to teach the virtue of humility, so favoured by the Rabbis."[48]

---

[48] *The Jerusalem Post Weekly,* Tuesday. January 25, 1972, "Tora and Flora," by L.I. Rabinowitz.

The hyssop dipped into the blood of the lamb is a picture of life given to them when delivered from death. It reminds us who have accepted our Passover Lamb Yeshua of that great love of God which offered a Sacrifice on our behalf that we might have Life out of His death (and resurrection). Oh, glorious day when the "blood" of God's Lamb was made effective to us on the doorposts of our heart the moment we believed! We then accepted God's great love which brought us Life out of death! *"For God so loved the world, that he gave his only begotten Son* [as a Sacrifice], *that whosoever* [Jew or Gentile] *believeth in him should not perish, but have everlasting life"* (John 3:16).

An *egg* is always placed on the Seder plate. Some say that the round egg, a symbol of mourning, is eaten in memory of either the destruction of the Temple, the exile of the Jews, or the death of Moses (perhaps all of these). Others say that the egg is a symbol of fertility. Another explanation for this custom is that, according to tradition, the eating of eggs was forbidden by Egyptian law at the time of the Exodus and therefore it is eaten at the Seder in celebration of *freedom*. Still another explanation: The *roasted* egg on the *Ka'arah* dish represents the daily "burnt offering" of ancient Israel. Some interpret the egg as a symbol of hope and *new* life as yet not manifest. Untermeyer, a Jewish writer, said that this was compared with the custom of eating *eggs* on Easter morning (a symbol also of *new* Life). To some, the egg tells of the hardness of Pharoah's heart!

A hard-boiled egg is at each place setting on *Seder* night. Each person around the table starts the meal after the first part of the service by dividing a hard-boiled egg, placing it in a bowl of salted water (which represents tears, and to some, symbolizes the Red Sea), mashing it in the liquid and then eating it. They are reminded of the suffering of their ancestors in slavery and the tears which they shed in their captivity. To us who have been delivered from bondage in "Egypt's land" the salt water symbolizes the tears of our Messiah Jesus in His earthly ministry. He is called "a man of sorrows and acquainted with grief." It was foretold that He would be "rejected of men" and His deepest grief was when *"He came unto his own and his own* [Israel] *received him not"* (John 1:11). Yes, He wept as He looked out over the city of the Jews and said:

> *"O Jerusalem, Jerusalem, which killest the prophets, and stonest them that are sent unto thee; how often would I have gathered thy children together, as a hen doth gather her brood under her wings, and ye would not!"* (Luke 13:34).

Oh, how He longs to gather Israel, even now, to Himself and give them His Life. Though He came to His own and His own received Him not, yet how He yearns for them to acknowledge their sins and accept Him as their long-awaited Messiah!

The *Haroseth* mixture is made so as to look like clay, cement or mortar. This reminds the Jewish people of their servitude as "brick-layers" under their taskmasters in Egypt.

"In the book of Exodus the Scriptures tell how the enslaved Hebrews were forced to build cities for the Egyptians. The names of two cities thus built are mentioned. Pithom and Raamses. In 1883 Pithom was uncovered, and later another archaeologist uncovered Raamses. Still more remarkable is the fact that in these uncovered cities of long ago it was found that the bricks in the lower levels have straw, while those farther up have stubble, and the highest levels have no straw at all. The Bible student will find the answer to this seeming mystery in Exodus 5, where the Egyptian taskmasters, in order to oppress the Hebrews more severely, took away the straw that formerly had been furnished them for brickmaking and yet required the slaves to produce the same amount of work. To fulfill this demand the Hebrews must have scattered through all the land, endeavoring to gather stubble for straw. All this minuteness of detail is confirmed by the bricks of cities uncovered by archaeologists some three thousand years later!"

—Malcolm P. Hinckley, *The Gospel Advocate*

The Shankbone of a Lamb

The Jewish people were commanded to take, on the 10th day of the month, a lamb for an house, a lamb without blemish, a male of the first year, and on the 14th day the whole congregation of Israel *"shall kill it in the evening"* (Exodus 12:1-6). (The expression "in the evening" is, in Hebrew, *bain ha-arbaiim,* "between the [two] evenings.") This command was given to protect them from death, and in order to keep the firstborn alive God gave a lamb-substitute to be slain in his place. For the destroying angel was to pass through the land of Egypt and slay all the firstborn, but when he saw the blood of the lamb upon the lintels and door-posts of the houses, he would know that the judgment of death had already been carried out in that home and he would *pass over* them.

Now I relate the saddest part of the Feast as observed by my Jewish people today. All they have to remind them of the Passover Lamb is a shankbone (or shoulder bone) which has been burnt over the fire. They place it on the table in a distinctive platter along with bitter herbs. (This was my experience before I accepted the true Lamb of God.) Every year they rejoice in their freedom from Pharaoh but they are still in slavery, for there is no lamb nor blood of the lamb in their houses and the penalty of death is still upon them! What a pity that the Jew does not see that "the Lamb" was a type of Him who was to come!

The excuse which some Jews give for not having the lamb at the Passover is that it is inconvenient and too, Leviticus 17:8-9 forbids the Israelite to sacrifice outside the Temple. Consequently, the orthodox Jew considers a *lamb* to be forbidden in Judaism since the Temple was destroyed, the sacrificial system has ceased, and it is impossible to carry out this command.

> "Since the destruction of the Temple in 70 AD, the Jews have used a shankbone of a lamb as a symbol of the paschal lamb. However, the dry, meatless, roasted bone nullifies the significance of the Passover service, because a Passover without a Passover *lamb* is nothing more than a feast of unleavened bread. The Jewish nation is now in exile from God, the temple was destroyed, the priesthood vanished, the sacrifices ceased, and for almost 2,000 years the Jews have not had a *genuine* Passover."   —Selected

However, there is one Jewish community that sacrifices lambs every year. These are the few hundred remaining *Samaritans* in Israel, the last remaining descendants of the people brought in by Assyria in 722 CE to replace the exiled Jews. (See more information about the Samaritans in my book *New Covenant Passover Haggadah*, "Variations in Celebrating the Passover Seder," pp. 4-5.)

One explanation of the reason that a lamb was used for the celebration of Passover:

> "The reason why a lamb was chosen as the sacrificial beast was that the Egyptians worshiped the ram, and the Children of Israel had to show publicly that they disavowed such idolatry before God would release them from bondage."[49]

The foregoing statement was made under the heading of "Passover Legends among the Jews." *That is what it is–just a legend*!

God commanded that they *kill* a lamb and roast it over the fire. Not a *live* lamb stood in front of the door to protect them; not a lamb beautified by man's adornments. Not a lamb with its life blood flowing through its body was commanded of the Jewish people to place before their homes; but a spotless, blameless, innocent lamb was to be *slain*, its blood shed and its meat eaten! The blood of this lamb was to be *shed* that *life* might come to Israel. The meat of the lamb was to be eaten for strength for their journey. It is through the *death*, not the *life* of the lamb that salvation is now given to those who believe.

But now, for convenience there is only a bone which is placed on the most expensive dish in the house. The Jewish people look upon it and think of that lamb they were to kill and eat before they journeyed

---

[49]Theodor Herzl Gaster, Professor of Comparative Religion at Dropsie College of Philadelphia, in his book on the *Passover*, page 49.

from Egypt to the Promised Land. They have just an old, dry bone; but we who have accepted Christ as our personal Saviour have partaken of the blood (life) and the meat of the *true lamb*!

As the Israelites were to strike the blood (*imprimatur*, official approval) on the doorposts for their soul's redemption and eat of the lamb's meat for the journey, so we who are followers of Messiah Jesus do apply His blood in faith to our heart's door for the deliverance of our soul from bondage to our enemy, and have also partaken of His "meat" for the redemption of our body from disease and pain, for strength and health for our journey through this wilderness life to the Promised Land! As the Israelites who had been slaves, beaten and starved, weak in body, and of whom it is recorded that (after eating of the lamb) there was *"not one feeble person among their tribes"* (Psalm 105:37), so we who had been enslaved under sin, now are strong to do exploits for *we have partaken of God's True Passover Lamb*!

Oh, that my Jewish people would realize as they read their own Jewish Bible (the *T'nakh* or Old Testament, particularly Exodus, the twelfth chapter) that the lamb they were to kill was a perfect type of Him who was to come who would deliver them from their sins! If only they would know Him whom to know rightly is Life Eternal! For this lamb was to be taken from the firstling of the flock, meaning "son of a year" for after it is a year old it is no longer a lamb but is a sheep. In other words, this lamb was to be in the prime of life, the strength of youth, to be the sacrifice. Consider this: The Messiah was the *firstborn* of Mary, the *firstborn* of the *new* creation! In the prime of His life, in the strength of His youth He was chosen as the Passover Sacrifice! He was the *firstling* of the flock!

This lamb my Jewish forefathers were to select was to be of the *male* sex. When the Messiah came to earth He did not appear as an angel, or an animal, but He came as a *man*!

This lamb was to be without spot or blemish. It was to be examined from the 10th day of Nisan to the 14th. According to Jewish writings there were 52 points of inspection by the priest. On the tenth of Nisan, when the Jews were selecting their lambs for the Passover, Jesus made His entry into Jerusalem through the Sheep Gate and automatically was set aside for the Lamb Sacrifice when the people refused to accept Him as their King. After He was set aside on that day He was on trial to see if He had any spot in Him. He was declared to be without blemish at the conclusion of His trial when Pilate said to the Jewish people assembled there: *"I find no fault in this man"* (Luke 23:4). At the very moment the Jews were gathering the lambs (which had been declared acceptable for the sacrifice) to be slain for the Passover ritual, the Messiah, in whom could be found no spot, again came through the Sheep Gate fulfilling the words of the Jewish prophet Isaiah:

"He was oppressed, and he was afflicted, yet he opened not his mouth: he is brought as a lamb to the slaughter, and as a sheep before her shearers is dumb, so he openeth not his mouth" (Isaiah 53:7).

Some Jews observe the day before Passover by fasting which they call *Ta'anis B'horim,* ("the fast of the firstborn") as an expression of their gratitude to God because He spared the firstborn of their forefathers in Egypt. The lamb was to die in the place of the firstborn of the Israelites. An innocent lamb which had never harmed anyone, which had not done any wrong, was to die so that the firstborn could live. One was to be killed so that another could be set free. And the Messiah of Israel (Yeshua), an innocent *Lamb,* who knew no sin, was slain in the place of the sons of earth that they might live, and that believing on Him as their Substitute, they could be set free! Halleluia!

This lamb of the Emancipation from Egypt was to die on a *cross-shaped stand* and *roast over the fire.*

> "In the roasting whole of the Paschal lamb, there was the necessity for a crosspiece because this 'roasting over the fire' could only be accomplished by suspending it upon a longitudinal pole with a transverse bar to spread open the body. When the Passover lamb was roasted, a spit was thrust lengthwise through its body, and another transversely from shoulder to shoulder. Every Passover lamb was thus transfixed *on a cross!* In like manner when Moses lifted up the brazen serpent (Numbers 21:8-9) it was not on a pole but on a *banner-staff;* i.e., *a cross.*"[50]

Christ (Messiah Yeshua) died upon a *cross-shaped stand* on Golgotha's brow as the wrath, the *fire* of God's judgment for sin was visited upon Him. Thus the prophecy concerning the lamb to be sacrificed on a cross and *roast over the fire* was fulfilled!

The lamb was to be killed at a specific time ordained by God: *"In the evening"* (Exodus 12:6). The Hebrew for "in the evening" here is "bain-ha-arbaiim" or "between the (two) evenings." (Also written as "at even" in Leviticus 23:5; Exodus 29:39 and 30:8.) This suggests the time, a point between the sun's declining west and its setting, about three p.m. In the temple service, the day was divided into quarters and the quarter between twelve and three was called the *minor evening oblation* while that between three and six was called the *major evening oblation.* "Between the evenings" then, means between those two periods, or three o'clock p.m. And so it was that the Messiah Jesus, at the ninth hour (Matthew 27:46), or at 3 p.m. (our time), literally "between the two evenings" gave up His spirit, saying first: *"It is finished [fulfilled]"*!

---

[50]A.T. Pierson, *Many Infallible Proofs,* p. 204.

The whole congregation of Israel (a type of those who would be redeemed by the substitute) was to kill this lamb. From the *Mishnah* we have this explanation: "The Passover offering is slaughtered in *three* divisions, for it is said, and the whole assembly of the Congregation of Israel shall kill it [i.e.] *'assembly,' 'congregation,'* and *'Israel'*." The entire world is guilty of Messiah's death. It was sin (*"ALL have sinned and come short of the glory of God"* Romans 3:23) which made it necessary for atonement to be made. Those who would be cleansed must bring a blood sacrifice. Messiah (Christ) was that *Sacrifice!*

✡ ✡ ✡ ✡ ✡ ✡ ✡

God's Division of the Lamb
Exodus 12:9

God specified that the division of the Lamb was to be "the head with the legs, and with the pertinence thereof." Although no individual Israelite could possibly eat a whole lamb, he had a whole lamb at his disposal. *"Every man according to his eating shall make your count for the lamb"* (Exodus 12:4). The enjoyment of the lamb was a question of appropriation, appetite, and capacity. The believer's enjoyment of Christ is along the same lines. Here, as elsewhere, *we only get what we appropriate.*

The various divisions of the lamb speaks of the varied aspects of the Person of Christ, and the different parts of God's Word. The *head* speaks of His wisdom and the prophetic parts of the Scriptures. The *legs* speak of the walk of Christ and the practical parts of the Word of God. The *inwards* speak of the affections of Christ and those devotional parts of the Bible that have a direct bearing on the heart of the child of God and are so necessary to sweet and intimate communion with God.

Let us who know our Messiah Jesus partake of the *entire* Lamb that we might be nourished and strengthened. May we not indulge in too much *head* or too much *legs*. Error largely consists of truth held out of proportion, undue emphasis on certain things, at the expense of others things equally important.

The same spiritual resources are available to every child of God as was given to Israel. The qualifications for those who were allowed to partake of the Passover were: those born in the family, those bought with a price, those who were circumcised (Exodus 12:44, 48). All these things are true of the children of God, both Jews and Gentiles. They have been born into the family of God (John 1:12-13). They have been redeemed by the blood of Christ (1 Corinthians 7:23). They have been spiritually circumcised (Colossians 2:11). These and these only have a right or are able to feed upon the Lamb!

This lamb was not to have any of its bones broken. The *Mishnah* states on Exodus 12:46: "He who breaks a bone of a clean Passover offering receives forty (lashes)." In contradiction to this (because the Mishnah did not pertain to *Gentiles*), it was the custom for the Roman soldiers to break the leg bones of those who hung upon the cross in order to speed their death. There were others who were crucified on that occasion 1,900 years ago. When the soldiers came to the two malefactors on either side of Jesus, they were still alive, therefore the custom of breaking the bones of their legs was carried out on them. But when the soldiers came to Messiah Jesus, they discovered He was already dead (from soul suffering and body pain); therefore they passed by Him, unknowingly observing the command of God concerning the Lamb: *"Neither shall ye break a bone thereof."* Fulfilled in every detail!

In the Word of God, the Messiah is named as the Head and those who believe on Him are called His Body. He desires and commands that this Body (His Church) be a healthy, strong, and holy body, not a body crippled and deformed with schisms and divisions, with backbiting and murmuring, with fightings, envyings and strife—***none of its bones broken***!

The Paschal Lamb was to be consumed the night it was killed; nothing was to be left for the next day (Exodus 12:10). The body of Yeshua, our Paschal Lamb, was not left on the Cross overnight. And when we accept Him as our personal Saviour, we cannot leave part of Him for another day; we cannot refuse His full and free salvation; we cannot lay aside any of His doctrine; but we must partake of the ***whole*** Lamb–His flesh *and* His blood–His deliverance for spirit, soul, and body!

> "On the 14th day of the month Nisan, the day of the Jewish Passover, at the very hour when the lamb was slain, the Lord Jesus Christ gave Himself a ransom for a world of sinners, an atonement for a world of sin. The 'lamb' was slain–not 'lambs'. Was there indeed but one lamb offered in all Israel? No, there were many lambs, many thousands of lambs 'a lamb for an house' as it is written. Yet God comprehended them all as but *one*, for after ordaining that a lamb should be slain for each household (and there were over 200,000 households in Egypt), He spake thus in Exodus 12:6: *'And the whole congregation of Israel shall kill it* [not 'them'] *in the evening.'* How marvelously God has in the Paschal Lamb set before us the promise and pattern of the sinless Lamb of God who would come and shed His own precious blood for the redemption of all who put their trust in Him!"   —*Selected*

O glorious day when a Lamb was taken for our house, who was the Substitute, who paid the death penalty for us by tasting of death in our place! Wonderful Lamb of God who shed His own precious blood as an atonement for our sins! O, blessed day when by faith that blood was applied to our heart's door! Death no longer has power over us. For God sees the blood of the Lamb. He knows we recognize and have accepted His Sacrifice; therefore, even as He has promised, that will He do: *"When I see the blood I will PASS OVER you!"*

THE AFIKOMAN *(Aphikoman)*

Now we arrive to the most interesting and astounding ceremony of the entire Passover celebration. It is repeated year after year in Jewish homes and looked upon as being very important, yet remains a *mystery* all the while. My grandfather, who had studied to be a Rabbi, and my great-grandfather who was a *Hasidic* Rabbi in Jerusalem before him, observed this ritual not understanding the true meaning hidden there. One day I inquired of my grandfather why we did these things and his answer was: "Because our forefathers did these things, that is the reason we also do these things."

In front of my grandfather was a container for Unleavened Bread, the outside of which was embroidered with gold thread. This he called "Matzah Tash" which means "Unleavened Bread Pocket." The usual practice was three *Matzot* each of which is covered separately in the folds of a napkin or special cover. But my grandfather used the most popular practice which was a bag with three compartments. We could see that this Matzah Tash was One, yet Three.

Breaking the Middle Matzah[51]

Before the Seder my grandmother had placed three "cakes" of unleavened bread in the Matzah Tash, each one separated and distinct from the other by the cloth of the compartments. During the ceremony which occurred in the early part of the Seder, my grandfather would put his hand into the second compartment and take out the *middle* loaf. He blessed it and broke it into two *unequal* pieces. The reason given for this middle loaf to be broken into *unequal* pieces is that it is impossible to break it *equally* because of the Matzah's perforated lines. In the Jewish Haggadah the explanation for breaking the Matzah is:

"A poor man does not feast over a whole loaf [the middle matzah?] because he is never certain that he will have food for the next meal. He takes a small piece [the smallest of the broken middle matza?], putting most of the bread [the largest piece?] away for later." —*Rav Hai Gaon*

---

*See *The Hasidic Movement*, p. 322.
[51]Sketch by Howard Morlock. ©copyright by *Bedrock Publishing*, 1977.

I see in this ritual a wonderful truth. There is a small piece and a large piece which came about by the breaking process. Since the middle matzah represents the Messiah of Israel (as also the other two in the Matzah Tash), the smallest broken piece tells of His first coming in humiliation and suffering; the largest piece tells of His return never to suffer again but enlarged in His power and glory!

The largest piece of the broken Matzah is called the *Afikoman* (also called *Tsafon* which means "hidden"). In the Jewish Haggadah which is read at the Passover services, we find this definition of "Afikoman": It is "the Greek word *'epikomos'* which signifies 'after banquet,' hence 'dessert'."

Although the Seder meal does have dessert (such as 12-egg sponge cake, macaroons, etc.) the *Haggadah* defines the Afikoman as "dessert" because nothing is to be eaten after it is eaten. The taste of the Afikoman is to *remain in the mouth*! We who know Messiah Jesus need no dessert of the world. We need no addition to the deliverance He purchased for us. We are satisfied with the Lamb! May the remembrance of His redemption remain in our lives forever!

"The *Yemenite* Haggadah shows an acrostic for the name *Afikoman*: [The initial letters of these words spell *afikoman*.]

nuts	א גוזים
fruits	פ ירות
wine	יַ יִן
roasted things	קְ ליות
and meat	וּ בשׂר
water	מַ ים
spikenard	נ רדים

All of the above and even other foods are forbidden to be tasted after eating the *afikoman*."

✡ ✡ ✡ ✡ ✡ ✡ ✡

"But there is another Greek word for 'Afikoman,' which gives a full and satisfactory explanation, and where violence is not at all necessary to give it meaning. It reads exactly as the Hebrew. What does it mean? According to Liddell and Scott's Greek Lexicon, the word 'Afikoman,' sometimes spelled 'Aphikomen,' derives from the second aorist (past tense) form *ikomen,* with the pre-formative *aph*, of a verb *'ikneomai'*—'I come.' *Aphikoman* means *'I came.'* Who came? The One, obviously, whom the broken Matzo represents, namely, the Lord Yeshua [Jesus], the true Pesah! In the Afikoman, therefore, the Lord Jesus calls to all who are waiting and hoping for the coming of the Messiah: 'Why do you wait any longer? I *came* already! Afikoman! Open your eyes of faith, and behold me. I am the True Passover. I shed my blood to shield you from death and give you eternal life. I stand in the place of your Passover because I am its fulfillment'!"

—Solomon Birnbaum, tract on *The Passover*; additions by Frank M. Boyd

My grandfather would hide the Afikoman between two pillows at the side of his chair. He uncovered the Matzot remaining on the *Ka'arah* plate and recited the blessing over it as he lifted it up before the family at the table. The service and the meal continued and after the meal his grandchildren were given an opportunity to find the Afikoman (or pieces of the Afikoman). For discovering it we were promised a prize, a reward, a gift which would be given to us at Pentecost (*Shavuot*) which occurred 50 days later. A Jewish explanation of this custom is:

"The Afikoman is 'hidden away' at the beginning of the service and a reward is given to the child that finds it. This is done to create interest among the young lest they become inattentive during the lengthy Seder service."[52]

Another Jewish explanation:

"In a deeper sense the hiding of the afikoman symbolizes that the Exodus was only the beginning of the process of redemption, and part of it is still *hidden.*"[53] [The Hebrew word for *hidden* is צפון *tsafon,* which is another word associated with the *afikoman* and is a part of the Passover Seder ceremony.]

We were supposed to watch for the *afikoman* as explained by our grandfather from the words of Exodus 12:17: *"Ye shall **observe** the feast of unleavened bread."* The literal rendering is *"You shall **watch** [guard] the Matzah."*

When the meal was finished my grandfather took the Afikoman which had been found, broke it and passed the pieces to each one present and we would eat it together. There is no food eaten after partaking of the Afikoman. The origin of this custom is traced to the Paschal lamb which was eaten on Passover night. *"Nothing was to remain until morning"* (Exodus 12:10). It was customary to reserve a small portion of the lamb to be eaten at the close of the meal. When sacrifices had ceased, a piece of the Matzah was eaten instead.

A custom that originated in the Middle Ages was to watch the Afikoman and keep it as a protection from "the evil eye." In some instances it was carried around by pregnant women who would hold

---

[52]Abraham Mayer Heller, *The Vocabulary of Jewish Life,* p. 97.
[53]Rabbi Joseph Elias, *The Haggadah/Passover Haggadah,* p. 64.

it while giving birth! Jews of Morocco believe that, during a voyage, the tossing of the afikoman into a stormy sea will ensure a calm and safe journey, for it is written:

"For he hath delivered me out of all trouble" (Psalm 54:9). מִכָּל צָרָה הִצִּילְכוּ and the initial letters of each word spell *Matzah* (מ צ ה)!

THE THREE MATZOT

According to the Haggadah, the Matzah Container (*Matzah Tash*) represented the Jewish Nation; the first Matzah being the Priests, the middle Matzah being the Levites, and the third Matzah being the Israelites, the "lay people." Some interpret two of the Matzot to represent the *Lehem Mishnah,* the double portion of the Sabbath and the holy days, and the third one called *Lehem Oni,* "the bread of affliction or poverty." Sometimes they are called by the names Abraham, Isaac, and Jacob. Why **three** *Matzot* is also explained: "Matzah must be eaten *three* times during the Seder: by *itself*, with *maror*, and as *afikoman*."

To the Jews the answer to the three Matzot is: because the Israelites who wandered in the wilderness for 40 years received a *double* portion of manna before the Sabbath it is traditional to have *two* loaves of *challah* on Shabbat and festivals. "But since *Matzah*, the only form of wheat we can eat for bread we need *two* pieces. We also need a piece between these two pieces that can be broken in two for the *afikoman*, the hidden *Matzah."*

The Cabalists called the three *Matzot* by the names of the three divisions of Israel: Cohen, Levi and Israel, to symbolize the unity of the Jewish people.

But why is it that not the first nor the third loaf but the *second* or *middle Matzah* is (1) removed from its place and (2) broken into two unequal pieces by the father; (3) why does he hide it; (4) why is a Gift or reward promised by the father to that one who discovers it; (5) why is it raised and revealed again, then participated in as the last part of the meal? Surely we could not say that the second Matzah, if Isaac, neither if Levi, fulfills these rituals!

At the Last Supper or Passover Seder which Messiah Jesus celebrated with His disciples, He explained all these ceremonies and symbols. He took the Matzah (the Unleavened Bread) and *recited a blessing over it*, the same blessing which is recited today at Passover time: *"Barukh attah Adonai Elohenu melekh ha-olam, ha-moitzeh lehem min ha-aretz."* "Blessed art Thou, O Lord our God, King of the Universe Who bringeth forth bread from the earth." We see the promise of the Resurrection in these words. In essence, Messiah was saying that He who is the Bread would be brought forth by God from the earth. He who is the Bread of Heaven was born in *Bethlehem*, which means "The House of Bread." He was broken and was raised from the dead out of the earth! Messiah Yeshua broke the Bread and passed it to His disciples saying: *"... This is my body broken for you, this do in remembrance of me ..."* He held the Cup and said: *"... This cup is the new testament in my blood: this do ye, as oft as ye drink it, in remembrance of me ..."* (1 Corinthians 11:24-25). It was not in remembrance of the Exodus from Egypt. It was in remembrance of a greater deliverance and a greater Deliverer than Moses. It was in remembrance of Him who brought us out of sin, Yeshua ha-Meshiach!

"Prior to His death Jesus ate the Passover Supper with His disciples. When he said, 'Take, eat; this is my body,' He was not giving them neat slices of bread. *He broke it before He gave it to them.* And I believe He demonstrated His broken body with a complete or central fracture.

"We should realize that Christ *tore* the bread apart *Himself* and *then* distributed it to His disciples. Here is a wonderful type! He broke His own body on the tree. He gave Himself. Christ did not die a martyr's death. Martyrs are bound and fettered. They cannot help themselves. Jesus said, *'Thinkest thou that I cannot now pray to my Father, and He shall presently give me more than twelve legions of angels'*? (Matthew 26:53)." —Author unknown

We who believe in Yeshua (Jesus) our Messiah know that the container for the Matzot represents God, for He is *one*; He is **Echad** (Hebrew for "united one," "a compound unity"). The *three* compartments with the *three* Matzot in this *one* container represent the manifestations of *one God* in the Father, the Son, and the Holy Spirit. *Three in one—a Tri-unity, a Trinity*! Each is distinguished in itself (as shown by the cloth which separates one Matzah from the other), yet cooperating together as *one*, even as we notice God, the Word, and the Spirit involved together in the Creation (see Genesis 1:1-2).

It is not the First Person of the Godhead, neither the Third Person of the Godhead, but the Second Person, the *"middle loaf,"* who left His place in glory, came down to this sin-cursed earth and tabernacled in the flesh (see John 1:1, 14). The Father *anointed and blessed Him* to preach good tidings to the meek, to bind up those who are broken-hearted, to proclaim liberty to the captives, and the opening of the prison to them that were bound (Isaiah 61:1). And after three short years of blessed ministry, His body was *broken* (crucified) even as He predicted: He was *hidden* in the grave; and though there is a tradition among the Jewish people that the disciples *stole* the body of the Lord Jesus and claimed that He rose from the dead, the Father above kept "watch" over the "Afikoman" and He only could raise it according to the prophecy!

On the *third* day Messiah Jesus *arose* victorious over death, "hell" ("hades"), and the grave! (See prophecy of Messiah's resurrection, Psalm 16:10 with 1 Corinthians 15:4.) Praise God, we do not have a dead Messiah! He is a living, resurrected and glorified Messiah! Death could not keep Him in the tomb! He tore the bars away! He is now *seated* at the right hand of the Majesty on high and some day very soon *will return* in the clouds of heaven, will be revealed, as it were, and all those who see Him and who believe in Him will *participate* in Him (the *Afikoman*) forever!

The disciples who believed in the Risen Lord were commanded to wait in the city of Jerusalem for the *Promise of the Father* and *50* days after the Passover Lamb had been slain and rose from the dead they received the *Gift of the Holy Spirit.* They had discovered the Afikoman and now received their reward of the Gift which the Father had promised! The Father said that we can receive anything He *promised* if we ask Him in the Name of His only begotten Son! We who believe in the risen Lord today, who have found Him whom our soul loves, can receive this same promise of the Father as was received at Pentecost. ("Pentecost" means "fifty" or "fiftieth" and is the name which Greek-speaking Jews called their Hebrew Feast of "Shavuot" "Weeks" or "Week of Weeks.")

Oh, my people Israel, Messiah has been *hidden* as was the Afikoman at your Passover Seders, and you have not as yet partaken of Him (many of Israel have accepted Him, however), but some day when He returns He will reveal Himself to you (as a nation), the veil of Moses will be done away from many more of you, and Messiah, the **afikoman**, will be distributed among you for your salvation!

According to the Jewish ritual of the Passover Seder, the table setting was to be as pictured on the following page:

Table Setting for Passover Seder

"(1) There was the meal, distinguished by special features, the most important of them the roasted lamb, the unleavened bread and the bitter herbs. (2) The youngest member of the company–the son if it was a family–had to ask what the strange ceremonies meant. (3) The leader of the company–the father if it was a family–had in answer to recount God's mighty deeds for Israel, beginning with shame (the heathen past and the slavery in Egypt) and ending with praise (the Exodus, Sinai, the holy land and the Messianic future)."[54]

Pause and meditate upon these great facts of this Feast of the Lord! Yeshua (Jesus) is the Great Emancipator from Egypt's bondage! He is the Great Deliverer from slavery to the enemy, Satan! The Messiah of Israel is the Unleavened Bread (the Matzah), the Staff of Life, the *Broken* Matzah, the Afikoman! Yes, He is the Fruit of the Vine, the Joy of Salvation! Yeshua is the Light of the World and in Him is no darkness at all! He is the Rest, the Freedom, the Peace! Messiah Jesus is the *true Passover, the Lamb slain from the foundation of the world to receive honor and glory and power and dominion forever and ever, Amen*!

---

[54]David Daube, *The New Testament and Rabbinic Judaism*, p. 187.

The following sketches were drawn for me in 1968 by **Howard Morlock**, a former student of mine at Seattle Bible College. Captions are mine.

THE THREE MATZOT OF THE PASSOVER SEDER

THE THREE MATZOT

For the Seder always there are 3 matzot, each piece distinct in itself, separated by a cloth– yet all together as ONE. – *Suggesting the Godhead. ONE God who is manifested in THREE Persons.* (See Genesis 1:1-4 which tells of God, His Word, and the Holy Spirit; also 3 Persons in One: Isaiah 48:16; 63:8-10.)

Middle Matzah Removed

The Father (Leader) puts his hand into the middle section and takes the Second Matzah out from its place. –*Suggesting the Second Person of the Godhead who left His place in glory, sent by the Father to earth.* (See Deuteronomy 18:18; John 1:1, 14.)

Middle Matzah Broken

The Father (Leader) breaks the middle Matzah into two unequal parts. –*Suggesting the death of the Second Person of the Godhead* (Isaiah 53:6,10; Psalm 22).

Hiding Middle Broken Matzah

The largest part of this middle Matzah (called "Afikoman") is "hidden" between two pillows on the chair at the Father's side. – *Suggesting the burial of the Second Person of the Godhead* (Isaiah 53:9).

Finding the Hidden Piece*

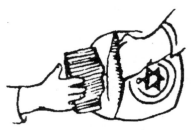

At the conclusion of the meal the children are given opportunity to find the Afikoman. The one who does find it puts it into a bag or specially designed container. It is kept "hidden" here until it is called for by the Father. —*Suggesting Jewish and Gentile believers have discovered Messiah, the Second Person of the Godhead whose body was broken for them according to the prophecy:* (Isaiah 53:5). They now can say: *"I have found Him of whom Moses in the law and the prophets did write, Jesus of Nazareth ..."* (John 1:45).

Father Asks for Afikoman*

The Father asks for discovery of the Afikoman to be made known and then promises a gift to that one who has found it. This reward is usually given at "Shavuot" which Greek-speaking Jews named "Pente-cost" meaning "Fiftieth" because it came 50 days after

Passover. —*Suggesting the Gift of the Holy Spirit or called "Promise of the Father" which is for all those who have found Him, that is, they believe in Yeshua as Messiah.* (See Isaiah 28:11; Joel 2:28, 29 with Acts 1:8, 2:4, 14-18.)

Father Distributes Afikoman

The "hidden piece" or the Afikoman which has been removed from its "hidden place," is uncovered or is revealed as it is taken by the Father. Now it is broken into pieces by him and distributed to the company as the last food to be eaten that night. — *Suggesting Messiah's resurrection* (Psalm 16:10; Acts 2:23-27), *His revelation, and then finally His "distribution" to all believers at His Second Coming* (Daniel 7:13, 14).

*Added to the ritual in more recent times.

CHRIST OUR PASSOVER

Thou Paschal Lamb, appointed
By God the Father's love;
That we, through His Anointed
Might all His mercy prove:
Through Thee we have salvation,
Life, pardon, peace obtained;
And praise with adoration
The Lamb for sinners slain.
Freedom from condemnation
Could only come by Thee,
Through Thy humiliation
And sufferings on the tree.
Thy weight of sorrow bearing
From Satan, man, and God,
And love to us declaring
Through Thine atoning blood.

We praise Thee, Holy Saviour,
That Thou didst suffer thus,
And in Thy loving favor
Endure the curse for us.
Through everlasting ages
All glory be to Thee;
While this each heart engages—
Thy love on Calvary.
We wait for Thine appearing
To chase the night away,
The welcome summons hearing
To call us hence away.
Thy saints will then in glory
Redeeming love proclaim,
While they rejoice before Thee
That "worthy is the Lamb."
—Selected

Let anyone who is hungry
come... HAGGADAH

THE JEWISH PASSOVER

All leaven from the home is cast,
The Paschal lamps are lit,
And children in a festive mood
Around the table sit:
For joy and sorrow intertwine
Tonight for Jacob's exiled line.
Set in white, the Paschal feast
A holy awe awakes,
As Israel's father, Hebrew-voiced,
The Exodus relates:
He blesses first the cup of wine,
Then reads the service line by line.
He praises God, and washes hands,
And breaks the middle cake, –
Old sorrow's threefold symbol
bread

Which Israelites partake.
He then invites Jews in distress
To come and Israel's hope confess.
Salt and water, finger-dipped,
Ten awful plagues recount,
As bitter tears from Hebrew eyes
To Pharaoh's throne-room mount;
And blows that fell on Israel's back
Return to Egypt's heart, alack!
Burnt and bare, a lamb's shankbone
Recalls the lamb once slain,
But as a bloodless sacrifice
The offering is vain!
No priest the Paschal lamb can slay
While from the temple courts away!

Parsley, hyssop's counterpart,–
Soft moss in Egypt grown,
The sprinkler of the Paschal blood,
As meekness here is shown;
For Israel, though a stiff-necked
race,
Will weep before *The Lamb's* kind
face.
An egg love's sacrifice denotes
And resurrection life,—
A symbol of the Red Sea crossed
And song displacing strife:
The Promised Land to faith appears
Where home's delightful prospect
cheers.
Wise and simple sons inquire,
"Why do we do these things?"
"Because from Egypt we come forth
Beneath Jehovah's wings."
The wicked son himself excludes
When to God's wonders he alludes.
Abram's call and Jacob's fear,
And Laban's Syrian hate,
And Joseph's safe and servitude
The Liturgies relate:
But through them all love's golden
thread
Shows Israel by Jehovah led.
Bitter herbs partaken, too,
Link Judah with the past;
But with the wine's inspiring joy
Old sorrows vanish fast;
And almonds breathe of hope
restored
With fervent love to God outpoured.

Supper eaten, grace is sung,
The broken cake brought up,–
The symbol-bread Messiah is,
His love is in the cup.
They tell us of the Coming One,
The King of Kings, God's Sinless
Son.
The vacant chair inspires a child
To open wide the door.
For good Elijah heralding

The King we should adore:
Ah once He came, and will again,
To empty Judah's cup of pain.
"Next year in Jerusalem," we say:
Lord God, so let it be!
For only in the Holy Land
Can Israelites be free,–
Jerusalem, though far away
Is loved as in King David's day.
And in this hope
the service ends
With symbol-songs of joy
Which leave the Jew in Gentile
lands
As merry as a boy,–
A foretaste of the Golden Age
Revealed on the Haggadah page.
—*Rev. Mark John Levy*

EASTER AND PASSOVER

Why on a different date each year?

The word "Easter" (*Eostre*) is taken from the name "Ishtar," Babylon's great goddess of the dawn and spring. Rather, this holiday should be properly called "Pesach" or "Passover," "The Feast of the Paschal Lamb" and more correctly: "Resurrection Day"!

"Easter" or "Resurrection Day" came from, or is the fulfillment of the *second day* of the Passover *Feast* ("Waving of Barley First-Fruits"), three days after the Passover Sacrifice. Since the Jewish calendar consisted of 12 *lunar* months (some 29 days in duration, some 30 days) or 354¼ days, and periodically (every three years, seven times in 19 years) another month added to bring it into line with the *solar* calendar, the dates for the Passover as well as the dates for Easter were shifted from year to year in relation to the Julian or Roman *solar* calendar.

In early church history there was a controversy between Jewish and Gentile believers as to a set date for this holiday. The Jews felt it should be observed on Nisan 14 (their Passover), no matter what day of the week it was. The Gentiles felt it should be on Sunday, the first day of the week. This dispute continued until the Fourth Century, the western churches celebrating the day on Sunday, the eastern churches on Nisan 14.

It was in AD 325 Constantine was responsible for the decision of the Nicaean Council that Easter should be observed on the first Sunday *after the full moon* following the vernal equinox (March 21). Because of the changes of the moon and the appearance of the full moon, as well as the decision that Easter *must* be on a Sunday, it falls on a different date each year.

CHART OF JEWISH CALENDAR

In the Jewish calendar, every month begins with the New moon and is composed of 29 or 30 days (alternately). The lunar month does not always begin on the same day as that of the solar year, and usually includes days from two different months according to the Western calendar.

NISAN (occurs in March or April)

Sun.	Mon.	Tues.	Wed.	Thu.	Fri.	Sat.	
				Passover – **14**		**15**	– Passover Sabbath

16 - Counting of the Omer begins.

Sun.	Mon.	Tues.	Wed.	Thu.	Fri.	Sat.	
16	**17**	**18**	**19**	**20**	**21**	**22**	– 1st Sabbath (of the omer)
23	**24**	**25**	**26**	**27**	**28**	**29**	– 2nd Sabbath
30	(15 Days of Counting the omer)						

IYAR (occurs in May)

Sun.	Mon.	Tues.	Wed.	Thu.	Fri.	Sat.	
	1	**2**	**3**	**4**	**5**	**6**	– 3rd Sabbath
7	**8**	**9**	**10**	**11**	**12**	**13**	– 4th Sabbath
14	**15**	**16**	**17**	**18**	**19**	**20**	– 5th Sabbath
21	**22**	**23**	**24**	**25**	**26**	**27**	– 6th Sabbath
28	**29**	(44 Days of Counting the omer)					

SIVAN (occurs in June) (see Esther 8:9 –third month)

Sun.	Mon.	Tues.	Wed.	Thu.	Fri.	Sat.	
		1	**2**	**3**	**4**	**5**	– *7th Sabbath*
6	*(Fiftieth Day of Counting)*			**"Weeks" or "Pentecost"**			

ᛋᚻᎪᏤᏌᎾᎢ (Pentecost)

Bible names for the Feast of Pentecost are: "Feast of Harvest" (Exodus 23:16); "Day of Pentecost," (Acts 2:1); "Feast of Weeks" (Exodus 34:22, Deuteronomy 16:10); and "The Day of First Fruits" (Numbers 28:26).

> "The counting of the Omer, begun on the *second evening* of Passover, comes to a close with *Shavuot*. Every evening during the seven-week interval, the 'Sefirah' or 'counting' is made."[55]

---

[55]Rabbi Abraham J. Karp, *How to Celebrate Shavuot at Home*, p. 12.

The custom of counting the *omer* ("a heap, a sheaf") is still observed by orthodox Jews in their synagogue. These days of counting begins on the eve of the second day of Passover and continues for 50 days until *Shavuot* ("Week of Weeks," "Seven Weeks"), the equivalent to the word, "Pentecost" or "Fiftieth" which Greek-speaking Jews gave to their holiday "Shavuot." This "omer" contains a small specimen of the first harvest, usually a sheaf of wheat. Before counting, the Rabbi prays: "Praised art Thou, O Lord, our God, King of the Universe, who has sanctified us by His commandments, and has commanded us to count the days of the Omer."

"The manner of counting is as follows: 'This day is the ___ day since the Omer.' In some congregations a tablet is suspended from the wall of the synagogue indicating the exact day of the Omer season."[56]

When the 50th day of counting arrives, the synagogues and homes are decorated with trees, plants and flowers, in commemoration of the first-fruits which they were commanded to bring as an offering to the Lord.

An interesting custom observed by some Jews is that of eating *Kreplach* (3-cornered dumplings) on Shavuot. The reason is to remind them of the Torah even during meals. For everything connected with the Law was of *Triplicate* nature: (1) *Torah* (**Law of Moses**, *Chumash*), (2) **Prophets**, and (3) **Holy Writings** (TeNaK), was given to *Israel* comprising (1) **Priests**, (2) **Levites**, and (3) **Israelites** through Moses, the **third** *child* of Amram, after **three days** of preparation, in the **third** *month* (Sivan)!

My grandfather tried to observe the Laws concerning the Sabbaths and other Holidays throughout the year. He read some instructions to us for observing Shavuot which were headed by the words: "Things to Remember." 1. The **3** days before *Shavuot* ["Yom Tov" "Good Day" referring to "Shavuot"] are the "Three Days of Preparation. 2. During these **3** days every Jew should get ready to receive the Festival of Shavuot in its true spirit. 3. When "Yom-Tov" occurs on Friday, the true spirit of the holiday should be prepared the day before. Then the following laws were added to the above: 4. It is forbidden to strike a match on Yom-Tov or turn on the electricity. 5. It is forbidden to put out a light on Yom-Tov. 6. It is forbidden to handle money on Yom-Tov, (either coins or notes). 7. It is forbidden to ride on Yom-Tov on any vehicle, such as a train, streetcar, bus, bicycle, etc. These last two laws my orthodox Jewish grandfather was very careful to observe and taught his grandchildren to do the same.

---

[56]William Rosenau, *Jewish Ceremonial Institutions*, p. 80.

Poems and songs are read along with reading of the Holy Scriptures. *Akdamuth* is a mystical poem written in Aramaic by Meir ben Isaac Nahorai. This beautiful hymn composed in the 11th Century is read (in the Ashkenazic liturgy) after the opening verse of the Torah reading on the *first day of Shavuot*. It celebrates the glory of God and the greatness of the Torah. The following stanza is a short excerpt from this festival poem (*Akdamuth*) of 90 stanzas:

> Could we with ink the ocean fill
> Were every blade of grass a quill
> Were the world of parchment made
> And every man a scribe by trade,
> To write the love of God above
> 'Twould drain the ocean dry,
> Nor would the scroll
> Contain the whole,
> Though stretched from sky to sky!
> —Translated by Israel Zangwill

The Jewish people call this day "Shavuot" or "Weeks" (Week of Weeks or Seven Weeks) because it comes seven *weeks* after Passover. They are reminded on that day of the Ten Commandments [sayings] which were given to Moses fifty days after the Passover lamb was slain for their redemption from Egypt and they had crossed the Red [Reed] Sea. This Feast is also known by the name "Day of Giving of the Law."

Since Jews feel that Israel was established as a nation on Shavuot, it is a custom among Jewry at this time to formally accept young men and women as active members of their faith. The Biblical scroll read on this festival is the Book of Ruth, because it tells of Ruth's acceptance of the true faith and the harvest of first-fruits in the fields of Boaz.

On the morning after the first day of Passover (the morning after the Sabbath) the High Priest in Israel was commanded to bring a "sheaf (*omer*) of firstfruits" and wave it "to and fro" in the Temple before the Lord. The Hebrew word for "wave" here denotes not a smooth motion but a "violent shaking."

Fifty days after the second morning of the Passover Feast, the Jewish people were commanded to celebrate this Feast. A new offering was to be brought to the Lord on that day and waved before Him by the High Priest. This new offering consisted of *two wave loaves of fine flour, baken with leaven.*

Josephus, Edersheim, and the *Mishnah* tell that the sheaf of barley harvest was *marked out by 3 men after the sunset on Nisan 14* which was the beginning of Nisan 15. They cut down a sheaf and brought it to the Temple to lay it before the Lord after they had dried it by fire. There it rested on the Sabbath day and the *"morrow after the Sabbath"* (the morning hour is implied) the priest would wave the sheaf before the Lord and begin to count the days to Pentecost.

If this is the case we see the Sheaf cut down is Messiah Jesus who was cut down from human life in the field of the world. The Sheaf laid up before the Lord after the testing of fire and resting in the Temple on the Sabbath is Messiah, who, after being cut down was *prepared for burial* and whose body rested on the Sabbath in the tomb. The Sheaf that was waved on high *"to and fro"* before the Lord a day after the Sabbath is Messiah who arose from death on the first day of the week! He is the *First-Fruits* of the resurrection (see 1 Corinthians 15:23)!

On the evening of the second day of Passover (early morning), three days after the Passover Lamb was slain, when the priest violently shook the single sheaf (omer) before God, there was an earthquake; by Divine power the tomb which held the body of the Passover Lamb (Messiah) was wrested open! *"On the morrow after the Sabbath,"* even as God had shown in symbol of the *omer*, Jesus, the Messiah arose!

After Messiah's resurrection, He remained fully forty days with His disciples after which He was taken into heaven. This testimony was established by more than 500 Jews who lived in and around Jerusalem, who saw the events that transpired and testified concerning them as we read in 1 Corinthians 15:6.

It was 50 days after the Passover lamb of the Exodus was slain and the Israelites had crossed the Red Sea when the Lord manifested His power and glory on Mount Sinai.

> *"And it came to pass on the third day in the morning, that there were **thunders and lightnings**, and a thick cloud upon the mount, and the **voice of the trumpet** exceeding loud; so that all the people that was in the camp trembled. And Moses brought forth the people out of the camp to **meet with God**; and they stood at the nether [below] part of the mount. And mount Sinai was altogether on a smoke, because the **LORD descended** upon it in **fire**: and the smoke thereof ascended as the smoke of a furnace, and the **whole mount quaked greatly**"* (Exodus 19:16-18).

It was 50 days after the True Passover Lamb was slain outside the gates of Jerusalem and had risen from the dead when the Holy Spirit manifested His power and glory:

> *"And when the **day of Pentecost** was fully come, they were all with one accord in one place. And suddenly there came a **sound***

*from heaven as of a rushing **mighty wind**, and it **filled all the house** where they were sitting. And there appeared unto them **cloven tongues** like as of **fire**, and it sat upon each of them. And they were all **filled with the Holy Ghost**, and began to speak with **other tongues**, as the Spirit gave them utterance"* (Acts 2:1-4).

Cloven tongues as of fire sat upon each of them!

On the *50th* day after Messiah had been crucified as the true Passover Lamb and had risen from the dead, God, the Holy Spirit, visited a group of waiting disciples in the Upper Room, the antitype of His visitation with Moses on Mount Sinai 50 days after the lamb of Egypt was slain and they left for the Promised Land! At Sinai, 50 days after the lamb of Egypt was slain and they were delivered from bondage (crossing over the Red Sea), there was the *trembling of the mountain* at the presence of God. In Jerusalem, 50 days after the Lamb of God gave His life and had wrested open the tomb, the waiting disciples felt the *trembling of the House*! At Sinai *noisy thunderings* were heard; at Jerusalem there was the sound of the *rushing wind*. At Sinai, *God's voice* was heard by Israel *as a trumpet* "exceeding loud." At Jerusalem, *the notes of the gospel* were heard through the *disciples* as they spoke with power the wonderful works of God.

Interesting Note: There were *120* in the Upper Room who received the infilling of the Holy Spirit. The number 120 occurs twelve times in the Bible and means "a number, a host or multitude." Man was given 120 years after Adam. Moses also reached this number. Later this was shortened to under 100 years. It is interesting to note that at the dedication of the Temple 120 priests blew silver trumpets and 120,000 sheep were sacrificed, etc. The only mention of this number in the New Testament is in Acts 1:15: *"The number of names together were about an hundred and twenty."*

Pictured here are 3 kinds of bread which מַצָּה Jewish people use today. (Top left position is *Matzah*, the Unleavened Bread for Passover. Top right position is **Lehem** meaning "Bread." This was leavened and could be white bread, rye, לֶחֶם pumpernickel, wheat, etc. And in the bottom חַלָּה position is **Hallah**, the ceremonial white bread for Sabbath, Weddings and other religious ceremonies except Passover. (*Hallah* and *Matzah* [forms] was unknown in OT and NT times.)

> *"And ye shall count unto you from the morrow after the sabbath, from the day that ye brought the sheaf of the wave offering; seven sabbaths shall be complete: Even unto the morrow after the seventh sabbath shall ye number fifty days; and ye shall offer a **new** meat [meal] offering unto the LORD. Ye shall bring out of your habitations **two wave loaves** of two tenth deals: they shall be of fine flour; they shall be **baken with leaven**; they are the firstfruits unto the LORD"* (Leviticus 23:15-17).

On the Day of Pentecost the priest waved *two loaves* "baken with *leaven*" before the Lord. Generally it was forbidden that leaven be brought with a sacrifice:

> *"No meat [meal] offering, which ye shall bring unto the LORD, shall be made **with leaven**: for ye shall burn **no leaven**, nor any honey, in any offering of the LORD made by fire"* (Leviticus 2:11).

But on this occasion there was a hidden meaning to the leaven. The *two loaves* represented the two peoples (Jew and Gentile) made *one* in the Messiah. And there was leaven (sin) in them both!

The Old Testament saints wrote about the great *secret* of the **two loaves**. They looked into and inquired concerning its meaning. From Genesis to Malachi it lay hid, like a golden thread, appearing in prophecy and prediction, in type, parable, offerings, and feasts. But it never was fully known until the time of Paul. The Holy Spirit revealed to this Jewish apostle that God's eternal purpose was to take from *both* Jews and Gentiles a people for His Name, that they would be made a *joint-body* in the Messiah. (See my book entitled: *Two Loaves– One Bread: Jew and Gentile in the Church.*)

God's Desire and Promise for Pentecost

> *"And the LORD spake unto Moses, saying, Speak unto the children of Israel, that they bring me an offering: of every man that giveth it willingly with his heart ye shall take my offering. And let them make me a sanctuary; **that I may dwell among them**"* (Exodus 25:1-2, 8).

God's desire ever has been "That I may dwell among them!" From the beginning, when man was first formed, the Creator has searched for a home! But did not the Lord of glory possess a home in heaven, surrounded by holy worshipping angels? Yes, God dwelt in the atmosphere of glory and honor, of holiness and purity. Yet He desired companionship; He desired communion and fellowship with the man He created in His own image! Therefore He sought for a dwelling place with him and came down to walk and talk with him "in the cool of the day."

But sin broke up God's "home" in the Garden of Eden. No longer could His desire for fellowship be realized, for God cannot abide where sin is!

When disobedience to the Divine Law severed that holy relationship between Adam and his God, there was provided a way of approach back into His presence. However, it was a "limited" fellowship, not the reality and the glory as it was before. Every time afterward that man would come into "fellowship" with his Maker, he brought a sacrifice and placed it upon the altar. In this way he could have holy Divine communion once more. These altars scattered here and there were the way of "dwelling" with God until Moses was called up to Mount Sinai. For 40 days and nights, God conversed with him there giving him laws and ordinances for the children of Israel as also the plan for the Tabernacle. Now God established them as a nation and gave the pattern which they, as his holy nation, were to follow.

In it all, the desire of God was: *"Let them build me a sanctuary that I may dwell among them"*! Oh, how He longed for a people in whom He could walk and talk and reveal Himself!

Why did the Lord choose a tent, in this instance, for His home? Why did not the Lord choose a palace, an elaborately decorated building? Was He not the God of the Universe and could He not provide Himself the most glorious house in which to live? It is true, He could have spoken the word, and the greatest, most beautiful and splendid home would have come into existence for Him. But again, why did the Almighty choose a tent? The answer lies in the fact that the Israelites were dwelling in tents! God came down to their level! He humbled Himself in that He would be like them! However, His tent was distinguished by certain symbolical features from the tents of Israel which surrounded it; yet the fact remains: the God who created the Universe dwelt in a tent with the children of Israel who dwelt in tents!

It was not God's plan that the Tabernacle in the wilderness be His permanent dwelling place. It was a shadow of better things to come. When Israel settled in Canaan the original Tabernacle was still in use right up to the time of the dedication of Solomon's Temple (1 Kings 8:4). In addition, David had made a second tent for the Ark

(2 Samuel 6:17, 7:6). When David came on the scene the Divine desire was placed in his heart:

> *"Surely I will not come into the tabernacle of my house, nor go up into my bed; I will not give sleep to mine eyes, or slumber to mine eyelids, **Until I find out a place for the LORD, an habitation for the mighty God of Jacob** "* (Psalm 132:3-5).

God spoke to David concerning this but could not grant him his request for David was a man of war. However, the Lord promised David through him a Temple would be built for His Name!

> *"Then he called for Solomon his son, and charged him to build an house for the LORD God of Israel. And David said to Solomon, My son, as for me, it was in my mind to build an house unto the name of the LORD my God: But the word of the LORD came to me, saying, Thou hast shed blood abundantly, and hast made great wars: thou shalt not build an house unto my name, because thou hast shed much blood upon the earth in my sight. Behold, a son shall be born to thee, who shall be a man of rest; and I will give him rest from all his enemies round about: for his name shall be Solomon, and I will give peace and quietness unto Israel in his days. He shall build an **house for my name**; ..."* (1 Chronicles 22:6-10).

David amassed a great amount of material for "the sanctuary" but it was his son, Solomon, who built it according to the Word of the Lord. It took seven years to build this magnificent structure for the dwelling place of the Almighty (1 Kings 6:37-38). Someone has calculated in the following list, that duplication of Solomon's Temple would cost over $87 billion (before inflation)!

Gold, silver, brass	$34,399,110,000
Jewels	34,399,110,000
Vessels of gold	1,876,481,515
Vessels of silver	3,246,720,000
Robes and vestments	10,385,440
Trumpets	1,000,000
Food for Workmen	344,385,440
Rough Materials	12,726,685,000

When this building was completed the "glory of the Lord filled the Temple" (2 Chronicles 5:14), the Shekinah dwelt between the cherubim over the Mercy Seat.

It is interesting to note that there were **120** who ministered in Solomon's Temple when the power fell and **3,000** could wash at the Laver at the same time! This foretells the **120** in the Upper Room ministering to the Lord on the Day of Pentecost when **3,000** persons were "washed" (saved)!

Why did God now dwell in a building instead of a tent? Could not He have placed a diamond studded throne upon a cloud and revealed His presence to the people from there? Yes, He could have, but God now dwells in a building because the Israelites themselves lived in buildings! He came down to where they were, to be like them! His Home at that time was distinguished from the rest, but nevertheless He dwelt in a building even as did the children of Israel!

God is everywhere but also lived in a Tent while His people were *wandering* but in a Temple when His people were *settled* in the Land. The beautiful Temple built by Solomon was not intended by God to be His permanent abiding place. This was only a temporary "house" to show forth the Better House to come!

The glory of the Lord departed from Solomon's Temple because of Israel's sin. God withdrew Himself from among the people and still His voice rang forth: *"Let them build me a sanctuary that I may dwell among them!"*

We read in Luke that the glory which departed from the Temple, returned.

> *"And there were in the same country shepherds abiding in the field, keeping watch over their flock by night. And, lo, the angel of the Lord came upon them, and the glory of the Lord shone round about them: and they were sore afraid. And the angel said unto them, Fear not: for, behold, I bring you good tidings of great joy, which shall be to all people. For unto you is born this day in the city of David a Saviour, which is Christ the Lord"* (Luke 2:8-11).

Here we see the Savior bringing back the glory that man's sin had driven away. His *body* became the *dwelling place of the Father*! Messiah Jesus was the antitype of the altars, the tent in the wilderness, and the Temple of Solomon! Between the cherubim over the mercy seat of His heart dwelt the Shekinah! He is the true Tabernacle which the Lord "pitched" (built) and not man. Everything about the Temple and the Tabernacle pointed to the Messiah Yeshua!

Why did the Lord choose a Man in whom He could dwell? Why did not the Almighty choose an angel or some other heavenly creature? Because the people of God were formed of the dust of the earth, limited and subjected to an earthly sphere; therefore the Great and Strong All-Sufficient One (El Shaddai) emptied Himself; He lowered Himself to dwell in a tent of flesh that He might be like them! He was distinguished from the rest of His brethren; nevertheless He tabernacled in human form like those He came to redeem!

Still it was not God's plan that even the Messiah would be His *permanent* sanctuary on earth. For after 33 years of tenting among men, it was necessary that He depart from them. Once more the people's sin destroyed God's Home among them. Still God's cry for a permanent sanctuary among His people was not fully realized.

When Messiah Jesus left His dwelling among men to ascend back to the Father, and before He went away, He promised:

*"And I will pray the Father, and he shall give you another Comforter, that **he may abide with you for ever**"* (John 14:16).

"... It is expedient for you that I go away: for if I go not away, the Comforter will not come unto you; but if I depart, I will send him unto you" (John 16:7).

The Messiah was limited in His body and could not be in more than one place at a time. He could not be present with all of His people at every moment as He so desired. But before the foundation of the earth in the mind of God was a plan for a Sanctuary that would not pass away, a House where He, by His Spirit, could dwell between the cherubim forever!

God would cleanse this Home first and then place His Spirit within. Here He would abide. This would be His sanctuary, His very own people He had redeemed! His desire would then be fulfilled.

From the Word of God in the New Testament we see that the word in Greek for *sanctuary* (*naos*) is used also for the temple in Jerusalem and of the believer's body—as in 1 Corinthians 3:16-17. And this is the sanctuary He wants us to prepare for His habitation forever!

God is not interested in fine edifices, beautiful cathedrals, and decorated churches for a place to abide. He is searching for the *believer* in whom He can come with His glorious presence, the Shekinah. God had been *over* men. In the Person of the Messiah, He was *with* men and by the Person of the Holy Spirit, He is *in* men.

Before Jesus ascended into heaven, He admonished His disciples, both men and women, even His mother Mary, to tarry (wait) in Jerusalem for *"the promise of the Father"* (Luke 24:49). He told them that God was *with* them, but He would be *in* them (John 14:17). While waiting in the Upper Room, these believers were preparing a sanctuary for the living God! The Lord Himself was waiting to take up His abode in the temple of His people.

The Israelites remembered that 50 days after the passover lamb of the Exodus was slain and they had crossed over the Red Sea three days later, God visited them with thunderings and lightnings on Mount Sinai, giving the Law to Moses, establishing them as a nation, and revealing the pattern of the Tabernacle. Now, 50 days after the True

Passover Lamb (the fulfillment of the type) was slain and crossed "the river of death," God would again visit His people and establish a *new* nation, write the law, not upon tables of stone, but on the fleshly tables of their hearts, and would enter *fully to abide* in the temple not made with hands!

Jews from all over the then-known world came to celebrate the Feast of Pentecost (Shavuot) according to the Word of the Lord. At the same time the Jewish believers in Messiah, a "despised" group, met in the Temple to wait for the promise of the Father in obedience to Messiah's command. While the people were preparing for *Shavuot* and remembering the institution of the nation of Israel, the Mosaic law, and the pattern of the Tabernacle, the followers of the lowly Nazarene were preparing for the advent of the promised Comforter. When the Comforter came and filled the temples of clay, God's desire for a permanent sanctuary was realized in the lives of believers everywhere who, by faith, receive this wonderful gift of the Holy Ghost. Not only *Jews* but *Gentiles* as well (the fulfillment of the *two loaves* baken with leaven) stand before the Lord in Jesus the Messiah as candidates for the promise of the Father (Acts 2:39).

> *"And that he might reconcile **both** unto God in **one** body by the cross, having slain the enmity thereby:* [At one time Jews were set apart from Gentiles as written in Numbers 23:9 but now are joined together by the cross!]

> *"And came and preached peace to you which were afar off* [the Gentiles] *and to them that were nigh* [the Jews]*; For through him we **both** have access by one Spirit unto the Father. Now therefore ye* [Gentiles] *are no more strangers and foreigners, but fellow-citizens with the saints* [of the OT and NT–Jews] *and of the household of God;And are built upon the foundation of the apostles and prophets, Jesus Christ himself being the chief corner stone; In whom all the building fitly **framed together** groweth unto **an holy temple in the Lord:** In whom ye also are builded together for an **habitation of God** through the Spirit"* (Ephesians 2:16-22).

> Note: "The Son honored the Passover by dying. The Father honored the Feast of the Wave Sheaf or First-Fruits by raising Christ from the dead. The Holy Spirit honored the Feast of Weeks or Pentecost by coming upon the disciples of Christ as they waited in the Upper Room."[57]

---

[57]H.K. Downie, *Harvest Festivals*, Chapter 6, p. 89.

ROSH HASHANAH (New Year)

The words *Rosh Hashanah* are translated as "Head of the Year." It is so called because it is the Jewish New Year's Day. (In Judaism there is a Civil or Agricultural year which begins in the Fall, and the Sacred New Year which begins in the Spring at Passover.) Rosh Hashanah occurs on the first day of Tishri (which usually falls in September). However, according to Exodus 12:2, *Nisan* was regarded as the "head" of the year, "the beginning of months."

A Rabbi Blows the Shofar (trumpet)

The words "New Year" are not found in the Bible, and in only one place (Ezekiel 40:1) does the Hebrew expression *Rosh Hashanah* ("Beginning of the year") occur. The first of Tishri is generally regarded by the Rabbis as the beginning of creation because the first word of the Bible *bereshith* (the Hebrew word for *in the beginning*) when scrambled reads *evetishri* or the *First of Tishri*!

Unlike the Gentile celebration of January 1, the Jewish people celebrate their New Year's Day in a very solemn way. They examine their record for the past year and make resolutions to do better the coming year.

> "Three books are open on Rosh Hashanah before the Creator, wherein the fate of the wicked, the righteous, and those of an intermediate class are recorded. The names of the righteous are immediately inscribed, and they are at once sealed 'to life'; the middle class are allowed ten days, till the Day of Atonement, to repent and become righteous; while the wicked are at once blotted out of 'the book of the living'."
> —*Rosh-Hashanah* 1:2, 16b, *Mishnah*

"Feast of Trumpets" was known as *Hag Hashofaret*, "The Shofar Festival" in the time of Philo of Alexandria (20 BCE-40 CE). The Bible calls it *Yom Tru'a,* "The Day of the Trumpet Blast." ("Shofar" literally means "hollow.")

In fulfillment of the command God had given them in Leviticus 23:24, which is ascribed to the New Year) Jewish people gather in the synagogue on Rosh Hashanah where the most prominent feature of the religious ceremonies is the blowing of the ram's horn, marking the preparation of the Festival. On this day the Jewish people feel that the purpose for the sound of the *Shofar* ("trumpet") is to arouse them to the serious contemplation of their sinfulness as well as to their duty to lead a godly life. Also they feel that the sounding of the *shofar* on Rosh Hashanah is to serve as a reminder of the ram sacrificed by Abraham in place of his son Isaac.

Jews have treasured the "shofar" throughout the ages as their "own" special musical instrument. The horn of any *kosher* animal, except that of a bull which is reminiscent of the Golden Calf incident, may be used to make a Shofar. However, it is the ram's horn that is most popular from the days of Israel in the Bible.

The ram's horn is blown as a summons to conscience to awaken and heed the call of duty. For this reason *Rosh Hashanah* is known as "The Day of the Sounding of the Horn." And because on that day it is concluded that God calls to memory the faults and sins of the past year, it is also known as "The Day of Memorial," and since the Jewish people feel that they are then on trial before the Judge of the whole earth, Rosh Hashanah is also known as "The Day of Judgment."

It is according to Jewish belief that there is a Recording Angel who records all the deeds, good and bad, of all individuals for future reward and punishment. Gabriel is generally regarded as this recording angel. (There is reference to the recording in *the book of remembrance* in Malachi 3:16.) On Rosh Hashanah (as on the Day of Atonement which follows ten days later) the prayer of the Jew to his God is that He would inscribe his name in "The Book of Life"!

THE SHOFAR

The trumpet (Shofar) is the ritual ram's horn of the Hebrews, the oldest known form of wind instrument, which makes a sound like a tuba. On days of repentance, in order to represent a man humbling himself, a crooked ram's horn is used. This is symbolic of a contrite heart repenting on the solemn days of Yom Kippur (Day of Atonement).

Michael Kaniel, in *Jerusalem Post Weekly*, explains the making of the Shofar in the following descriptive article:

"After the tip of the horn has been cut off, a narrow cylindrical bore is gouged out to the natural hollow of the horn. The horn is then heated directly or soaked in hot water to make it pliable, and gradually stretched and carefully shaped. The broad end is cut, and sometimes trimmed, occasionally in a zigzag pattern. The narrow end is then widened slightly to form a mouthpiece, by forcibly expanding the heated cut edge of the tip. The edges are then rubbed smooth, and the exterior is smoothed out by scraping.

"The end result is a conoid [like a cone] of more or less oval form, starting with a narrow, curved, somewhat flattened tube, and widening into a bell-shape or roughly parabolic [something bowl-shaped] form. When properly blown, the Shofar produces a deep, penetrating sound with a limited range of tones. There are three variations of these tones sounded on Rosh Hashana. The *tekia* is a smooth, continuous note, said to express joy and contentment; and the *tru'a* is a minimum of nine brief staccato 'toots,' indicating trepidation or sorrow; the *shevarim*–three short blasts–combines the above two. Altogether 100 blasts are sounded on each of the two days of Rosh Hashana."

SOUNDS OF THE SHOFAR IN THE SYNAGOGUE

The Shofar is used in the synagogue especially on *Rosh Hashana* ("Head of the Year," "Beginning the Year," or "New Year.") Also it is used on *Yom Kippur* ("Day of Atonement").

Following is material shown in CD JeMM, the Jewish Multimedia Magazine on CD ROM (with additions). This is advertised on the Internet at http://virtual.co.il. (We even heard the ritual sounds of the Shofar from this program!)

Name of the Notes and Explanation

Tekia, A straight trumpet-like blast. Described in the Mishnah (Tractate, Rosh Hashanah 4:9) as signifying kingship which is the major theme of Rosh Hashanah.

Teru'ah, Nine staccato notes blown in rapid succession, similar to the wail of a person crying in short bursts. According to one rabbinic interpretation, it represents a plea for mercy at the upcoming trial—another major theme of *Rosh Hashanah*.

Shevarim, Three short notes (each three beats long), reflecting an alternative rabbinic interpretation that *Teru'ah* should be a moan, not a cry. *Shevarim* means "broken."

Shevarim-Teru'ah, Because of the rabbinic differences over how *Teru'ah* should sound, Rabbi Abbahu of Caesarea introduced this compromise measure–the blowing of *Shevarim* and *Teru'ah* in unbroken sequence.

In the order of blowing at least three sets of shofar blasts are sounded, since the word *Teru'ah* appears three times in the *Torah*. Traditionally, 100 notes are sounded during the *Rosh Hashanah* service.

Tekia Gedolah, (The Great Blast), A long drawn-out note concluding each set of blowing during the Rosh Hashanah ceremony. The rabbis described it as a sign of "divine withdrawal," based on the verse: "When the Shofar sounds long, they [the people] shall come up to the mountain" (Exodus 19:13).
　　　　　—End of Information from *Virtual Jerusalem on CD ROM*

Saadya, a teacher of the 10th Century, holds that the Shofar reminds Jews of the creation, their duty to God, the revelation on Mount Sinai, the teaching of the prophets, the destruction of the Temple, the binding of Isaac as a sacrifice, imminent danger, the day of Judgment, the redemption of Israel, and the resurrection!

It was the voice of the Shofar at Sinai "exceeding loud" that made all Israel tremble, for they recognized it as the same sound as was heard in their religious services, and knew at once it must be the voice of God on the mount! (Exodus 19:16; 20:18. In this connection it is interesting to note John's description of God's voice in Revelation 1:10; 4:1.)

The *Baltokia* ("Baal Tekia"), the one who blows the Shofar, stands in the center of the synagogue on an elevation, his prayer shawl (*Tallit*) drawn far over his head. Holding the curved instrument pressed gently to his lips, with all his power he makes the Shofar sound clear and distinct. The Shofar has no metal mouthpiece, or stops. The natural horn is shaped by immersion but the nine sounds of alarm are created by holding the Shofar slantwise to the lips, and blowing with regulated force. The three principal sounds are: "Tekia, Terua, Shevarim (with Shevarim-Terua)." A series of 30 blasts continued in quick succession, is called *The Great Tekia*.

Jews claim that Maimonides records the Shofar as an instrument to awaken man from his sleep, and to bring him to a consciousness that there is a God who rules the universe. Rabbi Aaron ha-Levi of Barcelona says in his famous book, *Hachinuch*, that the Shofar, with the voice of awe in it, has the quality of inspiring the feeling in man of obedience which prompts him to repentance.

The blowing of Trumpets was a well-known institution in Israel. There were *two trumpets* (Numbers 10:1-10) and both are frequently mentioned in the Old Testament. The *khatsoserah* was a long, straight, *silver* trumpet. This was mainly used on festive occasions and times of holy joy and triumph. The *shofar* was curved like a *ram's horn* (Joshua 6:4) and had a deep, solemn note, which gave the idea of awe and trembling at the presence of the Lord, of judgment impending or deserved.

The trumpets were used to regulate all the movements of the people of Israel in the wilderness, by them they worshiped, marched, and made warfare. There were different notes for various occasions and the people, familiar with them, knew what to do when the trumpet sounded. The Psalmist David may have had this in mind when he said, *"Blessed is the people that **know** the joyful [trumpet] sound"* (Psalm 89:15).

While the Shofar is being blown in the Synagogue on Rosh Hashanah the following remarkably significant prayer is offered:

> "Merciful and gracious God, I have sinned against Thee, and done that which is evil in Thy sight. Have mercy on me and forgive all my transgressions, trespasses and sins, through *Yeshua*, the Prince of His Presence."[58]

In most of the prayer books of the present day the above prayer is omitted, and the following offered instead:

> "May it please Thee, O Lord God, and the God of our fathers, that Thou mayest accept it as the mediation through Elijah and Joshua, the Prince of the Presence, the Prince Metatron (Messiah), and that Thou mayest be filled with mercy towards us. Blessed art Thou, O Lord who art merciful."

The angel Metatron, according to Jewish theology, was he who discoursed with Moses (Exodus 3:2-15) and the angel in whom God placed His name. The following from the *Zohar* is of interest here. (The *Zohar*, "Illumination," is a mystical commentary on the Bible, written partly in Aramaic and partly in Hebrew):

> "There is a Man, if a Man He is, who is an Angel. This Angel is Metatron, the Keeper of Israel; He is a man in the image of the Holy One, blessed be He, who is an Emanation from Him [from God]; yea, He [the Metatron] is Jehovah. Of Him cannot be said, He is created, formed or made; but He is the Emanation from God."[59]

How fittingly this could be applied to Messiah Jesus!

An institution which is about 900 years old, known as *Tashlich* ("Casting Off"), is observed immediately following the afternoon services of the first day of the New Year. This ceremony is still a popular propitiatory rite observed by Jews on this day. In fulfillment of Micah 7:19, *"Thou wilt cast all their sins into the depths of the sea,"* Jewish men and women go to the edge of a running stream immediately following the afternoon services where the Shofar has announced the first day of the New Year, and shake their coats or empty their pockets of crumbs of food into the water. In doing so prayers are recited concluding with the words: "May God cast our sins into the depths of the sea!" This is done in preparation for the Day of Atonement (*Yom Kippur*) which follows ten days later.

In Biblical times the trumpet was used for various announcements, like that of the New Moon and Festivals (Psalm 81:3; Numbers 10:1-10; Isaiah 18:3), signals of alarms, the call to battle, the stopping of

---

[58]Rev. Dr. A. Th. Philips, *Prayer Book For the New Year* (1913), p. 100. (This prayer is in the Hebrew and not translated into English as are all the other prayers.)
[59]*Zohar*, chapter 67, page 130.

pursuit, for dismissal of the army or return home, the Year of Release, as a signal of victory (Jericho), and as an instrument in processions. It was blown also at the offerings presented to the Lord, for proclaiming of an important event such as the accession of a ruler to the throne, and to make known the start of a fast. In Israel's history it was sounded to warn the people of impending natural disasters such as floods, locusts, etc. and of invasion by foreign armies.

As the trumpet was a symbol of God's voice it is mentioned by our Jewish brother, Paul when he admonished Jewish and Gentile believers in Messiah to be sure of order in the church, speaking to edify, comparing confusion to the *uncertain sound of the Shofar*, the Trumpet (1 Corinthians 14:8).

> It is believed by orthodox Jews that "the Messiah's coming will be heralded by the arrival of the Prophet Elijah blowing the great Shofar of 'Our Liberation.' This tradition has been expressed in Jewish art by numerous illustrations in *Hagadot* and other manuscripts and printed books from early medieval times, showing the Messiah on a donkey approaching the walls of Jerusalem while sounding the Shofar, or the Messiah sitting on the donkey with Elijah proceeding him on foot and sounding the shofar."
> —Michael Kaniel in *Jerusalem Post Weekly*

On the first day of Tishri the Israelites were commanded by God to have a Memorial of the Blowing of *Trumpets* (Leviticus 23:24). It was to be a day in which *all the trumpets* that ever were blown (and the event connected with them) were to be remembered. Not only in past events but also in the future the trumpet will be used as a symbol of God's voice. Through the Jewish prophets God prophesied a very important event concerning these last days which is to be announced by the blowing of a trumpet:

> *"All ye inhabitants of the world, and dwellers on the earth, see ye, when he lifteth up an ensign [Flag of Israel] on the mountains; and when he **bloweth a trumpet**, hear ye"* (Isaiah 18:3).

> *"And he will lift up an ensign to the nations from far, and will **hiss** unto them from the end of the earth: and, behold, they shall come with speed swiftly:"* (Isaiah 5:26).

> *"I will **hiss** for them, and gather them; for I have redeemed them: and they shall increase as they have increased"* (Zechariah 10:8).

The word "hiss" here is compared to the sound of a *trumpet*. It has been translated into the English as "hiss" but is really the Hebrew word for "whistle." This is the "whistle" that will be heard around the world—not audibly but in the "heart of hearts" of the Jewish people. For God will gather them back to the land He promised would be theirs. God will *whistle* for them from the north, the south, the east and the west wherever they have been scattered in every nation under the sun. The people of Israel have been away from their land for 2,000 years but now they are home and continuing to be gathered there as God had promised!

And not very many days after the gathering of the Jewish people back to their land, there is another great event which will be proclaimed by the blowing of a *trumpet*! ***This event is going to rock this world as has never any event in her history!***

> *"For the Lord himself shall descend from heaven with a shout, with the voice of the archangel, and with **the trump** [trumpet] of God: and the dead in Christ [Messiah] shall rise first: Then we which are alive and remain shall be caught up together with them in the clouds, to meet the Lord in the air: and so shall we ever be with the Lord"* (2 Thessalonians 4:16-17).

> *"... We shall not all sleep, but we shall all be changed, In a moment, in the twinkling of an eye, at the last **trump**: for the **trumpet** [Shofar] **shall sound**, and the dead shall be raised incorruptible, and we shall be changed"* (1 Corinthians 15:51-52).

It is interesting to note that the Jewish Talmud sets forth prophecies concerning the coming of the Messiah and the end of the world, such as:

> "For six thousand years the world will continue, and in the seventh it will be destroyed." (*Tractate Sanhedrin*, Vol. 7 and 8, *R. Ketina*). "The world is to stand 6,000 years. Two thousand of confusion, two thousand the law, and two thousand ***The days of Messiah***" —*Sanhedrin*, fol. 97, Col. 1

The Eternal New Year began in the heart of him who accepted as his Saviour-Messiah, the Lord Yeshua (Jesus). At that moment the heart was changed and all his sins were cast into the depths of the sea. The trumpet of the Lord of Hosts sounded announcing this great event and a new name was written in the Lamb's Book of Life! This New Creation now is awaiting the sound of the Shofar which shall usher in that greatest of all events since the days of Messiah's flesh! Oh, glorious day when the Lord shall come for His own, both Jew and Gentile, who have accepted the redemption He purchased through His supreme sacrifice on the Altar of Calvary!

YOM KIPPUR (Day of Atonement)

Kapporas Schlagen
(Sacrifice for
Atonement)

*"And the LORD spake unto Moses, saying, Also on the tenth day of this seventh month there shall be a **day of atonement**: it shall be an holy convocation unto you; and ye shall **afflict your souls**, and offer an offering made by fire unto the LORD. And ye shall do no work in that same day: for it is a **day of atonement**, to make an atonement for you before the LORD your God. For whatsoever soul it be that shall not be **afflicted** in that same day, he shall be cut off from among his people. And whatsoever soul it be that doeth any work in that same day, the same soul will I destroy from among his people. Ye shall do no manner of work: it shall be a statute for ever throughout your generations in all your dwellings. It shall be unto you a sabbath of rest, and ye shall **afflict your souls**: in the ninth day of the month at even, from even unto even, shall ye celebrate your sabbath"* (Leviticus 23:26-32).

"One of the important Bible readings in the synagogue on *Yom Kippur* is taken from the Book of Isaiah (58:6-8):

'Is not this the fast that I have chosen? To loose the fetters of wickedness, to undo the bonds of the yoke, and to let the oppressed go free ... Is it not to deal thy bread to the hungry And that thou bring the poor that are cast out to thy house? when thou seest the naked, that thou cover him, And that thou hide not thyself from thine own flesh? Then shall thy light break forth as the morning, ... And thy righteousness shall go before thee' ..."

—Arthur Gilbert and Oscar Tarcov,
Your Neighbor Celebrates

The Lord asked a question of Israel: *"Is it such a **fast** that I have chosen? a day for a man to **afflict his soul**?"* (Isaiah 58:5; cf. Leviticus 16:29-31, 23:27, 32.) "Fasting" here is connected to the phrase, "*afflict his soul*" and in many instances in the Bible this is the root idea, especially on the *Day of Atonement*. In times of crisis the people of God fasted ("afflicted the soul") at God's instructions. To loose the bands of wickedness, to undo the heavy burdens, to let those who were oppressed go free, to break the yoke that binds, God's people were to fast. God would answer their cries when they, in their desperation and in obedience to Him they would call upon Him with fasting.

FASTING

Following are a few instances listed in Scripture to show the value of *fasting* and *prayer*:

Deuteronomy 9:18-26—Moses knew the value of *prayer*.

1 Samuel 7:3-11—Returning to God with *fasting* and *prayer*. God gave them victory over the enemy.

2 Samuel 1:12—*Fasting* on occasion of public calamity.

2 Kings 6:14-17—"And Elisha *prayed*."

2 Chronicles 7:14—If we meet these conditions the Lord is faithful to keep His promise.

2 Chronicles 15:2-4—If we seek Him, He will be found. If we forsake Him, He will forsake us.

2 Chronicles 16:9—The Lord is looking for someone to work through!

2 Chronicles 20:3, 15—A *fast* was proclaimed and the Lord came to the rescue.

Ezra 8:21-23—Ezra and his people *fasted* and *prayed*, and God protected them.

Nehemiah 1:4-7; 9:1—The young man knew the value of *fasting* and *prayer*.

Esther 4:3-16—*Fasting* and *prayer* saved a nation!

Psalm 35:13—*Fasting* is a humbling process.

Psalm 106:23—Moses stood in the gap.

Isaiah 37:15-20—Hezekiah took his trouble to the Lord, and the Lord fought his battle.

Isaiah 59:18—"He wondered that there was no intercessor."

Jeremiah 7:3—The Lord is pleading: *"Amend your ways and ye shall dwell in the land."*

Jeremiah 7:23—*"Obey my voice that it may be well with you."*

Ezekiel 22:30—*"And I sought for a man among them ... to stand in the gap."*

Daniel 9:3—Daniel *fasted* and *prayed* until the answer came.

Joel 1:14; 2:12-17—Here it is plainly stated what to do in time of crisis.

Jonah 2:2—He *prayed* and was delivered. (See also 1 Kings 8:38-39.)

Jonah 3:5-10—Even this godless king had faith to *fast* and *pray* to the God of Abraham!

Romans 15:4—*The Old Testament was written for our learning*! (1 Corinthians 10:6-11).

These are the words of Messiah Jesus: *"The days will come, when the bridegroom shall be taken from them, **and then shall they fast"*** (Matthew 9:15). He was speaking of His ascension into heaven after He had been taken from them in crucifixion. And they did "fast" as

He had prophesied. Then as a regular part of preparation for a special task or in waiting upon God for ministry, etc. It was the accepted duty of each disciple of the Lord to "afflict the soul" with fasting.

God commanded the Jewish people to keep a day of atonement, a day in which they shall mourn for their sins (*afflict their souls*), a day of covering, of forgiveness, in which they are to cease from their own labor and bring a sacrifice offering to God. The penalty for disobedience to this command (as also the command to observe the Passover), is the most terrible known to Jews, called *Kareth*, which means the cutting off of all connections with the people. According to the Rabbis, such a soul is condemned to the everlasting fires of hell. Although Jews believe there are three main ways of finding forgiveness, namely: by repentance (*T'shuvah*), by prayer (*T'fillah*), and by charity or alms-giving (*T'sedekah*), they feel they must particularly observe the *Day of Atonement* because of this Rabbinical interpretation.

According to the Jewish calendar, *Yom Kippur* is the most holy and terrible day of the year. It is called terrible because it is claimed that on that day God *seals* the decree which has been written down in the *Book of Remembrance*. Therefore all religious Jews repeat fervently in the synagogue on that day, the following prayer:

> "Remember us unto life, O King, who delightest in life, and inscribe us in the Book of Life for thine own sake, O Living God!"

Yom Kippur is translated from the Hebrew, *A Day of Covering*. The word *kippur* is taken from *kaphar* which literally means *to cover up* and is first mentioned in the Scriptures to describe the *pitch* which Noah used for the ark (Genesis 6:14). The Hebrew word for "pitch" is derived from this verb, because pitch covers that over which it is spread, and not only *conceals*, but *protects* it. By the atonement, the offerer's sins were covered, hidden from God's sight, and he himself was protected from its consequences.

According to God's requirements, only the High Priest in Israel could "make the atonement" for the people.

> *"And this shall be a statute for ever unto you: that in the seventh month, on the tenth day of the month, ye shall **afflict your souls**, and **do no work at all**, whether it be one of your own country, or a stranger that sojourneth among you: For on that day shall **the priest make an atonement for you**, to cleanse you, that ye may be clean from all your sins before the LORD"* (Leviticus 16:29-30).

THE HIGH PRIEST'S CLEANSING

"The High Priest's cleansing on the Day of Atonement: First the High Priest is conducted to the bath house. He bathes himself five times on this day; in addition, he washes his hands and feet ten times. These bathings and washings are performed in a special room in the Temple, near the Court of the Priests. The first bath, however, the one in the morning, takes place outside of the innermost court, beyond the water tower.

"Each time he bathes a curtain of byssus (costly linen) is spread between him and the people. He doffs his ordinary raiment, bathes, dons the golden vestments, washes his hands and feet in a golden basin, and starts the daily sacrifice. He performs it in his golden robes, and the congregation stands enthralled at the sight. From their point of observation, the High Priest is a glowing spectacle, with his golden diadem, the precious gems on his breast, and the golden bells which hang on the hem of his purple robe and which tinkle with every movement that he makes.

"He then goes into the anteroom in order to burn the incense on the golden altar, and to put the lamps of the Menorah in order. This ends the regular daily service; now comes the special Yom Kippur service, for which the High Priest dons garments of white linen.

"He is led to the bath house near the Court of the Priests. He washes his hands and feet, divests himself of his ceremonial golden robes, bathes himself, puts on the garments of white linen, and again washes his hands and feet."[60]

"The High Priest in Judaism is called 'Kohen ha-Gadol' or 'Kohen ha-Rosh.' Jews like to claim to be of the Priestly Tribe. When, in the course of the Jewish year, an occasion arises where the function of the High Priest is required, (as the High Priestly prayer on the *Day of Atonement*-Yom Kippur), a Jew by the name of *Cohen*, *Levi*, or *Katz* is called upon. A Jew by the name of *Cohen*, is by descent, thought to be a priest of the tribe of Levi ("Cohen" means "Priest"). The name *Levi*, of course, represents the *Tribe*. The name 'Katz' is taken as an abbreviation of two words, 'Righteous Priest' or 'Kohen Tsadek,' and a Jew by this name is considered to be a descendant of the High Priestly line."*

On the Day of Atonement it is believed that Moses returned from Mount Sinai with the second tables of the law and God forgave Israel of their first great sin. Even to the present time, Jews everywhere feel that by fasting and repentance for 24 hours in obedience to God's

---

[60]Hayyim Schauss, *The Jewish Festivals,* p. 134.
*From my book, *We Have a Great High Priest,* first edition, p. 88.

commandment, they are forgiven of all their iniquities and their names are written in the Book of Life.[61]

Most Jewish people know that the Old Testament, their T'nakh, tells of the Book of Life (see Exodus 32:32; Isaiah 4:3; Psalm 69:28; Daniel 12:1). The writer of the Book of Hebrews refers to the Old Testament saints, calling them *"the church of the Firstborn (Ones),"* *"Preeminent Ones")* *"enrolled in heaven"* (Hebrews 12:23). Also in the New Testament this *Book of Life* is referred to in Luke 10:20; Philippians 3:20 *"conversation is in heaven,"* *"citizenship"* or *"life"* (as written down) *"is in heaven,"* (Philippians 4:3; Revelation 3:5; 13:8; 17:8).

It is true that the Jewish people have no high priest and no sacrifice, yet they are so convinced of the need of an atonement, that rather than confess that they have absolutely none, they teach that repentance and the day itself will atone for all sin (*Hilchoth T'shuvah* c.i.2).

Before the Day of Atonement, the father of the household (who acts as High Priest) gathers the entire family and provides a sacrifice for them. This ceremony which is called *Kapporas Schlagen* ("slaying the sacrifice") is one of the most striking observances since the destruction of the Temple and is still performed by many orthodox Jews in the world.

The following is taken from the *Prayer Book For the Day of Atonement* with a revised English translation by the Reverend Dr. A.Th. Philips:

ORDER OF CAPUROTH (Kapporos)

"It is the custom to atone with fowl on the morning preceding the day of atonement, or a day before. Male persons take a rooster, female, a hen, and a pregnant woman takes both, a rooster and a hen. If there is no fowl, it is allowed to atone with money, provided the money is afterwards given to the poor. Before atoning, one says: 'A soul instead of a soul.' Then the following should be said three times: 'Children of men, such as sit in darkness and in the shadow of death, being bound in affliction and iron, He brought them out of darkness and the shadow of death, and brake their bands in sunder. Fools because of their transgression and because of their iniquities, are afflicted. *Their soul abhorreth all manner of food*; and they draw near unto the gates of death. Then they cry unto the Lord in their trouble, and he saveth them out of their distress, He sent His word and healed them and delivered them from their destructions. Oh that men would praise the Lord for his goodness, and for his wonderful works to the children of men! If

[61]See portion "God Wrote a Book," pp. 317-323.

there be a messenger with him and interpreter, one among a thousand, to shew unto man his uprightness: Then he is gracious unto him, and saith, Deliver him from going down to the pit: I have found a ransom.

"If one atones for himself, this is to be said three times: This rooster is going to be killed, and I shall be admitted and allowed to a long, happy, and peaceful life."

Hands are laid upon the fowl, before the individual ceremony, to transfer the sins upon it in keeping with the ritual of the high priest in the Tabernacle of old who laid his hands upon the sacrifice for the sins of the people of Israel. The fowl is then swung around the head three times after reciting Psalm 107:17-20 and Job 33:23-24. After this ritual the fowls are taken to an assistant Rabbi who kills them according to the rites of the oral law, and the meat is given to the poor.

Only a fowl is used in this ceremony of *Kapporas Schlagen.* No other animal would serve. This is because of the Hebrew word for "man." In Hebrew, "man" is called *gever*. If "gever" ("man") has sinned, "gever" must sustain the penalty of sin. But since the punishment is heavier than a man can bear, there is substituted for him a fowl ("cock"), which in the *Talmudic* dialect is also "gever." ("Gever," as "man," is found only once in the Talmud, *Yoma* fol. 20, col. 1). Here is an interesting note: In Zechariah 13:7 the *Shepherd* refers to the *man* ("Gever," "Warrior") who was smitten and is acknowledged by great Jewish commentators to be a Messiah reference!

On the eve of the Day of Atonement the traditional most beautiful and sacred chant in Hebrew, "Kol Nidre" ("All Vows") is sung in the synagogue. This is a prayer introduced by the *Marranos* who were forcibly converted to Christianity during the Spanish Inquisition. "Kol Nidre" is intended to nullify in advance all vows and promises which Jews have been forced to make, or have made hastily in emergencies of sorrow or passion:

"ALL VOWS and self prohibitions, vows of abstinence and promise, vows with self-imposed penalties and payments, which we may vow, swear, promise, and devote, from this day of Atonement unto the next day of Atonement (may it come to us in happiness), we repent them all, may they be held by the Almighty of no moment. May such vows be by him not considered as vows, nor such oaths, as oaths, nor such promises and obligations as binding. May they be all null and void, without power or binding force."

KOL NIDRE

(All Vows)

Kol Nidre—chant of ages,
Chant of Israel, chant of sorrow,
Measuring off the throbbing heart-beats
Of a people bowed in anguish,
Crushed by tyrants, thwarted, broken,
Wand'ring ever—homeless, weary.
Generations set your motif
Out of trials, hopes and yearnings,
Added each its variations
To your theme and to your cadence.
Diverse lands and diverse periods
Poured their soul into your music.
When we hearken with our hearts tuned,
We can hear the lamentations
Through time's corridor resounding;
We can see revealed before us
Heroes, martyrs, saints and scholars,
Loyal, steadfast sons of Israel
Sanctifying God, their Father.
Kol Nidre – chant of ages,
Chant of pain and chant of pathos,
Mingled with your notes of sorrow
Vibrant measures trill and quiver,
Rising to a great crescendo
With the Jew's undying spirit
As he raises 'loft his Torah,
Symbol of his faith and vigor.
Notes of joyous exultation
Crept into your dirgeful music
As with fortitude he cherished
All his fathers held most sacred.
While our hearts beat to your rhythm,
Stir us with new consecration
To our fathers' God, to serve Him
With our heart and soul and fervor.
Kol Nidre—chant of ages,
Chant of grief and chant of triumph,
Echoing, this night of mem'ries,
In the ears and heart of Israel,
Once again you draw together
All dispersed and all God's faithful
To return and humbly seek Him —
Suppliants for His grace and pardon.
Faced by grim, appalling forces
In these days of woeful living,
Do we plead before God's mercy
For His strength, His help, His guidance.

With your plaintive chant, Kol Nidre,
Rise our prayers to heaven ascending,
For a surcease of man's sorrows,
For the dawn of peace and freedom,
When all hearts are purged of hatred,
Passions, lusts that rend asunder.
Then all men will stand together
To acknowledge God, their Father.
—Morris Silverman,
High Holiday Prayer Book

Eight times during *Yom Kippur* the *Al Het* or *The Confessions* are made. At this part of the prayers, all the worshipers beat their chests and admit that they are guilty for many sins which are listed and which they read. Though each individual has not committed every specific sin, all as a united group are considered guilty for those of others, and therefore the prayer is in the plural and includes the nation of Israel. Confession is the main theme of the Yom Kippur service, for the Jewish religion teaches that if a man sincerely repents or regrets his misdeeds, he will be forgiven. The *Al Het* enumerates many kinds of sins such as dishonesty, cruelty, arrogance, gluttony, treachery, disrespect for parents, stubbornness, haughtiness, hardening of the heart, foolish speech, talebearing, etc. The whole category of sins is in the form of an acrostic of the 22 letters of the Hebrew alphabet.

Repentance on Yom Kippur

The services close with one long blast of the *Shofar* (Trumpet) followed by a great cry and fervent rocking to and fro in testimony to the oneness of the unity of Israel's God. It is considered an ill omen if the blast of the Shofar is not perfect. The three basic calls of the ram's horn on Yom Kippur are: *T'kiah*, a single sustained blast starting on a low note and rising nearly an octave on the musical scale; *Shevarim*, 3 very short *T'kios*, strung together; and *T'ruah*, nine staccato soundings of the low note, concluded by a high note. Originally, each call must have had some specific message for the listener, such as: *T'kiah*, like the army bugle call for "assembly." *Shevarim*, the equivalent for our "man your stations." *T'ruah*, the old cavalry's bugle "charge."

✡ ✡ ✡ ✡ ✡ ✡ ✡

BLOWING THE SHOFAR

A Rabbi blows the "Shofar"

Judaism has many superstitions which are related in the legends and lore of the writings by the Fathers. One legend is that of the *shofar*. It tells that when the shofar is blown during the High Holy Days, Satan becomes confused. The weird sound that proceeds forth from the shofar confuses him and he neglects for a time, at least, to accuse the Jews before God! Consequently, the Jews escape with lesser punishment!

The last feature of the *Day of Atonement* is the blowing of the *shofar*, the signal to return home in hope that God has written one's name in the Book of Life. It is only a hope; there is no assurance in Judaism.

When leaving the synagogue a ceremony of blessing the new moon takes place, for after the Day of Atonement, the Jew feels as if he were born anew!

"Shuva, Shuva"

Repentance plays a great part in the ten days from *Rosh Hashanah* until and concluding in *Yom Kippur* (Day of Atonement). God told Israel that the only way they could have peace with Him was through *repentance*. The Hebrew word for "repent" is "Shuva, Shuva." It means "turn around," "turn back." In other words, God says to the Jewish people: "Stop! Stop the direction in which you are going now and go back or *return* to your God whom you have forsaken."

This word, *shuva* or "repent," means more than just "to be sorry," but *to turn completely* in the opposite direction and proceed from there.

> *"Say unto them, As I live, saith the Lord GOD, I have no pleasure in the death of the wicked; but that the wicked **turn** from his way and live: **turn ye, turn ye** from your evil ways; for why will ye die, O house of Israel?"* (Ezekiel 33:11).

Every Jewish prophet of the Old Testament had a similar message of *repentance* for Israel. God had declared the Jewish people to be a sinful nation which needed to *turn back* to God. God even set aside this special day, the *Day of Atonement,* so that on that day, after they followed His directions in the ceremony, they would receive forgiveness of their sins.

Isaiah spoke of Israel's *turning* to God through the *Messiah*. He prophesied that this would happen:

*"And the Redeemer shall come to Zion, and unto them that **turn** from transgression in Jacob, saith the LORD"* (Isaiah 59:20).

Also Hosea prophesied of Israel's *repentance* in the last days:

*"Afterward shall the children of Israel **return**, and seek the LORD their God, and David [i.e., descendant of David] their king; and shall fear the LORD and his goodness **in the latter days**"* (Hosea 3:5).

When the Jewish prophet, John the Baptist, preached his message to the Jews of his day, it was the message of *repentance*. He declared to them: *"**Repent ye**: for the kingdom of heaven is at hand"* (Matthew 3:2). In other words, he said: *"Turn around*, turn your heart and mind back to God, for God's Messiah, the King of the Jews with His salvation, is here!"

When Messiah Jesus began to preach, he said the same thing as John did: *"Repent, for the kingdom of heaven is at hand"* (Matthew 4:17).

One must repent before he can have salvation. Jew and Gentile alike cannot be forgiven without first *turning around from his sins* and *turning back to God.* This is God's way for *everyone*, there is no other way! The first step to salvation is *repentance*. The second step is to believe in Jesus, as the Messiah. Gentiles must also go this way, for God is no respecter of persons. He has only **one** way, **one** salvation for both Jew and Gentile–**no exceptions**. *All* peoples must repent and believe in Jesus as their *Salvation*. (The name "Jesus" is translated from the Hebrew word "Yeshua" as the very word, **Salvation**! The first reference to "Yeshua" is in Genesis 49:18, *"I have waited for **thy salvation** [thy Yeshua], O Lord."* It is interesting to note that the Jerusalem and Jonathan Targums interpret this passage: "I have waited for thy Yeshua, O Yahweh." The writers of the Targums claim that these words are Messianic in content!)

The Jewish prophet Zechariah spoke about repentance: *"**Turn** ye unto me, saith the LORD of hosts, and I will turn unto you, saith the LORD of hosts"* (Zechariah 1:3).

And another Jewish prophet repeated these words: *"**Return** unto me, and I will return unto you, saith the LORD of hosts"* (Malachi 3:7).

One need not convert to a religion, to a church or to a new tradition and idea of religious men, but only *turn to God Himself* and believe in his heart that Jesus is his Messiah.

God had declared Israel to be a sinful nation which needed a Redeemer; God said that the people of Israel needed an atonement for their souls and that a Redeemer would come to make the atonement for them. The Jewish people were to observe this *Day of Atonement forever*:

> *"And this shall be a statute **for ever** unto you: that in the seventh month, on the tenth day of the month, ye shall **afflict your souls**, and do no work at all, whether it be one of your own country, or a stranger that sojourneth among you: For on that day shall **the priest make an atonement for you**, to cleanse you, that ye may be clean from all your sins before the LORD. It shall be a sabbath of rest unto you, and ye shall **afflict your souls**, by a **statute for ever**"* (Leviticus 16:29-31).

God had commanded sacrifices to be offered even before the giving of the Law! (See Genesis 15:9 where the sacrifices listed are the same as the animals which were offered under the Law of Moses!)

God gave the "recipe" to Israel as to how they were to have atonement.

> *"For the life of the flesh is in the **blood**: and I have given it to you upon the altar **to make an atonement** for your souls: for it is the **blood** that maketh **an atonement** for the soul"* (Leviticus 17:11).

Notice in above Scripture that *God* is speaking. He said that it is the (sacrificial) blood that atones for sin—not the blood of an angel, a man, a bull or a goat–but, since *God* is the One who is doing the speaking, it is *God* (who will come to partake of flesh and *blood*) who will give *His* blood or Life for an *atonement* for the soul.

We see a prophecy of Messiah in Leviticus 17:11. He would be innocent. He would be without sin but He would be the Substitute. Even as the innocent bulls and goats of the Old Testament ceremonies who "shed their blood"–would die–and by this death the sins of the people which had been imputed to them would die too so they would be forgiven, in like manner our sins were laid upon the Holy One of Israel; He gave up His life upon the Altar of Calvary as an Atonement for our soul. God, Himself, gave His own blood in the person of His Son! He said that He, Himself, would give His Life as a Sacrifice. He said that He, Himself, would give His *blood* as an atonement for the soul!

Oh, my Jewish people. No longer do you have to go to the synagogue once a year on Yom Kippur to receive forgiveness for your sins. No longer is it necessary for you to have a fowl for your substitute sacrifice. No longer need you afflict your soul with fasting in order to have salvation. You have a Day of Atonement forever and you will not be cut off from God if you will only believe. God has sent your Messiah Jesus to be your atonement, to be the forgiveness for your sin!

God pronounced a terrible decree upon those who did not have a day in which their sins were atoned for–a day in which they *afflicted their souls* and ceased from their work in order to worship God (Leviticus 23:29). This penalty was the most terrible that anyone could suffer. God said that if one did not have a Day of Atonement he would be *cut off* from the people of God *and* this implied that he would be cut off from God Himself! But God, in His mercy, has provided a way in which *everyone* can have a Day of Atonement, a way of forgiveness. It is through the *blood* of the Lamb, the Messiah of Israel, the Savior of the world!

Down through the years God had been revealing in types and shadows concerning that which was to come. The Jewish animal sacrifices were given in anticipation of the Great Sacrifice God had planned in Isaiah 53, which depicts the suffering Savior. (The Jewish people only saw the glory and triumph of the Messiah, but not the prophecies concerning His suffering for the sins of man.)

The blood of bulls or of goats was only a figure of *better* blood–better because from a greater and holier sacrifice! God is no longer pleased with the ancient sacrifices of the Old Covenant, for the fulfillment has already come in the person of Yeshua ha-Meshiach (Jesus, the Christ) who shed His precious blood on Calvary as the atonement for the sins of the world.

God ordained that not only the *Jews*, but the *Gentiles* as well, have a day in which their sins are forgiven, in which they are protected, preserved, and covered, in which they cease from their own labors, in which their souls are afflicted, or else, they too shall be forever cut off from God. This important Day was to be kept through the *shedding of blood* for *"without the shedding of blood* (of an appropriate sacrifice) *there is no remission of sin"* (Hebrews 9:22).

According to ancient Jewish interpretations (in the Talmud) not only was the sacrifice to be without blemish but the blood of that sacrifice was not supposed to congeal. This meant the blood was to be used in the ritual immediately after it had been shed. To accommodate for this it was known that in the Temple the basin to hold the blood of the sacrifice was pointed at the bottom to keep the Levite from setting it down, else the blood would congeal! We see, by this, that the Rabbis of the Talmud considered the blood of the sacrifice very carefully and necessary to complete the ritual on the Day of Atonement.

It is very important that the blood of the Supreme Sacrifice be considered very necessary to our salvation. The manner of obtaining that blood, the life of His flesh or humanity, was carried out in the way God prescribed and foretold. The shedding of Messiah's blood was done in a manner which was prophesied in the Hebrew Scriptures. It is blood of the sinless Lamb applied to our hearts' door by faith which sets us free!

CASTING OF LOTS

"Lots" of the OT is called *"The Sacred Dice"*

On the Day of Atonement under the Old Covenant, the High Priest would *cast lots* on two goats. This casting of lots was a divination. Some *divination* is condemned but some was approved of God. The lots (Urim and Thummim) are imitated in the gambling dice of the present day. Black (or to "show the *light*") for the *Urim* and white for the *Thummim* or "perfections." Even the sacred number "seven" is used in this gambling game! Without realizing it man has imitated sacred things and corrupted that which God has made!

> "The use of the lot as a means of ascertaining the will of Deity is referred to at least without expressed censure, ... with tacit approval in many parts of the Bible" (*International Standard Bible Encyclopedia*).

> *"And Aaron shall cast lots upon the two goats; one lot for the LORD, and the other lot for the scapegoat [Azazel]. And Aaron shall bring the goat upon which the LORD'S lot fell, and offer him for a sin offering"* (Leviticus 16:8-9).

The lot which would fall on one goat would be "slain unto the Lord." Then its blood would be carried by the same High Priest into the Holy of Holies and placed upon the Mercy Seat. The High Priest had already taken the blood of a bullock into the Holiest for himself. When he returned to the people after their atonement, it was the *second* time he had made his appearance before them! And so it is with the Greater High Priest who came *once* to give His *own* blood and then after the Father's acceptance of the Sacrifice when the sins of the people were forgiven, Yeshua ha-Meshiach would return at the appointed *second* time!

The goat which was slain unto the Lord and its blood shed, is typical of a new and living way into the presence of God in the Holy of Holies:

> *"For when Moses had spoken every precept to all the people according to the law, he took the blood of calves and of goats, with water, and scarlet wool, and hyssop, and sprinkled both the book, and all the people, Saying, This is the **blood of the testament** which God hath enjoined unto you. Moreover he sprinkled with blood both the tabernacle, and all the vessels of the ministry. And almost all things are by the law purged with blood; **and without***

*shedding of blood is no remission. It was therefore necessary that the patterns of things in the heavens should be purified with these; but the heavenly things themselves with better sacrifices than these. For Christ [Messiah] is not entered into the holy places made with hands, which are the figures of the true; but into heaven itself, now to appear in the presence of God for us: Nor yet that he should offer himself often, as the high priest entereth into the holy place **every year** with blood of others; For then must he **often** have suffered since the foundation of the world: but now **once** in the end of the world hath he appeared to put away sin **by the sacrifice of himself*** (Hebrews 9:19-26).

*And every priest standeth **daily** ministering and offering **oftentimes the same sacrifices**, which can never take away sins: **But this man** [Messiah], after he had offered **one sacrifice for sins for ever, sat down on the right hand of God;*** (Hebrews 10:11-12).

The other lot would fall upon the "scapegoat."

"And Aaron shall lay both his hands upon the head of the live goat, and confess over him all the iniquities of the children of Israel, and all their transgressions in all their sins, putting them upon the head of the goat, and shall send him away by the hand of a fit man into the wilderness: And the goat shall bear upon him all their iniquities unto a land not inhabited: and he shall let go the goat in the wilderness" (Leviticus 16:21-22).

The scapegoat would carry the sins of the people far from them; it was a substitute; it was made sin that the people might be excused from the penalty of their sins! And Yeshua ha-Meshiach (Jesus, the Christ) was the Scapegoat, for He was the Substitute who died outside the city of Jerusalem (*"in the wilderness,"* Hebrews 13:12) who carried our sins from us, made sin that we might be made the righteousness of God in Him! He has done more than "cover up" our sins. *He has blotted them out*! He has removed them as far as the east is from the west. He has cast them behind His back to be remembered against us *no more*!

KEMATSLIF ?

It is said by a Hebrew-Christian scholar that it is recorded once in Jewish literature for the High Priest on The Day of Atonement to sprinkle the blood not "upward or downward," but only *kematzlif*. The last letter "f" makes this word in its present form without sense and concerning its meaning even the great Jewish teacher and commentator Rashi confesses he could not understand. One famous writer states that the spelling of this word in the original must have ended with a "**v**" (ב "bet" pronounced as "**v**" without the dot or *dagesh* in the center) and not with an "**f**" (פ "pey" pronounced as "**f**" without the dot or dagesh in the center) which renders it ***kematzliV***, meaning *"in the fashion of a cross."* The High Priest was to sprinkle the blood vertically and horizontally, making the sign of the cross! This was a prophecy of the coming Messiah who would shed His blood in this manner, for He died upon a cross for the atonement of sins! It seems that later, because the word "cross" was offensive and the editors of this part of the service did not want it to be retained in Jewish literature, they changed one letter to another letter in the alphabet which sounded the same, thus making it *"kematzliF"*!

THE BLOOD-WAY OF APPROACH TO GOD

God ordained that the **blood** should be the *only* way of approach to Him. He revealed it in the very beginning to Adam and Eve in the Garden of Eden after they transgressed His law. God Himself slew an animal (a lamb for each), shedding its blood, made coats of the skin and with them clothed these sinners down to the ankles. They were covered through the shedding of blood, through the sacrifice of another.

The first parents taught their children, Cain and Abel, of this way of approach to God by blood sacrifice. Cain disobeyed and brought the work of his hands, arranging a beautiful altar to present to the Most High God. Abel obeyed the voice of the Lord through his parents, slew the "firstling" of his flock, shed its blood, and placed it upon his altar before the Lord. Looking at these two altars, the modernist would choose Cain's for it is beautiful to the eyes of the natural man. Abel's sacrifice is a "bloody" sight, not very pleasant to behold. But of the two, God chooses Abel's for there is the *shedding of blood* which pointed to a better Sacrifice to come.

When the Lord commanded the people of Israel concerning their deliverance from Egypt, He did not tell them to take a beautiful lamb, the most beautiful of all their flock, to tie a red ribbon around its neck and place it in front of their door, so that when the Destroying Angel would pass through the land and see the beautiful lamb He would spare the firstborn in that household. Neither did God tell the Israelites to gather their valuable possessions, take all their certificates, and medals, or list all their accomplishments and place them before the door and when the Angel saw all their possessions, talents and achievements He would "pass over" them. God did not instruct His people to list their doctrinal beliefs, their tithes and offerings, their knowledge of the Scriptures as though all this would redeem their firstborn from death. **No**! He commanded the people of Israel to take the firstling of the flock, an innocent lamb without spot or blemish, to *shed its blood by killing it*, place that *blood* upon the doorpost and then said: "When I see the **blood** *I will pass over you*"! That first Passover, they had to stay where the *blood* was, had to stay *inside* their houses (under the blood) until morning; they had **blood-protection**!

*"Much more then, being now justified by **his blood**, we shall be saved from wrath through him [Messiah]"* (Romans 5:9).

*"Neither by the blood of goats and calves, but **by his own blood** he entered in once into the holy place, having obtained eternal redemption for us. For if the blood of bulls and of goats, and the ashes of an heifer sprinkling the unclean, sanctifieth to the purifying of the flesh: **How much more shall the blood of Christ** [Messiah], who through the eternal Spirit offered himself without spot to God, purge your conscience from dead works to serve the living God?"* (Hebrews 9:12-14).

God has emphasized the need of the shedding of blood ever since the evil day in Eden. Ever since that day Eve and her daughters have been reminded of the necessity of the *shedding of blood to life*, both spiritual and physical. When a new life, a child or even an animal is born, it is accompanied by great suffering and bloodshed. All this reminds us of God's great plan of salvation in Messiah Jesus. How can we ignore or treat casually such a consistent plan?

Only the blood of God's Son can give life eternal. Not blood flowing in the veins of the man, even the perfect God-Man, but the blood *shed* of Him, who was with God in the creation of all things. Only such blood, the blood of *God's own life* (as a Man) ("the blood is the life thereof; I have given it") has power to purify an unclean soul and give a perfect body in the time of the resurrection so that we may appear unashamed at last in His very presence.

God introduces the ashes of a red heifer for the purifying of the flesh. (Ashes and water produce lye which is a good cleansing agent.) But as in the foregoing Scripture it is declared: *How **much more** shall the **blood of Christ** [Messiah], purge your conscience from dead works to serve the living God."*

The following prayer is uttered on the Day of Atonement by orthodox Jews:

"Our righteous anointed is departed from us; horror hath seized us, and we have none to justify us. He hath borne the yoke of our iniquities, and our transgression, and is wounded because of our transgression. He beareth our sins on his shoulder, that he may find pardon for our iniquities. We shall be healed by his wound, at the time that the Eternal will create him as a new creature. O bring him up from the circle of the earth. Raise him up from Seir to assemble us the second time on Mount Lebanon, by the hand of Yenon."[62]

The foregoing prayer is, to the enlightened believer in the Savior Jesus, explained this way: "Our righteous anointed" means our

---

[62]Dr. A.Th. Philips, *Prayer Book for the Day of Atonement*, p. 239.

righteous Messiah (the Hebrew for *anointed* being *Meshiah*) and hence the entire prayer pertains to Him. "Is departed from us" implies that He has already come. "He hath borne the yoke of our iniquities and our transgressions ... He beareth our sins on his shoulder that he may find pardon for our iniquities" means Messiah came to give His life a ransom for many (Matthew 20:28). He declared of the cup of wine at the last Passover which He celebrated with His disciples: *"This is my blood of the new testament which is shed for many for the remission of sins"* (Matthew 26:28). "The Eternal will create him as a new creature ... bring him up from the circle of the earth" signifies that God would raise the Messiah from the dead! "To assemble us the second time" refers to Messiah's second coming when He will gather all Israel to the Holy Land!

Before the foundation of the earth, in the mind of God there was set a Day of Atonement for both Jew and Gentile which was fulfilled 2,000 years ago on the Altar of Calvary! We who have accepted God's salvation can praise the Lord, saying: "Messiah Jesus is my change, He is my redemption for He was slain in order that I might be admitted to life everlasting."

Our wonderful Savior, by the sacrifice of Himself, has inscribed our names in the Book of Life and we shall never be separated from Him. No longer is it necessary that a goat or a bullock or even a fowl shed its blood for the remission of sins once every year, for God's Lamb shed His blood once and for all. Jew or Gentile who believes in Him can rejoice that there is a *Yom Kippur* (Day of Covering) for time and eternity, made possible through the perfect *Kapporah* (sacrifice) which is Yeshua (Jesus), the Son of the Living God!

SUKKOT (Booths or Tabernacles)

"Also in the fifteenth day of the seventh month, when ye have gathered in the fruit of the land, ye shall keep a feast unto the LORD seven days: on the first day shall be a sabbath, and on the eighth day shall be a sabbath. And ye shall take you on the first day the boughs of goodly trees, branches of palm trees, and the boughs of thick trees, and willows of the brook; and ye shall rejoice before the LORD your God seven days. And ye shall keep it a feast unto the LORD seven days in the year. It shall be a statute for ever in your generations: ye shall celebrate it in the seventh month" (Leviticus 23:39-41).

The Feast of Tabernacles was to be observed on the fifteenth day of the seventh month *Tishri* which falls in late September or early October. In Joel 2:23-24 the *first month* was the *agricultural* first month or the "beginning of the season" which would be the seventh month (Tishri) of the *sacred calendar.* This was the time for the fullness of the harvest when the wine and the oil was gathered in. The Hebrew word for this festival is *Sukkot* (Succot) which means "huts," "booths," or "tabernacles." It is one of the three great occasions upon which God commanded the people of Israel to assemble at the Temple at Jerusalem to present their sacrifices and offerings to Him. They were to bring their abundance to God. *"They shall not appear before me empty"* was His command (see Deuteronomy 16:16). They were to leave their homes and lands in order to go up to Jerusalem with the harvest from their fields, groves and orchards. So important it was that they go to Jerusalem with their offerings and with no burden of that which they left behind that God promised the protection of their lands from vandalism while they were gone (Exodus 34:24).

This celebration is also called *Hag-ha-Asif* ("Feast of Ingathering," see Exodus 23:16). Jewish people today observe it as a national holiday to memorialize the journey from the land of slavery to the Promised Land. It is the longest, happiest and most colorful of all the Jewish festivals of which it has been said by the Rabbis: "One who had not seen the festivity and rejoicing at Sukkot had never seen rejoicing in his life." This statement is taken from the Mishnah which says: "He who has not seen the Rejoicing of the Place of Water-Drawing has never in his life witnessed a real celebration." (*Mishnah Sukka V.* and *Gemara Sukka* 53a.)

This refers to the activities in the days of the second Temple when the high point of the festivities was the *Simhat Bet Hasho'eva*, the water-libation ceremony in the Temple ("Rejoicing of the Place of the Water-Drawing").

In Bible times, a specially appointed priest was sent to the Pool of Siloam with a golden pitcher to bring water to the foot of the altar where was a basin into which the water was poured. At the same time he poured wine from another pitcher so that both water and wine would mingle together and flow through special pipes back to the Brook of Kidron again. The pouring of the water signified the prayer for abundant rain which was necessary for the growth of their crops. Even today in the synagogue this practice of praying for rain is still observed on Sukkot.

The pouring of the water held another truth. Along with the physical interpretation, it applies in a spiritual sense, in that it prophesied the coming Messiah and the outpouring of the Holy Spirit. The water was poured in this manner until on the eighth day the Feast of Tabernacles was ended. This last day of Sukkot was called *Hoshannah Rabbah*, "The Day of the Great Hosanna." The pouring of the water on this day was climaxed amidst great rejoicing and praises to God. The priests blew the trumpets and the Levites sang songs, while the people, waving their *lulavs* (palm branches), chanted the *Great Hallel*. This Great Hallel was also chanted at the Feast of the Passover. The Hymn of Praise includes Psalms 113-118 and in it is found the word "Hosannah" translated from the Hebrew to mean "Save now." This foretold the salvation of Israel (and Gentiles) which was expected through the coming Messiah!

In the Jewish Prayer Book Sukkot has been called "Season of Gladness." Joy is the theme and is considered a religious duty by the Jewish people since they know God has commanded it: *"Serve the LORD with gladness. Come before his presence with singing"* (Psalm 100:2). (It is from this holiday of Sukkot that the Pilgrim Fathers in the 17th Century drew inspiration for our American *Thanksgiving Day*)! God commanded Israel three times to be joyful at the Feast of Sukkot: *"You shall rejoice before the LORD your God for seven days"* (Leviticus 23:40). *"You shall rejoice in your feast"* and *"You shall be altogether joyous"* (Deuteronomy 16:13-15).

BOOTHS

"Ye shall dwell in booths seven days; all that are Israelites born shall dwell in booths: That your generations may know that I made the children of Israel to dwell in booths, when I brought them out of the land of Egypt: I am the LORD your God" (Leviticus 23:42-43).

Today it is a custom among the Jewish people to dwell in a hut on Sukkot and to decorate it with various kinds of fruits and flowers. Every member of the family must take his turn in building the "sukkah" or "booth." These booths are erected in the yard or in the home and sometimes on the roof of the house. To some it serves as a permanent dwelling place during the seven days of the feast. Orthodox Judaism requires all the males to live in it, unless prevented by ill

Family Celebrating Sukkot

health. In southern climates the "Sukkah" is of such size as to enable the entire family to live in it during the seven days. The devout worshiper who returns home after the day-long fast on the Day of Atonement goes out into his yard and drives the first stake into the ground for his "sukkah." And having tended to this he would then break his fast anticipating the holiday of Sukkot with very real pleasure.

There is an entire volume of the *Talmud*, with numerous commentaries, devoted to the important law of *how to erect the booth*. Its dimensions are minutely described. No expenditure of money or labor is to be spared in the beautifying of this "dwelling."

The Four Species

Daily, except on the Sabbath, during the week-long Sukkot festival the observant Jew takes the "Arba Minim" ("Four Species") of plants in his hands in fulfillment of the commandment (Leviticus 23:40). The father and the members of his household take the Four Species into the family Sukkah (booth) in the morning and recite the required benediction. Then he carries them with him to the synagogue. At the appropriate times during the Hallel prayer, he waves these in all four directions, upwards and downwards to indicate that God's glory fills the whole universe. The willows are bound together for convenience in lifting them during the recitation. The worshiper

Arba Minim "The Four Species"

faces the east, holding the *Lulav* in the right hand, the *Etrog* in the left hand, waving east, south, west and north. The Talmud states that in this manner it was used in the Temple.

The "Four Species" are: 1. "Lulav," "palm fronds," 2. "Etrog," "fruit of citrus trees," 3. "Hadassim," "leafy branches," "myrtle springs," 4. "Aravot," "willows from the riverside." The Scriptures give the names as: *pine trees* (more correctly: *trees of oil,* or *olive trees*), the *palm*, the *myrtle* and *willows of the brook.* The **olive** (oil) speaks of the Holy Spirit power, the **palm** of victory, the **myrtle** of joy and gladness, the **willow** of tears and sorrow; this as a reminder of the past, not to cause sadness, but to enhance the joy of the present.

> The Four Species "were to remind Israel of the four stages of the wilderness journey: the *palm branches* representing the valleys and plains: the *boughs of thick trees*, the bushes on the mountain heights; the *willows*, the brooks from which God gave His people drink; the *citron*, to remind them of the good land the Lord had given them." —*Edersheim*

The *Etrog* is "the fruit of the Hadar tree." The word "hadar" is today used to refer to the *citrus fruit*, but the word also means *beauty, majesty, grandeur.* In almost all times and in nearly all countries, the "fruit of the Hadar tree" has been interpreted to mean what we call the *citron*, which looks rather like a slightly oversize lemon. The variety of Etrog used by the Yemenites is sometimes as big as a cantaloupe! But, unlike the lemon, the outer skin of the Etrog is covered with many little bumps, and the bumpier and the less lemon-like the Etrog is, the more beautiful it is considered by the Jew seeking perfection in his Etrog.

According to the *Midrash*[63] (the word "Midrash" is derived from *darash*, "to search, inquire, investigate, hence, to study, interpret, to expound–particularly Scripture), the Etrog (not the apple) was the forbidden fruit of which Eve ate and then gave Adam to eat in the Garden of Eden. Accordingly, it is sometimes the custom for the Jewish women to take a bite of the Etrog right after Sukkot, as a reminder and partial expiation of the first sin of the first woman!

Another Jewish description of the forbidden fruit is in the following:

> "*Ki tov ha-etz l'ma'achal—The fruit was good for food—* ridiculously low in cholesterol, calories and fat content, *ta'ava hu l'einayim—lustful for the eyes*—it was beautifully packaged, an esthetic delight, worthy of a gourmet's table, and finally, *nehmad ha'etz l'haskil—it was good for the mind,*—probably protein-rich to strengthen brain cells (Genesis 3:6)." —*The Jerusalem Post*

The importance of the Four Species commandment is found by the early appearance of the Four Species as a significant Jewish symbol, virtually as significant as the seven-branched Menorah (candelabrum). A Midrash explanation says the Four Species hint at the End of Days and the punishment of the wicked, the final War of Gog and Magog, the rebuilding of the Temple, and the *coming of the Messiah.* The Midrashic symbolism most quoted, however, links the Four Species to the Jewish People. Israel, the Midrash says, is made up of four types: learned men with good deeds to their credit; learned men possessing only scholarship but no good deeds; men possessing good deeds but no learning; and those lacking in both.

The Feast of Tabernacles is celebrated for *seven* days with an eighth day, which follows known as "Shemini Atzeres" ("Solemn Assembly"). "Solemn Assembly" is an imperfect translation, rather it is "Day of Restraint." The Revised Version gives it as "Closing Festival." The Hebrew word is taken from a word signifying *to bring to a close.* A ninth day, added in later centuries, is called *Shimchas Torah,* "Joy (Rejoicing) in the Law."

God commanded that the first day of Sukkot was to be a Sabbath and also the eighth day was to be a Sabbath (Shabbat). It is interesting that the Bible associates the Sabbath with the number *seven.* What the seventh day was to the week, the seventh month was to the year. The number "seven" is prominent in this last Feast on God's Calendar of Redemption. It was held in the *seventh* month and lasted for *seven* days. The offerings consisted of *seven* kids—1x7, *14* rams—2x7, *70* bullocks—10x7, *98* lambs—14x7, The total is 189 or 27x7!

[63]The *Midrash,* "exposition," is a homiletical commentary on the Hebrew Bible, that is divided into *Haggadah* and *Halachah.*.

SEVEN

In *Ripley's Believe It Or Not*

Seven is the holy number. There are 7 days in creation, 7 days in the week, 7 phases of the moon, every 7th year was Sabbatical, and 7 times 7 years was the Jubilee. There are 7 ages in the life of man, 7 divisions in the Lord's prayer, 7 Churches of Asia, 7 Graces, 7 Deadly Sins. The Apostles chose 7 deacons, Enoch, who was translated, was 7th from Adam. Our Lord spoke 7 times on the Cross, and after 7 times 7 days He sent the Holy Ghost. There appeared 7 golden candlesticks and 7 stars in the hand of Him that was in the midst; 7 lambs before the 7 spirits of God; the book with the 7 seals; the lamb with 7 horns and 7 eyes; 7 angels bearing 7 plagues, and 7 vials of wrath. The vision of Daniel was 70 weeks; and the elders of Israel were 70.

It is also true that the number *seven* tells of spiritual perfection; the number of the Holy Spirit's work. Seven is the sacred number. It is the mystical union of God with the world.

The Holy Spirit is the Author of God's work and *seven* is the ruling number as we find the Hebrew of Genesis 1:1—has only **seven** words. Genesis 1:1-2:3—the name of God is mentioned 35 times which is a multiple of *seven*. The Holy Spirit is the Author and Giver of life, and *seven* is the number which regulates every period of incubation and gestation in insects, birds, animals and man: 280 days for human (40x7); 21 days for a chicken (3x7); 14 for a robin (2x7); and in the following list. With animals the period of gestation is a multiple of *sevens*:

mouse is *21* days (3x7).
hare and rat is *28* days (4x7).
cat is *56* days (8x7).
dog is *63* days (9x7).
lion is *98* days (14x7).
sheep is *147 days* (21x7).

Since the Feast of Tabernacles was to begin on the 15th day of the month Tishri, and observed for *seven* days, this makes it end on the 21st day (3x7), *a triple of sevens*. Here we see the Sabbath as a Three-fold Rest or **rest** in the absolute sense for spirit, soul, and body. But immediately following this Seventh Day Sabbath (of the Feast of Tabernacles) was the *eighth day* which was also to be a *sabbath*. This speaks of the future earthly Messianic Kingdom when peace and righteousness shall rule and God's people (earthly Israel) will be observing the **Seventh-Day Sabbath** during that time, that is, resting in God and God resting in His people; then follows the new Day, the "new beginning," the *first day of Eternity,* a Sabbath forever!

God's purpose in the Feasts preceding the last one (Feast of Tabernacles) was to gather together a people for Himself that He might dwell in their midst. This purpose is repeated in the Feast of Tabernacles. He wants to *rest* in those He has redeemed. He wants to inhabit the praises of His people throughout eternity. The Feast foretells a Sabbath which will be for the people of God (Hebrews 4:9) when they will truly *rest* in Him and He will *rest* in His people, when His peace and righteousness will reign and when (God promised) *"they shall not hurt nor destroy in all my holy mountain"* (Isaiah 11:9).

Throughout the Old Testament Scriptures there are references to the period of Messiah's righteous reign. This Messianic Kingdom is yet *future* when He will truly be *King of the Jews*, as was prophesied He would be (Micah 5:2, [Hebrew text, Micah 5:1]).(He is not called *King* of the Church, but *Head* of the Church.)

It will be during the Messianic Kingdom on *earth* (the *Millennium*) when *all nations* (the *earthly* people) will keep the Feast of Tabernacles from year to year (Zechariah 14:16-19).

> *Note*: There are those who do not believe that there will be a Millennium in which this prophecy will be fulfilled. The term applied to them is **A**millennialism. The letter "a" with which "amillennial" begins is called in Greek *alpha privative* and represents the Greek letter prefixed to a word in order to give it a negative sense, as the Latin *non-* does in a word like "nonsense." The amillennial position is simply that there will be no millennium either before or after the return of the Lord Jesus Christ. ... This position contradicts the clear statement of Scripture as given in Revelation 20.[64]

The Messianic Kingdom or the "Kingdom of God" is explained in an interpretation given by J. Dwight Pentecost:

> "Throughout the Scriptures there seems to be a contradiction in the line of revelation concerning the kingdom over which God rules. On the one hand the kingdom is viewed as eternal and on the other as temporal, with a definite historical beginning, progress, and termination. Again it is depicted as both universal and local. Further, it is seen to be the direct administration of the sovereignty of God as well as the indirect administration through appointed sovereigns. It thus becomes necessary to see that *the kingdom over which God rules has two separate aspects, the eternal and the temporal, the universal and the local, the immediate and the mediated.*"[65]

During the Feast of Tabernacles and after the Millennial Temple is rebuilt the Lord will reinstitute the sacrificial system. For did not He command that these "shall be *forever*"? God's Word describes the

---

[64]From *The Chosen People Question Box II* by Dr. Henry J. Heydt, ThD., p. 199.
[65]J. Dwight Pentecost, *Things to Come*, p. 428, (*emphasis is mine*).

Millennial Temple which is to be rebuilt in the Kingdom Age during which time the worship of God will be implemented and animal sacrifices will be offered.[66]

> "The question is often raised, if Jesus' sacrifice was the only efficacious, once-for-all sacrifice to expiate sin (Hebrews 7:27; 9:12, 26), why should animal sacrifices, which could never take away sin (Hebrews 10:4), be offered during the Millennium? It is true that the sacrifices in the Millennial Temple will not expiate sin, just as the Mosaic offerings could not. We must conclude, therefore, that these offerings will be *memorial* in nature, similar to the Church in this age keeping the Lord's supper in remembrance of Christ's death."[67]

WHY I BELIEVE IN A MILLENNIUM

(The word *Millennium* from the Latin "Mille" [1,000] and "Annum" [year] has supplanted the Biblical word "Kingdom.")

1.   The Messianic *prophecies* have not been completely fulfilled as yet. The Millennium is the only logical time for this to occur. (The first coming was *literally* fulfilled, the second coming will be *literally* fulfilled.)

2.   It is the only logical way for God's promises to *Israel* to be completely fulfilled.

3.   The Sabbath days, garment fringes (*Tzitzit*), Feasts (God's *appointments*), sacrifices, priesthood, anointing oil, etc. have not been observed **forever** as God had commanded. The Millennium is the only logical time for this.

4.   It will complete man's testing. There were six testings of man through which man failed. This last one man will be tested and will also fail under an ideal government.

5.   The world will continue for 6,000 years and the Millennium (thousand) is the seventh. "*... that one day is with the Lord as a thousand years, and a thousand years as one day*" (2 Peter 3:8). In other words, the world will exist for six days and on the seventh day it will *rest*.

6.   The Millennium is the only logical time when the natural seed will be produced to inhabit the **new earth** throughout eternity.

THE LAND DURING THE MILLENNIUM

1.   Israel will become the particular inheritance of the Jewish people (Ezekiel 36:8, 12; 47:22-23; Zechariah 8:12). This is essential to fulfill Israel's covenants.

---

[66]See Ezekiel 46; cp. Isaiah 56:7; 66:20-23; Jeremiah 33:18; Zechariah 14:16-21.
[67]David Levy, *Israel During the Messianic Kingdom*, in "Israel My Glory," April/May, 1991 issue, p. 13.

2.   The land will be greatly enlarged in comparison to its former area (Isaiah 26:15; Obadiah 17:21; Micah 7:14). for the first time Israel will possess all of the land that God promised to Abraham (Genesis 15:18-21).

3.   The topography of the land will be altered (Ezekiel 47:1-12; Joel 3:18; Zechariah 4:7; 14:4, 8, 10). Instead of the mountainous terrain that characterizes Israel today, a great fertile plain will be formed at the Second Coming of the Messiah (Zechariah 14:4) so that Mount Zion will truly be "Beautiful for situation" (Psalm 48:2). This changed topography will permit a river to flow out of the city of Jerusalem and divide to the seas to water the land (Ezekiel 47:1-12).

4.   There will be renewed fertility and productivity in the land (Isaiah 32:15; 35:1-7; 51:3; 55:13; Ezekiel 34:27; 36:29,35). Then the plowman will overtake the reaper because of that productivity (Amos 9:13).

5.   There will be an abundance of rainfall (Isaiah 30:23-25; 35:6-7; Ezekiel 34:26; Joel 2:23-24; Zechariah 10:1). Throughout the Old Testament rain was a sign of God's Blessing and approval. The absence of rain was a sign of God's disapproval and judgment. The abundance of rain on the earth at that time will be a sign of God's blessing.

6.   The land will be reconstructed after being ravaged during the Tribulation period (Isaiah 49:19; 61:4-5; Ezekiel 36:33-38; Amos 9:14-15). The remnants of the destruction will be removed so that the earth may become clean again.

7.The land will be redistributed among the 12 tribes of Israel. In Ezekiel 48:1-29 this redistribution is outlined. The land will be divided into three portions by a line running from east to west all across its enlarged dimensions. The northern portion will be appointed to the tribes of Dan, Asher, Naphtali, Manasseh, Ephraim, Reuben, and Judah (vv. 1-7). The southern portion will be allotted to Benjamin, Simeon, Issachar, Zebulun, and Gad (vv. 23-27). Between the northern and southern portions will be an area known as the "holy oblation" –a portion of land set apart for the Lord (vv. 8-20). This area will be 25,000 reeds long and wide (vv. 8, 20), divided into one area 25,000 by 10,000 reeds for the Levites (Ezekiel 45:5; 48:13-14), another area of the same size for the Temple and priests (Ezekiel 45:4; 48:10-12), and a third area 25,000 by 5,000 reeds for the city (Ezekiel 45:6; 48:15-19).   —Unknown Author

THE CONSUMMATION OF GOD'S PLAN

The Feast of Tabernacles foretells the great consummation of God's purposes on *earth* in the *Kingdom,* (*i.e.,* the Millennium) when there will be rejoicing at the Great Ingathering of God's people from the north, the south, the east and the west. Here we see that great multitude of God's harvest–both Jews and Gentiles in *one*, carrying *Lulav* (palm) branches in their hands (Revelation 7:9) saying with a great voice:

"And I heard a great voice out of heaven saying, Behold, the tabernacle of God is with men, and he will dwell with them, and they shall be his people, and God himself shall be with them, and be their God" (Revelation 21:3).

"Today, numerous petitions for the salvation of Israel are received in the synagogue on *'Hoshana Rabba.'* While these petitions are voiced, the worshipers make seven circuits around the auditorium of the synagogue. Also on this day, the willow is shaken until the leaves fall off, which symbolizes the disappearing of sins. This also is expressive of the hope in resurrection and in the coming of the Messiah. As he shakes all the leaves off the willow stem till it is bare as a tree in winter, he anticipates that new life, fresh leaves, blossoms and fruit will come to the trees which have 'died' during the winter. So, too, it is the hope of these worshipers that new life and vigor will come to Israel in the days that are ahead."
—*Sukkos*, Rabbi Albert S. Goldstein

There was another outstanding feature of *Sukkot* besides the pouring of the water. The Temple was brilliantly illuminated at that time. The Jews who came to celebrate the Feast carried lights and torches. The Temple itself was lighted by the great golden lampstand and this combination of lights, torches and lampstand illuminated most of Jerusalem and surrounding areas.

It was on the last day of *Sukkot* (the Feast), the day of the *Great Hosannah*, while the people were rejoicing, while the water was being poured forth and the priests were blowing the trumpets, while the Levites were singing the Great *Hallel* ("Praise"), and the people were praying "Save now, I beseech thee Lord," that Yeshua (Jesus) stood in their midst to tell them that He was the answer to all their celebration!

"In the last day, that great day of the feast, Jesus stood and cried, saying, If any man thirst, let him come unto me, and drink. He that believeth on me, as the scripture hath said, out of his belly [innermost being] *shall flow rivers of living water.*

In the last day, that great day of the feast, Jesus stood and cried, saying, If any man thirst, let him come unto me, and drink. He that believeth on me, as the Scripture hath said, out of his belly [innermost being] *shall flow rivers of living water. (But this spake he of the Spirit, which they that believe on him should receive:)"* (John 7:37-39).

Messiah is the Rain for which the people prayed. He is the Light of the world, the Glory that fills the Temple. He is the Wine poured forth with the water, as also He is the Water of Life. Yeshua Ha-Meshiah (Jesus, the Messiah) is the Lord of the Harvest, the Great Ingatherer! Some glorious day there shall be a greater ingathering of a greater harvest which John describes:

*"After this I beheld, and, lo, a great multitude, which no man could number, of all nations, and kindreds, and people, and tongues, stood before the throne, and before the Lamb, clothed with white robes, and **palms** in their hands; And cried with a loud voice, saying, Salvation [Hosanna] to our God which sitteth upon the throne, and unto the Lamb"* (Revelation 7:9-10).

FEASTS OF THE LORD IN LEVITICUS 23
(As they occur in the T'nakh)[69]

Scripture	Harvest	Season	Month Name & Number	Date	Feast Which Occurs
Ruth 2:23	barley wheat	spring summer	Nisan (1st) Sivan (3rd)	Nisan 14-21, Sivan 6	Unleavened Bread
Ezra 3:4	corn, oil, wine	fall	Tishri (7th)	Tishri 1, 10, 15-22	Tabernacles
2 Samuel 21:9	barley	spring	Nisan (1st)	Nisan 14—21	Unleavened Bread
1 Samuel 6:13	wheat	summer	Sivan (3rd)	Sivan 6	Weeks (Pentecost)
Exodus 34:18, 22	barley wheat corn-oil-wine	spring summer fall	Nisan (1st) Sivan (3rd) Tishri (7th)	Nisan 14-21, Sivan 6, Tishri 1,10,15-22	Unleavened Bread, Weeks, Tabernacles
Judges 15:1	wheat	summer	Sivan (3rd)	Sivan 6	Weeks
Deuteronomy 31:10	corn— oil—wine	fall	Tishri (7th)	Tishri 1, 10, 15-22	Tabernacles
Exodus 23:14-17	barley wheat, corn-oil-wine	spring summer fall	Nisan (1st) Sivan (3rd) Tishri (7th)	Nisan 14-21, Sivan 6, Tishri 1,10,15-22	Unleavened Bread, Weeks, Tabernacles
2 Chronicles 7:(8,9)10	corn-oil-wine	fall	Tishri (7th)	Tishri 1, 10, 15-22	Tabernacles
1 Kings 8:2	corn-oil-wine	fall	Tishri (7th)	Tishri 1,10, 15-22	Tabernacles
Ruth 1:22	barley	spring	Nisan (1)	Nisan 14-21	Unleavened Bread

---

[69]Chart organized by Ruth Specter Lascelle, edited and formatted by Duane Bagaas.

SHIMCAS TORAH

"The Scrolls of the Law for reading in the synagogue was copied under very strict rules. It must be written on the skin of a clean animal and specially treated with gallnut and lime. The pages were squared and the lines ruled with a stylus.

Rejoicing of the Law

"Even the size of the margins was prescribed. The Torah must be readable. The space between the lines must be the same size as the letters. A scribe had to prepare himself by silent meditation before he began his work.

"He had to use a correct copy. He could not write a word from memory and he had to pronounce every word before he wrote it. Every letter must have space around it and must be so clearly drawn that even a school boy could distinguish it.

"Even greater care was exercised before the scribe could write the name of God. Each time he wrote it, he said "I intend to write the Holy Name." Once he started writing the Name he would permit no interruption. The Name could not extend into the margin.

"If an error was made it could not be erased. The entire page had to be rewritten! While the ink was drying the Name had to be covered by a cloth to keep the dust away.

Yad (Hand), the "Pointer" "The pointer in the reader's hand is shaped at its end in the form of a closed hand with an extended index finger. Even though the reader may know (as he frequently did) the entire passage by heart, he dared not trust his memory. He must see and read each word as he pronounced it.

"There are some who call this superstition. It is not superstition— it is reverence. I would that some modern translators of the Scriptures would use the same care in translating that the scribe used in copying, and the reader used in reading it!"
　　　　　　　　　—Author of above quote is unknown

Immediately after the Feast of Tabernacles, on the 23rd day of the seventh month, the Jewish people celebrate what is called "Shimcas Torah" or "Rejoicing of the Law." This is the jolliest day on the Jewish calendar. It is the day when the reading of the Torah is concluded in the synagogue every year and immediately afterward resumed. The custom of beginning to read Genesis at the same synagogue service as Deuteronomy is concluded, had its origin in the 14th Century, the reason being that Satan might say that the Jews, having finished the reading of the law were unwilling to begin reading it again. This custom is observed also so as not to bring the law to an end at any time!

On the "Day of Rejoicing Over the Law" special inducements are held out to the younger members of the congregation to participate actively in the public service. All assembled in the synagogue are called upon to pronounce the blessing over the reading of the Law, and even young boys participate. In the house of worship the scrolls of the law, dressed in beautiful velvet mantles of red, scarlet, blue and white, and ornate with golden embroidery and inscriptions, are taken out from the Ark of the law and placed lovingly in the arms of the men and boys. Little children holding flags and burning tapers extolling the Word of God follow in a procession up and down the aisles. The children have been reared and taught in the laws of Judaism which Jewish people feel is a religious commandment.

It is written in the Jewish sacred writings: "At five years, bound to the commandments; at 15 years, the study of the Talmud." Jewish children are expected to receive 300 hours of religious training throughout the year. So anxious have orthodox Jews been for their sons to be diligent pupils that they are careful to make the boy's first day at Hebrew school ("*Hader*" also spelled *Chader*) an occasion he will remember all his life. This custom also shows how deeply attached Jews have been to the Torah (Five Books of Moses) and how great has been their love of learning.

As the solemn procession circles the synagogue auditorium, those assembled there kiss the garment of the *scrolls*, or touch the *scrolls* with their fingers and then kiss their fingers. Among the Hassidim, at the age of 3 the child is taken to the *bet medresh* ("house of study"— particularly the Talmud and the Torah) where a dab of honey is placed on an *aleph* (the first letter of the Hebrew Alphabet) in the Torah and his finger placed upon it. Then his finger is brought to his lips to show him that the *study of God's Law is sweet!* They consider these scrolls "the lively oracles of God," as their most precious possession. Their forefathers lived and died to preserve these for the generations yet to come. Seven times they march around the synagogue rostrum, singing joyful hymns in honor of the Torah, *"Be glad and rejoice with the joy of the law."*

How sad is all this rejoicing over the law when we think of Israel's spiritual darkness! It is true that "unto them were committed the oracles of God" (Romans 3:2), however "eyes have they but they see not" and "blindness in part is happened unto Israel." When Israel's eyes are opened to behold their Messiah, then it will be *"Shimcas Torah"* indeed!

TISHA B'AV (The Ninth of Av)

One of the major fast days in Jewish tradition, and a day of historic *mourning* in Jewish life is the Ninth of Av (the Jewish eighth month). This is a fast day second in importance to the Day of Atonement (*Yom Kippur*) in the Jewish year. It once was kept in remembrance of the day in the year 586 BCE (Before the Common Era) when the mighty forces of the Babylonian armies under Nebuchadnezzar laid waste Jerusalem and slaughtered many of its inhabitants enslaving and exiling the survivors.

Mourning on
Tisha B'av

"According to tradition (*Taan.* 4:4) the decree concerning Israel's forty years of wandering in the wilderness was made on the Ninth of Av.

"It was on the Ninth of Av that the period of grace expired which was granted to the Jews of Spain in order that they might make up their minds whether they chose to convert to Christianity or to emigrate.

"It was in the fifteenth century, however, and especially after the expulsion of the Jews from Spain, that the extremely sad and somber character of the day began to take shape, together with all the mourning rites as they have since been practiced."[69]

It was on the Ninth of Av in the year 70 CE when the Romans swooped down on Jerusalem and destroyed the Second Temple and liquidated the Second Commonwealth in Israel. *Tisha B'av* today commemorates the destruction of the Second Temple rather than that of the First, recognizing the fact that the second destruction was the greatest catastrophe for the Jewish people. It is marked as a day of national gloom. In the synagogue the Book of Lamentations is recited to a plaintive melody and after the morning service, people usually visit the cemetery.

On the Ninth of Av in Jerusalem, devout Jews met at the Western Wall (Wailing Wall) before 1948 and when it was in the hands of the Arabs until 1967 they visited the Tomb of David, voicing their grief and pain over the fall of Jerusalem. Now again they wail and cry at the *Kotel* (the Western Wall) which is their possession once more.

According to Jewish tradition, *The Divine Presence* (*Shekinah*) has never departed from the Western Wall. And just as God never leaves the Wall, so the Jews feel they should never leave it for even one moment. There is always someone there in secret conversation with

---

[69]*The Universal Jewish Encyclopedia* edited by Isaac Landman.

his Creator. Even women are allowed at the Wall but according to orthodox Jewish tradition they are separated from the men by a fence.

"Memra" is similar to Shekinah. "Like the Shekinah, the Memra is accordingly the manifestation of God."[70]

In the Targum: "My Shekinah I shall put among you, my Memra shall be unto you for a redeeming deity." (*Tar. Yer.* to Leviticus 22:12.)

One of the recitations at the Wall is called *Tikkun Hatzot*, the midnight lamentation for the destruction of the Temple taken from Psalm 137: *"By the waters of Babylon, there we sat, yea we wept when we remembered Zion ..." "If I forget thee, O Jerusalem, let my right hand forget her cunning."* Another prayer at the Kotel is the 12th Credo of Rabbi Moses Ben Maimon: "I believe with a perfect faith in the coming of the Messiah and though He tarry, yet will I wait daily for Him to come"!

An uneven rectangle of 40-foot-high wall encloses the old city of Jerusalem (*IR Hakodesh, The Holy City*). This Wall is at least 400 years old (some portions, in fact, date back more than 1,000 years). On June 14, 1967 (*Shavuot* or Pentecost), the way to the Wall was opened for the first time. A quarter of a million Israelis walked from Mount Zion through the Dung Gate to renew their contact with this symbol of Israel and its long past. The *Western Wall* is called (by non-Jews) "The Wailing Wall" or "Wall of Tears." It is said that during the night and early morning, the large blocks of the wall are covered with dew as though the plants were weeping. According to tradition these plants weep with the mourners. Jewish people come here to mourn for the destruction of Jerusalem and to cry to God for the coming of the Messiah to rebuild the Temple. They kiss the stones and recite the 12th Article of Moses Miamonides which is a part of their Judaism:

Jews at the *Kotel*

"I believe, with a perfect faith, in the coming of the Messiah, and though He tarry, yet will I wait for Him to come."

---

[70]*The Jewish Encyclopedia*, p. 465.

PURIM (Feast of Lots)

"And Mordecai wrote these things, and sent letters unto all the Jews that were in all the provinces of the king Ahasuerus, both nigh and far, To stablish this among them, that they should keep the fourteenth day of the month Adar, and the fifteenth day of the same, yearly, As the days wherein the Jews rested from their enemies, and the month which was turned unto them from sorrow to joy, and from mourning into a good day: that they should make them days of feasting and joy, and of sending portions one to another, and gifts to the poor.

"And the Jews undertook to do as they had begun, and as Mordecai had written unto them; Because Haman the son of Hammedatha, the Agagite, the enemy of all the Jews, had devised against the Jews to destroy them, and had cast Pur, that is, the lot, to consume them, and to destroy them; But when Esther came before the king, he commanded by letters that his wicked device, which he devised against the Jews, should return upon his own head, and that he and his sons should be hanged on the gallows.

*"Wherefore they called these days **Purim** after the name of **Pur**. Therefore for all the words of this letter, and of that which they had seen concerning this matter, and which had come unto them, The Jews ordained, and took upon them, and upon their seed, and upon all such as joined themselves unto them, so as it should not fail, that they would keep these two days according to their writing, and according to their appointed time every year; And that these days should be remembered and kept throughout every generation, every family, every province, and every city; and that these days of **Purim** should not fail from among the Jews, nor the memorial of them perish from their seed"* (Esther 9:20-28).

To the present time, most Jewish people celebrate "The Feast of Lots," dancing and rejoicing, feasting and merry-making, for they remember a wonderful deliverance from their enemy on that day. This was a day when their forefathers were living in Persia and the Prime Minister, whose name was Haman, was defeated in his purpose to exterminate all the Jews who were then living within the kingdom. Through the intercession of a Jewish girl, the Jews were delivered from destruction. Her name in Hebrew was *Hadassah* which means *myrtle* for she was compared to the fragrance of this tree which pervaded the air, as so did her good virtues, her charm and beauty spread far and wide. She was also known as *Esther*, the Hebrew name of Persian derivation for *Venus* the brilliant morning star, because of her modesty and dazzling beauty.

Esther had been reared as his own daughter by her cousin, Mordecai (Esther 2:15). The real father of Esther was *Abihail*, the Uncle of Mordecai. When she was chosen by King Ahasuerus as his Queen, Mordecai commanded her not to reveal her identity as a Jewess to her husband or to any in the court (for fear of death), for the Jews were unpopular in Persia. Esther perfectly obeyed her foster-father in this command until the time came for the secret to be known. (Note: "Ahasuerus," generally held to be Xerxes I who reigned in Persia from 485 BC until 465 BC, not the Ahasuerus mentioned in Ezra 4:6 nor in Daniel 9:1 who was the father of Darius, the contemporary of Daniel. It has been suggested that "Ahasuerus" is more of a Title than a personal name.)

A wicked man by the name of Haman was made ruler over all the provinces in the kingdom by order of the King. He required that all people bow to him to give him homage, but Mordecai, being a Jew, could only bow before the God of Israel. This provoked the wrath of the Prime Minister by disobedience to his command. This enraged Haman to such a degree that he sought to destroy, not only Mordecai, but all the Jews in the province. He persuaded King Ahasuerus to decree the death of all Jews because *one* Jew did not bow to him.

Of all the books of the Old Testament there is none which has more of God in it than the Book of Esther, yet God is not once mentioned (in the King James version), but the *Douai* version does have the word once, in the seventh chapter, fourth verse: *"And would God we were sold,"* Esther is made to say. The best known fact about the Book of Esther, the "fact" that "the *Name of God* is not 'even' once named in this Book" *is not a fact at all*! The name *Jehovah* (JHVH or YHWH) appears *five times,* however, concealed in the original *Hebrew* in marvelous acrostic form! One cannot expect to find these Names in any translation, for acrostics cannot be translated.

THE DIVINE NAME IN THE BOOK OF ESTHER

In the ancient Hebrew Text of the Book of Esther the Sacred Tetragrammaton (ה ו ה י—YHWH) is hidden *five* times in acrostic form. A *sixth* acrostic is the Name *Ehyeh* (I AM). In three of the ancient manuscripts these letters of the acrostic are written larger than the rest of the text so as to stand out boldly on the scroll. In the Apocrypha a blundering attempt was made by a scribe to "improve God's perfect work" in the Book of Esther by an effort to correct the omission of God's Name! Another name for God which is simply the first and last letters of the Hebrew Alphabet which is (ת א Aleph-Tav also cannot be translated) is found 100 times in the Book of Esther!

Following are the places where the acrostic for YHWH is found in the book of Esther. (As an aid I have circled the letters of the Tetragram with arrows pointing in the direction they are to be read):

1. ←— את־ושתי המלכ ה לפני ו ולא־בא ה

    1:17—(commanded) "Vashti the queen to be brought in before him and she would not come"—uttered by the author of Esther.

2. —→ היא וכל הנשים יתנו

    1:20—"all the wives shall give"—uttered by Memucan.

3. ←— יבוא המלך והמן היום

    5:4—"let the King and Haman come this day"—uttered by Queen Esther.

4. —→ וכל־זה איננו שוה לי

    5:13—"This availeth me nothing"—uttered by Haman.

5. ←— כי־כלתה אליו הרעה

    7:7—"That there was evil determined against him."

6. —→ מי הוא זה ואי־זה הוא

    7:5—"Who is he and where is he"—uttered by King Ahasuerus. (This is an acrostic of EHYEH (I AM), **Asher Ehyeh** or *"that I AM."*

Jewish people explain the *casting of lots* on that occasion, like this: Haman, having been warned that all enemies of the Jews had in the past met with frustration, being superstitious, decided to cast lots to determine the most favorable day for the slaughter (of the Jews in Persia). The "lots" indicated that day to be the 13th day of the 12th month, *Adar*. But it turned out that Haman was hanged on the same gallows which he had previously prepared for *Mordecai*, and all the Jews escaped a terrible massacre. The next day, Adar 14, the victory was joyously celebrated.

ANTI-SEMITISM

Haman, a hater of the Jews, and Mordecai, the Jew, are not mere figures in history. Ever since there have been Jews, there have been Hamans who have ever been their enemies "bent on" their destruction. The Egyptians were the first people on record to institute anti-Semitic practices.

Hitler was the most recent hater of the Jews. He established the Nazi Party which, according to statistics slaughtered six million Jewish people. "Nazi" or "Natsi" is a popular abbreviation for a member of Adolph Hitler's *National Socialist German Workingmen's Party* "National Socialistiche Deutsche Arbeiter Partei" commonly designated by its initials NSDAP. The nickname "Nazi" originated from the German pronunciation of the first two syllables of the word *National*.

> "What is the real reason back of the attack on the Jewish nation? The answer is given in Revelation 12:13: The Dragon hates and persecutes 'the woman that brought forth the man-child (Messiah).' It is the old enmity of the serpent against the chosen vessel through which the Bruiser of his head was born into the world. But God uses the wrath of the dragon for His own purposes touching His people, as Joseph dealt with his brethren in the time of famine, speaking roughly to them, accusing them of being thieves, allowing the cup to be found in innocent Benjamin's sack, in order to awaken their slumbering consciences about the dark deed in the background of their lives, till they cried: 'We are verily guilty concerning our brother' as their sin rose up before them, like a spectre out of the grave of the past. This is the true inwardness of the wicked persecution of the Jews."
> —*Max Reich*

On the very first occasion that Satan is mentioned by name, he is described as standing up against Israel (1 Chronicles 21:1). This is the background of anti-semitism. Satan is the enemy of *all* mankind, but his hatred is directed particularly against the Jew.

The races of earth meet in Christ to discover they are brothers. The more they love the Lord, the more they love each other. The closer they get to Christ, the closer they are bound to *all* men. Hate cannot live in the light of the love of Christ!

Speaking to Israel (a literal people), God made some promises:

"Therefore all they that devour thee shall be devoured; and all thine adversaries, every one of them, shall go into captivity; and they that spoil thee shall be a spoil, and all that prey upon thee will I give for a prey" (Jeremiah 30:16).

"Thine hand shall be lifted up upon thine adversaries, and all thine enemies shall be cut off" (Micah 5:9).

In history, though plans for the destruction of the Jews have been carried out, yet God has kept His promise to deliver them from their enemies! Five times they were on the brink of complete annihilation:

(1) By the Pharaohs, 1571-1491 BC;
(2) Nebuchadnezzar, 588 BC;
(3) Haman, 510 BC;
(4) Antiochus Epiphanes, 170 (or 164) BC, and;
(5) Titus, AD 70.

And even though they are now estranged from God He still protects them as He promised He would: Note the Six-Day-War of 1967! He said: *"I am the LORD, I change not; therefore, ye sons of Jacob are not consumed"* (Malachi 3:6).

God promised Abraham:

"And I will make of thee a great nation, and I will bless thee [the nation that comes from him], *and make thy name great; and thou shalt be a blessing: And I will bless them that bless thee, and curse him that curseth thee: and in thee shall all families of the earth be blessed"* (Genesis 12:2-3).

Of course we realize that all those who have accepted the Messiah Jesus as their own personal Saviour are the children of Abraham *by faith* (however, Christians are not considered a *nation* historically), and this promise may be applied *spiritually* as well as literally, but as the promise at first was made to a literal people, the Jews, so must there be a literal fulfillment to these same literal people! Let us examine the Scriptures and discover vain efforts against the Jew— vain, because of God's promises to Israel:

1. The King of Egypt could not diminish him (Exodus 1:9-12).
2. The waters of the Red Sea could not drown him (Exodus 14:13-31).
3. Balaam could not curse him (Numbers 23:8).
4. The great fish could not digest him (Jonah 1:17; 2:10).
5. The fiery furnace could not devour him (Daniel 3:16-28).
6. The gallows of Haman could not hang him (Esther 5:14; 8:1-2).
7. The nations could not assimilate him (Esther 3:8; Numbers 23:9).
8. The dictators cannot annihilate him (Isaiah 14:1-2; 1 Chronicles 17:21-22).

The reason: 'Because the LORD saith: 'For I am with thee, saith the LORD, to save thee: though I make a full end of all nations whither I have scattered thee, yet will I not make a full end of thee' (Jeremiah 30:11).

—H. M. Mael, *Jewish Life*

The Psalmist uttered a great truth when he said concerning Israel: *"He* [the Lord] *hath not dealt so with any nation"* (Psalm 147:20).

Intercession for Jews

When Mordecai discovered the plot of Haman, he appealed to Queen Esther to intercede for her people to save them from destruction. She refused at first for she knew in revealing her identity as a Jewess and to appear before the King without being called, she would be put to death. How unlike the Messiah who was quick and obedient to do the Father's will, revealing His identity as the Son of God, though He knew it meant certain death for Him! Mordecai asked the second time saying that if she did not consent, there would be deliverance from another source: *"... And who knoweth whether thou art come to the kingdom for such a time as this?"* (Esther 4:14).

Esther then consented to the request of Mordecai, adding: *"If I perish, I perish"*! She was willing to die for her people's salvation. The Messiah was not only willing, but *did* die in order that His people would be saved from eternal destruction! Esther instructed the Jews through Mordecai to fast for three days and three nights and she also with her handmaidens would do the same. This reminds us of the words of our Messiah who stressed the importance of deliverance when He said: *"These* [things] *come not out but by fasting and prayer."* He, the Deliverer Himself, *fasted and prayed* for 40 days and nights to loose the chains that bind, to set the captive free, to deliver those in bondage, to save from destruction! God's chosen fast of Isaiah 58:6 was obeyed by Messiah, and the promise of deliverance because of His obedience to this fast was fulfilled as well.

When the three-day fast was ended and Esther appeared before the King on the third day, he lifted his scepter which was a sign of his approval. (The law for the destruction of the Jews which had been decreed by the King could not be reversed according to the *Law of the Medes and Persians*, but the King dispatched news letters to permit the Jews to defend themselves on the appointed date.) Esther's petition was granted; the Jews were saved; Haman was hanged on the gallows he had prepared for Mordecai. (The gallows was 50 cubits high [the Hebrew cubit is 18 inches] or 75 ft. to emphasize the depth of animosity and hatred of Haman toward Mordecai.)

Esther Before the King

Mordecai commanded the Jews to *"make the Purim-days as days of feasting and gladness, and of sending portions to one another, and gifts to the poor"* (Esther 9:22). Therefore, the Jew not only displays his faith in God, but also the generosity of his heart. To the Jew, faith and charity are essentials in the celebration of this holiday. On *every* festival the poor are remembered, and surely they are never neglected on Purim.(The Purim *Seudah* [Feast] of today is traditionally celebrated to recall the royal banquet centuries ago where Queen Esther revealed herself as a Jewess to King Ahasuerus and saved her people from destruction).

Towards evening, before Purim has set in and before the reading of the *Megillah* (Scroll of Esther), the Jewish person begins to provide means for taking care of the poor. It is customary for every Jew to give half the monetary unit current in the country, to commemorate the half-shekel the Jews were accustomed to give for the buying of the public sacrifices during the existence of the Temple in Jerusalem.

(*Megillah* is a word applied to four other Biblical books: the Song of Songs, Ruth, Ecclesiastes and Lamentations, which are read in the synagogue during the 3 pilgrimage festivals and on the Ninth of Av, the day commemorating the destruction of both Temples. But only the *Scroll of Esther* is referred to by Jews [from the *Mishnah*] as the *Megillah*. An entire Tractate[71] of the Talmud, called "Megillah" is devoted to the laws of Purim.)

The activity of sending portions to one another on Purim is called *Shaloch Monos*. Everybody, man and woman alike, must send at least *two* gifts to one of their friends, no matter whether this friend is rich or poor. By giving gifts the Jew remembers the gift of salvation given him through Queen Esther. And how can we, who are followers of our Messiah Jesus, help but rejoice and give cheerfully to the spreading of the Good News when we remember the wonderful Gift of salvation given us through the Supreme Sacrifice of Calvary!

On this day of merrymaking and masquerading, the Jews even permit men to wear women's clothes, and women those of men. The devout Jew knows that this act is otherwise strictly forbidden by the law of Moses (Deuteronomy 22:5) but this law is relaxed on Purim when a carnival spirit takes over. Carnivals, masquerades, general merriment and revelry have become the mood of the day. Boys and girls walk from house to house in grotesque masks and indulge in all kinds of fun at Purim.

Queen Esther wore a "mask," that is, she hid her identity as a Jewess, which is the reason for this masquerade. Our Messiah Yeshua wore a "mask of flesh" and to many of His own, He was not recognized as the promised One of God: *"He hath no form nor comeliness and when we shall see him we shall not desire him"* Isaiah prophesied of Him (Isaiah 53:2). They knew not that their God was visiting them disguised in the form of a Man, but to those who believed in Him, the "mask" was lifted; His identity was revealed to them by the Holy Spirit as the long-awaited Redeemer of Israel and the Saviour of the world!

On this holiday of joy, three-cornered breads or cakes are eaten which are filled with poppy-seeds or with chopped prunes and raisins. These have become known as *Hamantaschen* ("Haman's Pockets") for when the Jewish people eat them, they remember Haman's destruction even to his pockets!

---

[71]One of 63 *massektot*, "little books" of the Talmud.

The Jew reveres the synagogue where he worships his God, and he permits nothing to be done or said there which might show contempt for the holy place. But on Purim, when he makes sport (jest) of the Hamans of the past and of the present, the Jew allows and sometimes even encourages conduct which on other days would not be permissible in the synagogue.

Coming to the house of worship, the children are given toy pistols and rattles of all kinds, commonly known as *gragers*. The entire book of Esther (called the *Megillah*) is read through in the synagogue. At the mention of the name of Haman, the children begin shaking their rattles and shooting their guns, while the adults hiss, stamp and shout, until the place is alive with noise.

In the 13th Century in France and Germany, the custom was introduced of writing the name of Haman on two smooth stones to be knocked or rubbed together until the name was blotted out. Some wrote (in chalk) the name of Haman on the soles of their shoes, and at the mention of the name by the reader, stamped with their feet as a sign of contempt, while the adults shouted "May his name be blotted out." As the reader continues to read and pronounces the name of Esther or Mordecai, the congregation recite: "Blessed be Esther, blessed be Mordecai."

The followers of Messiah have a greater deliverance than the Jews of old, a greater enemy than Haman, but a greater Deliverer than Queen Esther. We, who know the Mighty Conqueror, remember His promise that we also shall be conquerors over every foe. He who has all power in heaven and earth declared to all who believe upon Him: *"Behold, I give unto you power to tread on serpents and scorpions and over all the power of the enemy, and nothing shall by any means hurt you"*! (Luke 10:19).

Even as the Jews, by their action in stamping under their feet their enemy Haman, we can do the same with Satan in the Name of Yeshua (Jesus)! And when we remember the Deliverer Messiah as the Jews remember Queen Esther, we can praise Him even as did David:

"... Bless the LORD, O my soul: and all that is within me, bless his holy name. Bless the LORD, O my soul, and forget not all his benefits: Who forgiveth all thine iniquities; who healeth all thy diseases;" (Psalm 103:1-3).

HANUKKAH (Dedication)

It is said that the word, Hanukkah, itself tells of the date for its observance: *"Hanu,"* meaning "rested" and *"kah,"* meaning "25." It was on the 25th of Kislev that the Jewish people "rested" from their enemies at that time in history. *Hanukkah* was also called "Festival of Lights" by Josephus[72] because of the many lights involved in the Feast. The first Hanukkah was observed 2,100 years ago. (See *I Maccabees* for the historical account.)

Father using the "Shammas" to light the fourth candle on the *Hanukkiah.*

To the Jewish people there is much significance in the idea of *lights,* one of them is relative to *marriage*: "From every human being there rises a light that reaches straight to heaven. And when two souls that are destined to be together find each other, their streams of light flow together, and a single brighter light goes forth from their united being." (*Baal Shem Tov*).

> *"And thou shalt command the children of Israel, that they bring thee pure oil olive beaten for the light, to cause the lamp to **burn always**. In the tabernacle of the congregation without [outside] the veil, which is before the testimony, Aaron and his sons shall order it from evening to morning before the LORD: it shall be a statute **for ever** unto their generations on the behalf of the children of Israel"* (Exodus 27:20-21).

Sometime near the celebration of Christmas the Jewish people observe an eight-day holiday known as "Hanukkah" (Hebrew word meaning "Dedication") in memory of the rededication of the Temple in 164 BC by Judas Maccabeus after it had been polluted by Antiochus Epiphanes, the Syrian king. ("Epiphanes" means "illustrious." The Jews renamed him "Epimanes" or "madman" for he tried to make himself like God.)

Judas (Judah or Jehudah) means "praise of God"; *Maccabeus* (Maccabee) means "Hammerer" because of the blows he struck for freedom. George Washington, who had studied the Book of the Maccabees, in the battle against the British who outnumbered the American army, used the Maccabee's strategy of a dummy camp to fool their outnumbered enemies!

> "The name 'Maccabee,' ... may be derived from the Hebrew *makkabhah*, 'hammer'; *makhbi*, 'an extinguisher'; or from the first

---

[72]*Jewish Antiquities* XII.7.

letters of the Hebrew sentence, '*Mi Khamakhah Ba-elim YHWH*' 'who among the gods, O Lord, can be likened unto thee' inscribed on the Maccabean banner in the word MaKHBiY."[73]

In 175 BC King Antiochus in Syria tried to force the Jews to give up their faith and to adopt Greek customs. He persecuted the Jews who refused to do this. Antiochus Epiphanes converted the Temple to worship of Zeus, the dominant Greek god. He looted the temple and ordered all Jews to bow down to the idols placed there. He brought in a sow (called "the abomination of desolation" by Josephus) and placed her on the Holy Altar in desecration of God's Holiness. He brought waste and destruction, desecrated the vessels of the Lord in debauchery and drunkenness and put out the "Ner Tomid" ("Perpetual Light").

The Hasmoneans, the Maccabee family, led the Jews in a revolt. After several years of fighting, Judah and his men drove the Syrians out. On the 25th of Kislev (exactly 3 years after the defilement of the Sanctuary) in the year 165 BC they made their entrance into the Temple and rededicated it to the service of God.

In the Temple the priests left a light burning in obedience to the command of God, but when they prepared to rekindle this light after the victory, they found that there was only enough oil to last one day. This discovery was a catastrophe to the Jewish people for God's command could not then be carried out. Search was made for the oil for this Lamp. The oil must be pure and prepared under the care of the High Priest and sealed with his seal. No pure oil could be found nor could any be prepared before eight days. The small jug of oil bearing the seal of the High Priest might suffice for only one day, but according to the Jewish people's tradition a *miracle* occurred, and the oil lasted for a full eight days!

> (There is no good *historical evidence* for the Hanukkah *legend* concerning the miracle of the burning oil! The problem with the above story is that none of the most ancient sources for the history of Hanukkah (I, II Maccabees and Josephus) mention the miracle. That does not mean that it never happened. It just means that the earliest and best sources for the history of Hanukkah never mention it. The miracle is first mentioned in the *Talmud*, compiled about five or six hundred years after the first Hanukkah.)
> —*First Fruits of Zion*, December 1996

There have been some additions to the orthodox ritual, but it is principally observed in the synagogue and the home by the lighting of candles set in an eight-branched Menorah to commemorate the miracle and the victory. In the book of Exodus, where the story is

---

[73]*International Standard Bible Encyclopedia,* p. 283.

told, the Hebrew word *Menorah* has been translated *candlestick*. The light it gave forth came not from candles but from purest olive oil. "Menorah" means "a place of light." The Hanukkah Menorah also contains an additional holder for the candle called *Shammas* (Servant) with which the others are lighted. The custom is to burn one candle the first evening, two the second; progressively increased each evening until all *eight* are lit on the eighth night. Before the candles are lighted there are blessings recited and singing follows afterwards extolling God as Israel's Deliverer. The most popular hymn on Hanukkah is *Maoz Tsur* ("Rock of Ages"). (This hymn is different from the Christian hymn of the same name.)

It is so significant that the eight candles of the Hanukkah Menorah are not lighted with a match but with another candle called the *Shammas* (Servant). Then after the Servant has given its light to all the others it is put in a high place or a special place of honor in the candelabra. We see in this action a beautiful picture of the only Servant (of God) who was exalted after He had given His light to His people. In the words of Isaiah (49:7) we find Him described: *"Thus saith the LORD, the Redeemer of Israel, and his Holy One, to him whom man despiseth, to him whom the nation abhorreth, to a **servant** of rulers, Kings shall see and arise, princes also shall worship, ..."*

God exalts His Servant, Messiah Jesus, and causes kings and princes to bow down before Him. Messiah is the only *Servant* who is worthy to be given a position of honor! Messiah, the Servant (Isaiah 52:13-15 and Philippians 2:6-8) is the One sent of God to bring us the light of salvation. Of the Messiah it is written: *"The **light of Israel** shall be for a fire, and his holy one for **a flame**"* (Isaiah 10:17).

The eight-branched Menorah also represents the people of God who are "the lower lights." The Word of God calls Messiah's followers "lights" (Ephesians 5:8) who are to let their light so shine before men that their good works would be seen and the Father glorified (Matthew 5:16).

The Word of God describes the Messiah Yeshua as "The Light of the World." He came as a *Servant* ("Shammas") to light every man who comes to Him, and all who come to Him shall no longer walk in darkness but shall have the Light of Life! This Light, who is the Messiah, shines not for one night only or for eight nights, but He is *Ner Tomid*, **The Perpetual Light** who shall shine forevermore!

A carol of thanksgiving for this Light is found in the book of Isaiah:

*"The people that walked in darkness have seen a great **light**: they that dwell in the land of the shadow of death, upon them hath the **light** shined"* (Isaiah 9:2).

THE DRIEDEL GAME

 A popular game is played at this season to remember the miracle of light. Tops (called *Driedels*) are spun in this celebration. The top (also called *Trendel*) is shaped like a cube, on each of the lateral sides of which is found a Hebrew letter. The four Hebrew letters are: *Nun* (נ), *Gimmel* (ג), *Heh* (ה), and *Shin* (ש), the initials of the words which constitute the sentence *Nes Gadol Hayah Sham* or "A Great Miracle Happened There."

The Word of God is given to us to remember our wonderful Messiah. *He* is the *Miracle* that happened. In fact *Miracle* is one of His Names! The English word "Wonderful" in Isaiah 9:6 is translated from the Hebrew word "Pele" which means "Miracle." He is God's *Sign* or *Miracle* as in Isaiah 7:14, and when He comes into our lives we experience God's Salvation so that we can say with joy: *"Nes Gadol Hayah Sham! A great miracle happened there!"* (In *Gematria* [numerology] the initial Hebrew letters of "A Great Miracle Happened There" have the number value of *358* which is the same numerical value as the name *Messiah*!)

John 10:22 tells of One who walked on Solomon's Porch on this day (Feast of Dedication) who has won a victory for us greater than that of Judah Maccabeus. He has loosed us from the hands of our enemy, Satan, and has cleansed the once polluted temple by the ministry of His Holy Spirit. We, who are redeemed, rejoice in the Gift of all gifts, not only at the Feast of Dedication, but every moment of our lives when we remember the victory He wrought for us and the miracle of the Everlasting Light in our souls. Halleluia!

DEDICATION

(On December 3, 1994 I gave the following message at the Rock of Israel Conference in Fairfield, Ohio on the occasion for the dedication of ROI Headquarters' Building to the Lord.)

The word *dedication* has been occupying my thoughts recently and I have been researching for the meaning, not only in Dictionaries and Commentaries but most of all in the Word of God. I wanted to know its meaning. How was it celebrated? What and who were involved in it and what significance does it have for us today? This word is defined from the world's viewpoint as "set apart for a certain purpose," or "wholeheartedly given to a cause." We speak of one who has given of himself, his money, his work, his possessions, and his time to a certain project as a dedicated person. The world has dedication celebrations honoring some person, a new building, the erecting of a statue, or an outstanding painting, etc.

Let us look for a better definition of this word from the Bible. There were many *dedication* celebrations recorded in God's Word. The list goes on and on concerning the dedication of various things, people who were honored, little Samuel was dedicated to the Lord by his mother, Hannah. Then there was the dedication of the Temple, The Wall of Jerusalem, The Stone or Pillar of Jacob. We remember the story of that Dedication (Genesis 28:22; 31:13). God met with Jacob and because Jacob was a dedicated man he poured oil upon the stone where God appeared to him. God refers to this act of dedicating the pillar (stone) for His house as *anointing*. The anointing with oil set the stone apart from the others as something unique, something associated with God and *dedicated* to Him.

The most outstanding Dedication in the Bible was of the Tabernacle. The description is found in the 7th chapter of Numbers which is composed of 89 verses, the longest chapter next to 176 verses of Psalm 119. (The Geneva Bible of 1775 was the first to use italics and the first to be divided into verses.) Nevertheless it is the second longest chapter of the Bible.

After the Altar (which represented the entire Tabernacle) was anointed, it was *dedicated*–set apart for God's use. The dedication celebration lasted 12 days. There were 12 princes who dedicated the Altar, one prince a day. That is, on 12 successive days, a different prince brought similar gifts and offerings. although the offerings of the princes were identical, each is separately recorded by inspiration. (Read Numbers 7:1-17 to get the picture.)

On another occasion the Jewish people showed their generosity for the work of the Tabernacle. God had requested that they bring an offering for the building of the Tabernacle. It is recorded that they not only brought that which God had required of them, but they brought free will offerings every morning as well. They had to be stopped from bringing–they brought too much (see Exodus 36:3, 5-7)!

In this matter of giving I recall an offering which was hilariously given by a congregation. My brother was a missionary in Haiti and had come home on furlough. He conducted a service in a church near our hometown of Ventura, California. In answer to the pastor's question for any need on the field Hyman mentioned that a refrigerator was the outstanding need among other things. After Hyman's message the pastor requested that the congregation bring an offering for the field. They immediately responded by singing and almost dancing down the aisles to the "collection plate." The pastor of the church had to stop them from bringing!–Remember, Hyman?

Solomon's Temple, called the House of the Lord, was involved in a *dedication* celebration.

*"Then the king and all the people offered sacrifices before the LORD. And king Solomon offered a sacrifice of twenty and two thousand oxen, and an hundred and twenty thousand sheep: so the king and all the people **dedicated** the house of God"* (2 Chronicles 7:4-5; also see 1 Kings 8:63-64.)

Reading further we find that Solomon held a feast at this time of dedication. A great congregation gathered for the occasion which lasted for 14 days, 7 days for the Feast of Tabernacles and 7 for the *Feast of Dedication* with an eighth day added for both Feasts (see verses 8 and 9).

Another *Dedication* Celebration was at the Jerusalem Wall recorded in Nehemiah:

*"And at the **dedication of the wall of Jerusalem** they sought the Levites out of all their places, to bring them to Jerusalem, to keep the **dedication** with gladness, both with thanksgivings, and with singing, with cymbals, psalteries, and with"* (Nehemiah 12:27).

As we read further in this portion of Scripture we notice that there was a great crowd of people along with the Levites and singers who were brought from quite a distance to celebrate the dedication of Jerusalem's Wall. Some of us here tonight have come from a distance, from California, Texas, Chicago, Washington, and other distant places to celebrate this particular *dedication*. As we read in this chapter we find that those gathered for that holy event were involved in worship, singing, rejoicing, playing of different instruments, feasting, the reading of God's Word, and in a great offering–all which we have done and will do tonight!

Then the *Dedication* of David's house followed the *pattern,* for there was singing: David sang the hymn he composed recorded in Psalm 30. There was feasting, rejoicing, prayer, and the Word of God at this House Dedication.

The Tabernacle Dedication was a pattern for all the dedications. There was an anointing first of all. Then the dedication followed which was a setting apart for God, for His use. There was singing, rejoicing, praying, feasting and God's Word was given. The *dedication* was completed by an offering.

Yeshua was involved in all the Dedications. He is the One who anointed the Temple by His presence. In fact His Title, *Meshiach* means *anointed.* He is the Dedicated One who dedicated the Tabernacle, the Temple, David's House, Jerusalem's Wall, and every article of furniture in the Tabernacle. He is the greatest Donor to the work of the Sanctuary, for He gave of Himself. He celebrated all the Feasts of the Lord and the Dedication of the Altar (called *Hanukkah*).

*"And it was at Jerusalem the **feast of the dedication,** and it was winter. And Jesus walked in the temple in Solomon's porch"* (John 10:22-23).

The Anointed One, no doubt observed the dedication of the Altar, the dedication of houses, of His own life to God, of any new building, and the dedication of the House of God, the Temple. We have just read of one particular instance when Yeshua, the Anointed One, observed the Feast of *Hanukkah* which occurred in combination with the Feast of Tabernacles. Yeshua was present at Jerusalem during the Feast of *Hanukkah* and delivered a discourse from Solomon's Porch of the Temple to the assembled multitude. (It is recorded once in Scripture that He did this, but He must have observed it many times before since He observed all the "Feasts" of the Lord as well as all God's commandments given to Israel.) During this Feast of Hanukkah He was asked: *"If you are the Messiah, tell us plainly."* We do not read of what was His offering on that occasion but as all the Jewish people were commanded of God to do so He followed the Pattern of Dedication. Most importantly He brought Himself who is the fulfillment of all the offering which the twelve princes and others brought at the Feast of Dedication of the Altar in the Tabernacle.

Because of our Lord Jesus we can dedicate this building to God. Because of Him who is the Anointed One, we can be anointed as the building is anointed, given to God for His use. Because of Him we can offer not only our finances, our possessions, but best of all we can offer ourselves in dedication to this work of the Rock of Israel Ministries. Let us allow the anointing oil to flow upon us to set us apart for this work of the ministry to the lost sheep of the House of Israel. Let us pray that through this building with its rooms, its offices, its personnel, there will proceed anointed material, anointed evangelists and service that will reach many to the Lord Yeshua ha-Meshiach!

—End of Message on Dedication

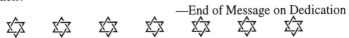

DOES THE BIBLE SPEAK OF CHRISTMAS?

It is widely believed that Christmas is really a pagan festival which the church adopted when Christianity became the official religion of the Roman Empire. There are those who point out it could not have been in winter, and that the Bible does not tell us to celebrate it.

In Haggai, chapter 2, is a promise to the Jews of a surpassing blessing, the date of its commencement being stressed no less than three times—*the 24th day of the ninth month.* The promise was unfulfilled by the time of Judas Maccabeus, so to ensure that the prophecy would not go by default, he chose this date to *rededicate* the Temple after it had been defiled by Antiochus Epiphanes.

The occasion was celebrated with great rejoicing and festivity, lamps being lit and singing and dancing taking place in the streets. This is the *Feast of the Dedication*, referred to in John 10:22, which Jesus attended and which is stated to have been in the winter. The ninth month is also shown to be in the winter, in Jeremiah 36:22.

The occasion is still celebrated by the Jews of our time with an 8-day festival beginning on the 24th of Kislev. It is called "Hanukkah," or "The Festival of Lights."

After the rebuilding of Jerusalem, the Jews were scrupulous to avoid any suggestion of paganism. Judas Maccabeus was the champion of Jehovah against Grecian paganism. Any festival inaugurated under his auspices is therefore beyond suspicion.

Since Jesus himself celebrated this festival, it must have had divine approval.

Judas Maccabeus ruled from about 166 to 160 BC. The promise of the *Great Blessing* had not been fulfilled by then; and in view of the tragic history of the Jews since that date, it is evident the Dedication was not the true fulfillment of the prophecy. We have to look elsewhere for the fulfillment or accept that the promise was not honored.

The ninth month in the Jewish calendar is Kislev, which corresponds roughly with December. The Jewish calendar varies with the moon. As a result, Kislev varied from a week or two earlier to a week or two later than December, the average incidence of the 24th day of the ninth month, Kislev, corresponding with the 24th of December, Christmas Eve.

So we see that the promise to Haggai must have been the promise of the Nativity, that the date corresponds with Christmas Eve, that it was in the winter, and that Jesus honored this time of festivity by attending the celebration at Jerusalem.

—L. Martin in *Elim Evangel*

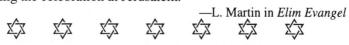

MY NOTE ON THE CHRISTMAS DATE

No one knows for certain the date of Messiah's birth, but here is something to think about: There must be conception, of course, before a birth. When God promised that *the* Virgin shall *conceive* and bear a child (and in connection with the very first promise of a coming Redeemer as the *woman's* seed), He referred to a ***miracle***; i.e., by the words *Behold* and *Sign*. It is not the *birth* of Messiah but His *conception* that is the *Miracle*!

There are three direct references to the miracle conception of Messiah in the T'nach (OT). The first one is in Genesis 3:15 which states that the Redeemer would be "her seed." No woman has seed. It is the man only of whom it can be said he has seed; i.e., "the seed of Abraham."

The next promise of the miracle *conception* is in Isaiah 7: 14 where God foretold that a *sign* (*oth*) or *miracle* will come to Israel. This miracle is that *the* *virgin* (without the aid of a man) shall *conceive* and bear a child.

We read in Jeremiah 31:22 of this miracle the Lord Himself will perform: *"... for the LORD hath created a **new** thing in the earth, ... a **woman** shall compass a man ..."*

The Hebrew word for "compass" is *savav* and means "to turn," "to go about," "to encompass," "to alter or change." The *Piel* form of "savav" is *tesovav* and which appears here in this verse making the tense future. In other words, the prophet was really saying that the Lord, in the future, will *create* a *new* thing in the land (earth)–*never done before–(and* it is the LORD only who *creates*). Jeremiah was implying that God will cause a woman to *alter the natural course of generation* by "conceiving seed" without the man and that she will bear a Man (*geber*) or *Mighty Man,* a Warrior, a Valiant Man, who is none other than the Messiah! (*Geber*—"Mighty Man." This term, Mighty, is used of God in Isaiah 9:6.)

Matthew 1:18 relates these words: *"Now the **birth** of Jesus was on this wise ..."* Preceding this verse it is recorded that the *man **begat*** but now the wording changes. ***Birth***, in Greek here, is *gennesis, genesis* or "beginning," and is related to the word *gennao*, "to beget" referring to *conception*. Further on in the last part of the 20th verse we read: *"... that which was **conceived** in her is of the Holy Ghost."* In other words, God ***created*** the Seed which was miraculously "planted" in her womb. With God *all* things are possible!

Again, it is not the birth but the conception of Messiah which is the ***miracle***. This w*as the actual day Messiah Jesus **began** in His humanity*!

What was the first month of the year to the Jewish people? God said it was to be Nisan, our March or April. Why was it the beginning (see Exodus 12)? It was the beginning because *a **lamb*** was taken for sacrifice, for Passover. The *beginning* of the *Lamb of God* in the womb of Mary could have been in the

Messiah was born as "The Lamb"

month when *a lamb was taken for a house,* the month Nisan. The period of human gestation is 280 days which, counting from the conception in Nisan, would be Kislev, the *ninth* month of the Jewish Calendar which coincides with our December! (It takes 4 months and 7 days of gestation for a *lamb* to be born. Since lambs were born in the month Nisan, this means they must have been conceived in the month Kislev, which coincides with our December! Both of these periods then coincide with conception and birth—both in the animal and in the human world!)

The *ninth* month is shown to be *winter* in Jeremiah 36:22. Since we see that Yeshua (Jesus), the Lamb, honored the 25th day of the month Kislev or The Feast of Dedication (*Hanukkah*) by walking on Solomon's Porch in *Winter, it* attests to the fact that mild weather conditions prevailed at that time of year so that He could do this. (Also, the shepherds could have "kept watch" over their flock (for the "birthing" of the lambs) *even in winter* when the angels announced to them at that time the birth of Messiah, the King of the Jews)!

Note: Solomon's Porch—an *exterior* structure forming a covered approach to the entrance of the building. It also is called a "portico" or "roofed colonnade." This portico was the scene where Jesus taught at The Feast of Dedication (John 10:23) and where multitudes gathered after the healing of the lame man (Acts 3:11). It was then mild weather conditions permitting these people even in *winter* to be on the *outside* of the building with Jesus!

Messiah died as "The Lamb"

CHAPTER FOUR

MESSIAH OF ISRAEL

The Name "Messiah"

"The name Messiah is used a total of *four* times in the Bible, two times in each Testament. These instances are: Daniel 9:25-26 which verses state the time of the birth and death of the Messiah, plus the purpose of His death as a Substitute to bear the sin of the world; John 1:41, *"...We have found the **Messias** which is, being interpreted, the **Christ**."* Lastly, John 4:25, *"... I know that **Messias** cometh, which is called **Christ**: when he is come he will tell us all things."* Clearly, these passages are not isolated, but are cross-referenced to both testaments.

"There are many Old Testament references to Messiah where the English translation is *anointed*. Some of these are typical and the word *meshiach* is in the construct form, but the words and the passage nonetheless are definite witnesses to the title, Messiah. Psalm 2:2, *"The kings of the earth set themselves, and the rulers take counsel together, against the LORD, and against his **anointed*** [Meshiach],* " is a prime example. A few others are 1 Samuel 2:10, and 12:3, and Lamentations 4:20, all of which are typical references to the Messiah."   —Author unknown

An interesting note is found in the Talmud concerning the *Name* of the Messiah:

"Seven things were formed before the creation of the world: The Law, Repentance, Paradise, Gehenna, The Throne of Glory, The Temple, and the *name of MESSIAH*."[74]

MESSIAH IN THE HEBREW SCRIPTURES

God is not a man that He would lie, so when He makes a promise He will keep it. He says what He means and He means what He says! In the T'nakh (OT) we read many prophecies concerning the coming Messiah. God anointed holy men of Israel to write these promises. The Bible shows many pictures of one Supreme Person who was to come. The central figure in the Scriptures is the Messiah of Israel, the Savior of the world. We see Him on every page of the Torah, the Law of God. Every incident or person mentioned in the Old Testament points to Him and in some way brings out a greater revelation of Him.

---

[74]*P'Sachim*, fol. 54, col. 1. (Emphasis is mine.)

When we read the New Covenant Scriptures we notice that Jesus, the Messiah referred to the T'nakh many times as pictures of Himself. After He had been resurrected from the grave and was walking with two of His disciples on the road to Emmaus, He lovingly rebuked them for their sadness over His crucifixion:

> *"Then he said unto them, O fools, and slow of heart to believe **all that the prophets have spoken**: Ought not Christ [Messiah] to have suffered these things, and to enter into his glory?"* (Luke 24:25-26).

He rebuked them for not believing all the prophetic pictures of Himself. Then He continued speaking to them repeating what the prophets said:

> *"And beginning at Moses and all the prophets, he expounded unto them in **all the scriptures** the things concerning himself"* (Luke 24:27).

Did you notice Jesus the Messiah said that *all* the Scriptures speak of Him? The Scriptures to which He referred was the T'nakh (OT). There was no New Testament at that time. The New Testament did not appear until about 20 years after Jesus was crucified and was resurrected.

If you would study the New Testament you would find that in it there are one hundred and ninety references to the Torah or the Five Books of Moses; one hundred and one references to the Psalms; one hundred and four references to the book of Isaiah and thirty references to the minor prophets. In all, there are six hundred thirty nine references or quotes from the T'nakh in the New Testament! Over and over again we find the words: "it is written," or "that it might be fulfilled which was spoken by the prophets," or "as the Scripture saith," or "according to the Scriptures."

Any open-minded Jewish person will be convinced beyond a shadow of a doubt that there is only one person in all the Universe who can possibly fit into all the details of prophecy of a Messiah found in his own T'nakh, the Holy Scriptures. *Daniel* tells of His coming before the second destruction of Jerusalem. *Moses* declared that the Messiah was to appear while Judah "held the Sceptre" as the royal tribe of Israel. The Sanhedrin was the law-making body of Judah before they were dispersed. *Micah*, the Jewish prophet, wrote that Messiah was to come from the line of *David*. Moses wrote He must be a descendant of *Abraham*, of the Tribe of *Judah* and from the family of *David*. *Isaiah*, the Jewish prophet, declared that the Lord would give a supernatural sign concerning the conception of Messiah. His conception and birth would be like no other because it would be of a miraculous nature. *Jeremiah*, as well as *Isaiah*, wrote that the

Messiah was to have a human and divine nature. *Jeremiah* said He would be righteous and would be called by the name "The LORD our Righteousness." *Isaiah* wrote that He would be a child born to Israel and would be called "The Mighty God (Warrior, God-man)," "The Prince of Peace."

My Jewish people might object to the fact that Messiah was not only human but divine. Yet should they study their own *T'nakh* (OT) they would discover that God appeared in *human form* to Abraham, to Jacob, to Manoah, to Joshua and others. Many Scripture portions relate this fact of the human and the divine in the person of the Messiah.

Daniel, Isaiah, and others prophesy that the Messiah is to come to atone for the iniquities of the people and to bring in everlasting righteousness. David wrote, in the Psalms, of the Messiah's death, resurrection and coming again! And we could go on with many portions of the T'nakh but space here is insufficient. However, we will conclude by quoting Peter's message of 2,000 years ago to his own Jewish brothers: It is still a message to my Jewish people today:

> *"But those things, which God before had showed by the mouth of all his prophets, that Christ [Messiah] should suffer, he hath so fulfilled. Repent ye therefore, and be **converted**, that your sins may be blotted out, ...; And he shall send Jesus Christ [Messiah], which **before was preached unto you:** ..., which God hath spoken by the mouth of all his holy prophets since the world began.*

> *"Yea, and all the prophets from Samuel and those that follow after, as many as have spoken, have likewise foretold of these days. Ye are the children of the prophets, and of the covenant which God made with our fathers, saying unto Abraham, And in thy seed shall all the kindreds of the earth be blessed. Unto you first God, having raised up his Son Jesus, sent him to bless you, in turning away every one of you from his iniquities"* (Acts 3:18-21, 24-26).

ONE SOLITARY LIFE

"Here is a young man who was born in an obscure village, the child of a peasant woman. He grew up in another village. He worked in a carpenter shop until He was thirty, and then for three years He was an itinerant preacher. He never wrote a book. He never held an office. He never owned a home. He never had a family. He never went to college. He never put His foot inside a big city. He never traveled two hundred miles from the place where He was born. He never did one of the things that usually accompany greatness. He had no credentials but Himself. While He was still a young man, the tide of public opinion turned against Him. His friends ran away. He was turned over to His enemies. He went through the mockery of a trial. He was nailed to a cross, between two thieves. While He was dying, His executioners gambled for the only piece of property He had on earth, and that was His coat. When He was dead, He was laid in a borrowed grave through the pity of a friend. Nineteen centuries wide have come and gone, and today He is the central figure of the human race, and the leader of the column of progress.

I am far within the mark when I say that all the armies that ever marched, and all the navies that ever sailed, and all the parliaments that ever sat, and all the kings that ever reigned, put together, have not affected the life of man upon this earth as has that one solitary life." —Anton Darms, in his *The Jew Returns to Israel*

The illustration shown here is from inside the cover of *Biblical Archaeology Review*, November/December issue, 1995.

The name of Jesus in other languages:

Mongolian: *Ecyc*
Russian: *Hhcyc*
Crotian: *Isus*
Spanish: *Hesús*
Old English: *Iesus*
Poetic: *Jesu*

SPEAKING THE NAME "JESUS CHRIST"

I am not opposed to the tactful use of the Hebrew equivalent of *Jesus Christ* when it is appropriate in witness. (In this book I have used both the Hebrew and English terms.) To *insist* on using *Yeshua ha-Meshiach* or *Yeshua* **instead** of *Jesus, Jesus Christ* or the *Lord Jesus* at **all** times by Jewish and Gentile believers, is Biblically incorrect. The *English* translation of the *Brit Hadasha* gives the name "Jesus," "Christ," "Jesus Christ," and "Christ Jesus."

We expect *Hebrew* to be spoken in present-day Israel. But in the United States, American Jews speak the *English* language, with less than 10 percent having even a knowledge of Hebrew. Also the language spoken in foreign countries is of that particular country and not where–for the most part–Hebrew is spoken at all. A few examples: the Russian name for Jesus is *Esues* and for Christ is *Xhristoes*, the Spanish *Haysus*, the Greek *Ieosus*, the Hebrew *Yeshua* or *Yehoshua*, etc. Also, the Scriptures have been translated into *all languages*, so demanding that Christians (whether they be Jew or Gentile) *always* use the Hebrew *Yeshua ha-Meshiach* instead of the English *Jesus Christ* or in the other languages of the world, is disconcerting and inappropriate. It is written that *"at the name OF Jesus* [not the name "Jesus" itself but the name OF Jesus, that is, the name belonging to

Jesus—and He has many names—] *every knee should bow ... And that every tongue should confess that Jesus Christ is Lord, to the glory of God the Father"* (Philippians 2 :10-11).

PROPHECY AND FULFILLMENT

"The mother (the Jews) of Messiah drags, weary, forlorn
Across mighty wastes, unconsoled in her quest.
Like a grief-heavy shadow, dark, dumb, and worn,
She seeks for the son who was reft from her breast.
"She raises her hands, silent as doom,
Eyes questing from slow-moving cloud to cloud;
Lord, why did you set a son in my womb,
And straightway uproot him? Her soul it is bowed.

"Mother of griefs, your sorrow is mine.
My brethren are orphan where you are bereft.
Give strength to your heart in all winds that flow,
And no longer be silent! Rend heavens for a sign;
Let your wail shake God's throne and no quiet be left
Till *Messiah* is brought back to earth below!"

—*Translated from the Hebrew by I.M. Lack*

TWO MESSIAHS

According to the Talmud Jews expected two Messiahs: *Meshiah ben Joseph* and *Meshiah ben David*.

"We are told that both Moses and Aaron spoke to Pharoah about freeing the Jews. Someone asked the great 19th-century forerunner of 'practical Zionism,' Rabbi Shmuel Mohilever, why God needed two emissaries. He answered: 'The Final Redemption, too, will be brought about by *two* Messiahs—Messiah, son of Joseph and Messiah, son of David.' The questioner repeated his question, and Rabbi Mohilever replied: *'One to take the Jews out of Exile, the other to take Exile out of the Jews'.*" [75]

The Old Testament tells that the hopes of Israel were centered on two great events: the coming of God's Kingdom, and the coming of a Man who would bring this Kingdom to pass. This Man would please God and would bring His people to rest and deliverance from the enemy. Thirty-six prophets made predictions concerning Him, either

---

[75]*Yalkut Moshe*, by Moshe Hacohen Gordon, Tel Aviv, Avraham Tzioni, publisher, 5728.

about His birth, His spirit, His miracles, His relationship with other peoples, His death, His resurrection, or about some other phase of His life. This Man, who fulfills the visions and hopes of the Psalmist and the Prophets, is the Messiah or "The Anointed One." He comes from the line of David, from Abraham, Isaac and Jacob. It was prophesied He would come:

1. From the *Human Family* of ADAM-Genesis 3:15
2. From the *Race Line* of SHEM-Genesis 9:25-27
3. From the *Patriarch Line* of ABRAM-Genesis 18:18
4. From the *True Heir Line* of ISAAC-Genesis 21:12
5. From the *National Line* of JACOB-Genesis 28:3-4
6. From the *Tribal Line* of JUDAH-Genesis 49:10
7. From the *Kingly Line* of DAVID-Psalm 132:11
—Arranger of above quote unknown

Many are the Jews who, upon first arriving in the Holy Land, went to the Western Wall ("Kotel") to pray and lament. They struck their faces toward the wall and wet the stones with their tears and cried: *"Oh, God send us the Messiah!"* A Jewish religionist wrote: "Ultimately, it is not only we who are waiting for the Messiah. It is the Messiah who is waiting for us!"

Jews have been waiting and yearning for the coming of One who would deliver them from their countless enemies and set up His everlasting Kingdom. Many have been their disappointments through the years, for false prophets have laid claim to the title of "The Anointed One." In all, 35 such impostors have been listed in Jewish history! Just a few outstanding false Messiahs are listed here.

FALSE MESSIAHS

Among the first of these false Messiahs mentioned in the annals of antiquity was a man by the name of *Theudus*. Josephus, the Jewish historian speaks of him. So does the Patriarch Gamaliel mention him as recorded in Acts 5:36. Theudus led his 400 followers in an unsuccessful rebellion against the Romans. He was beheaded after his defeat and capture.

The Jews, under the Roman yoke, were deceived by a man named *Simon* who made fabulous promises of deliverance to the people and who was hailed as the God-sent Savior. Among his many followers, made up of all classes of the nation, was the famous Rabbi Akiba with thousands of his students. He announced *Simon* as the Messiah, calling him *Bar Kochba* ("Son of a Star"), applying to him the prediction of Numbers 24:17 *"There shall come a star out of Jacob."* In the year AD 131 the nation rallied to his battle-cry when he became the leader of an uprising. Defending this man, the Jews lost between 500,- to 600,000 souls. It was too late when this famous Rabbi and the others with him, discovered their ominous mistake. They denounced him, calling him *Bar Kozba* ("Son of a Liar"). The people's hopes ended in disaster. Judah was lost; they were taken captives into slavery and were dispersed all over the great Roman empire.

In the year 1660, there was a messianic pretender named *Shebethai Zvi* who aroused great expectations among the Jews of Europe. Their hopes were dashed to the ground when he turned Mohammedan to save his life.

THE TRUE MESSIAH

In searching the Scriptures there can be no doubt as to who Messiah is! From a careful study of the Gospels we cannot fail to see that the Hebrew Scriptures (which were often quoted by the Messiah Himself) describe Him in every detail!

> *"And beginning at Moses and all the prophets, he* [Jesus] *expounded unto them in all the scriptures the things concerning himself"* (Luke 24:27).

The true Messiah must be the Messenger and Mediator of a New and Everlasting Covenant which includes Gentiles as well as Jews. He must also unite in Himself all the God-ordained offices that exist in Israel, being a prophet (lawgiver and leader) like Moses, a High Priest and Mediator like Melchizedek, and a King like David, besides being the Saviour and Lord of all that ever will be saved. (Deuteronomy 18:15; Isaiah 55:4, 33:22; Psalm 110:1, 4; Zechariah 6:12-13; Jeremiah 33:1, 4-18.) The true Messiah must be the Redeemer of man's spirit, soul (mind), and body. (Job 19:25-26; Psalms 16:9-11 and 17:15, 31:5, 19 and 72:13-14; Isaiah 26:19.)

> *"**What think ye of Christ** [Messiah]"?* (Matthew 22:42). Here are some answers given by persons named in the *Brit Hadasha*:
>
> *Pilate*: "I find no fault in Him at all."
> *Judas*: "I have sinned in that I have betrayed *innocent* blood."
> *Centurion*: "Truly this was the Son of God."
> *John the Baptist*: "The Lamb of God which taketh away ... sin."
> *John*: "He is the bright and morning star."
> *Peter*: "Thou art the Christ, the Son of the Living God."
> *Thomas*: "My Lord and my God."
> *Paul*: "The excellency of the knowledge of Christ Jesus my Lord."
> *Angels in heaven*: "A Saviour which is Christ the Lord."
> *Father in heaven*: "My beloved Son in whom I am well pleased."

"What think ye of Christ?" is the test
To try both your state and your mien,
You cannot be right on the rest,
Unless you think rightly of Him.
                    –Selected, From *American Messianic Fellowship*

There are many prophecies contained in the Old Covenant Scriptures concerning the Coming One. We cannot list them all since they are so numerous. However, in the following pages just a few are mentioned.

DATE OF MESSIAH'S COMING

*"The sceptre shall not depart from Judah, nor a lawgiver from between his feet, until **Shiloh** come; ..."* (Genesis 49:10).

"Shiloh," "tranquil," "secure," "peaceful." In the above Scripture it is an epithet of the Messiah and can have no other meaning. The interpretation of the word, "Shiloh" is that of "pacifier" or "peacemaker." It is similar to the word "Shalom" or "peace," "peaceful," "prosperous," "secure" which is also a designation of the Messiah. See Micah 5:5, *"and this man shall be the peace"* i.e., the author of peace (cf. Ephesians 2:14).

The Jewish people no longer are rulers; the staff has departed from them. Therefore Messiah had to come before the dispersion of AD 70.

"Know therefore and understand, that from the going forth of the commandment to restore and to build Jerusalem [after the Babylonian captivity] *unto the Messiah the Prince shall be seven weeks* [seven sevens of years], *and threescore and two weeks:* [two sevens of years, about 483 years] *..."* (Daniel 9:25).

According to this prediction, the Divine Messiah must have come about 2,000 years ago. The prophet Daniel said that 70 weeks ("sevens of years") were determined concerning God's people, from the going forth of the commandment to rebuild the walls of Jerusalem until the coming of the Messiah, the Prince. (There are several methods of calculating chronologically this period, but they all run their course before the crucifixion of Jesus.)

"And after threescore and two weeks [sevens of years] *shall Messiah be cut off* [executed], *but not for himself: and the people* [Romans] *of the prince* [Titus] *that shall come shall destroy the city* [Jerusalem] *and the sanctuary* [temple]; *and ... unto the end of the* [age] *war desolations are determined* (Daniel 9:26).

Here Daniel gives definite and exact measurement as to the time of Messiah's coming. He had to come during the second Temple, before AD 70. Since the second Temple has been destroyed, it must be clear to any unprejudiced mind that the time for the coming of the Messiah has come and gone; and since God's Word cannot be broken, it follows that He must have come. Who could He have been? Who has met the time specifications for His coming? However, Jewish people go not by their own T'nakh but by the Talmud's prediction: "Mashiah will come when one generation is either wholly innocent or wholly guilty."   —*Talmud, Sanhedrin* 98a

> *"Behold, I will send my messenger, and he shall prepare the way before me: and the Lord, whom ye seek, shall suddenly come to his temple, even the **messenger of the covenant**, whom ye delight in: behold, he shall come, saith the LORD of hosts"* (Malachi 3:1).

The Hebrew prophet, Malachi, who lived about 400 BC, stated that the Messiah would come to the temple; and since Malachi lived after the destruction of the *first* temple, he then was referring to the *second* temple.

During the construction of the second temple, Haggai, another great Hebrew prophet, predicted that the glory of the latter temple would be greater than of the former, (Haggai 2:2-9.)" *... and the desire of all nations shall come"* (Haggai 2: 7). The Second Temple could only be greater in glory than the First by the coming of God's Holy Servant, *The Desire of All Nations.* No other reason could be given to make it greater! *"Therefore will he give them up, until the time that she which travaileth hath brought forth: ..."* (Micah 5:3).

God assured the Jewish people through the prophet that He would not allow the enemy to destroy them until *Immanuel* ("God With Us") would be born of that appointed virgin who would travail (Isaiah 7:14). The Jewish Temple, where were kept the genealogical records of the royal family of the House of David, had to exist so that Messiah's descent could be proven.

> "The very existence of Israel into 'houses' presupposes among them the existence of well-authenticated genealogies."[76]

Those records proved that the Messiah Jesus is the descendant of David and that He is the One concerning whom God spoke through the prophets. But after Yeshua, the son of David, was born and fulfilled His mission, God permitted the Temple (the place where the records were kept) to be destroyed. The people were scattered all over the world so that no one Jew on earth is absolutely certain now of any

---

[76]*Jewish Encyclopedia*, Vol. V, p. 597.

tribal descent. Only the Messiah Jesus can trace His lineage to David since Matthew secured His genealogical data before the destruction of the Temple in AD 70!

TO BE OF THE TRIBE OF JUDAH

"And there shall come forth a rod out of the stem [stock] *of Jesse* [father of King David], *and a Branch shall grow out of his roots: And the spirit of the LORD shall rest upon him, ..."* (Isaiah 11:1-2).

"The word 'stem' or 'stock' refers to a sawed off tree trunk, implying that the royal family would lose its prestige; therefore we see the significance of the birth of Jesus, the son of Judah and of David, in obscurity in a stable in Bethlehem."
—Dr. Keith L. Brooks, *Prophecy Magazine*

We discover in the New Testament, the very first verse concerning the genealogy of Messiah: *"The book of the generation of Jesus Christ, the son of David, the son of Abraham"* (Matthew 1:1). The Messiah was to be a member of the *Jewish* line, of the seed of Abraham and David, as it is written, else the many prophecies were not fulfilled in Him.

Mary (Miriam), the mother of Jesus, was of the seed of David, but could not give her firstborn a claim to the Kingship because she did not come from the *royal* line of Solomon. She was a descendant of David, to be sure, through Nathan, Solomon's brother, but this was not the *royal* line which must come through a male heir. The Messiah must not only be able to trace His right to the throne of David through the *natural* seed, but also through the *royal, legal* line, which God had accepted, the line of Solomon.

Therefore we have *two* genealogies of the Messiah in existence today, one in Matthew and the other found in Luke. In Luke we have His *human* genealogy through His mother, Mary and in Matthew we have His *royal* line through Joseph, His father in the eyes of the law.

Now both Joseph and Mary were descendants of Abraham and of King David. Mary's line was the *human* line, the natural one; and Joseph's line was the legal, the *royal* line. It is the genealogy of Joseph then which proves the *legal* right for Jesus to be the King of Israel and His right to the throne of David.

But God had pronounced a curse upon *Jeconiah*, the son of *Jehoiakim*, of the line of David. No king who was born of his line would be permitted to sit upon the throne. Joseph came from the line of Jeconiah and legally possessed the right to the throne, but was denied this honor because of God's curse on the descendants of Jeconiah. The Messiah must be of the seed of David through this line of Solomon. God found a way by which Jesus could be the *legal* heir to the throne through the *royal* line of Solomon and yet be the Son of David *according to the flesh!* By virtue of His foster-father Joseph, Jesus had the legal claim to the throne and He also had claim through natural birth, because He was the son of Mary, who was also in the line of King David!

God nullified the curse of Jeconiah by bringing together these two Jewish young people, Joseph and Mary, from all the people in the world, that Jesus might fulfill every requirement to be *both* the King of Israel and the Saviour of mankind! It could not be that Joseph was His natural father, for no child born of the line of Jeconiah could sit upon the throne, but Jesus must still be the seed of David. This God provided for by choosing in the person of Mary as His mother, a direct descendant of David! God brought together the *only two persons* who could possibly have met every condition by which Christ could be the sinless Son of man and still be the heir to David's throne! Had God chosen any other woman but the virgin Mary, the plan would have completely failed. Had He espoused her to any other man but Joseph, it would have failed as well!

TWO GENEALOGIES OF JESUS, THE CHRIST

"A favorite point of attack on the Bible for those who deny its divine origin and inerrancy is the two varying genealogies of Jesus Christ. Not only is this a favorite point of attack by unbelievers, but it is also a point that often puzzles earnest students of the Bible. It is perfectly clear that the two genealogies differ widely from one another, and yet each is given as the genealogy of Christ. How can they by any possibility both be true? One has recently written me on this question in these words: 'Two genealogies of Jesus are given, one in Matthew and one in Luke, and one is entirely different from the other. How can both be correct?'

A very simple answer to this apparently difficult question is this:

1. The genealogy given in Matthew is the genealogy of Joseph, the reputed father of Jesus, His father in the eyes of the law. The genealogy given in Luke is the genealogy of Mary, the mother of Jesus, and is the human genealogy of Jesus Christ in actual fact. The Gospel of Matthew was written for Jews. All through it Joseph is prominent, Mary is scarcely mentioned. In Luke, on the other hand, Mary is the chief personage in the whole account of the Saviour's conception and birth. Joseph is brought in only incidentally and because he was Mary's husband. In all of this there is a deep significance.

2. In Matthew Jesus appears as the Messiah. In Luke He appears as 'the Son of Man,' our Brother and Redeemer, who belongs to the whole race and claims kindred with all kinds and conditions of men. So in Matthew the genealogy descends from Abraham to Joseph

and Jesus, because all the predictions and promises touching the Messiah are fulfilled in Him. But in Luke the genealogy ascends from Jesus to Adam, because the genealogy is being traced back to the head of the whole race and shows the relation of the second [last] Adam to the first.

3. Joseph's line in Matthew is the strictly royal line from David to Joseph. In Luke, though the line of descent is from David, it is not the royal line. In this Jesus is descended from David through Nathan, David's son indeed, but not in the royal line, and the list follows a line quite distinct from the royal line.

4. The Messiah, according to prediction, was to be the actual son of David according to the flesh (2 Samuel 7:12-19; Psalm 89:3-4, 34-37; 132:11; Acts 2:30; 13:22-23; Romans 1:3; 2 Timothy 2:8). These prophecies are fulfilled by Jesus being the son of Mary, who was a lineal descendant of David, though not in the royal line. Joseph, who was of the royal line, was not His father according to the flesh, but was His father in the eyes of the law.

5. Mary was a descendant of David through her father, Heli. It is true that Luke 3:23 says that Joseph was the son of Heli. The simple explanation of this is that Mary being a woman, her name according to Jewish usage, could not appear in the genealogy, males alone forming the line, so Joseph's name is introduced in the place of Mary's, he being Mary's husband. Heli was his father-in-law, and so Joseph is called the son of Heli, and the line thus completed. While Joseph was son-in-law of Heli, according to the flesh he was in actual fact the son of Jacob (Matthew 1:16).

6. Two genealogies are absolutely necessary to trace the lineage of our Lord and Saviour Jesus Christ, the one the royal and legal, the other the natural and literal; and these two genealogies we find— the legal and royal in Matthew's Gospel, the Gospel of law and kingship; the natural and literal in Luke's, the Gospel of humanity.

7. We are told in Jeremiah 22:30 that any descendant of Jeconiah could not come to the throne of David. Joseph was of this line, and while Joseph's genealogy furnishes the royal line for Jesus, his son before the law, nevertheless Jeremiah's prediction is fulfilled to the very letter, for Jesus (strictly speaking) was not Joseph's descendant and therefore was not of the seed of Jeconiah. If Jesus had been the son of Joseph in reality, He could not have come to the throne, but He is Mary's son through Nathan and can come to the throne legally by her marrying Joseph and so clearing His way legally to it.

As we study these two genealogies of Jesus carefully and read them in the light of Old Testament prediction, we find that so far from constituting a reason for doubting the accuracy of the Bible they are rather a confirmation of the minutest accuracy of that Book. It is amazing how one part of the Bible fits into another part when we study it thus minutely. We need no longer stumble over the fact of two genealogies, but discover and rejoice in the deep meaning of the fact."[77]

Jesus was born of a Jewish mother, lived the life of a Jew under the law of Moses, died a Jew, is coming again to sit upon the Throne of "His Father David" who was a Jew, and rule over *Israel* as *King of the Jews* ("ruler in Israel") according to the prophecy.

It must be understood that Jesus was *The Universal Man* as intimated in His genealogy. There were other than Semitic strains (Tamar and Rachab or Rahab, Canaanites; Ruth, a *Moabitess*, etc.). The Jewish people then, are not *exclusively* of one racial strain. However, Jesus was a descendant of that nation that came from Abraham, Isaac, Jacob (Israel) Judah and David, who were known in the Bible as *Hebrews, Israelites,* or *Jews.*

Note: Ruth the Moabitess originated from what we today term as an act of incest. The word Moab means *mai-av* (from *father*). The father referred to is Lot who, given wine to drink, sleeps with both his daughters for they wanted to preserve or propagate the race (Genesis 19:33-37). This incident occurred *before* the Law was given which prohibited such an act. In contrast, *after* the law of Moses had been given, the Messiah was conceived in an act of immaculate conception, a supernatural spirit descending from above (Matthew 1:18, Luke 1:34-35).

---

[77]R.A. Torrey, *Difficulties in the Bible,* pp. 98-100.

MESSIAH'S TWO GENEALOGIES
Chart designed by Ruth Specter Lascelle

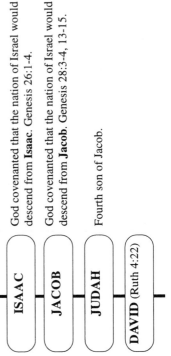

GOD	
ADAM	The first Father of the **Human Family**. Genesis 2:7, 19.
NOAH	The second Father of the **Human Family**. Genesis 5:32.
SHEM	Son of Noah, Father of the **Semitic Division of the Human Family**.
ABRAHAM	God covenanted that the nation of Israel would descend from **Abraham**. Genesis 12:1-3.
ISAAC	God covenanted that the nation of Israel would descend from **Isaac**. Genesis 26:1-4.
JACOB	God covenanted that the nation of Israel would descend from **Jacob**. Genesis 28:3-4, 13-15.
JUDAH	Fourth son of Jacob.
DAVID (Ruth 4:22)	

1. The Messiah would come in the **HUMAN FAMILY LINE OF ADAM**. Genesis 3:15.

2. The Messiah would come from the **RACE LINE OF SHEM**. Genesis 9:27 - (God shall dwell in the tents of *Shem*.)

3. The Messiah would come from the **PATRIARCH LINE OF ABRAM**. Genesis 12:1-3; Genesis 18:18.

4. The Messiah would come from the **TRUE HEIR LINE OF ISAAC**. Genesis 15:4; 17:19-21; 21:12; 26:4.

5. The Messiah would come in the **NATIONAL LINE OF JACOB**. Genesis 28:3-4, 13-15.

6. The Messiah would come from the **TRIBE LINE OF JUDAH**. Genesis 49:10.

7. The Messiah would come from the **KINGLY LINE OF DAVID**. 2 Samuel 7:12-15; Psalms 89:3-4; 132:11.

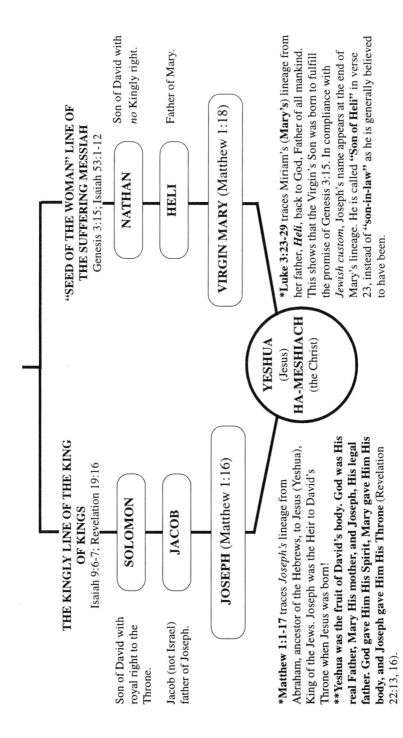

THE KINGLY LINE OF THE KING OF KINGS

Isaiah 9:6-7; Revelation 19:16

SOLOMON

Son of David with royal right to the Throne.

JACOB

Jacob (not Israel) father of Joseph.

JOSEPH (Matthew 1:16)

"SEED OF THE WOMAN" LINE OF THE SUFFERING MESSIAH

Genesis 3:15; Isaiah 53:1-12

NATHAN

Son of David with *no* Kingly right.

HELI

Father of Mary.

VIRGIN MARY (Matthew 1:18)

YESHUA (Jesus) **HA-MESHIACH** (the Christ)

*Matthew 1:1-17 traces *Joseph's* lineage from Abraham, ancestor of the Hebrews, to Jesus (Yeshua), King of the Jews. Joseph was the Heir to David's Throne when Jesus was born!

Yeshua was the fruit of David's body. God was His real Father, Mary His mother, and Joseph, His legal father. God gave Him His Spirit, Mary gave Him His body, and Joseph gave Him His Throne (Revelation 22:13, 16).

*Luke 3:23-29 traces Miriam's (Mary's) lineage from her father, *Heli*, back to God, Father of all mankind. This shows that the Virgin's Son was born to fulfill the promise of Genesis 3:15. In compliance with *Jewish custom*, Joseph's name appears at the end of Mary's lineage. He is called **"Son of Heli"** in verse 23, instead of **"son-in-law"** as he is generally believed to have been.

SCRIPTURAL PROOF JESUS WAS A JEW

1. In prophecy Messiah was to be a Jew like unto Moses from among Moses' people, his brethren: **Deuteronomy 18:18**. Moses was a descendant of Jacob, the Jew. (Jacob was the father of Levi. Levi was the father of Kohath, Kohath, the father of Amram, Amram, the father of Moses.) Jesus is compared to Moses in Hebrews 3.

2. The brothers of Jesus, according to the *flesh*, were Jews (**Romans 9:4-5**, first see 3rd verse).

3. *Isaiah 9:6*, "Unto US (the Jews) a child is BORN."

4. To be a son (descendant) of *Jewish* King David "Stem of Jesse") *Isaiah 11:1* with *Luke 1:68-69*). Jesus was called "Son of David" (*Matthew 1:1*) in His genealogy.

5. He was to be of the Tribe of Judah. (*Genesis 49:10* cf. *Hebrews 7:14*). All Israel was reckoned by genealogy (*1 Chronicles 9:1*).

6. He was born of **The Jewish** virgin—"Ha-almah," "*the* virgin." *Isaiah 7:14* Mary (Miriam), a *Jewess*. Messiah was to be "made of a woman"—not made of a woman *and* a man). *Galatians 4:4* (with *Jeremiah 31:22*). The virgin birth was prophesied in *Genesis 3:15*. "Her" *seed*. Seed always is of the man, but here, *seed* of a *woman*!

6. To be born in the *Jewish* City of David. *Micah 5:2* (Hebrew text is Micah 5:1), *Luke 2:11*.

7. Messiah was made under subjection to the OT Law: *Galatians 4:4*—"made under the law."

THE LAW OF MOSES

1. A Jewish son was to be redeemed by a lamb substitute: *Exodus 13:13*. It is called *Pidyon Haben* or "Redemption of the (firstborn) Son." It was to remind Israel of that first redemption when they were slaves in Egypt and God commanded this was to be done. Jewish people still celebrate "Pidyon Haben" (see Chapter 2, "Jewish Customs and Ceremonies"). Mary and Joseph observed this ceremony for Jesus. *Luke 2:22-23*.

2. The Covenant of Circumcision (*Brit Milah*) is a ceremony 4,000 years old and still in force today among Jews. This "Brit Milah" ceremony was commanded by God for the Jewish people in *Genesis 17:9-14* and in *Leviticus 12:3*. This was carried out for Jesus as we read in *Luke 2:21* and He was given a name at the time of His circumcision.

3. The Jewish mother was to be purified after the birth of her child (Leviticus 12:6-8) to remind of original sin. At the time of her purification she was to offer a sacrifice, either a lamb, a young pigeon or a turtle dove (Luke 2:22, 24). Mary, the mother of Jesus was too poor to bring a lamb so, according to *Leviticus 5:7*, she brought two young pigeons. But in reality she brought the *true* Lamb!

JESUS AND THE LAW

1. He knew the Law.
2. He taught the Law in the synagogues.
3. He was respected as a teacher of the Law. *Matthew 23*.

Symbol of the "Law of Moses"

4. He was given the honor to read from Isaiah in the synagogue. If He was *mamzer* (illegitimate) as some claimed, He would not be allowed this honor.

(See Deuteronomy 23:2 and Zechariah 9:6.) Only a *Jew* would have been asked to read in the synagogue. Only those of learning and note would be permitted to do so. Jesus was a Teacher of the Law and was recognized as such. He was called "Rabbi" (John 1:38), or "teacher" by use of the Greek word, *didaskale* or "Master."

5. He said He did not come to destroy the Law. *Matthew 5:17-20.*

6. Messiah Jesus observed the Law perfectly. He was made under authority of the Law as a *Jew*. *Galatians 4:4*.

7. He recited the *shema* in reply to the question:
"What is the first commandment"? *Mark 12:28-29*

8. Messiah Jesus followed the Jewish religion. He instructed His followers to "listen to their teachers." He respected the teachers of the Law and said of them: "They teach with authority as successors to Moses," "they sit in Moses' seat." *Matthew 23:2*

9. Messiah favored the Law of Moses so highly that He reprimanded the Jews for not properly keeping it. *John 7:19*

The modern Rabbis make *teaching* their work more than preaching. So also did Jesus, the Rabbi of Rabbis! His teaching occurred more times than did His preaching.

JESUS AND TZITZIT (Fringes)

The commandment to the Jewish people (men) to wear fringes in the corners of their garments was observed by Messiah Jesus. (The commandment: Numbers 15:38-41; Deuteronomy 22:12, fringes and ribbon of blue with Matthew 9:20; Luke 8:44.) Matthew 9:20; 14:36; 23:5 suggests that the "border" of the garment were the traditional "tzitzit" prescribed by the Law. And since Jesus was made under the authority of the law He would observe this commandment. According to Edersheim Jesus wore the fringes[78] (*tzitzit*) in the borders of His garments.

---

[78]Alfred Edersheim, *Life and Times of Jesus the Messiah, Vol. I*, p. 409.

Jesus rebuked the religious Jews, not for wearing the garment with *the fringes*, but for *enlarging the borders* (which held the fringes) to be seen of men. Jewish teachers of the Law all wore a seamless garment. This was prophesied of the Messiah in Psalm 22:18. It was fulfilled in Matthew 27:35; John 19:23-24.

JESUS, THE JEW

The Samaritan woman recognized and called Him a Jew (John 4:9). Jesus classed Himself with the Jews when He said of Himself and His people: "*We* know what *we* worship." And "Salvation is of the *Jews*" (John 4:22). The Greek text of John 4:22 is literally: "*The salvation is out from the Jews.*" In other words He said: He, Himself, who is *Salvation*, comes out from the Jews, that is, *He is a Jew* and *He brings salvation to all peoples*! Jesus made it clear to the Samaritan woman who had no dealings with the Jews, and vice versa, that **salvation** comes from the Jews and this **Salvation is Jesus!** Our redemption is inseparably tied up with the *Jews*! Simeon held the baby Jesus in his arms and called Him by that name: "*Salvation*" (Luke 2:30). (The Hebrew for "Jesus" is "Yeshua" and it is translated many times in the Hebrew Scriptures as "Salvation".) *Salvation* (*Yeshua*–Jesus) is connected with the fact that in the flesh, **He was a Jew**!

TO BE BORN IN BETHLEHEM

Micah indicates the birthplace of the Messiah of Israel as Bethlehem Ephratah, which was about six Roman miles southwest of Jerusalem and was also the birthplace of David. There were two cities by the name of Bethlehem, so this one in Judah is distinguished by the added name from the Bethlehem which belonged to the tribe of Zebulun (Joshua 19:15-16). The word *Bethlehem* means *House of Bread* and *Ephratah* comes from the root meaning *fruitful*, thus both names refer to the fertility of the region.

Ah yes! The Messiah is that *Bread* that came down out of Heaven, who was born in *The House of Bread* and is *The Fruitful One* as it was prophesied.

What an insignificant little town was Bethlehem. At all times it was "among the least" in Judah, so small that the Rabbis do not even refer to it in detail. It is not mentioned among the cities of Judah in Joshua 15, nor is it in the list of cities of Nehemiah 11. Yet this city is known the world over, has inspired men and women to compose poetry

---

[79]Sketch designed by Ruth Specter Lascelle.

and music, given artists a majestic picture to paint, provided material for many books, thrilled the hearts of millions through centuries, and has brought the one bright hope into a dark and dying world. Why? Because God said of this city through the prophet:

> *"But thou, Bethlehem Ephratah, though thou be little among the thousands of Judah, yet out of thee shall **he** come forth unto me that is to be **ruler in Israel**; whose goings forth have been from of old, from everlasting"* (Micah 5:2, Hebrew text is 5:1).

In this poor, obscure town One was to be born who could take the foolish things of this world and confound the wise, who by His coming could transform the unlovely into a thing of beauty, who could by His very presence compel the learned to bow in humility before Him, and kings to lay their authority at His feet!

Though He was to be *Ruler* (or King) in Israel, the Messiah was meek and lowly in heart. His birth did not take place in a royal palace nor was it in Rome, the greatest city of the then-known world. God chose for His birthplace, a stable in the smallest town in Judah. But when the Saviour was born there, this unnoticed city became important; an unlovely town was transformed, and the "least" became the "greatest."

Today, the Messiah Yeshua is still searching for a place in the heart of the insignificant, the unlovely, the "least" of all the people. He desires to take up His abode there within such hearts. And when the great Transformer does enter the human heart, He will (in a sense) do with that useless, worthless life as He did with the little town in which He was born!

Bethlehem, "the House of Bread," the City of David, is important, beautiful and famous because it was the birthplace of a King 2,000 years ago. We who have opened the door of our hearts to Him and allowed Him room to be born there (though poor and unworthy as we are) can rejoice, for we realize that God in His love, has spoken and fulfilled His promise to us concerning our individual lives: *"But thou ... though thou be little ... out of thee shall He come forth ... that shall be ruler ... whose goings forth have been from of old from everlasting."*

According to the prophet Micah, the Messiah was to be born in the city of Bethlehem and was to be King (ruler) of the Jews. *"Whose goings forth have been from of old from **everlasting**"* indicates He was to have existed before He came to earth in a human body. In Psalm 72:17 the Messiah's *"name shall be continued as long as the sun."* In Hebrew it reads: "Liphneh Shemesh Yinon Sh'moh," meaning literally, *"Before the sun was his name Yinon."* The Targum renders this passage: "Before the sun had been created His Name had been prepared and all nations will be blessed in His merits." This is the only occurrence in Scripture of the word *Yinon* and all ancient commentators agree it is a name of Messiah (see Proverbs 8:22-24).

Also from this passage on *Yinon* the word "Shiloh" comes, to which many Jewish scholars admit as referring to Messiah. (*Sanhed.* 98b, also *Onkelos*, and the two Jerusalem Targums, etc.) Compare also Ezekiel 21:26-27 with Genesis 49:10. Perhaps a better translation of *Shiloh* might be *Sheloi*. It was a custom of the ancient fathers in Israel to explain words in acrostic form after their initial letters. The letters of the word "Shiloh" (rather "Sheloi") lend themselves (in Hebrew) to mean: *"His Name shall be continued as long as the sun."*

The fulfillment of Messiah's birthplace is found in the New Testament. Herod demanded where he could find the King of the Jews.

> *"And they said unto him, In **Bethlehem** of Judaea: for thus it is written by the prophet, And thou **Bethlehem**, in the land of Juda, art not the least among the princes of Juda: for out of thee shall come a Governor, that shall rule my people Israel"* (Matthew 2:5-6).

According to the prophecy, Messiah was to be born in the city of David, but the two persons whom God intended to play the leading role and to use in His great redemption were in the town of Nazareth! However, the Lord God Almighty caused a heathen Emperor to issue an order that would compel Joseph and Mary to register in Bethlehem! (Luke 2:1-3).

The prophecy declared that the virgin-born Son of God was to "come forth" from Bethlehem, and so it was, but what *part* of Bethlehem? The Bible intimates that the place of His birth would be "The Tower of the Flock." This village is located on the *northern fringe* of Bethlehem and about three miles south of Jerusalem. Where do we find this prophecy? In the words of the prophet Micah:

> *"And thou, **O tower of the flock**, the strong hold of the daughter of Zion [the Jews], unto thee shall it come, even the **first dominion**; the **kingdom** shall come to the daughter of Jerusalem"* (Micah 4:8).

TOWER OF THE FLOCK

What is "the first dominion" and "the kingdom?" It can be none other than the King of the Jews ("*Ruler* in Israel"–Micah 5:2, 5:1, Hebrew text) who will come to "the daughter of Jerusalem" (Israel)." Where will this Messiah come from? *The Tower of the flock* !

> "It would be natural for Joseph, unable to find room in the inn and with Mary ready to give birth, to retrace his steps to the stable at *Migdal Edar* which he had doubtless passed a short while before

on entering Bethlehem. Benjamin, son of Jacob, had been born there. It would serve for the birthplace of the Son of God.

Migdal Edar literally means *tower of the flock*. It was the place in ancient Israel where *sheep were raised for ceremonial slaughter* at the nearby Temple. These shepherds, who raised lambs for sacrifice, doubtless lived in expectation of the day when God's Lamb would appear. And what better place for Jesus to be born than at the very spot where lambs were raised for sacrifice? Was He not, in truth, "*... the Lamb of God, who taketh away the sin of the world*" (John 1:29)? He would be born where lambs were born and die where lambs died.

Migdal Edar, *Tower of the Flock* Near Bethlehem

—Marv Rosenthal in *Israel My Glory* magazine

TO BE THE SON OF GOD

*"Who has established all the ends of the earth? What is his name, and what is **his son's name**, if you know?"* (Proverbs 30:4, Isaac Leeser's translation).

*"Do homage to the **son** lest he be angry and ye be lost on the way; for his wrath is speedily kindled. Happy are all they who put their trust in him"* (Psalm 2:12, Isaac Leeser's translation).

The disciples of Jesus, who were Jews, accepted Christ as the Son of God. He was proclaimed to be the Son of God by the angels at His birth. He was acknowledged to be the Son of God even by devils (Matthew 8:28). God declared Christ to be His Son, saying: *"This is my **beloved** son, hear him"* (Mark 9:7). "Beloved" is also the meaning of the name, ***David***. Does this imply here that God was declaring: "This is my son *David*, hear Him!"?

God gave a promise to David:

"And when thy days be fulfilled, and thou shalt sleep with thy fathers, I will set up thy seed after thee, which shall proceed out of thy bowels [loins], *... and I will stablish the throne of his kingdom **for ever**. I will be his father, and he shall be my **son**. ..."* (2 Samuel 7:12, 17).

The declaration "my son," cannot refer exclusively to Solomon, for two reasons. First, we do not find anywhere in the Scriptures that Solomon is called God's Son. Second, the definite expression *forever* which is used in connection with that Son's Kingdom, does not apply to any of the Kings of Israel for they have passed from the scene long ago. But, evidently, without a doubt, it is a prophecy referring to the *seed of David,* the promised Messiah, and of Him God says, *"He will be **my son**."*

GOD IN HUMAN FORM

*"And Jacob was left alone; and there wrestled a **man** with him until the breaking of the day. And he said, Let me go, for the day breaketh. And he said, I will not let thee go, except thou bless me. And he [the man] said unto him [Jacob], What is thy name? And he said, Jacob. And he [the man] said, Thy name shall be called no more Jacob, but Israel: for as a prince hast thou power with God and with men, and hast prevailed"* (Genesis 32:24, 26-28).

Here we see that Jacob wrestled with a **man**. But in verse 28, we are informed that he wrestled with none other than **God**! Then, to commemorate this wonderful experience, Jacob called this place *Peniel* ("face of God"), *"For, I have **seen God face to face**, and my life is preserved"* (Genesis 32:30). Jacob recognized the fact that this "man" with whom he wrestled was God Himself!

Most Jewish people cringe at the mention of the fact that one can see God and live. Yet in the foregoing Scripture we learned that this was the experience of Jacob. Also Moses, the great Lawgiver of the Jews relates a similar instance in his own life and others:

*"Then went up Moses, and Aaron, Nadab, and Abihu, and seventy of the elders of Israel: And they saw the God of Israel: and there was under his feet as it were a paved work of a sapphire stone, and as it were the body of heaven in his clearness. And upon the nobles of the children of Israel he laid not his hand: also **they saw God**, and did eat and drink"* (Exodus 24:9-11).

In these verses Moses declared that he, Aaron, Nadab, Abihu, seventy elders, and the children of Israel saw the God of Israel. After seeing Him they were able to eat and drink, which testifies to the fact that though they had seen God they were still alive.

Here I feel that a definition of the two names "Jacob and Israel" by a Hebrew teacher would be helpful:

"Jacob (יעקב) was so called because he was born clutching the heel (עקב) of Esau, which our Sages, interpret as a sign that in time to come, after Esau will have been brought to *heel*, Israel will reign as opposed to an elevated state. The ordinariness flows from the [Hebrew] letters ע ק ב (heel), a relatively insignificant part of the body. But even in this lowly, mundane state when Jews are involved in secular affairs, G-d's presence, represented by the letter ' י ' is evident" (*Lekutei Torah* on Numbers 24:5). It is interesting, to note in passing, that the Jew is, in many languages, referred to by the letter ' י '–thus *Jude, Jood*.

"The name 'Israel' was bestowed upon Jacob after he had fought with the angel: [God] [Genesis 32:29] ('for you have striven with angels and with men and have prevailed') The name ישראל is thus derived from שׂרה, meaning 'ruling' or 'being superior.' It also contains the letters ראשׁ 'head,' a significant part of the body. "ישׂראל" can also be analyzed into שׁיר קל [shir kol], a song to G-d, which sums up the role of Israel as being to serve G-d, to sing praises to Him, as it is written: ... ("The people which I formed for Myself, that they might sing my praise") [Isaiah 43:21]."[80]

We notice that "the Angel of the Lord," who is God, appeared frequently in the Old Testament times *as a man*. That being the case, it should not be difficult for a Jew who has studied his own Jewish Scriptures, to believe that the Messiah was none other than God manifested in the flesh! God had promised Israel:

> *"Behold, I will send **my messenger**, and he shall prepare the way before **me**: and the Lord, whom ye seek, shall suddenly **come to his temple**, even the messenger of the covenant, whom ye delight in: behold, **he shall come**, saith the LORD of hosts"* (Malachi 3:1).

The Messiah is called "Lord" in this prophecy. Note also that He is called "The Messenger of the Covenant." The term "messenger" in the Hebrew text is *Malach* which is the common word for "angel." (The term: "The Angel of the Lord" is used 41 times in the Hebrew Scriptures. One example, Genesis 16:7-13.) By this we learn that the Messiah is *The Angel* who is none other than God Himself. He is the Angel who "saves" and "redeems," spoken of in Isaiah 63:9. The Angel is the Messiah who came to save and redeem. He is "The Messenger of the Covenant," (the New Covenant), prophesied and promised by God in Jeremiah 31:31-32.

Why must God appear as a *man*? Because sin required the death penalty. Man, who is a sinner, could not redeem himself. God, in His own Person, must be a Substitute to pay the ransom price in man's place. But God alone could not die; He lives "forever and forever" (Psalm 90:2). Therefore, the Redeemer of mankind must become man in order that He could be made sin and *die* (see Hebrews 2:9; 1 Peter 1:18-19). The Redeemer could not be *only* man either for if He was He would have been involved in sin Himself through Adam (Romans 5:12). Also, if He was only man, there would be no sacrifice that would be appropriate for *all* humanity. In order then, to meet all the requirements in the case, there had to be a *God-Man,* to meet both man's need and God's requirements of a Savior.

---

[80]Rabbi M. Glazerson, *Sparks of the Holy Tongue*, pp. 38-39.

TO BE BORN OF A (THE) VIRGIN

"Therefore the Lord himself shall give you a sign; Behold, a virgin [ha-almah—the virgin] shall conceive, and bear a son, and shall call his name Immanuel" (Isaiah 7:14; see with Matthew 1:21).

In the context of this passage there is the law of double reference, for Isaiah 7:16 does not seem to "match" to a coming Messiah and Isaiah 8:3 seems to fulfill the prophecy. Isaiah 7:14 implies that there is coming a *type* of Immanuel in the near future as proof that God is with His people to deliver them. Yet it is also a prophecy in the more remote future of One to come who will be both God and man. He will deliver His people from human enemies as well as from sin and guilt (Matthew 1:22-23 refers to Isaiah 7:14).

God gave the Jews a miraculous sign by which they would know their Messiah even at His birth! Let us examine this prophecy closely. God told them He is going to give a *sign* (in Hebrew, *oth*). *Oth* also means "a wonder" "a miracle." In other words, it is plainly stated that God will perform a *supernatural act*! If the coming of the Messiah was by an ordinary birth, it would not be such a miracle!

The common objection to the virgin birth springs from a refusal to believe that God could or would upset the biological processes. In other words, we say no human being was ever born without a human father and mother. Yet Adam and Eve came into the world not through human channels, but by a Divine miracle of creation! Another miraculous birth occurred with Sarah, "who had ceased to be after the manner of women" in whom it was an utter physical impossibility to bring forth a child; yet of whom was born Isaac according to the promise of the Lord! The angel asked a question at the time of Abraham and Sarah's doubt which should satisfy anyone having difficulty with the fact of the virgin birth: *"Is **anything** too hard for the LORD?"* (Genesis 18:14).

This Child born of the virgin was to be called "Immanuel." Isaiah 7:14 declares it is *God* who gives this name. When, in the Scriptures, the *parents* give a name to their child, it is associated with their hopes and dreams for the child (also connected with circumstances at the time of birth), but when *God* is the One who gives a name it is actually the character of the person since God is the only one who knows all things. When God said that the virgin's child would be called *Immanuel*, He was prophesying concerning the Messiah's *actual* Person, His character and office, *who He really would be*! "Immanuel" means "God-With-Us," therefore God said of this One to be born of the virgin that actually He would be *God*; *i.e.*, the God-Man!

Messiah's name also was to be "Shiloh" (Genesis 49:10), also "Yenon" meaning "Continued" (Psalm 72:17), and "Jehovah

[*Yahweh*], Our Righteousness" (Jeremiah 23:6), yet when He was on earth He never was called these names. They were (as was *Immanuel*) names to tell of His character, who He was to be, and the purpose for His Being. Meaning of names and not just the giving of names is stressed in the Bible. The names "Immanuel" and "Yeshua" both imply Deity, the first meaning "God With Us" (His actual Person) and the second, "Jehovah Saves" or "Salvation" (His work of redemption)!

The article *the* virgin (not *a* virgin as it is erroneously translated into the English) points back to the prophecy in Genesis 3:15 when God spoke to the serpent:

> *"And I will put enmity between thee and the woman, and between thy seed and **her seed**; it shall bruise thy head, and thou shalt bruise his heel."*

Here "her" seed is in the singular number, meaning that One person born of the woman shall bruise the head of Satan and shall overcome him. Anyone able to overcome Satan must be stronger than Satan, that is: He must be stronger than a mere man. He must be God. This gives us the reason for the virgin birth. He could not be "God-with-us" if He had a human father. Thus we see that God Himself will come in the form of a man to be this Deliverer, this Redeemer!

ALMAH AND BETHULAH

These two words in the course of 30 centuries of their use, have undergone change in meaning so that today it would seem almost as though their definitions are reversed. The earliest use of *almah* in Scripture is found in Genesis 24:43. Rebecca is called an "almah." When she is referred to as *bethulah*, it is followed by the clause: *"and a man did not know her,"* implying that in other instances a "bethulah" may be a woman who is married, as in Joel 1:8, *"Lament like a virgin* [Bethulah]*, girded with sack-cloth over the husband of her youth."*

In various places in Scripture Israel is called by the name "Bethulah," a young woman, pictured as in a state of marriage in relation to God. Rashi,[81] the chief Jewish commentator in the Hebrew Bible whose pronouncements, to a pious Jew, are final, also renders "almah" in Isaiah 7:14 by "virgin." The same rendering of "virgin" in Isaiah 7:14 is given in the more recent translation of the Hebrew by Isaac Leeser.

The Hebrew word "almah" is taken from the root "alam," which means "to hide," "to conceal." There could hardly be a more fitting

---

[81]Rashi is the abbreviation of **R**abbi **S**olomon **Y**itschoki, 1040-1105, the most distinguished commentator on the Bible and the Talmud. Also see Rashi on Isaiah, p. 27, Warsaw Edition 1902.

basis for a word meaning "virgin." This implies a young woman untouched by a man. Women from the beginning had given birth to children from the union of the male sperm and the female cell; this was the *natural* process for life to be brought forth into the world and was not a miracle in the sense of Isaiah's prophecy. The wonder which God promised in the Messiah's birth would be entirely unheard of and an impossibility on the part of man to perform! A child was to be born of the *seed of the woman* instead of the seed of the man! This miraculous *sign* of the Messiah was prophesied 750 years before its fulfillment which is recorded in Matthew 1:18-23 and again in Luke 1:26-35.

It is a well-known biological fact that the seed comes from the *male*, not the female. Genealogy is always reckoned by the male line in the Holy Scriptures. But there is one exception. In promising the coming of a Redeemer, Moses foretold He was to be the *"seed of the woman"* (Genesis 3:15. See also Jeremiah 31:22). This is the *only time* in Scripture anywhere that a man is ever said to be the seed of the woman. The line runs through the male, not through the female. We are said to be the offspring of Adam. The Messiah alone stands apart from all as *The Seed of the Woman*, implying immediately that He would have no human father! For according to the Old Testament prophecies, the true Messiah must be a Jew and yet in a very special way the Son of God; that is, He must be Deity incarnate. To make this possible, Messiah must be supernaturally conceived by the Spirit of God and born of a Hebrew virgin, that He might be the promised "seed of the woman" (not of the man) and yet strong enough to bruise (crush) the head of Satan, the father of all sin, suffering, sorrow, death, and separation from God.

There are some who would have us believe that *almah* means *any* young woman, whether single or married; but how can it be a miracle for a *married* woman to conceive and have a child? Furthermore, when 70 Jewish scholars translated the Old Testament into Greek (called *Septuagint* or the Hebrew Title: *Targum Ha-Shibim* meaning *Translation of the Seventy*. One *Targum* is an Aramaic version of the Hebrew Scriptures) about 275 BC, they translated *almah* by using the Greek word *parthenos* which has only *one* meaning, that of "virgin," indicating that they understood the significance of the prophecy!

The word "almah" cannot mean a young married woman as some religious leaders and teachers say, for we find the same Hebrew word in the following Scriptures unmistakably referring to pure maidenhood:
1.   *"Behold, I stand by the well of water; and it shall come to pass, that when the virgin* [almah] *cometh forth to draw water,...."* (Genesis 24:43).

2. *"And Pharaoh's daughter said to her, Go. And the maid [almah] went and called the child's mother"* (Exodus 2:8).

3. *"The singers went before, the players on instruments followed after; among them were the* damsels *[alamoth—plural of almah] playing with timbrels"* (Psalm 68:25; Hebrew text is verse 26).

4. *"The way of an eagle in the air; the way of a serpent upon a rock; the way of a ship in the midst of the sea; and the way of a man with a maid* [almah]*"* (Proverbs 30:19).

5. *"Because of the savour of thy good ointments thy name is as ointment poured forth, therefore do the virgins* [alamoth—plural of almah] *love thee"* (Song of Solomon 1:3).

6. *"There are threescore queens, and fourscore concubines, and virgins* [alamoth—plural of almah] *without number"* (Song of Solomon 6:8. *Rashi* definitely describes "almah" as "virgin" in Song of Solomon 1:3 and 6:8).

The foregoing six references with Isaiah 7:14 are the *only* passages of Scripture where the words "almah" or "alamoth" are mentioned!

The Messiah was to come by human birth according to Isaiah the Jewish prophet who was moved upon by the Holy Spirit to write:

"For unto us a child is born, unto us a son is given: and the government shall be upon his shoulder: and his name shall be called Wonderful, [Miraculous/Miracle], Counsellor, The mighty God, The everlasting Father, The Prince of Peace" (Isaiah 9:6).

"The government shall be upon his shoulder." The prophecy God gave through Isaiah is: "the key of the house of David will I lay upon his shoulder; ..." (Isaiah 22:22). An ancient custom to confer the authority to rule was symbolized by a ceremony of laying the keys of a principal city upon the shoulder of its future King. By this act the king was inducted into his office.

The Hebrew text of Isaiah 9:5 reads:

"For unto us a child is born, unto us a son is given: and the government is upon his shoulder: and his name shall be called Wonderful Counsellor of the mighty God, of the everlasting Father, Prince of Peace"
—Translation by Alexander Harkavy,
Hebrew Publishing Company

Isaiah foretells that the "child born" to (Israel), is the *son* who is given (by God). He will have a name associated with His office of Governor (Ruler) in Israel. No child of mere human beings would be given such names as "Mighty God," "Father of Eternity," etc. "A child is born" tells of His humanity; "A son is given" tells of His Deity. Names of Deity are ascribed to this One who will be ***born*** of Israel!

TO BE PROPHET, PRIEST AND KING

God promised that Messiah would be a PROPHET

The Old Testament (*T'nakh*):

*"I will raise them up a **Prophet** from among their brethren, like unto thee [Moses], and will put my words in his mouth; and he shall speak unto them all that I shall command him. And it shall come to pass, that whosoever will not hearken unto my words which he shall speak in my name, I will require it of him"* (Deuteronomy 18:18-19).

The New Testament (*Brit Hadasha*):

*"And he shall **send** Jesus Christ, which before was preached unto you: For Moses truly said unto the fathers, A **prophet** shall the Lord your God raise up unto you of your brethren, like unto me [Moses]; him shall ye hear in all things whatsoever he shall say unto you. And it shall come to pass, that every soul, which will not hear **that prophet**, shall be destroyed from among the people"* (Acts 3:20, 22-23).

The Old Testament:

A prophet who proclaimed the Word of God must be anointed. The word "Messiah" means "anointed." The Old Testament (T'nakh) states in the words of the Messiah:

*"The spirit of the Lord GOD is upon me; because the LORD hath **anointed** me to **preach** good tidings unto the meek; he hath sent me to bind up the brokenhearted, to **proclaim** liberty to the captives, and the opening of the prison to them that are bound;"* (Isaiah 61:1).

The New Testament:

*"And Jesus returned in the power of the Spirit into Galilee: ... And he taught in their synagogues, ... and, as his custom was, he went into the synagogue on the sabbath day, and **stood up for to read**. ... he found the place where it was written, **The Spirit of the Lord is upon me**, ... And he closed the book, ... And he began to say unto them, **This day is this scripture fulfilled in your ears**"* (Luke 4:14-17, 19-21).

*"Then those men, when they had seen the miracle that Jesus did, said, This is of a truth **that prophet** that should come into the world"* (John 6:14).

God promised Messiah would be a PRIEST

The Old Testament:

*"And I will raise me up a **faithful priest**, that shall do according to that which is in mine heart and in my mind: and I will build him a **sure house**; and he shall walk before mine anointed **for ever**"* (1 Samuel 2:35).

*"The LORD hath sworn, and will not repent, Thou art a **priest for ever** after the order of Melchizedek"* (Psalm 110:4).

The New Testament:

*"Wherefore, holy brethren, ... consider the Apostle and High Priest of our profession, Christ Jesus; Who was **faithful** to him that appointed him, ... But Christ [was faithful] as a son over his **own house**; whose **house** are we, ..."* (Hebrews 3:1-2, 6).

*"And no man taketh this honour unto himself, but he that is **called of God**, as was Aaron. So also Christ glorified not himself to be made an **high priest**; but he that said unto him, Thou art my **Son**, to day have I begotten thee. As he saith also in another place, Thou art a **priest for ever** after the order of Melchisedec"* (Hebrews 5:4-6).

The Old Testament:

*"And take thou unto thee Aaron thy **brother**, ... from among the children of Israel, that he may minister unto me in the **priest's** office, ..."* (Exodus 28:1).

The New Testament:

*"Wherefore in **all things** it behoved him [Jesus] to be made like unto his **brethren**, that he might be a merciful and **faithful high priest** in things pertaining to God, to make reconciliation for the sins of the people"* (Hebrews 2:17).

God promised that Messiah would be a KING

The Old Testament:

*"Behold, the days come, saith the LORD, that I will raise unto **David** a righteous Branch, and a **King** shall reign and prosper, and shall execute judgment and justice in the earth. In his days Judah shall be saved, and Israel shall dwell safely: and this is his name whereby he shall be called, **THE LORD OUR RIGHTEOUSNESS**"* (Jeremiah 23:5-6).

*"But thou, Bethlehem Ephratah, though thou be little among the thousands of Judah, yet out of thee shall he come forth unto **me** that is to be **ruler** [King] **in Israel**; whose **goings forth** have been from of old, from **everlasting**"* (Micah 5:2-5:1, Hebrew text).

The New Testament:

"..., and shalt call his name JESUS [Yeshua or "Salvation"]. *He shall be great, and shall be called the **Son** of the Highest: and the Lord God shall give unto him the **throne** of his father **David**: And he shall reign over the **house of Jacob for ever**; and of his kingdom there shall be no end"* (Luke 1:31-33).

*"Now when Jesus was born in Bethlehem of Judaea in the days of Herod the king, behold, there came wise men from the east to Jerusalem, Saying, Where is he that is born **King of the Jews**? for we have seen his star in the east, and are come to worship him. ...* [Herod] *demanded of them* [the Jewish religious leaders] *where* **Christ** [Messiah] **should be born. And they said unto him, In Bethlehem of Judaea: for thus it is written by the prophet,"** (Matthew 2:1-2, 4-5).

Conclusion

In the first chapter of the Book of Hebrews, the first through the third verses, Messiah is referred to as *Prophet*, *Priest* and *King*:

*"God hath in these last days **spoken unto us by** [in] **his son.**"* This is Messiah, the ***PROPHET*** who not only speaks the Word of God but *is* the very Word of God in the flesh! (John 1:1, 14);

"When he [Messiah] *had by himself **purged** our sins ..."* This is Messiah, the High ***PRIEST*** offering Himself a Sacrifice for our sins;

*"... sat down on the right hand of the **Majesty** on high."* This is Messiah the **KING** who sat down on the Throne of God!

TO BE LIKE MOSES

"And the LORD said unto me [Moses], *... I will raise them* [Israel] *up a Prophet from among their brethren, like unto thee, and will put my words in his mouth; and he shall speak unto them* [Israel] *all that I shall command him. And it shall come to pass, that whosoever will not hearken unto my words which he shall speak in my name, I will require it of him"* (Deuteronomy 18:17-19).

Moses, of all prophets, is considered by Jews as the greatest, and even today in the religious vocabulary of the children and adults, Moses' name is mentioned more often than any other person. He led the children of Israel out of bondage into the promised land. And Israel's Messiah was to lead His people out of bondage to sin into the freedom of the Kingdom of God. In promising that the Messiah was to be like *Moses*, God added His judgment for those who would not receive Him.

"Messiah" means "Anointed" in Hebrew, and in the Greek this same translation is true of the name "Christ." He was "anointed" to be a ***prophet like Moses***. (God made His *ways* known to *Moses*, His *acts* to the Children of Israel, Psalm 103:7.) The following prophetic statements and historic incidents have dovetailed into the lives of both Moses and Christ. This surely could not come either by chance or fraud:

Each born at a time when Israel was under the rule of a Gentile King.
Moses, Exodus 1:8-10. **Christ**, Luke 2:1-3.
Placed by their mothers in very unusual baby beds.
Moses, Exodus 2:3. **Christ**, Luke 2:7.
Strangely saved from death when the king sought the lives of Hebrew infants.
Moses, Exodus 1:22;2:1-2. **Christ**, Matthew 2:13, 16.
Rescued in childhood.
Moses, Exodus 2:2-10. **Christ**, Matthew 2:14-15.
Reared by daughters of a kingly line.
Moses, Exodus 2:5-8. **Christ**, Luke 1:30-33.
Brought up in the homes of men who were not their fathers.
Moses, Exodus 2:9-10. **Christ**, Matthew 1:18-25 and Acts 7:21-22.
Fled the land of their birth because of the wrath of the king. **Moses**, Exodus 2:15. **Christ**, Matthew 2:13.
Returned to the land of their birth and performed many and mighty miracles there.
Moses, Exodus 4:19-21 and Deuteronomy 29:2-3. **Christ**, Matthew 2:19-20 and Matthew 4:23-24.
Contended with evil masters.
Moses, Exodus 7:11. **Christ**, Matthew 4:11.
Criticized and spoken against by their kinsmen.
Moses, Numbers 11:16-17. **Christ**, John 7:3-5.
Both had 70 helpers.
Moses, Numbers 11:16-17. **Christ**, Luke 10:1.
Appointed 12 men and sent them on special missions.
Moses, Numbers 13:1-2, 17, 21, 25. **Christ**, Matthew 10:1, 5-8.
In spite of their greatness and position, both were men of deep humility and meekness.

Moses, Numbers 12:3. **Christ**, Matthew 11:28-30.

Both discredited.

Moses, Numbers 12:1-2. **Christ**, Luke 17:12-19.

Both fasted 40 days.

Moses, Exodus 34:28. **Christ**, Matthew 4:2.

Both able to heal the worst disease known to men, viz., leprosy. **Moses**, Numbers 12:9-14. **Christ**, Luke 17:12-19.

Both controlled the sea.

Moses, Exodus 14:21. **Christ**, Matthew 8:26.

Provided a cure for the serpent's bite.

Moses, Numbers 21:8-9. **Christ**, John 3:14-15; I Peter 2:24.

Both made intercessory prayers.

Moses, Exodus 32:32. **Christ**, John 17:9.

Both endured murmuring.

Moses, Exodus 15:24. **Christ**, Mark 7:2.

Both provided deliverance for the nation of Israel through the shedding of blood.

Moses, Exodus 12:3,7,12-13. **Christ**, Hebrews 9:11-15.

Both spoke as oracles.

Moses, Deuteronomy 18:18. **Christ**, John 8:26; 12:49.

Both fed multitudes.

Moses, Exodus 16:15. **Christ**, Matthew 14:19-21.

Volunteered to die for their people. Moses was not permitted to die; Messiah was obliged to die.

Moses, Exodus 32:31-34. **Christ**, John 10:11,17,18; Romans 5:8,10,11.

Both had radiant faces.

Moses, Exodus 34:32-35. **Christ**, Matthew 17:1-3.

Both died in a manner previously determined by God.

Moses, Deuteronomy 34:5-6. **Christ**, Psalm 22:16; I Corinthians 15:3-4.

Both established Memorials.

Moses, Exodus 12:13. **Christ**, Luke 22:19.

Both reappeared after death.

Moses, Matthew 17:3. **Christ**, Acts 1:3; I John 5:1.

Both divinely chosen deliverers.

Moses, Exodus 3:7-10. **Christ**, Acts 7:25; John 3:16.

Rejected by Israel, both turn to the Gentiles.

Moses, Exodus 2:11-16. **Christ**, Acts 7:25; 18:5-6; 28:17-28.

During rejection, both gain a Gentile bride.

Moses, Exodus 2:16-21. **Christ**, Matthew 12:14-21; II Corinthians 11:2; Ephesians 5:30-32.

When they return to appear to Israel, both accepted.

Moses, Exodus 4:29-31. **Christ**, Romans 11:24-26; Acts 15:14-17.

TO ENTER JERUSALEM HUMBLY

"Rejoice greatly, O daughter of Zion; shout, O daughter of Jerusalem: behold, thy King cometh unto thee: he is just, and having salvation; lowly, and riding upon an ass [donkey], *and upon a colt the foal of an ass* [donkey]*"* (Zechariah 9:9). [This is the way it is written in the Talmud: "Poor and riding upon a donkey in Zechariah 9:9 refers to the Messiah." *Bereshith R.* 56 and 75.]

It was the custom since the first king of Israel for the appointed king to ride upon a donkey into the city (see 1 Kings 1:33, 35, 38). Soon after the year AD 32 or thereabouts, Jesus literally fulfilled the prophecy of Zechariah by riding up to the city of Jerusalem on the colt of an ass (donkey). (Genesis 49:10-11 shows that Jacob knew of this peculiar Messianic sign.) The New Testament account of that ride refers to the prophecy in Zechariah 9:9. *"All this was done, that it might be fulfilled which was spoken by the prophet ..."* (Matthew 21:4).

JERUSALEM IN THE LIFE OF MESSIAH

Luke 2:21. Circumcised in the Temple.
Luke 2:46. In the Temple talking to religious leaders.
Matthew 23:37-38. Predicts destruction of Jerusalem.
Luke 9:51. He suffers in Jerusalem.

Matthew 21:1-9. Acclaimed King at His entrance.
Matthew 26:47-56. Arrested.
Matthew 27:26. Condemned.
Matthew 27:35. Crucified.
Matthew 28:1-15. Risen
Mark. 16:19. Ascended to heaven.
Acts 1:11. Coming Again.
Luke 21:24. Predicts oppression of Jerusalem.
Zechariah 9:9. Jerusalem to be the City of the Savior.
Zechariah 12:3. Jerusalem to be a source of contention.
Isaiah 65:18-19. Jerusalem to be redeemed.
The New Jerusalem Revelation 21:2-5, 23-24.

TO BE DESPISED AND REJECTED OF MEN

"He is despised and rejected of men; a man of sorrows, and acquainted with grief: and we hid as it were our faces from him; he was despised, and we esteemed him not" (Isaiah 53:3).

Charles Hadden Spurgeon, prince of preachers, wrote:

"'A man of sorrows'– the expression is intended to be very emphatic, it is not 'a sorrowful man,' but 'a man of sorrows,' as if He were made up of sorrows, and they were constituent elements of His being. Some are men of pleasure, others men of wealth, but He was a 'man of sorrows.'

Our Lord is called 'a man of sorrows' for peculiarity, for this was His peculiar token and special mark. We might call Him 'a man of holiness'; for there was no fault in Him: or a 'man of labours,' for He did His Father's business earnestly; or 'a man of eloquence,' for never man spake like this man. Yet had we gazed upon Christ and been asked afterwards what was the most striking peculiarity in Him, we should have said: His sorrows. Tears were His insignia, and the cross His escutcheon. He was the warrior in black armor; He was the lord of grief, the prince of pain, the emperor of anguish. Born in a stable, sorrow received Him, and only on the cross at His last breath did sorrow part with Him. His disciples might forsake Him; but His sorrows would not leave Him. He was often alone without a man, but never alone without a grief."

He was called Jesus of *Nazareth*. Every indication seems to point to the conclusion that the Hebrew word for Nazareth here is *Netzer* meaning *Branch* or a *Bush* (see Isaiah 11:1 and Isaiah 53:2). Nazareth then, is a "town of bushes," a name of contempt in contrast to a "city of trees" or the "cedars of Lebanon." *Notzri* or *Nazarene* is descriptive of the *lowliness* of the Messiah, a theme frequently elaborated upon in the pages of prophecy.

See Matthew 2:23. The word *Nazareth* is taken from *netzer* found in the text quoted from Isaiah 11:1. Different from *Nazarene* is

"Nazarite" from the word "nazir," "a consecrated one," "a devotee." ("Nazirah"—female *Nazir*). Rashi says of the word, *Nazir*: "keeping away from something (to God)." One could be a *Nazir* or "separated one" without taking the vow of a Nazirite as in Numbers 6. Messiah was a true *Nazir* or "consecrated one." He needed not to take the vow for His life was already consecrated to God. There are present-day Nazirs in Israel, both men and women (Nazirah). A section of the Talmud, the treatise "Nazir," is devoted to Nazirite vows.

TO BE BETRAYED

"For it was not an enemy that reproached me; then I could have borne it: ... But it was thou, a man mine equal, my guide, and mine acquaintance. We took sweet counsel together, and walked unto the house of God in company" (Psalm 55:12-14).

*"And one shall say unto him, What are these wounds in thine hands? Then he shall answer, Those with which I was wounded in the house of **my friends**"* (Zechariah 13:6).

"Yea, mine own familiar friend, in whom I trusted, which did eat of my bread, hath lifted up his heel against me" (Psalm 41:9).

The most unpredictable thing in the entire story of Jesus was that He would be sold to His enemies by one of His choice followers, yet Zechariah was bold enough to make this prediction, and the records reveal that it was done just as the prophet foretold:

*"And forthwith he [Judas] came to Jesus, and said, Hail, master; and kissed him. And Jesus said unto him, **Friend**, wherefore art thou come? Then came they, and laid hands on Jesus, and took him"* (Matthew 26:49-50).

*"And while he [Jesus] yet spake, behold a multitude, and he that was called Judas, **one of the twelve**, went before them, and drew near unto Jesus to kiss him. But Jesus said unto him, Judas, **betrayest** thou the Son of man with a kiss?"* (Luke 22:47-48).

TO BE SOLD FOR 30 PIECES OF SILVER

*"And I said unto them, If ye think good, give me my price; and if not, forbear. So they weighed for my price **thirty pieces of silver**. And the LORD said unto me, **Cast it unto the potter**: a goodly price that I was prised at of them. And I took the thirty pieces of silver, and **cast them to the potter in the house of the LORD**"* (Zechariah 11:12-13).

The prophecy of Zechariah tells that the Messiah was to be sold for 30 pieces of silver and that these coins were to be cast to the potter in the house of the Lord. We read of the fulfillment in the *Brit Hadasha* (NT). Notice that in both the prophecy and the fulfillment it is stated that the price was *30 pieces;* they were of *silver*; they were *thrown down*; they were *cast down in the house of the Lord*; and the money was used to purchase *the potter's field!*

> *"Then Judas, which had betrayed him, when he saw that he was condemned, repented himself, and brought again **the thirty pieces of silver** [each piece worth about 64 cents, before inflation] to the chief priests and elders, Saying, I have sinned in that I have betrayed the innocent blood. And they said, What is that to us? see thou to that. And he **cast down** the pieces of silver in the **temple**, and departed, and went and hanged himself. And the chief priests took the silver pieces, and said, It is not lawful for to put them into the treasury, because it is the price of blood. And they took counsel, and bought with them **the potter's field**, to bury strangers in. Wherefore that field was called, The field of blood, unto this day. Then was fulfilled that which was spoken by Jeremy the prophet, saying, And they took the thirty pieces of silver, the price of him that was valued, whom they of the children of Israel did value; And gave them for the potter's field, as the Lord appointed me"* (Matthew 27:3-10).

(Note: The word, *Jeremy*, in above quote is not found in some manuscripts. Instead some versions read "Zechariah" and others do not have either name. "Jeremiah" could have been added by a copyist; cf. Zechariah 11:13.)

TO SUFFER

	Prophecy	*Fulfillment*
To be forsaken by His disciples.		
	Zechariah 13:7	Matthew 26:56
	Psalm 35:11	Mark 14:27
To be falsely accused.		
	Psalm 27:12	Matthew 26:59-60
	Psalm 109:2	
To be scourged in the judgment hall.		
	Psalm 129:3	Matthew 27:27-30
To be smitten and spit upon.		
	Isaiah 50:6	Matthew 26:67
	Psalm 35:15, 21	Matthew 27:30
To be silent before His accusers.		
	Isaiah 53:7	Matthew 27:12, 14
	Psalm 38:13	
To be wounded and bruised.		
	Isaiah 53:5	Matthew 27:26, 29

✡   ✡   ✡   ✡   ✡   ✡   ✡

TO BE CRUCIFIED

Twenty-five Old Testament prophecies bearing on the betrayal, trial, death, and burial of the Messiah were uttered by many different voices at different times during the five centuries from 1000 to 500 BC, yet they were all literally fulfilled within 24 hours on the day of Christ's crucifixion! The following are just a few of these prophecies:

Prophecy	Fulfillment
To be executed by the piercing of the hands and feet.	
Psalm 22:16	Luke 23:33
To be executed with criminals.	
Isaiah 53:12	Mark 15:27-28
To pray for His persecutors.	
Isaiah 53:12	Luke 23:34
The people shake their heads at Him.	
Psalm 109:25	Matthew 27:39
To be ridiculed while dying.	
Psalm 22:7-8	Matthew 27:41, 43
People to be astonished.	
Psalm 22:17	Luke 23:25
To part His garments; to cast lots for His cloak.	
Psalm 22:18	John 19:23-24
To cry "My God, my God, why hast Thou forsaken me?"	
Psalm 22:1	Matthew 27:46
Gall and vinegar to be given Him.	
Psalm 69:21	John 19:28-29
To commit Himself into God's hands.	
Psalm 31:5	Luke 23:46
Friends to stand afar off.	
Psalm 38:11	Luke 23:49
His bones not to be broken.	
Psalm 34:20; Exodus 12:46	John 19:32-36
His heart to be broken.	
Psalm 22:14	John 19:34
His side to be pierced.	
Zechariah 12:10; 13:6	John 19:35-37
Darkness to cover the earth.	
Amos 8:9	Matthew 27:45
*To utter the words, "It is finished" ("It is **done**").*	
Psalm 22:31	John 19:30

Note: An interesting observation of the words: "It is finished" stated in John 19:30 is defined by W.E. Vine:

> "'Tetelestai,' a Greek word implying the perfect completion of that goal of man's redemption set forth in the *Old Testament* in prophecy, type and symbol. The work of redemption in these Old Testament representations was all accomplished or 'done' by Messiah in His Life, Death and Resurrection. 'Tetelestai,' from the word 'Teleo,' to finish, to bring to an end ('Telos,' 'an end'), frequently signifies, not merely to terminate a thing, but to carry out a thing to the full. 'Teleo,' 'to end,' signifies among its various meanings *give effect to*, and is translated *fulfill*."[82]

The 22nd Psalm which foretells the crucifixion of Messiah gives the words He will utter on the cross, though in different form: *"He hath **done** [asah] this"* (Psalm 22:31). The New Testament word is *Tetelestai* as above (John 19:30).

The arrest, trial, crucifixion and death of Jesus appear to have occurred in the brief space of about 15 hours during the fateful 14/15th day of Nisan in the year AD 29, 30, or 33. The oldest prophecy of Messiah's crucifixion is found in Genesis 3:15 where the Lord spoke to the serpent saying that the serpent would bruise the Messiah's heel but that the Messiah would (with His heel) crush (bruise) the serpent's head. This literally was fulfilled when the nails were driven through Messiah's feet, thus bruising His heels (John 19:18). At that time the serpent's head also was bruised (John 12:31-33)!

> *"... My God, my God, why hast thou forsaken me? why art thou so far from helping me, and from the words of my roaring?*
> *But I am a worm, and no man; a reproach of men, and despised of the people.*
> *All they that see me laugh me to scorn: they shoot out the lip, they shake the head, saying,*
> *He trusted on the LORD that he would deliver him: let him deliver him, seeing he delighted in him.*
> *Many bulls have compassed me: strong bulls of Bashan have beset me round.*
> *They gaped upon me with their mouths, as a ravening and a roaring lion.*
> *I am poured out like water, and all my bones are out of joint: my heart is like wax; it is melted in the midst of my bowels.*
> *My strength is dried up like a potsherd; and my tongue cleaveth to my jaws; and thou hast brought me into the dust of death.*
> *For dogs have compassed me: the assembly of the wicked have enclosed me: they pierced my hands and my feet.*
> *I may tell all my bones: they look and stare upon me.*
> *They part my garments among them, and cast lots upon my vesture"* (Psalm 22:1, 6-8, 12-18).

---

[82]W.E. Vine, *Expository Dictionary of New Testament Words*, p. 22 under "Accomplish" and p. 135 under "Fulfill."

Crucifixion was the most disgraceful death that a man could die, called a "slave's punishment" as it was mostly used for that class. A citizen could not be crucified. The crimes for which this was the penalty were treason, sedition, desertion (in the case of soldiers), perjury, robbery, assassination and piracy. A tablet, stating the crime, was fixed to the top of the cross. The suffering was excruciating, and death was hastened by breaking the leg bones. Convicted persons never died from bleeding on the cross. They died from asphyxiation. As the body sagged in weakness, it became impossible to exhale. The prisoner had to straighten his legs and raise his body or stop breathing. Thus crucifixion was a slow rising and falling for hours.

When a murderer of our day is condemned to death, he not only has the fair treatment of the people until his hour is come, but he is put out of the way in the easiest manner. But it was not so with Jesus. He was perfectly innocent, yet He was spit upon, smitten, given vinegar to drink, scourged, mocked, and then nailed to a cross, His life wearing away little by little to increase the suffering. He died in terrible agony and as He was dying even God forsook Him!

Crucifixion was an act which was evil and not good, a curse and not a blessing. In men's thoughts it has been associated with weakness and mockery, looked upon with disdain and disgust. The cross is shunned. It is despised. There the Crucified was spit upon, condemned, and taunted by both Jew and Gentile alike.

WHO WAS RESPONSIBLE FOR MESSIAH'S DEATH?[83]

For the correct answer to the above question we do not inquire of any man but turn to the true Word of God which prophesies of the coming rejected Messiah of Israel and plainly tells us who would be His executioners:

> *"Why do the heathen rage, and the people imagine a vain thing? The kings of the earth set themselves, and the rulers take counsel together, against the LORD, and against his anointed, ...,"* (Psalm 2:1-2).

Any student, understanding Bible language, will know immediately that whenever the word "heathen" is mentioned it means unbelievers who were *Gentiles* at that time; that the word "people" refers to *Israel* (the Jews). The "kings of the earth" in the days of the execution of the Messiah, were *Gentiles*. The "rulers" were the Jewish religious leaders of the Jews. "His anointed," of course, is the English translation of the Hebrew word "Messiah" and the Greek word "Christ."

---

[83] Also in my book *On What Day Did Christ Die?* under the caption: "Who Was Responsible for the Death of Christ?," Appendix II, pp. 111-116.

From the foregoing Scripture then, we conclude that both Jews and Gentiles would be against God and His Messiah. In the book of Acts we discover the fulfillment of this prophecy:

*"Who by the mouth of thy servant David hast said, Why did the heathen rage, and the people imagine vain things? The kings of the earth stood up, and the rulers were gathered together against the Lord, and against his Christ. For of a truth against thy holy child Jesus, whom thou hast **anointed**, both Herod, and Pontius Pilate, with the **Gentiles**, and the **people of Israel**, were gathered together, ..."* (Acts 4:25-27).

The Gentiles

Since the Gentiles are the first group mentioned in the foregoing Scripture, we will consider them first.

*"But we speak the wisdom of God in a mystery, even the hidden wisdom, which God ordained before the world unto our glory: Which none of the **princes of this world** knew: for had they known it, **they would not have crucified the Lord of glory**"* (1 Corinthians 2:7-8).

As we have learned, the *princes* at the time of Christ were *Gentiles*. Rome, a Gentile city, controlled all the laws and governments of the then-known world. She had power to sentence criminals, slaves, foreigners, and traitors. Pilate, who was governor over the Jews, was a *Gentile*.

"Tarquin the Proud" introduced *crucifixion* to the Roman world from Phoenicia in the Sixth Century BC, therefore it was a *Roman* method of execution. The *Jewish* method was stoning (also burning, strangling, beheading for murder) according to the Law of Moses. There were 32 capital crimes, for which there were four forms of execution. For the crimes of murder and apostasy from Judaism to idolatry, the punishment was beheading. Criminals convicted of the other 30 capital crimes were put to death by stoning, burning or strangulation. The 22nd Psalm prophesies of the *Roman* manner of Messiah's death centuries before Rome ever came into power, 250 years before this form of execution was known and 1,000 years before it was fulfilled! In this Psalm, through David, the Messiah predicts His own crucifixion, even to the cry He would utter on the cross: *"My God, my God, why hast thou forsaken me?"* (Psalm 22:1) Also (as mentioned before and I repeat), the word: *"He hath **done** this"* in verse 31, which from the Greek New Testament is *Tetelestai* or *"It is finished* [done]*"* (John 19:30).

Particularly notice the verses Psalm 22:12-18:

12. *Many bulls have compassed me: strong bulls of Bashan have beset me round.*

13. *They gaped upon me with their mouths, as a ravening and a roaring lion.*
14. *I am poured out like water, and all my bones are out of joint: my heart is like wax; it is melted in the midst of my bowels.*
15. *My strength is dried up like a potsherd; and my tongue cleaveth to my jaws; and thou hast brought me into the dust of death.*
16. *For dogs have compassed me: the assembly of the wicked have enclosed me: they pierced my hands and my feet.*
17. *I may tell all my bones: they look and stare upon me.*
18. *They part my garments among them, and cast lots upon my vesture."*

In the 16th verse the Messiah (Christ) points out that the "dogs" and the "wicked" pierced His hands and His feet. (The translation from the Hebrew reads: "like a lion they threaten my hands and my feet.") We have learned that the Jews were God's "people," or the believers, and all who were not of "the commonwealth of Israel" were unbelievers, "heathen," "dogs," the "wicked." Dogs are incapable of receiving anything from heaven and the Gentiles were "strangers and foreigners" to God at the time of this prophecy. (Today, the word "Gentiles" simply means they are not Jews.) Messiah referred to the Gentiles as "dogs" on several occasions, but one in particular:

> *"For a certain woman, whose young daughter had an unclean spirit, heard of him, and came and fell at his feet: The woman was a Greek[Gentile], a Syrophenician by nation; and she besought him that he would cast forth the devil out of her daughter. But Jesus said unto her, Let the* **children** *first be filled: for it is not meet to take the children's* **bread***, and to cast it unto the* **dogs**" (Mark 7:25-27).

The "children" were the Jews, the "bread" was anything they received from God, and of course, the "dogs" were the Gentiles at that time. But thank God, now there is *no difference* between the Jew and the Gentile, *Both* can come to the Father in heaven through Yeshua ha-Meshiach (Jesus, the Christ) for the middle wall of partition is broken down and the enmity done away in the Sacrifice on Calvary. However, we are considering complicity in the death of the Messiah and we find in His own words that the Gentiles were to pierce His hands and His feet!

At the time of Christ, the world was under the rule of Rome This *Gentile* power determined the laws of the land and carried out the death sentence by crucifixion. Pilate was governor of Judaea. He was a Gentile. He endeavored to escape from consenting to Christ's execution but the Jews threatened to report him to Caesar. Afraid of losing his position as governor, he pronounced the death sentence for Jesus.

The most tragic part of the crucifixion was carried out by Pontius Pilate, a Gentile, to whom Jesus was delivered. The decision was utterly in his hand, yet after having declared He was innocent, he cowardly decreed His death. (John 19:6-8, 19). He ordered his soldiers to crucify Jesus as the King of the Jews. This verdict was a *legal murder*, based upon falsehood. The crucifixion could only be carried out by the *Romans*. According to Josephus, Herod was tried for murder after the crucifixion of Jesus, because he "hath thereby transgressed our law, which hath forbidden to slay any man, even though he were a wicked man, unless he had been first condemned to suffer death by the Sanhedrin."

When the Messiah of Israel came to earth, He repeated the prophecy of His death to His disciples:

> *"And Jesus going up to Jerusalem took the twelve disciples apart in the way, and said unto them, Behold, we go up to Jerusalem; and the Son of man shall be betrayed unto the chief priests* [Jews] *and unto the scribes* [Jews], ***and they shall condemn him to death***, *And shall deliver him to the **Gentiles** to mock, and to scourge, and to crucify him: ..."* (Matthew 20:17-19).

Notice the divine accuracy of this prediction: The *Jewish leaders* were to betray, condemn and deliver Christ over to the Gentiles. The *Gentiles* were to mock, scourge, and crucify Him. We will see further how the *Gentile's* part was fulfilled even as the Lord had said.

> *"Then the **soldiers of the governor** took Jesus into the common hall, and gathered unto him **the whole band of soldiers**. And **they** stripped him, and put on him a scarlet robe. And when **they** had platted a crown of thorns, they put it upon his head, and a reed in his right hand: and they bowed the knee before him, and **mocked** him, saying, Hail, King of the Jews! And they spit upon him, and took the reed, and smote him on the head. And after that they had mocked him, they took the robe off from him, and put his own raiment on him, and led him away **to crucify him**"* (Matthew 27:27-31).

No Jew was permitted in the army of Rome. These soldiers consisted mostly of Italians, some Gauls (the present-day French), some Britons (the present-day American and British), and some Germans. In other words, this was a *Gentile*, not a Jewish army. So it is that the *Gentiles* carried out in detail the prediction of the Messiah-Savior concerning them in His own death. They mocked Him; they scourged Him; and they actually crucified Him!

The Jews

Another group besides the Gentiles who were responsible for the crucifixion of Messiah Jesus were the "people" of Israel. Judas was a

Jew. However, we must remember that the rest of Messiah's disciples, who loved Him and would have died for Him, were Jews as well! Messiah Yeshua chose twelve men to be with Him in His ministry. One who was trusted to carry the money bag, the treasurer of the group, one who dined with the Messiah, was prophesied to *betray* Him:

> *"Yea, mine own familiar friend, in whom I **trusted**, which did **eat of my bread**, hath lifted up his heel against me"* (Psalm 41:9).

> *"For it was not an enemy that reproached me; then I could have borne it: ... But it was thou, a man **mine equal**, my guide, and mine acquaintance. We took sweet counsel together, and walked unto the house of God in company"* (Psalm 55:12-14).

This was fulfilled as we read in the New Testament:

> *"And forthwith he [Judas] came to Jesus, and said, Hail, master; and kissed him. And Jesus said unto him, **Friend**, wherefore art thou come? Then came they, and laid hands on Jesus, and took him"* (Matthew 26:49-50).

> *"But Jesus said unto him, Judas, **betrayest** thou the Son of man with a kiss?"* (Luke 22: 48).

Betrayal speaks of mistrusted friendship. Jesus called Judas His *friend*. But Judas *betrayed* and *delivered* Jesus over to the Gentiles according to the prophecy!

THE FALSE ARREST AND ILLEGAL TRIAL[84]

(The following information on the *False Arrest and Illegal Trial* was taken from the writings of Rabbi A. U. Michelson, [former Jewish Judge in Germany], Pastor of First Hebrew-Christian Synagogue, Los Angeles, California who credited some of his material he received from the *Babylonian Talmud: Sanhedrin 1,* ch. IV. *Mishnah*; David Baron, *The Doctor of the Law*; J.E. Spooner, *The Unlawful Trial of Jesus*; Edersheim, *The Trial of Messiah*; Frank J. Powell, *The Trial of Jesus Christ*.)

The unfair trial of Christ is not found recorded outside of the Gospels, for the Sanhedrin, knowing they acted illegally, were afraid to keep a record of it!

According to the *Mishnah*, there were three Courts of Law in Jerusalem: the Greater Sanhedrin, the Lesser Sanhedrin composed of 23 members, and an Inferior Court or "Petty Court," "Court of the

---

[84]Also in my book *On What Day Did Christ Die?*, pp. 117-122.

Three" composed of 3 members. The Greater Sanhedrin composed of seventy one judges, was the Supreme Court of Appeal.

The Sadducees were the wealthy political aristocrats of the Jewish people. In the time of Jesus, the Temple and all local government was in the hands of the Sadducean priests. The Sadducees dominated the Sanhedrin. They derived great wealth from the business side of the Temple services, involving as it did the sale of cattle and birds for the sacrifices and the changing of money from Roman to Jewish currency. The Sadducees were particularly incensed when, on the Monday before His arrest, Jesus drove the money lenders and cattle dealers from the Temple.

The chief priests, elders and officers of the Temple arrested Jesus. Now it was a law at that time based upon the old law of Moses (Deuteronomy 17:6-7) that it was not legal for any member of the Sanhedrin to be an arresting officer. It was also illegal to arrest anyone after sundown no matter how bad a criminal he was, unless he were caught in the very act. He was absolutely safe under the law, until the following day. And then he could be arrested only by the witnesses. Furthermore, Jesus was really arrested by Judas and through his instigation, which under the law was not justified:

"Thou shalt not go up and down as a talebearer among thy people: neither shalt thou stand against the blood of thy neighbour: I am the LORD" (Leviticus 19:16).

A witness had to be a person of good character; he was forbidden to take a bribe. A Gentile could not be a witness. An accomplice or accessory could not be a witness under any circumstances. Thus Judas could neither be a witness, nor arrest, because he was a companion, a traitor, a talebearer.

To take Jesus before Annas at night to be interrogated was absolutely illegal under the law, both because it was at night, and because no one person could legally interrogate either the accused or a witness. The Examining Board of the Sanhedrin had to consist of three to seven men; no one person could independently interrogate a witness or an accused person. It was also a law that a man could not incriminate himself, in other words, he could not suffer punishment or take a punishment upon his own confession; it had to be supported by the testimony of two or three witnesses (Deuteronomy 17:6; 19:15; Numbers 35:30).

The Sanhedrin could not have a trial before their Sabbath. Further, no trial could be held on a feast day, and this was the Passover week, in which every day was a feast day.

It was after midnight when Caiaphas questioned Jesus who remained silent. As High Priest, Caiaphas could not interrogate any witness and could not express an opinion. Contrary to the law he placed Jesus under oath and he sought to interrogate Him before any witness had been interrogated. Caiaphas, illegally putting Jesus under oath, said: *"I adjure thee by the living God that thou tell whether thou be the Christ the Son of God"* (Matthew 26:63). This question Jesus would answer because He could not deny Himself and He, therefore, replied: *"Thou sayest."* Then the High Priest expressed himself which he had no right to do, saying, *"You have heard him. He is guilty of blasphemy"* (Matthew 26:65; Mark 14:63-64; Luke 22:71).

The Sanhedrin violated the law on another term, when they spit in His face and struck Him. They committed physical violence (Mark 14:65). No judge could lay his hands on either a witness or the accused, or in any way violate his person.

Another illegal act was when Caiaphas at the end of the trial rent his garment which was prohibited (Leviticus 21:10). The reason for this was that his priestly garment stood for the sacredness of his office.

It was personal feeling and jealousy which set the religious leaders against Jesus. For instance: when they saw that He was able to heal the incurable, they tried to charge Him with witchcraft (Matthew 9:24; 12:24; Mark 3:22; Luke 11:15). When He healed the man with the withered arm, they took occasion to impute to Him the profanation of the Sabbath (Matthew 12:9-13; Mark 3:1-6; Luke 6:6-11). When the Pharisees and Sadducees invited Him to dine with them, all their questions were directed to catch some words out of His mouth that they might accuse Him (Luke 11:37-57). When He reminded them that the Temple was God's house of prayer for all people (Isaiah 56:7), but they made it a den of thieves, they sought how they might destroy Him (Matthew 21:12-16; Mark 11:15-18; Luke 19:45-47). Their bitterest anger, however, which they could not restrain was when He raised Lazarus (John 11:43-45), for their own eyes gave them witness to the greatness of Jesus.

—*End of article by Pastor A. U. Michelson*

It was the Passover custom to release a prisoner from the jail in remembrance of the freedom given to the Israelites on that first Passover. The Jews were given the choice as to which of two prisoners would be set free:

> *"But the chief priests* [Jews] *and elders* [Jews] *persuaded the multitude* [Jews] *that they should ask Barabbas, and destroy Jesus. The governor answered and said unto them, Whether of the twain will ye that I release unto you? They said, Barabbas. Pilate saith*

*unto them, What shall I do then with Jesus which is called Christ? They all say unto him, **Let him be crucified** [Here the Jews were condemning Jesus to death]. And the governor said, Why, what evil hath he done? But they cried out the more, saying, **Let him be crucified**"* (Matthew 27:20-23).

Barabbas was a vile criminal according to the record: *"Who for a certain sedition made in the city, and for murder, was cast into prison"* (Luke 23:19). He deserved the sentence of death, but the Messiah who was innocent, who went about doing good, healing all those oppressed of the devil, took this murderer's place on the cross. Barabbas was set free because the Lamb of God offered Himself as a Substitute. Barabbas was loosed from the prison house and allowed to live because there was One who died in his stead. The Redeemer of mankind was the offering for sin, and though a man be vile, even as was Barabbas, a captive in the prison house of sin, he can come to the Savior who will break the chains that bind him. God can and will loose the prisoner and bring him into the freedom of His wonderful Salvation! So it is, according to the divine prediction, the Jews *betrayed, condemned* Jesus and *delivered* Him over to the Gentiles to *mock*, to *scourge*, and to *crucify* Him.

There are other Scriptures which seem to imply only Jews were to blame for the Messiah's death (Acts 2:22-37; 4:8-10; 7:51-52; 2 Thessalonians 2:14-16). One particular portion of the Bible in the Old Testament actually names the Jews for the crucifixion of Messiah:

*"And I will pour upon the **house of David**, and upon the **inhabitants of Jerusalem**, the spirit of grace and of supplications: and **they** shall look upon me [look unto me] whom **they** have pierced, and **they** shall mourn for him, as one mourneth for his only son, ...* (Zechariah 12:10)

*"In that day there shall be a fountain opened to the **house of David** and to the **inhabitants of Jerusalem** for sin and for uncleanness. And one shall say unto him, What are these wounds in thine hands? Then he shall answer, Those with which I was wounded **in the house of my friends**"* (Zechariah 13:1, 6).

According to the law an accomplice in a murder today is considered as guilty as the murderer. One hiring a crime done is as though he carried out the actual deed. The Gentiles were "hired" by the Jews to crucify Messiah Jesus. **Both** are guilty!

Though the Lord names both Jews and Gentiles as His executioners, yet it is the delight on the part of some who are uninformed to point an accusing finger only at the Jewish people. The crucifixion of Christ is used as a target for Jew-hatred and persecution. But we cannot judge the Jews for rejecting their Messiah any more than we can condemn the Gentiles for actually crucifying Him, for (as the prayer of the Messiah on the cross indicates), they did so in ignorance and Christ is ready to forgive *all* who come to Him and acknowledge their sin before Him!

It was the Pharisees (not all of them), the Sadducees who were against Him–and only a few individuals who could find room in the limited space of Pilate's court who shouted: "Crucify Him!" We note that of the 4.5 million Jews who existed in the day of Jesus, only 1.5 million lived in the "Holy Land" and in Jerusalem. The Jews that were scattered throughout Pontus, Galatia, Cappadocia, Asia, and Bithynia, and other places of their dispersion were not involved in the crucifixion of Jesus. God in His compassion was using as few as possible of His creatures to accomplish His purpose so that the doors of grace might remain open to all the rest of His children.

Though Judas (Messiah's "trusted friend" turned to be His bitterest enemy) was a Jew, yet the rest of the apostles were Jews as well. They would have given their lives for the Master! According to the Record, the first Christians, saints and martyrs who gave their lives for Christ, were *Jews.* The New Testament church of Christ consisting of 3,000 Jews was established in Jerusalem in the very heart of *Jewry.*

"The careful reader of the crucifixion story will find that standing beneath the cross were not only the fickle and easily goaded and misguided mob, which shouted: 'Crucify, crucify,' but also 'a great company of people, and of women, which also bewailed and lamented him ...' (Luke 23:27-28)."   —Victor Buksbazen

Many claim that the persecution and the suffering visited upon the Jews today is because at the hour of crucifixion the people of Israel shouted: *"Let His blood be upon us and upon our children."* This was a wicked prayer (if it could be called a prayer) spoken by unbelieving men. *The blood of Jesus does not cry out for vengeance*! It was shed for cleansing from sin. The Lord took no notice of the aforementioned request for it was said in ignorance. Rather His great compassion was expressed when He cried: *"Father forgive them, for they know not what they do"*!

Israel, as a nation, would have been doomed and no Jew could ever be saved, *had they known He was the Messiah* and had rejected Him. When thousands of Jews were saved at Pentecost (Shavuot), the Lord's prayer of forgiveness on the cross was answered and is continued to be answered whenever a Jewish person (or Gentile) accepts Him as their Salvation!

The Devil

However, there is another party responsible for the death of Jesus. We read of him in the very first promise of a coming Messiah. Speaking to the serpent, God said:

> *"And I will put enmity between thee and the woman, and between thy seed and **her seed** [Messiah]; it shall bruise thy head, and thou shalt bruise his heel"* (Genesis 3:15).

The serpent (Satan) was to bruise the heel of the Redeemer and, according to the prophecy, this was done. Literally, in no other death but in crucifixion, would the heel of an individual actually be bruised! Messiah's heel was nailed (bruised) to the cross. It was fulfilled as His "heel" crushed the head of the Serpent (defeated him by His death) and that "heel," in crushing the Serpent's head was "bruised" according to the prophecy!

It is Satan who seeks to thwart God's plan, to confuse the minds of the people. Satan it is who entered into the heart of Judas, planted hatred and aroused jealousy in the Sadducees and Pharisees. He stirred up and promoted Messiah's crucifixion.

Jesus

But could not Jesus, as the Messiah, defend and deliver Himself from this death? Yes, He could have, but in doing this He would have opposed the whole plan of God for the salvation of the world. In refusing to go to the cross of shame, He would have failed in His task as Redeemer of mankind. Yeshua ha-Meshiah (Jesus, the Christ) was responsible also for His own execution! The Scripture states:

> *"And being found in fashion as a man, he humbled himself, and became obedient unto death, even the death of the cross"* (Philippians 2:8).

He voluntarily, willingly gave His life as He said:

> *"I am the good shepherd: the good shepherd giveth his life for the sheep. Therefore doth my Father love me, because I lay down my life, that I might take it again. **No man taketh it from me**, but I lay it down of myself. I have power to lay it down, and I have power to take it again. This commandment have I received of my Father"* (John 10:11, 17, 18).

Jesus was not forced to die. He consented to it, for His Father had so commanded. When Peter took a sword and used it to defend his Master, Jesus rebuked him: *"Put up thy sword into the sheath: **the cup which my father hath given me, shall I not drink it?**"* (John 18:11).

It was prophesied in the Old Testament (*T'nakh*) that the Messiah would give Himself over to suffering and death: *"I gave my back to the smiters, and my cheeks to them that plucked out the hair, I hid not my face from shame and spitting"* (Isaiah 50:6). Yes, Jesus gave His head to wear the thorns for you; He gave His cheeks to be smitten for you *"He giveth His cheeks to him that smiteth him"* (Lamentations 3:30). He gave His eyes to weep over your sins; His tongue to pray for you; His back to be ploughed for you, *"The plowers plowed upon my back; they made long their furrows"* (Psalm 129:3). He gave His side to the spear for you; His hands to the cruel nails, His soul, an offering all for you. Yes, He clothed Himself in a human body that He might have it to offer (Hebrews 10:5, 9, 10). He became possessed of a human heart that it might be broken. He partook of blood which flowed in His veins in order that He might give it for the life of the world!

God

But there is another party without whom there could have been no crucifixion scene, for it was by the determinate counsel and foreknowledge of *God*, that the Messiah was "cut off." Jews and Gentiles "were gathered together" against Jesus *"to do whatsoever thy* [God] *hand and thy* [God] *counsel determined before to be done"* (Acts 4:28). God Himself was responsible for the death of Christ! In the very beginning it was *God* who slew an animal in the Garden of Eden, shedding its blood, in order to make coats of the skin to cover Adam and Eve. This prefigures the Supreme Sacrifice which the great Creator was to give for the redemption of the world. Before the first creation it was in the mind of the Father that the Messiah would come to be a Substitute, to die in order that those believing on Him could live. The Lamb was slain *before* the foundation of the earth by the determinate counsel of God!

> *"... the LORD hath laid on **him** [Messiah] the iniquity of us all. Yet it pleased **the LORD** to bruise **him** [Messiah]; **he** hath put **him** to grief: when **thou** [the Lord God] shalt make **his soul** an offering for sin, ..."* (Isaiah 53:6, 10).

Who bruised the Messiah, put Him to grief, and made His soul an offering for sin? *The Lord God!* The Messiah Himself foretold that *God* would put Him to death: *"And thou* [referring to God] *hast brought me into the dust of death"* (Psalm 22:15). God could have prevented that awful scene at Golgotha! He could have sent a legion of angels in defense of Jesus, but (as it is written): *"He spared not His own Son;* Why? Because He *delivered Him up for us all"* (Romans 8:32).

At the trial of Jesus, Pilate declared to Him that he had the power to release or to crucify Him. Jesus answered: *"Thou couldst have no power at all against me, except it were given thee from above"* (John

19:11; Hebrews 10:5, 9, 10). Not only did God give power to Pilate, but to the Jews and the Gentiles, using them as human instruments to accomplish His purpose. God gave power to Satan that he might push forward this execution. And yes, God gave power to Jesus to lay down His life! *"God so loved the world that he **gave** His only begotten Son* [as a sacrifice] *that **whosoever*** [Jew or Gentile] *believeth on him should not perish, but have everlasting life"* (John 3:16)!

The crucifixion is not a record of an historical misunderstanding; not a tragic event which ended in defeat. The cross is a fulfillment of a divine decree made before the foundation of the world! The death of the coming Messiah is prophesied and we see the manner of that death portrayed in type and symbol throughout the Old Testament! The furniture of the Tabernacle of Moses, which was designed by God, also was directed by God to be placed in the formation of a *cross*! When the Israelites were commanded to take up the Tabernacle to travel to another place which the Lord would show to them, they were to march with the furniture in *cross* formation. When the people of Israel were to observe that first Passover in Egypt, they were to kill an innocent lamb, then take the blood and strike it, not just in any manner they pleased, but on the two sideposts and the upper doorpost of their houses. Taking the blood from the basin on the threshold to the upper doorpost and on the two sideposts shows us that it was struck in the fashion of a *cross*!

Everyone

"The crucifixion is an event in which the whole world took part. Jewish disciples and well-wishers forsook Him and fled; Gentiles spat upon Him and mocked Him. Jews delivered Him to Pontius Pilate; Gentiles nailed Him to the cross. Jews cried, 'Crucify!' Gentiles gambled on His vesture. Christian Jews wept at the foot of the cross; Gentiles crushed the crown of thorns on His brow. Christian Jews brought costly spices; Gentiles offered Him vinegar and gall. Christian Jews were His pallbearers; Gentiles pierced His side. Thus Jews *and* Gentiles crucified our Lord."

—*A. J. Kligerman*

THE GUILTY ONE

"Who plaited the crown of thorns for His brow?
Some Roman soldier, nameless now.
Who hewed the Cross from the grim pine-tree?
Some Jew, a carpenter as was He.
Who forged the nails He was fastened with?
He knew no better, poor nameless smith.
Nameless all, for the sin and shame
Were done by the one that bears my name."

—Father Hugh Blunt, LL.D.

The story is told of a man who dreamed of seeing Jesus being led out to be scourged. He saw the Saviour's back laid bare and a rough soldier inflicting bloody stripes upon His flesh. Again and again the lash rose and fell. At length the sleeper could bear no more. In his dream he rushed forward, caught the upraised hand, spun the soldier around, and–looked into his own face!

No one is exempt from responsibility in the death of Messiah! Though the 53rd chapter of Isaiah, the Jewish prophet, is written concerning the Messiah of Israel and Israel's rejection of Him, yet it deals also with *all* sinners in relation to the Saviour:

> *"Surely he hath borne **our** griefs, and carried **our** sorrows: ... But he was wounded for **our** transgressions, he was bruised for **our** iniquities: the chastisement of **our** peace was upon him; ... for the transgression of **my people** was he stricken. Therefore will I divide him a portion with the great, and he shall divide the spoil with the strong; because he hath poured out his soul unto death: and he was numbered with the transgressors; and he bare the sin of **many**, ..."* (Isaiah 53:4, 5, 8, 12).

Someone has given an answer to the question: "Who Crucified Christ"? "The *Gentile* gave the order, the *Jew* gave the consent, the *devil* pushed it, *God the Father* willed it, *Christ* Himself allowed it, and *our sins* made it necessary."

The entire world is guilty before God of the crucifixion of Christ. His suffering and death was necessary for our salvation. According to the Divine Plan the *Innocent One* must die in order that we might live. He must be made sin in order that we might be made righteous. He must suffer the wrath and judgment of the Almighty God in order that we might be reconciled to our Maker. This One who is the Substitute, the Sacrifice and Ransom is Jesus, the Messiah and we (Jew and Gentile) who believe upon Him by accepting Him into our heart are pardoned for our sin and receive His life and righteousness!

TO BE BURIED IN A RICH MAN'S TOMB

Old Testament prophecy:

> *"And he made his grave with the wicked, and with **the rich** in his death [deaths]"* (Isaiah 53:9).

New Testament fulfillment:

> *"When the even was come, there came a **rich man** of Arimathaea, named Joseph, who also himself was Jesus' disciple: He went to Pilate, and begged the body of Jesus. Then Pilate commanded the body to be delivered. And when Joseph had taken the body, he wrapped it in a clean linen cloth, And laid it in his **own new tomb**, which he had hewn out in the rock: ..."* (Matthew 27:57-60).

TO RISE FROM THE DEAD

"For thou wilt not leave my soul in hell [sheol, the place of departed spirits]*; neither wilt thou suffer [permit] thine Holy One [Messiah] to see corruption"* (Psalm 16:10).

Since David did not experience a bodily resurrection from the tomb, it is obvious that he (called a prophet in Acts 2:30; see with verse 29) was writing of someone else, the "Holy One." Peter, another Jew who believed in his Messiah, preached to the Jews on the day of Pentecost saying:

"Him [Messiah], *being delivered by the determinate counsel and foreknowledge of God, ye have taken, and by wicked hands have crucified and slain:* **Whom God hath raised up, having loosed the pains of death***: because it was not possible that he should be holden of it. For David speaketh concerning him, ... Because thou wilt not leave my soul in hell, neither wilt thou suffer thine Holy One to see corruption.* [David] *spake of the resurrection of Christ, that his soul was not left in hell, neither his flesh did see corruption. This Jesus hath* **God raised up***, ... "* (Acts 2:23-25, 27, 31-32).

"The LORD [יהוה] *said unto my Lord* [אדני]*, Sit thou at my right hand until I make thine enemies thy footstool"* (Psalm 110:1). (Quoted in Matthew 22:44 and Luke 20:42.)

Psalm 110 was written by David, the King. He had no earthly lord, therefore he was referring to the divine Lord above who was speaking to his incarnated Lord (Messiah). The passage also implies that *Adonai* would be rebuffed by His enemies, that He would *ascend into heaven*, and that He would come a second time (see also Psalm 68:18).

"And when he [Christ] *had spoken these things, while they beheld, he was taken up; and a cloud received him out of their sight"* (Acts 1:9).

"For David is **not ascended** *into the heavens: but he saith himself, The Lord* [Yahweh] *said unto my Lord* [Adonai]*, Sit thou on my right hand, Until I make thy foes thy footstool"* (Acts 2:34-35).

TO COME A SECOND TIME

"I saw in the night visions, and, behold, one like the Son of man came with **the clouds** *of heaven, and came to the Ancient of days, and they brought him near before him. And there was given him dominion, and glory, and a kingdom, that all people, nations, and languages, should serve him: his dominion is an everlasting dominion, which shall not pass away, and his kingdom that which shall not be destroyed"* (Daniel 7:13-14).

The first time Messiah came, He walked the earth in humiliation; the *second* time He is coming in a blaze of glory! The first time He came to die; the second time He will come to die no more. He came first to redeem; when He returns He will claim those He has redeemed. He came once that His heel might be bruised by Satan; He must come again to crush the serpent's head and with a rod of iron to dash His enemies to pieces. He came once to wear a crown of thorns. It is prophesied He will come again to wear the royal diadem of universal dominion. The first time, nails were hammered through His hands. When He returns He will grasp the scepter of sovereignty and shall reign forever!

Orthodox Jewish theology teaches that there will be two Messiahs. One is to be from the *House of Joseph* who will be killed as He leads Israel against the Russian army invading the land of Israel (Ezekiel 38 and 39) and after the Jewish people repent God will provide the second Messiah from the *House of David* who will bring peace and righteousness to the nation. This is the way the ancient Jewish commentators (in the Talmud) explain the two descriptions of Messiah in the T'nakh such as Zechariah 9:9 and 12:10 where He is described as lowly and who will be pierced to death (Meshiah Ben Joseph), and in Daniel 7:13 where He comes with the clouds of heaven (Meshiah Ben David).[85]

On the average, one out of every 30 verses in the Bible declares the *Second Coming* of the Messiah. To every mention of His first coming, His return is stated *eight* times!

> *"And when he* [Messiah] *had spoken these things, while they beheld, he was taken up; and a* **cloud** *received him out of their sight. And while they looked stedfastly toward heaven as he went up, behold, two men stood by them in white apparel; Which also said, Ye men of Galilee, why stand ye gazing up into heaven? this* **same Jesus***, which is taken up from you into heaven,* **shall so come in like manner as ye have seen him go into heaven**" (Acts 1:9-11).

These two men in white apparel were angels who announced the return of Jesus. The angels were not mistaken when they announced the Messiah's first advent.

Enoch down to the last prophet declared the second advent of Messiah Yeshua. The Holy Spirit, by the mouths of the apostles, repeatedly said: "Jesus is coming again."

When the disciples were troubled because they were informed that Yeshua would leave them, He comforted them with these words:

> *"Let not your heart be troubled: ye believe in God, believe also in me. In my Father's house are many mansions* [abiding places]*: if it were not so, I would have told you. I go to prepare a place for you. And if I go and prepare a place for you,* **I will come again**,*

---

[85]Talmud, *Succah 52:1.*

and receive you unto myself; that where I am, there ye may be also" (John 14:1-3).

God's Word is true. Heaven and earth shall pass away, but His Word shall stand forever. *"God is not a man, that he should lie; neither the son of man, that he should repent: hath he said, and shall he not do it? or hath he spoken, and shall he not make it good?"* (Numbers 23:19).

When the followers of the Messiah-Jesus asked Him when He would return He described to them the events which are now, in our day, transpiring before our very eyes. He said:

"For many shall come in my name, saying, I am Christ; and shall deceive many. And ye shall hear of wars and rumours of wars: see that ye be not troubled: for all these things must come to pass, but the end is not yet. For nation shall rise against nation, and kingdom against kingdom: and there shall be famines, and pestilences, and earthquakes, in divers places. All these are the beginning of sorrows. And because iniquity shall abound, the love of many shall wax cold. But he that shall endure unto the end, the same shall be saved. And this gospel of the kingdom shall be preached in all the world for a witness unto all nations; and then shall the end come" (Matthew 24:5-8, 12-14).

"For there shall arise false Christs, and false prophets, and shall show great signs and wonders; insomuch that, if it were possible, they shall deceive the very elect. Behold, I have told you before. Wherefore if they shall say unto you, Behold, he is in the desert; go not forth: behold, he is in the secret chambers; believe it not. For as the lightning cometh out of the east, and shineth even unto the west; so shall also the coming of the Son of man be" (Matthew 24:24-27).

*"And then shall appear the sign of the Son of man in heaven: and then shall all the tribes of the earth mourn, and they shall see the Son of man **coming in the clouds of heaven** with power and great glory"* (Matthew 24:30; compare with Daniel 7:13-14).

Some may term the second coming of the Messiah an experience of death, but His first coming did not mean death to the Jews, rather, it meant *more abundant life*! At His second coming, the enemy *death* will be swallowed up in victory, those who are dead in the Messiah will arise, will *live* again!

There are those who may term the second appearing of Messiah Yeshua as a spiritual coming, as an apparition, a ghost; but the promise is: *"This **same** Jesus."* When He ascended into heaven, He was flesh and bones. After His resurrection, He appeared to His disciples who thought He was a ghost. Jesus admonished them to handle Him and see, for, He said: *"A **spirit** hath not flesh and bones such as ye see me* *have."* He will also have the marks of the wounds in His body, for Thomas (doubting this to be the Lord) was permitted to touch the pierced hands and side of Jesus to confirm His identity as Lord and Saviour. Yes, this *same "flesh-and-bones Jesus"* shall come again as He promised He would!

Many false Christs are in the world today even as Jesus had warned His followers there would be in the last days before His return. But a true disciple of the Lord is not deceived by them. God, by His holy angels, declared that *"this same Jesus shall so come in like manner as ye have seen him go into heaven."*

How did He go away? On a cloud—*"a cloud took him out of their sight"* (Acts 1:9, literal). He is coming back with *clouds.* He ascended *suddenly* and *miraculously.* He is returning *suddenly* and *miraculously.* While He was ascending into heaven, His disciples were *watching* Him go away. He is returning for those who love His appearing, who not only have the knowledge of His second coming, but who are *watching,* who are waiting with great longing, who are living lives consecrated to God in anticipation of that glorious event!

In view of that which is taking place around us, that which our Lord described would occur just before His Second Advent, each of us who have accepted Jesus as our Messiah and personal Saviour can *"Look up, and lift up our heads, for our* [complete and final] *redemption draweth nigh!"*

THE COMING OF HIS FEET

In the crimson of the morning,
in the whiteness of the noon,
In the amber glory of the day's retreat,
In the midnight robed in darkness,
or the gleaming of the moon,
I listen for the coming of his feet.
I have heard his weary footsteps on the sands of Galilee,
On the Temple's marble pavement on the street,
Worn with weight of sorrow
falt'ring up the slopes of Calvary,
The sorrow of the coming of his feet.
Down the minster-aisles of splendor,
from betwixt the cherubim,
Thro' the wond'ring throng with motion strong and fleet,
Sounds his victor tread, with a music far and dim.
The music of the coming of his feet.
Sandalled not with shoes of silver,
girdled not with woven gold,
Weighted not with shimmering gems and odors sweet,
But white-winged, and shod with glory

as in the Tabor light of old,
The glory of the coming of his feet.
He is coming, oh, my spirit! with his everlasting peace;
With his blessedness immortal and complete;
He is coming, oh, my spirit! and his coming brings release!
I am living for the coming of his feet.

—*Selected* [86]

SCARS OF CRUCIFIXION

Shalom Aleichem!

This was the way I would greet my students when I was an Instructor at Seattle Bible College for 23 years. "Shalom Aleichem" means "Peace (be) to you." They would answer by turning the two words around saying "Aleichem Shalom"! Turning the two words around in response to my greeting would mean: "to you peace" or "the same to you"! This is the greeting heard in Israel and all around the globe. It is like "hello" and "good-bye."

To define that beautiful word "Shalom" would involve much time so I will give just a brief explanation. Shalom does not only mean the absence of war. One word in Hebrew can have several English translations since it has a three-letter root and from the root many words are formed. Shalom means peace, prosperity, health, strength, harmony, contentment, etc. So when we say "Shalom aleichem" we are saying "May you have health, prosperity, strength, harmony, contentment, and so on.

Our Lord Jesus is named "Sar-Shalom," "Prince of Peace." He is the One who gives health, strength, harmony, prosperity and contentment. He always greeted His disciples this way and even after His resurrection we learn of this *special* greeting to His disciples.

> *"Then the same day at evening, being the first day of the week, when the doors were shut where the disciples were assembled for fear of the Jews, came Jesus and stood in the midst, and saith unto them,* **Peace be unto you**" [Shalom Aleichem] (John 20:19).

> *"And when he had so said, he showed unto them his* **hands** *and his* **side**. **Then** *were the disciples glad, when they saw the Lord. Then said Jesus to them* **again, Peace be unto you** [Shalom Aleichem]: *as my Father hath sent me, even so send I you"* (John 20:20-21).

Jesus greeted His disciples with "Shalom Aleichem." Then He showed them His hands and his side. They recognized their Lord from this and in response, said: "My Lord and my God." What was in

---

[86]Quoted from Clarence Larkin's *Dispensational Truth*, p.125.

His side and in His hands that made Him recognizable as their Lord? The *scars of the crucifixion*! Jesus could say "Shalom Aleichem" because He purchased peace for them when He gave Himself a sacrifice on Calvary! And He will have these scars *forever,* the only thing that man has put in heaven.

My Jewish people will recognize their Messiah by His wounds when He appears to them at His second coming. God promised Israel:

> "And I will pour upon the house of David, and upon the inhabitants of Jerusalem, the spirit of grace and of supplications: and they shall look upon me [אֵת aleph-tav] whom they have **pierced**, and they shall mourn for him, as one mourneth for his only son, and shall be in bitterness for him, as one that is in bitterness for his firstborn" (Zechariah 12:10).

At the time my Jewish people look upon Him (*Aleph-Tav*) whom they have pierced they ask a question of the Lord:

> "And one shall say unto him, What are these **wounds** in thine hands? Then he shall answer, Those with which I was **wounded in the house of my friends**" (Zechariah 13:6).

We know *Sar-Shalom*, the Prince of Peace, with the *scars of crucifixion* in His hands and side! Because our Lord purchased peace for us on the Cross of Calvary we can repeat His words of greeting to one another: *Shalom Aleichem*, "Peace be unto you."

SIGN OF THE RED HEIFER

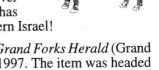

Something is happening relative to the coming of the Messiah which is causing a stir among *religious* Jews especially. Rabbis say, "It's a miracle! *A red heifer has been born in Israel*! It is believed to be a *sign of the long-looked-for Messiah*! For the first time in over 2,000 years, a ritually perfect red heifer has been produced—born on a farm in northern Israel!

News of the event was printed in the *Grand Forks Herald* (Grand Forks, North Dakota, USA) on May 30, 1997. The item was headed by the words:

HOLY COW?
Red heifer creates a sensation in Israel:
SIGN OF MESSIAH OR JUST A COW?
by Dina Kraft, Associated Press

KFAR HASIDIM, Israel–Some claim she is a harbinger of the Messiah. Some call for her destruction. Others find the attention she is getting ridiculous.

Ten-month-old Melody, believed to be the first red heifer born in the Holy Land in two millennia, seems happy just lying around in the shade. But the debate over her theological import is one of the more bizarre signs of the growing rupture between religious and secular Israelis.

"The red heifer is one of the most important signs that we are living in a special time," said Gershon Solomon, head of a group dedicated to rebuilding the ancient Jewish Temple, destroyed by the Romans in 70 A.D.

In ancient times, the ashes of a red heifer were mixed with spring water to purify high priests before they entered the Temple. There are fears some extremist groups might interpret Melody's birth as a sign the time is right to rebuild the Temple on the site that now houses some of the holiest shrines in Islam.

... Shmaria Shore, the Rabbi of this agricultural village in northern Israel, said hundreds of Israelis and tourists have flocked here to catch a glimpse of Melody. [He] said pure red heifers seem to have died out in Israel since the post-temple period, and that it is rare to see a red heifer without white or black spots. He took pains to point out that Melody, who is a darkish red, may not be the genuine article because of several imperfections. ... [87]

REJECTED STONE BECOMES CHIEF CORNERSTONE

It is prophesied that Israel who had rejected their Messiah when He came the first time will one day accept Him.

"The stone which the builders refused is become the head stone of the corner" (Psalm 118:22).

"... The stone which the builders rejected, the same is become the head of the corner?" (Luke 20:17).

Jews interpret Psalm 118:22 as the following:

"Israel is called a *stone* (Genesis 49:24) and the nations of the world are the *builders* who never appreciated Israel's role in their survival. The builders; *i.e.*, the rulers of the nations, despised the Jews; they demanded the Jews be expelled or annihilated, but when redemption arrives, all nations will realize that Israel is the cornerstone of the world" (*Radak*).

The true interpretation is concerning the relationship of Messiah and Israel. The nation of Israel is represented as the builders, the rejected Stone is their Messiah. At Messiah's first coming He was rejected by His people Israel but they will accept Him when He returns!

---

[87] Also see my *We Have a Great High Priest* in section "Ashes of a Heifer," pp. 121-125.

TO REVEAL HIMSELF TO ISRAEL, TO FORGIVE AND DEFEND THEM

"For I will gather all nations against Jerusalem to battle; and the city shall be taken, and the houses rifled, and the women ravished; and half of the city shall go forth into captivity, and the residue of the people shall not be cut off from the city. And his [the Lord's] feet shall stand in that day upon the mount of Olives, which is before Jerusalem on the east, and the mount of Olives shall cleave in the midst thereof toward the east and toward the west, and there shall be a very great valley; and half of the mountain shall remove toward the north, and half of it toward the south. ... and the LORD my God shall come, and all the saints with thee. And the LORD shall be king over all the earth: in that day shall there be one LORD, and his name one" (Zechariah 14:2, 4-5, 9).

"And it shall come to pass in that day, that I will seek to destroy all the nations that come against Jerusalem. And I will pour upon the house of David, and upon the inhabitants of Jerusalem, the spirit of grace and of supplications: and they shall look upon me whom they have pierced, and they shall mourn for him, as one mourneth for his only son, and shall be in bitterness for him, as one that is in bitterness for his firstborn. In that day shall there be a great mourning in Jerusalem, as the mourning of Hadadrimmon in the valley of Megiddon" (Zechariah 12:9-11).

"In that day there shall be a fountain opened to the house of David and to the inhabitants of Jerusalem for sin and for uncleanness. And one shall say unto him, What are these wounds in thine hands? Then he shall answer, Those with which I was wounded in the house of my friends" (Zechariah 13:1, 6).

From the foregoing Scripture verses we understand that when the nations of the world shall center their attack on the Jews at Jerusalem, the Messiah Jesus will return to earth to defend Israel against her enemies for the last time, to reveal Himself to these Jews who had been blinded as to His Messiahship. He will identify Himself as the Lord of glory through the marks of the wounds in His hands and His feet. He will forgive those who repent of their sin, judge the nations who mistreated Israel, establish His kingdom on the new earth with all His saints (Jew and Gentile), and rule and reign forever! Even so, come quickly, Lord Jesus!

✡   ✡   ✡   ✡   ✡   ✡   ✡

CHAPTER FIVE

RELATED JEWISH ITEMS

LUACH (Calendar)

The calendar of the Jews is based on the movements of the moon. On the last day of the month, people in ancient Jerusalem would watch the sky, and the head of the Sanhedrin and several of the elders, assembled in the Temple courtyard all that day, would be waiting for the news. Those first to notice the slightest crescent would rush to the Temple and inform the Sanhedrin. When–after questioning the witnesses as to the position, size and shape of the crescent–the officials were convinced that the evidence was correct, the Shofar (trumpet) would be blown and the beginning of the next month announced.

In ancient times also, the Jews kept record of the years by some important event or by the reign of a king. The Bible contains many such expressions as "in the fourth year of Solomon's reign over Israel," and "in the first year of Cyrus, king of Persia," and "two years before the earthquake." The present form of the Jewish calendar was fixed by Hillel II about 360 AD.

Today, every time there is a new moon, the Jewish people begin a new month. It should be remembered that the Jewish day begins at sunset and ends the following sunset. All holidays, therefore, begin in the evening. To be more exact, the day, reckoned from evening to evening, begins when three stars are visible, about 25 minutes after sunset.

The phases of the moon change approximately every seven days (God's perfect number), seven days in the week. In the Bible, the days are called by their numbers. First, Second, Third, and so on. In modern Israel (where Hebrew is spoken and Jews are free to follow their own customs) the days are called by their numbers. The Seventh day, of course, is called "Shabbat" ("Shabbos") or "Sabbath," which means "rest," as it has been since ancient times.

According to the Bible, the Israelites counted the years from the Exodus from Egypt. Even as late as the time of King Solomon, the book of Kings speaks of the building of the Temple, *"in the year 480 after the Exodus from Egypt."* When Solomon's Temple was destroyed, a new chronology was started. Today (1992) the Jewish Calendar counts from the Creation of the world; *i.e.*, the land of "Palestine" was made the Nation of Israel on May 14, 1948 or *5th Iyar,* 5708 CE (Common Era).

Early Jews used the Scriptures to calculate the date of Creation as **3761 BCE** (Before the Common Era). A Jewish man who lived in the First Century in Rome by the name of *Varro* calculated this date. (To find the Hebrew year, add 3761 to the civil year to arrive at the present *Jewish* year.)

The Jewish Calendar, as it now exists, is based on astronomical principles. It differs from the ordinary calendar because its unit still is the month, not the year. Twelve lunar months compose a year and comprise altogether 354¼ days. The solar year, or the time it takes the earth to make one revolution about the sun, is 365¼ days, or roughly eleven days more. In order to harmonize the lunar and solar years, a 13th month, called *Second Adar* is added in the Jewish calendar seven times in 19 years; i.e., on the third, sixth, eighth, 11th, 14th , 17th, and 19th. Each of these years is a leap year.

The names of the twelve months are: *Nisan, Iyar, Sivan, Tammuz, Ab* (Av), *Elul, Tishri, Heshvan, Kislev, Tebet, Shebat* and *Adar*. These names were borrowed from the Babylonians. Only four months with their *Hebrew* names are mentioned in the Scriptures: Abib, Ziv, Ethanim, Bul. *Abib*, grain in the ear, just ripening; *Ziv* refers to the beauty and splendor of the flowers in spring; *Ethanim* means "perennial," probably referring to living fountains; *Bul* means rain or showers, being the month when the rainy season commenced.

The Jewish Calendar

Month of the Civil or Agricultural Year	Occurs in
1. Tishri	September-October
2. Heshvan	October-November
3. Kislev	November-December
4. Tebet	December-January
5. Shebat	January-February
6. Adar (plus VeAdar in Leap Years)	February-March
7. Nisan (Abib) (1st month of sacred year)	March-April
8. Iyar	April-May
9. Sivan	May-June
10. Tammuz	June-July
11. Ab (Av)	July-August
12. Elul	August-September

The Lord God is Eternal but He created Time. He is the Author of the days and the nights, for He divided the light from the darkness. He spoke the planets into space and placed the sun, moon, and stars in the heavens. He made the first, the second, third, fourth, fifth, sixth, and seventh days. The Eternal God made these seven days to correspond to earthly time, the seventh, speaking forth the Lord's Perfect Day of rest when righteousness would cover the earth as the waters cover the sea. God's "time" calendar for man is correct in every detail, but someday it will be done away, for time will merge into eternity. There will be no need of the stars, no need of the light, for the Lamb that was slain before the foundation of the earth will be the Sun, Moon, the Bright and Morning Star, and the Light which shall shine undimmed forevermore!

SOME IMPORTANT DATES IN JEWISH HISTORY

Abraham .... BCE 2000
Moses 1400
Exodus from Egypt 1200
Kingdom of David 1013-973
Solomon 1000
Fall of Kingdom of Israel 722
Destruction of First Temple (Solomon's) 586
The Maccabean Revolt 168-165
Destruction of Second Temple (Herod's) .... CE 70
Last stand of Jews at Masada .... CE 73
Jerusalem Talmud 350
Babylonian Talmud 500
Miamonides 1135-1204
Expulsion of Jews from Spain 1492
First Zionist Colonization by Russian Jews 1882-1903
First Zionist Congress led by Theodor Herzl .... Aug. 1897
Balfour Declaration 1917
   (Great Britain pledged the development of Palestine
   as a National Home for the Jews.)
British Rule 1918-1948
The 52-member League of Nations gave Great Britain the
   Mandate of Palestine 1922
Bloody rioting between Arabs and Jews .... Aug. 1922
Nazi persecution of Jews in Europe 1933-1945
Iraq to Haifa Pipe Line is Opened .... Jan. 1935
World War II; Holocaust in Europe 1939-1945
Peel Commission recommend partition of land .... July 1937
Jewish Brigade formed as part of British forces 1944
Israel Declared a Nation at Tel Aviv .... May 14, 1948
Israel Accepted as Nation by United Nations .... May 11, 1949
Internationalization of Jerusalem by Decision
   of United Nations .... Dec. 7, 1949
Israel Declares Jerusalem Capital of the State 1950
Adolph Eichmann tried and executed in Israel
   for his part in the Holocaust 1962
Israel attacks Egypt-The Six-Day War .... June 2-7, 1967
Victory of Israel Over Egypt .... June 7, 1967
Yom Kippur War 1973
Israel Rescues Hostages at Entebbe .... July 4, 1976

Israel and Egypt sign Peace Treaty .... March 26, 1979
Jerusalem Great Synagogue Dedicated
    (cost $14 million) .... August 4, 1982
Operation Moses, immigration of Jews
    from Ethiopia 1984
Operation Solomon, airlift of Jews from Ethiopia,
    full diplomatic relations with the Holy See 1994
Israel-Jordan Peace Treaty signed 1994
Prime Minister Rabin assassinated at peace rally;
    Shimon Peres became prime minister 1995

DECLARATION OF THE ESTABLISHMENT OF THE STATE OF ISRAEL

ERETZ ISRAEL[88] was the birthplace of the Jewish people. Here their spiritual, religious and political identity was shaped. Here they first attained to statehood, created cultural values of national and universal significance and gave to the world the eternal Book of Books.

After being forcibly exiled from their land, the people kept faith with it throughout their Dispersion and never ceased to pray and hope for their return to it and for the restoration in it of their political freedom.

Impelled by this historic and traditional attachment, Jews strove in every successive generation to re-establish themselves in their ancient homeland. In recent decades they returned in their masses. Pioneers, *ma'pilim*[89] and defenders, they made deserts bloom, revived the Hebrew language, built villages and towns, and created a thriving community, controlling its own economy and culture, loving peace but knowing how to defend itself, bringing the blessings of progress to all the country's inhabitants, and aspiring towards independent nationhood.

In the year 5657 (1897), at the summons of the spiritual father of the Jewish State, Theodor Herzl, the First Zionist Congress convened and proclaimed the right of the Jewish people to national rebirth in its own country.

This right was recognized in the Balfour Declaration of the 2nd November, 1917, and re-affirmed in the Mandate of the League of Nations which, in particular, gave international sanction to the historic connection between the Jewish people and Eretz-Israel and to the right of the Jewish people to rebuild its National Home.

The catastrophe which recently befell the Jewish people–the massacre of millions of Jews in Europe–was another clear demonstration of the urgency of solving the problem of its homelessness by re-establishing in Eretz-Israel the Jewish State, which would open the gates of the homeland wide to every Jew and confer upon the Jewish people the status of a fully-privileged member of the comity of nations.

---

[88]*Eretz-Israel* (Hebrew), the Land of Israel, Palestine.
[89]*Ma'pilim* (Hebrew), immigrants coming to Eretz-Israel in defiance of restrictive legislation.

Survivors of the Nazi holocaust in Europe, as well as Jews from other parts of the world, continued to migrate to Eretz-Israel, undaunted by difficulties, restrictions and dangers, and never ceased to assert their right to a life of dignity, freedom and honest toil in their national homeland.

In the Second World War, the Jewish community of this country contributed its full share to the struggle of the freedom and peace-loving nations against the forces of Nazi wickedness and, by the blood of its soldiers and its war effort, gained the right to be reckoned among the peoples who founded the United Nations.

On the 29th November, 1947, the United Nations General Assembly passed a resolution calling for the establishment of a Jewish State in Eretz-Israel; the General Assembly required the inhabitants of Eretz-Israel to take such steps as were necessary on their part for the implementation of that resolution. This recognition by the United Nations of the right of the Jewish people to establish their State is irrevocable.

ACCORDINGLY WE MEMBERS OF THE PEOPLE'S COUNCIL, REPRESENTATIVES OF THE JEWISH COMMUNITY OF ERETZ ISRAEL AND OF THE ZIONIST MOVEMENT, ARE HERE ASSEMBLED ON THE DAY OF THE TERMINATION OF THE BRITISH MANDATE OVER ERETZ-ISRAEL, AND, BY VIRTUE OF OUR NATURAL AND HISTORIC RIGHT AND ON THE STRENGTH OF THE RESOLUTION OF THE UNITED NATIONS GENERAL ASSEMBLY, HEREBY DECLARE THE ESTABLISHMENT OF A JEWISH STATE IN ERETZ-ISRAEL, TO BE KNOWN AS THE STATE OF ISRAEL.

WE DECLARE that, with effect from the moment of the termination of the Mandate, being tonight, the eve of Sabbath, the 6th Iyar, 5708 (15th May, 1948), until the establishment of the elected, regular authorities of the State in accordance with the Constitution which shall be adopted by the Elected Constituent Assembly not later than the 1st October, 1948, the People's Council shall act as a Provisional Council of State and its executive organ. the People's Administration, shall be the Provisional Government of the Jewish State, to be called "Israel."

THE STATE OF ISRAEL will be open for Jewish immigration and for the Ingathering of the Exiles; it will foster the development of the country for the benefit of all inhabitants; it will be based on freedom, justice and peace as envisaged by the prophets of Israel; it will ensure complete equality of social and political rights to all its inhabitants irrespective of religion, race or sex; it will guarantee freedom of religion, conscience, language, education and culture; it will safeguard the Holy Places of all religions; and it will be faithful to the principles of the Charter of the United Nations.

THE STATE OF ISRAEL is prepared to cooperate with the agencies and representatives of the United Nations in implementing the resolution of the General Assembly of the 29th November, 1947, and will take steps to bring about the economic union of the whole of Eretz-Israel.

WE APPEAL to the United Nations to assist the Jewish people in the building-up of its State and to receive the State of Israel into the comity of nations.[90]

---

[90]*Comity of nations*: courteous recognition accorded by one nation to the laws and institutions of another.

WE APPEAL — in the very midst of the onslaught launched against us now for months — to the Arab inhabitants of the State of Israel to preserve peace and participate in the upbuilding of the State on the basis of full and equal citizenship and due representation in all its provisional and permanent institutions.

WE EXTEND our hand to all neighbouring states and their peoples in an offer of peace and good neighbourliness, and appeal to them to establish bonds of cooperation and mutual help with the sovereign Jewish people settled in its own land. The State of Israel is prepared to do its share in common effort for the advancement of the entire Middle East.

WE APPEAL to the Jewish people throughout the Diaspora to rally round the Jews of Eretz-Israel in the tasks of immigration and upbuilding and to stand by them in the great struggle for the realization of the age-old dream — the redemption of Israel.

PLACING OUR TRUST IN THE ALMIGHTY, WE AFFIX OUR SIGNATURES TO THIS PROCLAMATION AT THIS SESSION OF THE PROVISIONAL COUNCIL OF STATE, ON THE SOIL OF THE HOMELAND, IN THE CITY OF TEL-AVIV, ON THIS SABBATH EVE, THE 5TH DAY OF IYAR, 5708 (14th MAY, 1948).

David Ben-Gurion

Daniel Auster	Golda Myerson [Meir]
Mordekhai Bentov	Nachum Nir
Yitzchak Ben Zvi	Zvi Segal
Eliyahu Berligne	Rabbi Yehuda Leib
Fritz Bernstein	Ha-Cohen Fishman
Rabbi Wolf Gold	David Zvi Pinkas
Meir Grabovsky	Aharon Zisling
Yitzchak Gruenbaum	Moshe Koloday
Dr. Abraham Granovsky	Eliezer Kaplan
Eliyahu Dobkin	Abraham Katznelson
Meir Wilner-Kovner	Felix Rosenblueth
Zerach Wahrhaftig	David Remez
Herzl Vardi	Berl Repetur
Rachel Cohen	Mordekhai Shattner
Rabbi Kalman Kahana	Ben Zion Sternberg
Saadia Kobashi	Bekhor Shitreet
Rabbi Yitzchak Meir Levin	Moshe Shapira
Meir David Loevenstein	Moshe Shertok

Published in the *Official Gazette,* No. 1 of the 5th Iyar, 5708
(14th May, 1948).

FLAG OF ISRAEL

"The flag of the Jewish nation was formally adopted by the Zionists in 1898. Isador S. Donn of London and Jacob B. Askowith of Boston, Massachusetts, early in the Nineties, without knowing of each others' efforts, worked out the same general design."
—Jacob DeHaas, Editor,
Encyclopaedia of Jewish Knowledge

It is white with two horizontal stripes of blue, in the center of which is an interlaced double triangle called "Mogen David" or "Shield of David." The standards of the 12 tribes of Israel are mentioned in the Bible; the ensign of Judah with its lion in the center is described in later books.

Flag and National Emblem of Israel

"The national flag of the State of Israel is white with two Yale-blue bands extending the full length of the flag. In the center of the wide white stripe is a shield of David, made of six Yale-blue bands, forming two equilateral triangles with their bases parallel to the two blue bands."[91]

The present flag of Israel was modeled after the *Zionist* flag which was displayed for the first time at Basel, Switzerland during the First Zionist Congress in 1897. The designer of the *Zionist* flag was David Wolfsohn (1856-1914) who was the President of the World Zionist Organization after the death of President Theodor Herzel. Mr. Wolfsohn designed the Zionist flag after the *tallit*, the prayer shawl of Judaism. He said he wanted to "open and expand this shawl before the eyes of the nations of the world as a symbol of the Zionist dream and hopes."

FLAGS OF ISRAEL IN THE BIBLE

Numbers 2:2 (also Numbers 3) tells of Israel's tribal locations and their flags (banners). There were to be 4 symbols on the flags taken from Ezekiel's vision of the "living creatures" (Ezekiel 1:10) called "cherubim" elsewhere and imitated in Revelation 4:7.

The 12 tribes of Israel were to encamp in the configuration of a square during their wilderness trek. The four Camps (composed of three tribes each), the Camp on the East headed by Judah (verses 3 to 9) whose symbol was the ***lion*** (Genesis 49:9), the Camp on the South

---

[91]*Encyclopaedia Britannica*, p. 348.

headed by the tribe of Reuben whose symbol on his banner was a *man* (Deuteronomy 33:6), the Camp on the West headed by the tribe of Ephraim (verses 18 to 24) whose banner bare the symbol of the (bull) *ox* (for the two prominent tribes Ephraim and Manasseh, of the double portioned inheritance of their father Joseph, Deuteronomy 33:17), and the Camp on the North headed by the tribe of Dan (verses 25 to 31) to whom was given the symbol of Scorpio, which, in the ancient Egyptian Zodiac was a snake. However, when the time came to hoist the symbol of the snake, Ahiezer refused and chose instead the symbol of an eagle. Also according to a Jewish interpretation the name for *eagle* closely resembles the term for serpent in Hebrew, Genesis 49:17. Therefore instead of the serpent, an eagle is the symbol on the flag of Daniel. According to *Unger's Bible Dictionary:*

> "Dan's position in the journey was on the north of the Tabernacle, with Asher and Naphtali. The standard of the tribe was of white and red, and the crest upon it, an eagle, *the great foe to serpents*, which had been chosen by the leader instead of a serpent, because Jacob had compared Dan to a serpent. Ahiezer, substituted the eagle, the destroyer of serpents, as he shrank from carrying an adder upon his flag."[92]

Camp of Judah   Camp of Reuben   Camp of Ephraim   Camp of Dan

(The sketches above are by artist Howard Morlock and taken from my book entitled: *A Dwelling Place For God.*)

According to some Bible commentaries the four evangelists of the gospels have these symbols as representing the theme for their illustration of Messiah Jesus: Matthew, the LION; Mark, the OX, Luke, the MAN; John, *the EAGLE.* The evangelists' symbols derive from two sources: the Old Testament *cherubim*, particularly Ezekiel's vision of a single four-sided figure with the faces of a lion, a man, an ox and an eagle (Ezekiel 1:10); and John's vision of God's throne enveloped by four separate creatures: a lion, an ox, a man and an eagle (Revelation 4:7). These four creatures later became the conventional symbols for the canonical Gospels.

✡   ✡   ✡   ✡   ✡   ✡   ✡

---

[92]Merrill F. Unger, *Unger's Bible Dictionary*, pp. 235-236.

THE MOGEN DAVID IN THE FLAG OF ISRAEL

The two triangles at the center of the flag are of blue and are, not as seems apparent, one triangle atop another, but are intertwined, signifying proximity and strength in their relationship one with the other. It was used by Jews in the Third Century. It is also found on a Hebrew seal discovered in Sidon and dating from the Seventh Century BC. It begins to appear frequently on synagogues from the 16th Century on, when the influence of the Cabalistic Isaac Luria was spreading. It also appears side by side with the Menorah, which until then had been regarded as the *Shield of David*.

Today, the "Mogen David" ("Shield of David") is found in the Synagogues, and is perhaps the most popular symbol on Jewish ornaments. It has been officially accepted as the badge or symbol of Judaism and appears on each thing that is definitely associated with the Jewish people. During World War I it was colored red and used by Jewish organizations doing military relief work, as equivalent to the Red Cross. The symbol was accepted by the American and Allied governments as an insignia ranking with the Red Cross to be worn by all those attached to the Hadassah Medical Unit dispatched to Palestine in 1918. Even at the present time The Red Shield of David, used on ambulances in the land of Israel, serves in the same manner as does the insignia of the Red Cross Society. This design is a distinguishing mark on the tombstones of fallen Jewish soldiers and is worn as an armband by Jewish Army Chaplains.

On the catacombs near Rome, where Jewish people are buried, the insignia "Mogen (sometimes spelled *Magen*) David" is found as also on the wall surrounding the city of Jerusalem. This "badge of Judaism" was adopted by the Jewish Publication Society as their official device nearly 100 years ago.

According to tradition this insignia was commonly used as a Seal for official communications. In Medieval times it was known as "The Shield of David and Abraham." Mentioned in the work of Peter Gaster entitled "The Holy and the Profane,"[93] there are some who claim its origin with Abraham because of God's promise to him: *"After these things the word of the LORD came unto Abram in a vision, saying, Fear not, Abram: I am thy **shield** [Mogen], and thy exceeding great reward"* (Genesis 15:1).

The Shield of David (more popularly known as the "Star of David") is linked to the Name of the Lord (יהוה Yod, Hei, Vav, Hei)

---

[93]A good description and history of the Mogen David is found in Peter Gaster's *The Holy and the Profane* in the portion entitled "The Shield of David" on pages 217-221.

which Jewish people do not pronounce. The Name is called "Tetragrammaton" and frequently has appeared in the center of the *Mogen David* which custom was observed for centuries. In the middle of the 12th Century, Judah Hadassi mentions the *Shield of David* in his work entitled *Eskol Ha-Kofer*. Here with the "Star of David" are the names of angels accompanying the inscription: *"Tetragrammaton protect thee."*

Interesting Note: George Washington ordered the symbol of 13 stars on the reverse side of the National Seal so arranged in five rows (one-four-three-four-one) as to create the outline of the six-pointed Star (Mogen David) to honor the Jew, Haiim Solomon, who literally financed the U.S. Government through the Revolution!

It has been suggested that the combination of the triangles is taken from the ancient Hebraic signature of King David. The three Hebrew letters of his name, Daled (ד), Waw (ו), Daled (ד) by extension, compose a double triangle!

Jewish teachers have held that the six points of the star represent the omnipresence of God in all six earthly directions: east, west, north, and south, also up and down.

The Hebrew term *Mogen David* itself is made up of exactly *six* letters. Orthodox Jews claim that each point of this star stands for a Hebrew word spelling out the *Shema*, the Jews' Great Confession of the oneness of their God found in Deuteronomy 6:4.

Others feel that when drawing the inner diagonals of the star one would come upon 12 triangles which symbolize the position of the 12 tribes of Israel as encamped around the Tabernacle in the Wilderness.

There are those who maintain that there is an association between the six points of the star and the six measures of barley Boaz gave to Ruth, which supports the fact that *six* great people would stem from Ruth, foremost among these being King David.

It has been interpreted to denote the seven days of the week. The hexagon in the center, the most complete figure, was the Sabbath; the six outer triangles, the six week days.

There are those who interpret it as representing the six heroes of Israel: Abraham, Isaac, Jacob, Joseph, Moses, and Aaron. There are still others who consider it as a prophecy of the coming Messiah who is scheduled to arrive after *6,000 years*. In this connection they claim the prophecy of Balaam: *"There shall step forth a **star** out of Jacob, And a sceptre shall arise out of Israel"* (Numbers 24:17).

To some Jewish scholars, the triangle pointing downwards to the earth, represents man who is a triune being: body, soul, and spirit. The triangle pointing upwards toward heaven, according to a Jewish history of it, represents the Godhead, a mystery which they feel will be explained when the Messiah comes! The "Mogen David" is rich in tradition and means much to every true Jewish heart.

When we, who believe in Yeshua ha-Meshiah (Jesus, the Christ) look upon the Mogen David, there is presented to us a beautiful picture of the relationship of the Triune God with the man He created in His own image. We also see in the triangle pointing downwards from heaven a type of our God who came to earth in the form of a man as it was prophesied He would; the triangle pointing upwards toward heaven, the Messiah reaching God for us. Also in the intertwining of these two triangles it is brought to our attention the close fellowship of man with his God which was made possible by the reconciliation accomplished on the Altar of Calvary!

Map of Jerusalem

Jerusalem Covenant

As of this day, Jerusalem Day, the twenty-eighth day of the month of Jyar in the year five thousand seven hundred fifty-two; one thousand nine hundred and twenty-two years after the destruction of the Second Temple; forty-four years since the founding of the State of Jsrael; twenty-five years since the Six Day War during which the Jsrael Defense forces, in defense of our very existence, broke through the wall of the city and restored the Temple Mount and the unity of Jerusalem; twelve years since the Knesset of Jsrael reestablished that Jerusalem, "unified and whole, is the Capital of Jsrael"; "the State of Jsrael is the State of the Jewish People" and the

Capital of Israel is the Capital of the People of Israel. We have gathered together in Zion, national leaders and heads of our communities everywhere, to enter into a covenant with Jerusalem, as was done by the leaders of our nation and all the people of Israel upon Israel's return to its Land from the Babylonian exile; and the people and their leaders vowed to "dwell in Jerusalem, the Holy City."

Once again, "our feet stand within your gates, O Jerusalem— Jerusalem built as a city joined together" which "unites the people of Israel to one another," and "links heavenly Jerusalem with earthly Jerusalem."

We have returned to the place that the Lord vowed to bestow upon the descendants of Abraham, Father of our Nation; to the City of David, King of Israel; where Solomon, son of David, built a Holy Temple; a Capital City which became the Mother of all Israel; a metropolis for justice and righteousness and for the wisdom and insights of the ancient world; where a Second Temple was erected in the days of Ezra and Nehemiah, in this city the prophets of the Lord prophesied; in this City the Sages taught Torah; in this City the Sanhedrin convened in session in its stone chamber. "For there were the seats of justice, the Throne of the House of David," "for out of Zion shall go forth Torah, and the Word of the Lord from Jerusalem."

Today, as of old, we hold fast to the truth of the words of the Prophets of Israel, that all the inhabitants of the world shall enter within the gates of Jerusalem: "And it shall come to pass at the end of days, the mountain of the House of the Lord will be ell established at the peak of the mountains and will tower above the hills, and all the nations shall stream towards it." "Each and every nation will live in it by its own faith; for all the nations will go forward, each with its own Divine Name; we shall go in the name of the Lord our God forever and ever." And in this spirit the Knesset of the State of Israel has enacted a law: the places holy to the peoples of all religions shall be protected from any desecration and from any restriction of free access to them.

From this place, we once again take this vow: "If I forget thee, O Jerusalem, may my right hand lose its strength; may my tongue cleave to my palate if I do not remember you, if I do not raise up Jerusalem at the very height of my rejoicing."

And with all these understandings, we enter into this Covenant and write": We shall bind you to us forever; we shall bind you to us with faithfulness, with righteousness and justice, with steadfast love and compassion. We love you, O Jerusalem, with eternal love, with unbound love, under siege and when liberated from the yoke of oppressors. We have been martyred for you; we have yearned for you, we have clung to you. Our faithfulness to you we shall bequeath to our children after us. Forevermore, our home shall be within you.

_____in certification of this covenant we sign_____

(Signatures of the following were shown on the original document.)

Speaker of the Knesset   Chief Rabbi (Ashkenazi)
Chief Rabbi (Sephardi)   Deputy Prime Minister
Chairman Ministerial   Deputy Minister of Jerusalem Affairs
Committee for Ceremony   Chief of Staff Six Day War
Mayor of Jerusalem   Minister For Education and Culture
Representative of Bereaved Families for the Battles of Jerusalem
Prime Minister   President State of Israel
President Supreme Court   Deputy Prime Minister
Chairman World Zionist Organization
Deputy President Supreme Court.

The foregoing Document appeared in the magazine *Perhaps Today*, November/December 1993 issue.

JERUSALEM

Israeli Prime Minister Benjamin Netanyahu who was honored at the National Unity Coalition Breakfast in Washington, D.C. along with other remarks, said:

Jerusalem Lives (חי) !

"*Jerusalem* is the City of David, the city which the nation of Israel has cherished as its capital for three thousand years. And it is something that defies all rational explanations. The connection of the Jewish people to its land and to its eternal city has broken all laws of history. Today some describe it as 'Arab East Jerusalem.' No! This is the place where David ruled. This is the place where Isaiah prophesied his eternal prophecies. This is the place where I walk and feel my ancestors' stones on those paths on that ground. Jerusalem was, is, and will always be the capital of Israel."

—Quoted from *Friends of Israel Gospel Ministry, Inc.*
newsletter of May 22, 1997

THE FIVE BOOKS OF MOSES, THE TORAH

Hebrew Titles

1. *Bereshith*–"In the Beginning"
2. *Shemo*–"Names" "Now these are the *Names*"
3. *Vayikra*–"And Called" "And the Lord called"
4. *B'midbar*–"In the Wilderness"
5. *Devarim*–"Words" "These be the words"

English Titles

1. *Genesis*–"Beginning"
2. *Exodus*–"Going Out" or "Departure"
3. *Leviticus*–"Levite's" or "the Priest's"
4. *Numbers*–Israelites 2 *numberings*
5. *Deuteronomy*–2nd Law (Repetition of 10 commandments and added laws.)

THE SCROLL OF THE LAW AND ISRAEL'S HIGH PRIEST

When the Ark ("Aron ha-Kodesh," "The Holy Ark") is opened in the Synagogue the Torah Scrolls are seen with their crowns of finely worked silver upon them. On these crowns are ornaments called *rimmonim* which means "pomegranates" an ancient symbol of life and fruitfulness. According to the *Midrash*, there are exactly 613 seeds within a pomegranate, corresponding to the number of *mitzvot* prescribed in the Torah. ("Who wants to count them?")

On most of these crowns and pomegranates or *rimmonim* on the Torah Scrolls there are little tinkling *bells* hanging in various openings so that when the Torah is moved there is heard a sweet and pleasing sound. (Israel's ancient High Priest wore *bells* with *pomegranates* on his robe of blue according to God's commandment in Exodus 28:34.) The roller of the Torah scroll is called *Etz Hayyim* ("Tree of Life"). See Proverbs 3:18. The Torah has a silver *breastplate* called by the Hebrew name *Hoshen* and is sometimes decorated with jewels even as was the breastplate of the High Priest of ancient Israel (Exodus 28:15-21).

THE COMPLETION OF THE OLD TESTAMENT

Flavius Josephus (his Roman name. His Hebrew name was *Yosef ben Mattiyahu*), the Jewish historian (100 AD) assures us that there were but 22 books that made up the Sacred Scriptures (the same 39 books of the Old Testament), but Jews today accept the fact of **24 books in the Holy Scriptures.**

"For we have not an innumerable multitude of books among us [Jews] ... only *twenty-two* books, which contain the records of all the past times; which are justly believed to be divine ... It is true, our history hath been written since Artaxerxes very particularly, but hath not been esteemed of the like authority with the former by our forefathers, because there hath not been an exact succession of prophets since that time; and how firmly we have given credit to these books of our own nation is evident by what we do ... no one has been so bold as either to add anything to them, to take anything from them, or to make any change in them; but it is become natural to all Jews immediately, and from their very birth, to esteem these books to contain Divine doctrines, and to persist in them, and, if occasion be, willingly to die for them ..."[94]

THE HEBREW BIBLE

Jewish people do not think in terms of "Testaments" when referring to their Bible. To them the Hebrew Scriptures (OT) is divided into three divisions: The *Torah* (*law*, made up of Genesis, Exodus, Leviticus, Numbers, and Deuteronomy which are the five books of Moses), the *Neviim* (*prophets*, comprised of the historical books Joshua, Judges, 1 and 2 Samuel, 1 and 2 Kings, the major prophets Isaiah, Jeremiah, Ezekiel, and the minor prophets Hosea, Joel, Amos, Obadiah, Jonah, Micah, Nahum, Habakkuk, Zephaniah, Haggai, Zechariah, and Malachi), the *Ketuvim* (*writings*, divided into the Wisdom Books of *Psalms*, Proverbs, and Job, and the *Megilot* consisting of Song of Songs, Ruth, Lamentations, Ecclesiastes, and Esther; also the prophets, Ezra, Nehemiah, and Daniel, as also the history books of 1 and 2 Chronicles).

We call the first part of the Bible by the term "Old Testament" which is composed of 39 books, yet the Hebrew Scriptures (the *T'nakh* תַנַ"ךְ) is arranged into *24* books. The 12 minor prophets are counted as one book, the books of 1 and 2 Samuel, 1 and 2 Kings, and 1 and 2 Chronicles are each considered as one book.

The NT bears witness to the three-fold division of Scripture in Luke 24:44, where Messiah Jesus refers to all things written concerning him "in the *law* of Moses, and in the *prophets*, and in the *psalms*." Here, as in many other places, the Lord used a Hebraism. In our modern language, he probably would have used a phrase like, "in the entire Old Testament," in the *T'nakh* (תַנַ"ךְ).

The Law, in familiar order, is comprised of the *Pentateuch*–the five books of Moses, **The Law**. These are followed by **The Prophets** in chronological order: The Earlier Prophets: Joshua, Judges, 1 and 2 Samuel and 1 and 2 Kings, and The Later Prophets: Isaiah, Jeremiah, Ezekiel, Hosea, Joel, Amos, Obadiah, Jonah, Micah, Nahum, Habakkuk, Zephaniah, Haggai, Zechariah and Malachi. After these we find **The Writings**, which include Psalms, Proverbs, Job, Son of Solomon, Ruth, Lamentations, Ecclesiastes, Esther, Daniel, Ezra, Nehemiah and 1 and 2 Chronicles. (Chronicles is the last book of the Hebrew Scriptures.)

---

[94]"Against Apion," I.8, in *The Life and Works of Flavius Josephus,* translated by William Whiston.

Originally, the book of Psalms was placed right after the book of Ruth which is the account of David's godly Gentile grandmother. Most of the Psalms were composed by David and it was thought that logically his writings ought to follow his genealogy which is found at the close of the book of Ruth. Nevertheless, perhaps due to its prominent place in Jewish life and thought, eventually the book of *Psalms* was placed first in "Ketuvim," *The Writings.*

T'NAKH (תנ״ך), THE HEBREW SCRIPTURES

Key to the following Outline: Numbers to the left of the title indicate order and number of the *24 books of the Hebrew Bible.* The numbers in brackets to the right of the Title indicate the order and number of the English "Authorized Version."

A. **TORAH** (Law)
    1. Bereshith (Genesis) [1]
    2. Shemot (Exodus) [2]
    3. Vayikra (Leviticus) [3]
    4. B'midvar (Numbers) [4]
    5. Devarim (Deuteronomy) [5]
B. **NEVI'IM** (Prophets)
(a) Nevi'im Rishonim (Early Prophets)
    6. Yehoshua (Joshua) [6]
    7. Shofetim (Judges) [7]
    8. Shemuel (Samuel)
        Shemuel Alef (1st Samuel) [9]
        Shemuel Bet (2nd Samuel) [10]
    9. Melakhim (Kings)
        Melakhim Alef (1st Kings) [11]
        Melakhim Bet (2nd Kings) [12]
(b) Nevi'im Aharonim (Later Prophets)
    10. Yeshayah (Isaiah) [23]
    11. Yirmeyah (Jeremiah) [24]
    12. Yehezke-el (Ezekiel) [26]
    13. Teray 'Asar (12 Prophets)
        Hoshea (Hosea) [28]
        Yoel (Joel) [29]
        Amus (Amos) [30]
        Obadyah (Obadiah) 31]
        Yonah (Jonah) [32]
        Michah (Micah) [33]
        Nachum (Nahum) [34]
        Habakkuk (Habakkuk) [35]
        Tsefanyah (Zephaniah) [36]
        Chagai (Haggai) [37]
        Zecharyah (Zechariah) [38]
        Malakhi (Malachi) [39]

C. **KETUVIM** (Writings) (Greek–*Hagiographa*)
(a) Former Writings
        14. Tehillim (Psalms) [19]
        15. Mishle (Proverbs) [20]
        16. Iyob (Job) [18]
(b) Hamaysh Megillot (Five Rolls)
        (For reading at 5 Jewish Festivals)
        17. Shir Hashirim (Song of Songs) [22]
            (Pesach)
        18. Roos (Ruth) [8]
            (Shavuot)
        19. Ekhah (Lamentations) [25]
            (Tishah B'av)
        20. Kohelet (Ecclesiastes) [21]
        21. Ester (Esther) [17]
            (Purim)
(c) Later Writings
        22. Danyel (Daniel) [27]
        23. Ezra (Ezra) [15]
            Nechemah (Nehemiah) [16]
        24. Dibre Hayamim (Chronicles)
            Dibre Hayamim Alef (1st Chronicles) [13]
            Dibre hayamim Bet (2nd Chronicles) [14]

OUTLINE LESSON OF THE HEBREW SCRIPTURES

I.   **THE WORD, TANAKH** (T'nakh)
    A. Its Origin
       1. Messiah's division of the Bible, Luke 24:44
       2. Refers to three sections of Hebrew Scriptures.
    B. Divisions of T'nakh
       1. *Torah*—Law of Moses
          (The word *Torah* signifies *teaching* or *doctrine*. According to Jewish tradition the Torah was in existence in heaven and was merely brought down to Moses at Mount Sinai! Another story in the Talmud relates that God offered the Torah to all the nations of the world, but all refused it except Israel!)
       2. *Nevi'im*—Prophets
       3. *Ketuvim*—Writings, (*Psalms* begin the remainder of the T'nakh; see arrangement of The Hebrew Scriptures under *Ketuvim*).
    C. Acrostic of **T N K**.
       1. Or *acronym*—a word formed from the first (or first few) letters of several words.
       2. Acrostics popular with Jewish scholars.
       3. Definition of "acrostic."
          a. Greek—"akros,"—"end," "stichos,"—"line"
          b. Encyclopedia of Jewish Knowledge: "Poetic compositions in which an initial, middle or end letter of each line form a name or phrase."

4. Some acrostics in the Bible:
    a. Alphabet acrostic—Psalm 119, Psalm 25 and Psalm 34
        1) Psalm 25 and 34 have 22 verses—one to each letter
            of the alphabet in order.
        2) Psalms 111 and 112—each verse in two parts
            following alphabetical order.
    b. Most of the Lamentations of Jeremiah are acrostics, some
        of the chapters repeating each letter one or more times.
    c. Last chapter in Proverbs—initial letters of its last 22 verses
        in alphabetical order.
    d. T'nakh
        T orah $\left.\begin{array}{l}\end{array}\right\}$ **TeNaK**
        N eviim
        K etuvim
5. Other Acrostics (or acronyms)
    a. **R** abbi **M** oses **B** en **M** iamon (**RaMBaM**)
    b. Aleph-Mem-Tav
        1) First, Middle, Last letters of Hebrew Alphabet. E M T
            —**EMeT** or Truth
    c. **R** abbi **SH** olomon **Y** itschoki—**RaSHY** (Rashi)
    d. **B** a'al **SH** em **T** ov—**BeSHT**, "Master of the Good Name."
    e. CHABAD (**CHaBaD**)
        "Chabad" ("Habad") is an acronym for **Chochmoh,
        Binah, Daath**—the Hebrew words, "*wisdom, understand-
        ing* and *knowledge*," the three components of the human
        intellect. *Chabad* is that branch of the chassidic movement
        which was founded approximately 200 years ago by Rabbi
        Shnuer Zalman of Liadi in Eastern Europe. See *Chabad*
        (*wisdom, understanding* and *knowledge*) in Exodus 31:3.
    f. The early Christians, as is evident by the catacombs in
        Rome, commonly used acrostics in epitaphs. A favorite
        secret symbol of their unwavering faith, under the fires of
        persecution, was the outline drawing of a fish. The Greek
        word for FISH is ICHTHUS. And this is put into the
        following acrostic:

I eosus	Jesus	
CH ristos	Christ	
TH eou	God's	
U ios	Son	
S oter	Saviour	

⊂ANON OF SCRIPTURE

"The early Christian church used a very convenient word to
explain the admissibility or the inadmissibility of a book into Holy
Scripture. It spoke of the 'canon' of Scripture. The word 'canon'
means a 'rod,' (a measuring rod). Thus modern scholars will speak
of the ancient discussions as to the canonicity of a certain book,
namely, *its right to be admitted in the Bible.*

"There is no Hebrew word corresponding to the words *canon* and *canonical*, though, of course, the scholars who arranged the Bible had the idea or the thought of 'canonical.' They used a phrase which is meant to be its equivalent, but the phrase is a very strange one to us. They said frequently that 'holy books defile the hands' (*m. Yadaim iii*, 5), or, when they wanted to say that a certain book was *not sacred*, they would dismiss it with the statement that it *did not defile the hands.*

"It is a little difficult to explain how that phrase, 'to defile the hands' came to mean what we now call 'canonical.' When hands were defiled through ritual impurities they required formal washing. The Rabbis meant, therefore, that the touching of sacred books required washing of the hands. They had a general practice, or precedent, for the practice of washing the hands after touching sacred objects. For example, the high priest on the Day of Atonement, when he put on his various types of sacred garments, was required to wash his hands after handling them. This was a symbol of sacredness. Applying it as a test for sacred books, they accomplished two purposes. Applying first, they guaranteed against careless and irreverent handling. Second, they indicated that the books were so sacred that whoever touched them could not then proceed to touch ordinary profane objects without making a distinction by washing his hands. At all events, this was their phrase which is equivalent to our modern phrase, 'canonical.' If a book were sacred, it required a ritual washing of the hands after one touched it and before one touched any other object.

"*The Tosefta* (an early Talmudic book parallel to the Mishnah) uses the phrase 'to defile the hands' in the following quotation: 'The blank margins of books and the books of the heretical sects do not defile the hands. The books of Ben Sirach and all the books that were written after them do not defile the hands" (*Tosefta Yadaim* II, 13). This passage indicates that the phrase 'to defile the hands' describes the sacredness of a Biblical book. It also indicates that the date of a book's composition was a test of its admissibility into the Bible."[95]

INTERESTING FACTS CONCERNING THE SCRIPTURES

There are 263 Old Testament quotes in the New Testament; 376 quotes are less direct=639 (slightly varied by some expositors).

The formula of quotations is most generally: *"that it might be fulfilled,"* or *"It is* ['has been'] *written."* The word is *"gegraptai"* which means *"it has been written and remains written"* (see John 10:35 w/Matthew 24:35). Also the words: *"The Scripture cannot be*

---

[95]Solomon B. Freehof, *Preface to Scripture,* pp. 16, 17.

broken" to be compared with Isaiah 40:8, *"... the word of our God shall stand for ever."* Whenever the Hebrew Scriptures are referred to in the New Testament (Covenant) the phrases are: "the Scripture saith" *"according to the scriptures"* and as above: "It is written," "that it might be fulfilled," etc. The writers of the New Testament refer to the T'nakh (OT) in the following: Acts 15:15 *"by the mouth of David hath said,"* Acts 4:25, (in the Psalms), Acts 2:35, etc. Messiah Jesus used the phrase *"by the Holy Ghost,"* Mark 12:36. *"The Holy Ghost said"* or *"The Holy Ghost by ..."* in relation to the Word of God.

In the New Testament there are 190 references to the 5 books of Moses, 101 references to the Psalms, 104 references to book of Isaiah, 30 references to minor prophets. Messiah Jesus constantly referred to the Tanakh since the New Testament did not appear until perhaps 20 years after Messiah's death and resurrection. He entered and ended His earthly ministry referring to the Scriptures; i.e., Matthew 4:4, 7, 10; Luke 24:46. He accepted Scriptures (Mark 7:6, 9-10, 13) as the very Word of God. He referred to the Scriptures when He said to His disciples: *"Have you not read in the **book of Moses"***(Mark 12:26 w/ Matthew 12:3, 19:4) and *"What did **Moses** command you?"* (Mark 10:3). Messiah also taught His followers: *"You search the Scriptures ... His Word ... they bear witness of me"* (John 5:38, 39).

THE WORD OF GOD

"Is like Gold and sweetening like Honey (Psalm 19:10);
Refining like Fire and breaking like a Hammer (Jeremiah 23:29);
Dividing like a Sword and discerning like a Critic (Hebrews 4:12);
Nourishing like Milk and developing like Meat (Hebrews 5:12-14);
Revealing like a Mirror (James 1:23-25);
Reproducing like a Seed (Matthew 13:3) and
Cleansing like Water (Ephesians 5:26)."

—Dr. Henry J. Heydt

A BIT OF CHRONOLOGY

Genesis V

Adam lived	930	years;	
Adam was	130	years old when	Seth
was born; which was	800	years before	Adam
died. Seth was	105	years old when	Enos
was born	695	years before	Adam
died. Enos was	90	years old when	Cainan
was born; which was	605	years before	Adam
died. Cainan was	70	years old when	Mahalaleel
was born; which was	535	years before	Adam died.
Mahalaleel was	65	years old when	Jared was
born; which was	470	years before	Adam died.
Jared was	162	years old when Enoch was born;	
which was	300	years before	Adam died.
Enoch was	65	years old when	Methuselah
was born; which was	243	years before Adam died.	
Methuselah was	187	years old when Lamech	
was born; which was	56	years before Adam died.	

Lamech could have talked with Adam 56 years of his life, 874 years from creation.

Lamech was	182	years old when
Noah was born	56	years of that time,
Adam lived; or	126	years after Adam's death Noah
was born. Adam's age was	930	years.
Noah was	600	years old at time of the flood

(Genesis 7), which makes .... 1,656 years from creation to the flood, computing Adam's age and Noah's age at the time of the flood, and the 126 years between Adam and Noah.

The following will show some of the questions easily answered by the preceding order of reckoning:

*Did Lamech die before or after the flood?

Lamech was	182	years old when Noah was born,
and Noah was	600	years old at the time of the
flood, which makes	782	years to the flood; but
Lamech was only	777	years old when he died;
Lamech therefore died just	5	years before the flood.

*Did Methuselah die before or after the flood? He just escaped the flood.

Methuselah was	187	years old when
Lamech was born;	777	was Lamech's age when he died,
thus	964	years was Methuselah's age 5

years before the flood.

*How long before the flood did Adam die?

	1,656	are the years from creation to
the flood.	930	was Adam's age when he died;
therefore he died.	726	years before the flood.

Adam could have dandled on his knee all his children and grand-children down the line to Lamech. All could have heard from Adam's own lips the story of the Fall. Lamech, Noah's father, lived 56 years during Adam's life. He could have attended Adam's funeral, after which he lived 721 years.

Is Genesis 3:15 all that Adam is supposed to know about the gospel and the plan of redemption before he died? We have every reason to believe that God gave Adam a clear revelation of the same, as exemplified in the life of his son, Abel; all may not be able to see or believe this; for the benefit of those who do not, we direct you to the first column of figures which shows that Adam lived 308 years during Enoch's life, with whom he might have talked about God and his wonderful experience in walking with Him, and his prospective translation; Enoch was a preacher of righteousness (Jude 14). Enoch lived 365 years, 308 years of this time Adam lived, but Enoch did not begin to walk with God until 65 years of his life had expired (Genesis 5:21,22). Adam died 57 years before Enoch was translated. Just how long could Adam have talked with Enoch about walking with God? The answer is found incidentally in the first column of figures.

Lovingly Dedicated to the Young Bible Student,
by CORA CHILSON FANNON (Pasadena, California)

THE MOST IMPORTANT CHAPTER IN THE BIBLE
Genesis 3

You may not agree with the heading of this study, but we believe that we are right in the statement, and for several reasons. First, if we take Genesis 3 out of the Bible we have absolutely no reason for the eleven hundred eighty-six [1,186] chapters which follow it. If sin did not come into the world as recorded in Genesis 3, then certainly God would not be so foolish as to write eleven hundred eighty-six chapters to tell how sin must be cared for. If we take the third chapter of Genesis out of the Bible, we might as well take the nineteenth chapter of John out, also.

The nineteenth chapter of John is one that deals with the cruci-fixion of Christ, but if sin did not come into the world as recorded in Genesis 3, then certainly Jesus Christ did not need to go to the Cross, for the only reason for Calvary was human sin. Further-more, whenever you show us a man who denies the historicity of Genesis 3 we will show you a man who denies salvation by blood.

The Greatest Text

Again, we believe Genesis 3 to be the most important chapter in the Bible because it contains a verse which is the seed plot of the whole Bible. We refer to Genesis 3:15. These are the words of God to Satan after the fall of man. "And I (God) will put enmity between thee (Satan) and the woman (Eve), and between thy seed (the seed of the serpent) and her seed (the seed of the woman): it (the seed of the woman) shall bruise thy (Satan's) head, and thou (Satan) shalt bruise his (the seed of the woman's) heel."

The rest of the Bible is nothing but an expansion of this verse. We can follow the truth of this verse through the Old Testament out into the New, and see it coming to its consummation in the very last chapter in the Book of the Revelation.

We consider Genesis 3:15 one of the greatest texts in the Word of God. It includes John 3:16, but much more. It is the first prophecy of the Lord Jesus Christ and was uttered by God in judgment against the serpent very soon after that being had accomplished the fall of man.

In this verse we have the first and second comings of Christ. In the first coming His heel was bruised. In His second coming the Serpent's head is to be crushed. The heel and the head of this verse are not literal. They are figures of speech bringing to us the thought of the earth life of Christ represented by the heel, and the rulership of Satan represented by the head. Many, many times in Scripture, God used the figure of the foot to set forth the life we live. Satan is spoken of in Scripture as the "prince of this world" and the "god of this age." Note that in this verse the second coming of Christ is mentioned before the first coming.

In this verse we have the virgin birth of Christ. By "the seed of the woman" Christ is meant, of course. He is the only One of all the millions of earth who stands out as the seed of the woman. He is not the seed of Adam. Human fatherhood cannot enter in at all. The man who does not believe in the virgin birth of Christ must cut Genesis 3:15 out of the Scriptures.

In this verse we have the death of Christ. "Thou shalt bruise his heel." This refers to the suffering and death of Christ which was accomplished by Satan—and through a literal bruising of the heel! Satan entered into Judas to accomplish his evil purpose.

In this verse we have the resurrection of Christ, for the Seed of the Woman who is put to death by the Serpent afterward crushes and destroys the one who put Him to death.

In this verse we have the enmity between the seed of the serpent and the Seed of the woman. This is an enmity between anti-Christ and Christ. You are now in Revelation 19 where you see the outcome of this enmity. The Christ is victorious. The beast and false prophet are both cast alive into the Lake of Fire.

In this verse we have the enmity between Satan himself and the Seed of the Woman. The crushing of the head of the serpent means more than the crushing of a bony skull; it means the over-throw of Satan's plans and plots, policies and purposes, and you now in the last chapters of the Book of the Revelation, for therein is the record of this accomplishment.

In this verse we have the declaration of Satan's failure. "I will put enmity between thee and the woman." There is no doubt that Satan planned that these two in the Garden of Eden, with all the multiplied millions of descendants, should be his slaves forever, but God planted within the heart that faith faculty which should be able to resist the devil and bring freedom from his bondage.

In this verse we have regeneration, for certainly there has never been enmity between anyone and Satan unless that one has been born from above. The mind of the flesh is always enmity against God and only through the Spirit is there enmity against Satan.

The importance of this chapter is seen in the fact that we have in it, in type, for the first time in Scripture, salvation through the blood of a substitute, and through the faith of a man. It pictures in a very vivid way salvation from sin by the grace of God.

There are some who say that Genesis 3 is nothing but an old Babylonian myth or fable, but wherever you find man today you will find thorns and thistles just as Genesis 3 says—and this is not fable, but fact.

There are some who say that Genesis 3 is nothing but an old Babylonian myth or fable, but we have seen men in city and country, in field and factory, in mine and mountain earning their bread by the sweat of their face just as Genesis 3 says—and this is not fable, but fact.

Genesis 3 gives us the history of the entrance of sin into the world and into the human race, and the chaotic condition in the world today can be explained on no other grounds. Sin is not a theory but a fact, tragic and stubborn. We can never appreciate the awfulness of it until we look at Calvary.

—Robert L. Moyer,
The Most Important Chapter in the Bible

GOD WROTE A BOOK

I was amazed to discover while studying the Holy Scriptures that there is a Book God Himself has written. *No, it is not the Bible.* The *Bible* has been written by *holy men of old* who were God-inspired (2 Timothy 3:16). Though the Book God wrote is *not* the Bible, the

Bible mentions it 12 times.[96] In these passages God's Book is mentioned under various terms being called "thy book" and "my book," "the book of the living," "the book of life," "the Lamb's book of life" and "the book of life of the Lamb." These terms are all applied to the "Book of Life" but this does not mean that, because there are various titles, each one is a separate Book. For example, we have several names for the Bible: the Holy Scriptures, the Oracles of God, the Law and the Prophecies, the Word of God, the Sword of the Spirit, and others. So we have several names for the Book that God has written.

What was written in God's Book besides the names of all the redeemed? We learn the answer to this question in the words of David, the Psalmist:

*"I will praise thee; for I am fearfully and wonderfully made: marvellous are thy works; and that my soul knoweth right well. My substance was not hid from thee, when I was made in secret, and curiously wrought in the lowest parts of the earth. Thine eyes did see my substance, yet being unperfect; and in **thy book all my members were written**, which in continuance were fashioned, when as yet there was none of them. How precious also are thy thoughts unto me, O God! how great is the sum of them!"* (Psalm 139:14-17).

David said that all his substance or members of his body which God had fashioned He wrote in His book even before these members were actually created! Not only does this pertain to David but it refers also to each one of us. Even the "hairs of our head are numbered" (see Matthew 10:30; Luke 12:7)! Think of the millions of people who have been born into the world since the beginning of time, each having a head of hair (some without) and each little hair God has numbered. It is written in His Book! As David exclaimed "how marvellous are His works!"

In connection with the foregoing subject, I thought of my Computer which I have been using to write all of my books. We are living in the age of the Computer which man has invented. What a complicated "machine" with all its many parts! I asked my daughter, Wuffy Evans and my son, Duane Bagaas, a Computer "Expert," how many parts does the Computer have and their reply was "A BaZillion." Those who work on Computers might know the names of each of these "BaZillion" parts, but this does not half compare to the human brain which God has created, named and written in His Book!

Do you know modern science teaches that the mind has *13 billion cells*? Each cell has 25,000 connections and we receive input at the

---

[96]Exodus 32:32-33; Psalm 69:28;109:13; Daniel 12:1; Luke 10:20; Philippians 4:3; Revelation 3:5; 13:8; 17:8; 20:12, 15; 21:27; 22:18-19.

rate of seven billion inputs per second. Someone has said that the brain is a Master Computer unequaled by the invention of man! Only God could accomplish this remarkable work of "art" and write it in a book!

Adam had a computer-like mind that was far superior to ours today. It was created a perfect brain with computer memory circuits unaffected by decay, breakdown, aging, deterioration, death. Adam could think; he could reason; he could understand. He demonstrated this by his astonishing capability of naming all the creatures on earth according to their specific nature and purpose. All this God wrote in His book!

David exclaimed: "I am fearfully and wonderfully made." When we consider the descriptions which *man* has given concerning the human body we also make the same exclamation! The following is one of these descriptions:

"The human *body* is a wonderful living machine. There are 20,000,000 little mouths or lacteals that suck food as it passes through the 32 feet of intestines. There are 263 bones, 600 muscles, 970 miles of blood vessels, 30 pounds of blood or about six quarts, or one fifth of the entire weight, which makes a complete circuit every two minutes.

"The *heart* is a pump about four by six inches in size and beats 70 times a minute, 4,200 times an hour, 36,792,000 times a year, and at each beat four ounces of blood are expelled from the heart, which is about 16 pounds a minute, 12 tons a day, 4,000 tons a year, 240,000 tons in sixty years. It is a ceaseless organ, day and night, and pumps in a day what is equal to lifting 200 tons one foot high.

"The *lung* capacity of an adult is 320 cubic inches with 600,000,000 air cells that take in about 2,400 gallons of air a day. Air cells exceed 20,000 square inches, an area nearly equal to a floor of a room twelve feet square.

"The *brain* of a man weighs about three pounds and two ounces, and that of the woman two pounds and 12 ounces. About 10,000,000 *nerves* are connected with it directly or by spinal marrow.

"Each square inch of *skin* contains about 3,500 sweating tubes, each of which may be likened to a drain pipe one-fourth of an inch long, making a total length of 201,155 feet or about 40 miles.

"The *nose* smells and distinguishes instantly about 6,000 different odors. The *ears* have 20,000 hairs to tune in on every known sound and can register and distinguish them instantly. The *jaw* has a 40-pound pressure. The *tongue* has 400 cups that can taste any known thing and relay it to the brain at once. The *voice* can travel across the world in about four-hundredths of a second.

"A 200-pound body contains about one-fourth ounce of iron, one-fifth ounce of sugar, two ounces of salt, 24 pounds of coal (in carbon form), 10 gallons of water, one-tenth drop of iodine, two pounds of phosphorus, 112 cubic feet of oxygen, 60 of nitrogen, 561 of hydrogen, and seven pounds of lime, or about 98¢ worth of chemicals."[97]

Just think: God has written a Book in which the preceding account is included for everyone who is born (as well of those not yet born) into the world!

My Jewish people believe there is a Book of Life (*Sefer ha-Hayyim*) in heaven. On Rosh haShanah (New Year) and on Yom Kippur (Day of Atonement) devout Jews pray that their names would be written there. A Jewish writing explains:

"It was anciently held that the names of the righteous were recorded in heaven, and to have one's name expunged from it was a Divine sentence of death. Later, an eschatological significance was given to the concept, and to be written in the Book of Life meant to be inscribed for immortality in the World to Come which followed the ***Messianic Age***. A Book of Death in this connexion [*sic*] was set beside the Book of Life. An annual inscription for temporal life or death was associated with New Year's Day, made absolute on the Day of Atonement."[99]

To Jews the accepted salutation on the Jewish New Year is *Leshanah Tovah* which means "Happy New Year." Many employ the fuller form: *Leshanah tovah tikosev* meaning "May a good year be inscribed in your behalf" *i.e.*, in the Book of Life.

"According to a Jewish tradition God inscribes names in the Book of Life on the New Year and on the Day of Atonement God's signature or seal is attached to the blessed inscription. Hence, the meaning of the full *Rosh Hashanah* greetings: May you be inscribed for a good year. In the *Yom Kippur* greeting the word *vetechosem* is added i.e.—May the inscription for a good year be signed and sealed in your behalf."[100]

Those who are redeemed by the Lamb need not wonder, neither request their names to be written in God's Book of Life since it is certain that their names are there because they have accepted God's redemption in Messiah Jesus! God's book is also called "The Lamb's Book of Life" ("The Book of Life of the Lamb") and the "Book of the Living." In it is written the names of His redeemed people since

[97]Finis Jennings Dake, *God's Plan For Man, Part I: The Origin of All Things,* pp. 17-18. Also quoted in my *Pictures of Messiah,* pp. 219-220.
[98]Scroll sketched by Howard Morlock. Illustration formed by Duane Bagaas.
[99]Schonfield, Hugh. *A Popular Dictionary of Judaism,* p. 37.
[100]Abraham Mayer Heller, *The Vocabulary of Jewish Life,* pp. 20-21.

Book of Life" ("The Book of Life of the Lamb") and the "Book of the Living." In it is written the names of His redeemed people since the world began as well as the specified "members" of each person's body! Also written in the book God wrote is a record of his wanderings and the tears that he shed. We read this in David's Psalm:

> *"Thou tellest my **wanderings**: put thou my **tears** into thy bottle: are **they** not in **thy book**?"* (Psalm 56:8).

This Book (not the Bible) is given several Titles which are referred to in the Scriptures as follows: Moses called it *"thy book which thou hast written"* (Exodus 32:32). He believed that names written in this *book of life* could be blotted out because of sin. He interceded for Israel and mentioned *God's Book:*

> *"Yet now, if thou wilt forgive their sin—; and if not, blot me, I pray thee, out of **thy book which thou hast written**"* (Exodus 32:32).

David called it *"the book of the living"* and he also believed that a person's name in this book could be erased because of sin. He prayed concerning his enemies:

> *"Let them be **blotted out of the book of the living**, and not be written with the righteous"* (Psalm 69:28).

Paul mentioned *the book of life* when he wrote of his fellow-laborers:

> *"And I entreat thee also, true yokefellow, help those women which laboured with me in the gospel, with Clement also, and with other my fellowlabourers, **whose names are in the book of life**"* (Philippians 4:3).

God, who wrote the Book of Life referred to the fact that once a person's name is written in this Book does not guarantee the fact that it always will be there but can be blotted out due to sin (Exodus 32:33) and so did Messiah Jesus believe this:

> *"He that overcometh, the same shall be clothed in white raiment; and I will **not** blot out his name out of **the book of life**, but I will confess his name before my Father, and before his angels"* (Revelation 3:5).

Paul called God's Book *"the book of life"* (Philippians 4:3) which is found also in the following verses of Scripture:

> *"And all that dwell upon the earth shall worship him, whose names are not written in **the book of life of the Lamb** slain from the foundation of the world"* (Revelation 13:8).

> *"The beast that thou sawest was, and is not; and shall ascend out of the bottomless pit, and go into perdition: and they that*

*dwell on the earth shall wonder, whose names were **not** written in **the book of life** from the foundation of the world, when they behold the beast that was, and is not, and yet"* (Revelation 17:8).

*"And I saw the dead, small and great, stand before God; and the **books**[101] were opened and **another** book was opened, which is **the book of life**: and the dead were judged out of those things which were written in the **books, according to their works**"* (Revelation 20:12).

There are several books opened besides the *Book of Life*. One of these is called "the book of remembrance":

*"Then they that **feared the LORD** spake often one to another: and the LORD hearkened, and heard it, and a **book of remembrance** was written before him for them that feared the LORD, and that thought upon his name"* (Malachi 3:16).

Whenever we think of our wonderful Lord and we reverence Him, speaking often of Him, this is recorded in "the book of remembrance." It is not clear that the Lord Himself wrote this book for as it is said it was written before (in front of) Him. According to Jewish belief there is a Recording Angel who records all the deeds, good and bad, of all individuals for future reward and punishment. And this, they believe is called "the book of remembrance."

*"And whosoever was not found written in **the book of life** was cast into the lake of fire"* (Revelation 20:15).

*"And there shall in no wise enter into it any thing that defileth, neither whatsoever worketh abomination, or maketh a lie: but they which are written in **the Lamb's book of life**"* (Revelation 21:27).

*"And if any man shall take away from the words of the book of **this** prophecy, God shall take away his part out of **the book of life**, and out of the holy city, and from the things which are written in **this book**"* (Revelation 22:19).

Notice in the above Scripture verse that mention is made concerning several books: *Book of this prophecy* (referring to the Book of the Revelation), also the *book of life* and **this** book.

Messiah Jesus spoke of God's Book when He spoke to His disciples about their joy in the work of deliverance:

*"Notwithstanding in this rejoice not, that the spirits are subject unto you; but rather rejoice, because **your names are written in heaven**"* (Luke 10:20).

Paul wrote a letter to the Hebrews, mentioning the Book God wrote:

---

[101]Several books were opened. How many–it is impossible to know.

"To the general assembly and church of the firstborn, which are **written in heaven,** *and to God the Judge of all, and to the spirits of just men made perfect,"* (Hebrews 12:23).

Thank God, I know that my name is written by God in the Lamb's Book of Life because I have been redeemed! Oh, that the prayers of my Jewish people on their New Year (*Rosh HaShanah*) and on their Day of Atonement (*Yom Kippur*)will be answered which they pray: "Remember us unto life, O King, who delightest in life, and inscribe us in the Book of Life for thine own sake, O Living God!"

EXPLANATION OF FRONTISPIECE

The photograph shows my great-grandfather, Lipeh Saltzman, who was one of the *Hasidim* (from the singular word, *hasid*, meaning "pious" [one]. The word *Hasid* refers to a Jew of extreme piety.) Notice his parted beard and side-curls, which were and still are the mark of a very devout Jew. The side-curls are called *peyot* (sing., *peyah*: "edge," "side," "curl," "lock," "point of the beard") and are worn in obedience to God's command *"...neither shalt thou mar the corners of thy beard."* The hair is not cut, in observance of the command: *"ye shall not round the corners of your heads."* These commands against heathen practices are found in Leviticus 19:27 and 21:5.

The fur-trimmed hat, called a *shtreiml*, which centuries ago was the distinguishing head cover of the Polish aristocracy, is today an emblem of the Hasidim. The shtreiml is another sign of Jewish respect and devotion to God.

The clothing Rabbi Saltzman is wearing is the everyday dress of the *kohanim* (priests) at that time. It was worn with a belt and could be used for ordinary service in the synagogue, but at prayer times and when officiating in the Temple he would also wear the "tallit" (prayer shawl) over his garments. Instead of the "tallit," sometimes he would wear a long-sleeved white robe called *Kittel* by the Hasidim. It was worn by the pious on New Year's day (Rosh Hashana), the Day of Atonement (Yom Kippur), and at Passover Seders (services at the meal times of the first and second nights). Also this "kittel" was used as a burial shroud.

The embroidered sash-belt over his coat is from the commandment of God to His priests concerning their garments in Old Testament days as they ministered in the Tabernacle (see Exodus 28:8).

Rabbi Saltzman ministered in Jerusalem during the last days of his life. According to the Talmud, "One who lives in Jerusalem has a share in the life to come." Before he left Russia for Jerusalem, his youngest son, Avram, pleaded with him to leave a portrait of himself

~ 323 ~

with the family since never again would they see him in person. (They knew he was going to the Holy Land to live his last days.) So, at the insistent pleas of his son, this photo was taken. It is the only photograph of the Rabbi, because he was otherwise careful to obey the First Commandment of God prohibiting any likeness or image of things in heaven or on earth. The Hasidim of Israel, as well as elsewhere, observe this commandment today.

THE HASIDIC MOVEMENT

"The *Chasidic* [Hasidic] movement founded by the Baal Shem [Master of the Name], (1700-1760) brought a new spirit into Jewish life at a time when Judaism served the needs of men of learning but failed to satisfy in full measure the spiritual needs of the less learned. *Chasidism* emphasized:

Hasidim in Worship

(1) The emotional expression of Judaism as opposed to its legal and intellectual phases,
(2) The Omnipresence and Immanence of God,
(3) The superiority of faith over learning,
(4) The potential worthiness of man, even in the lowest strata of human society.
(5) The potency of prayer in the spirit of selflessness expressed by emotional outbursts accompanied by the swaying of body and vociferous chanting. (*Hislahavus*—enthusiasm is the term adopted by *Chasidim* to describe this method of worship.)
(6) Greater religious importance of Jewish womanhood, and
(7) Personal loyalty to the *Tsadik*, the spiritual leader."[102]

In opposition to those who had forsaken the strict observance of the Torah (the Law) and had partly assimilated themselves to Hellenism, a movement of orthodox Jews called "Hasidim" (from the singular form, "hasid" meaning "pious") originated at about the beginning of the Second Century BC in Palestine (called *Israel* today). According to Jewish historians, in Mishnaic times (the Maccabean period), the Hasidim were militant, anti-Roman Pharisees mentioned as "a company of Hasideans," a transliteration of "Hasidim," in I Maccabees 2:42 and 7:13, also in II Maccabees 14:6. They joined Judah Maccabee in a revolt against Antiochus Epiphanes and his religion of idolatry which he was trying to force upon the Jews. From these Hasidim sprang various groups of devoted followers of the Torah, including the Pharisees and Essenes.

---

[102]Abraham Mayer Heller, *The Vocabulary of Jewish Life*, p. 233.

In the 18th Century the Hasidic philosophy of the original Pharisees was revived in Podolia on the *old* Polish-Turkish border. It is regarded by most Jews as the greatest Jewish revivalist movement of all time. This began among the priestly leaders but spread also to the laymen. Its founder was Israel ben Eliezer (1700-1760) who was called "the Besht" (initials of "Baal Shem Tov") or "Master of the Good Name." This title was given to those persons who have been credited with the power of working miracles by means of possessing the secret of the true pronunciation of the sacred Four-Lettered Name of God–YHWH or JHVH called–*The Sacred Tetragrammaton.* He taught against asceticism and self-affliction, claiming this as unacceptable in God's sight, and preached the hallowing of all passions to only delight in the service of God. His purpose was to establish a small, selected and highly exclusive school of men dedicated in the life of holiness, purity, unworldliness and spirituality. He instructed his pupils that there was joy to be expressed in the presence of God and that worship performed joyously brought God near. This led to physical ecstasy, dancing and religious singing expressed with enthusiasm. Through this kind of life the Hasid would be able to realize his aspiration to acquire the gift of possession by the "Ruach ha-Kodesh" (the Holy Spirit) and to attain a super-soul. The Hasid discovered in his religion a source of unquenchable joy.

It is surprising to learn that the long black coats and large furry hats worn by the Hasidim originated among **non-Jews**. These were high ranking Polish *Gentiles* who wore such clothing hundreds of years ago, *but it was forbidden to the Jews* at that time!

Baal Shem Tov (the "Besht") became known as a healer and as a traditional miracle-worker using the secret Divine Name (YHWH) by which he performed wonders. By means of incantations, prayer and magical formulae he would heal the masses that came to him. He stressed the Omnipresence of God and was instrumental in fore-shadowing the idea of the *Zaddik* (literally, the *Righteous*, which was applied to all Hasidic leaders) the *High Being*, mediator between God and His people.

A *Hasid* Rejoicing in Worship (holding Kiddush cup)

Since the Hasidim in their zeal for their beliefs stressed the sincere love for God and the effectiveness of prayer *rather than knowing the Talmud*, the Rabbis opposed "the Besht" who was their leader, his lack of Talmudic learning and his magical practices. In spite of this opposition he rapidly gained in authority and fame and he continued in his ministry over a period of 25 years.

The *Karaim* or *Karaites* of Israel today is another Jewish sect (founded by *Anan* in the latter part of the Eighth Century) who rejected the Rabbinic laws and the Talmud's interpretations of the Scriptures. They accept the Bible laws in a literal sense only.

Those who followed traditional religion from the Talmud were scandalized by the doctrine of exhibited joy which was an important part of the Hasidic movement. At one point of the persecutions arrayed against them, the Hasidim were accused of plotting the overthrow of the government which resulted in their imprisonment in 1798. After a long investigation the government officials of Russia (which now had incorporated most of Poland) found nothing objectionable in their teachings, either politically or morally. They were liberated from the prison and granted full freedom to practice their religion.

Today (1997) there are Hasidim in various parts of the world but mostly centered in Jerusalem, Israel, and the movement is spreading in revival once more. There is a Hasidic community in the Williamsburg neighborhood across the East River from Manhattan in New York which became a refuge for *thousands* of East European Hasidic Jews, survivors of the Nazi holocaust.

The Hasidic community in Jerusalem is known by the name *Meah Shearim* ("One Hundred Gates"). They believe that the present State of Israel, since it was founded by *men* and not the Messiah Himself, actually delays His coming! Another peculiarity of the Hasidic Jew is: he speaks Yiddish. He feels that Hebrew is too holy to be spoken and will be used when Messiah comes. Until that time Hebrew is used only for the study of the Holy Books.

As has been stated, this movement of the Hasidim is growing more and more in these last days before the return of Yeshua ha-Meshiach, the greatest of all Miracle Workers whose Name is Wonderful (Miraculous), Counsellor (of the) Mighty God, the Father of Eternity, the Prince of Peace (Isaiah 9:6)!

THE STORY OF THE ALPHABET

"So far as human knowledge is concerned, writing was in existence for thousands of years before the alphabet was invented. It is a matter of general knowledge that the signs invented for the alphabet are derived from the Greek, and that those who formulated them borrowed in turn from the Phoenician. Until lately the Phoenicians enjoyed the credit of being the originators. The archaeological evidence now suggests that the Phoenicians derived the alphabet from the *Israelites*."[103]

Until the second decade of the 20th Century, the earliest known examples of the Semitic alphabet were found in what is known as the

---

[103]Sir Charles Marston, *The Bible Comes Alive*, p.165. See Appendix of this book on page 284 for Alphabet forms.

Moabite Stone, an inscription of Mesha, King of Moab, dating from the Ninth Century BC. In this Moabite Stone, and also in Egyptian hieroglyphics, we discover *pictures* symbolizing the letters of their alphabet which is similar to the ancient Hebrew and Aramaic. The pictures (pictographs or hieroglyphics) became sounds. The Hebrew Alphabet is composed of 22 letters and therefore only 22 sounds with their accompanying pictures had to be learned by the student in early times. (Imagine the Chinese school children who have to learn something like 2,000 pictures of their alphabet in order to read fluently)!

✡ ✡ ✡ ✡ ✡ ✡ ✡

HEBREW עברית (IVREIT)

The Semitic language is a group of languages composed of Aramaic, Hebrew, Arabic, and Assyrian. Most of the nations who spoke these tongues were descended from Shem, the son of Noah. These are closely related languages; perhaps they came from one ancient original tongue. The language of the people of Israel in the Bible was *Hebrew*. But the Jews were taken into captivity. Settling in Palestine (The word Palestine is a corruption of the word Philistina referring to the Philistine invaders from the Greek Islands who settled the coastal area of the land. Palestine is now *Israel*), they began to use the speech of the people around them, which was *Aramaic*. (Aramaic is still being spoken in three tiny Syrian villages: Malloula and two others nearby. The villagers neither read nor write it; it is passed on by word of mouth from one generation to another. They are Christian, the rest of Syria is predominantly Moslem according to a newspaper item dated February 27, 1966.)

Hebrew was retained for use in the Temples. The Scriptures were first read in *Hebrew*, and were then generally translated into Aramaic so that everyone could understand. Aramaic is the language most akin to Hebrew (referred to as "a degeneration of Hebrew"), and it became the common Jewish language about 300 BC.

> The actual historical fact is that the Hebrew-Phoenician alphabet is the mother of practically all the alphabets now being used in the world. ... The English alphabet we now use is directly descended from this Hebrew-Phoenician alphabet. The names of the English letters are actually fragments of old Hebrew words which were used as the names of the letters.[104]

Recently it has been discovered by etymologists that Hebrew and English are profoundly connected and *all languages* are a "scrambled form of man's original tongue (Hebrew)."

---

[104]Edward Horowitz, *How the Hebrew Language Grew*, Thomas Jefferson High School (Hebrew Department) Brooklyn, New York.

Hebrew was the language of educated Jews after the captivity, when many of the uneducated spoke Chaldee (Aramaic, more correct). See Nehemiah 8:8. Paul used the Hebrew language and not Chaldee when he spoke from the stairs after his arrest at Jerusalem (Acts 21:40; 22:2). The Lord Jesus Himself spoke to Paul in the Hebrew tongue (Acts 26:14).

Abba Eban, Israel's Minister of Foreign Affairs, said: "Israel is the only nation in the world that speaks the *same tongue*, upholds the same faith, and inhabits the same land as it did three thousand years ago." —*The Pentecostal Evangel*, September 12, 1976

Hebrew is called a "pure" language since God chose it for the writing of His Holy Word. It is "Leshon ha-Kodesh," "The Holy Tongue." Godly Jews have always had a great respect and reverence for the very letters of the Hebrew *Scriptures*. It is "pure" also, because there are no swear or slang words in this language and the worst oath in Hebrew against anyone is: "That your name be obliterated"!

(When we say the word "alphabet" we are speaking three languages: *Alpha*, Greek; *Bet*, Hebrew; *Alphabet*, English!) Hebrew letters are important in themselves for not only do they portray significant things, but also each letter has numerical value. Messiah Himself spoke of the importance of the Alphabet in connection with the Word of God when He mentioned the *jot* (yod) and the *tittle* (little horn) in Matthew 5:17-18. (Hesychius explained the "tittle" as the mark made at the beginning to write a letter of the alphabet.) Messiah Jesus said that not the smallest Hebrew letter (yod) or any part of a Hebrew letter would be changed or pass away from the law until all be fulfilled. By this He said that the Law of God would not change. Every detail of God's law must be fulfilled to the very letter. And it *is* fulfilled completely in the Lord Yeshua (Jesus) who is *every letter of the Hebrew Alphabet*! (See my *Pictures of Messiah*, Chapter Four, "Messiah in the Hebrew Alphabet," p. 107.)

The first Hebrew alphabet only recorded the Consonants of the Hebrew and left it up to the reader's memory to supply the appropriate vowel sounds. ***The first verse of the Bible*** would have looked something like the following forms:

Below is the same verse in modern day Hebrew with vowel points (*nikudit*) added:

בְּרֵאשִׁית בָּרָא אלהים אֵת הַשָּׁמַיִם וְאֵת הָאָרֶץ

The ancient Hebrew alphabet consisted of 22 letters–all consonants. Some say it is made up of 20 consonants, seven vowels, and five final letters.[105] It is commonly supposed that these letters were used Biblically in the Sixth Century.

The old Phoenician alphabet gave way to the square Aramaic characters of the modern Hebrew which possibly came into use as early as the time of Ezra. These consonants, forming words, (though some consonants were used as vowels) were difficult to pronounce and therefore in the Seventh Century (possibly 700 or 750 AD) vowel signs which are called "nikudit" (plural form of the singular noun, "nikudah") were invented by Jewish scholars of Tiberius, Palestine who were called *Masoretes*. These vowel signs were placed under, over, or within the letters so they might be more easily read. The Bible written with the consonants pointed with vowel signs is called the "Masoretic Text" since it was the Masoretes who supplied these marks.

There are no common letters in Hebrew; all are capitals. The words are written from right to left as in all original languages. However, a recent archaeological discovery revealed that the oldest Hebrew was written left to right!

"A report coming from Tel Aviv, Israel in August of 1976 stated that an ancient Hebrew script was found which was composed of 80 letters arranged in five lines and included an entire line of the Hebrew alphabet similar to the modern one. It is believed that the script is a hundred years older than the famous Gezer Calendar of the late 10th century BCE [BC]. The new discovery has led scholars to believe that the ancient Israelites (in 1000 BC) probably copied their alphabet from the *Canaanites* and not from the Phoenicians, as previously believed. The tablet was discovered at the site of an ancient farming settlement of the 12th century BCE [BC]. This ancient settlement has been identified with *Even Ha'ezer*, mentioned in chapter 4 of Samuel 1. The archaeological team was led by Kochavi, head of the archaeology department at Tel Aviv University, and Moshe Garsiel, director of Land of Israel Studies at Bar-Ilan University."

—*The Jerusalem Post*, September 1976

To make it understandable to the human mind, God used man's alphabet to describe our all-inclusive Messiah-Jesus. As man's language in the written Word of God is only understood by the intellect through the human alphabet, so God's language in the Living Word is only revealed by the Holy Spirit through the Heavenly Alphabet, the Lord Yeshua ha-Meshiach (Jesus, the Christ)!

---

[105] Abraham Heller, *Vocabulary of Jewish Life*, p.196.

There are more than a dozen passages in the *T'nakh* (OT) composed on the principle of the Hebrew alphabet: Psalms 111, 112, 119; Proverbs 31:10-31; Lamentations 1, 2, 3, 4, etc. The Hebrew Alphabet is more clearly seen in the 119th Psalm which emphasizes the Alphabet with the Word of God. This Psalm is called an *Alphabetical Acrostic*. It is composed of 22 sections corresponding to the 22 letters of the Hebrew Alphabet. Each section has 8 verses. These 8 verses all begin with that letter of the Alphabet by which it is headed. The Psalm is a *Messianic Symbol,* each letter portraying Messiah Jesus. Each form, shape, and number value to these letters tell of Him who is the First and the Last, the *Alpha* and the *Omega*, the *Aleph* and the *Tav*, the A and the Z, the Beginning and the Ending. He is the Alphabet of the Word of God to define every *word* and the *letters* of every word in God's Holy Book! When Messiah walked the earth He was the Word of God in the flesh (John 1:1, 14)!

✡ ✡ ✡ ✡ ✡ ✡ ✡

Hebrew in the United States

So close did the early American pilgrims live to the spirit and ideals of the Bible that almost all children born to them were given Hebrew or Biblical names. At one time they had harbored the idea, and almost adopted the plan, to make Hebrew their official language in the new world so as to break completely their language ties with their mother country, England, and thus start life anew on these shores. Hebrew thus almost became the official language in America!
—*Israel's Remnant* magazine, 1967

Hebrew Words

Of all the thousands of words now used in modern Hebrew only 800 come from the Holy Scriptures. In the entire Hebrew Bible there are only 8,000 words, 2,000 of which appear once. This interesting data comes from a study published by Prof. Haim Rabin entitled *The Historical Sources of the Hebrew Language*. According to Prof. Rabin, modern Hebrew contains no more than 60,000 words. In addition to the aforementioned 800 words found in the Tenakh there are also some 14,000 words stemming from the Rabbinical literature and the writings of Israel's sages. Since the renascence of modern Hebrew language, a great many being newly coined technical expressions.
—*B'nai Brith Messenger*, 1976

~ תא ~

THE ALEPH-TAV
(Tav also spelled *Tau* or *Taw)*

It is quite common to take the first and last letters of a word as an *abbreviation* for the complete word. Such is *the abbreviation of the Alphabet*–all inclusive. The first and the last letters of the Hebrew Alphabet are combined and this combination is found many times in the original Old Testament Scriptures (*T'nakh*) but cannot be translated. Some unconverted Hebrew students have attempted to translate it and have even placed vowel signs beneath the letters in order to be able to pronounce it, but they do not know the true meaning and significance of it. The often-occurring untranslatable "abbreviation" of the Hebrew alphabet in the Old Testament, the Aleph-Tav, hints at the fact that it is *more than a language term*!

The abbreviation (particle) *Aleph-Tav* is found in countless places in the Hebrew Old Testament, and any attempt to translate it appears futile. A Rabbi of prominence in his day (Rabbi Noach of New York) regarded as an authority, said that when this particle was used with nouns it has the suggestion of inclusiveness.

In the first verse of Genesis (the Hebrew text) we find this particle two times. It is written before the word "heavens" and before the word "earth." This first and last letters of the Hebrew alphabet stands before heavens and earth after the word "created" as though that which is created is "everything from A to Z." Aleph-Tav is used to stand *symbolically* for the beginning and the ending, the whole extent of the thing such as: God blessed Israel from Aleph to Tav in Leviticus 26:3-13, but curses from Vav to Mem in Leviticus 26:14-43. Also, Abraham observed the whole law from Aleph to Tav!

Why did God, the Holy Spirit, inspire the writers of the Hebrew Scriptures to intersperse this "combination," abbreviation, or particle hundreds of times throughout the First Testament? Surely it has a very important part in the Word of God because of the numerous instances in which it is found. Surely there is a reason for its prominence, for every Word of God is in its proper place! God had His hand in the making of the Hebrew Alphabet. His Name ("Aleph-Tav") shows His completeness and thoroughness in everything He has said and done.

Let us discover some very striking instances where the combination first-and-last letters of the Hebrew Alphabet are written in the Hebrew Scriptures:

Genesis 4:1. English translation: *"I have gotten a man from the LORD."* In this verse the particle *Aleph-Tav* is translated as *"from."* What Eve really said (according to the Hebrew text) was: *"I have acquired a man,* [Aleph-Tav] *the LORD"*! The particle *Aleph-Tav* stands before the singular, personal name of the *Lord*, the sacred *Tetragram* (יהוה YHWH)! Eve thought she had given birth to the Messiah who had been promised (Genesis 3:15).

Isaiah 41:4. (Here God declares His Name). The English translation is *"I the LORD, the first, and with the last; I am he ..."* The particle *Aleph-Tav* is translated as "with." The Lord is the first and last letters of the Hebrew Alphabet meaning He is the entire Alphabet, the All-Inclusive One!

Zechariah 12:10. English translation is: *"... and they shall look upon me whom they have pierced."* The particle *Aleph-Tav* has been translated as "whom." Isaac Leeser's translation is "they shall look up toward me." The translation of Alexander Harkevy is "they shall look up unto me." Both these Jewish translators add the words: "for everyone whom they have pierced." It is apparent that these translators did not want to recognize that it is the *Lord* who was pierced! The Aleph-Tav is a Person! a *Divine* Person since in the preceding verse (Zechariah 12:9) the Lord promised to pour out the spirit of grace and supplications upon the House of David and in this verse He affirmed that *He* is the One whom they have pierced. Can you not see the *Aleph-Tav* is another Name for our blessed Lord Yeshua (Jesus)? He is the First and the Last, the Beginning and the Ending. There is no letter before Aleph and there is no letter following Tav!

Another Name with the *Aleph-Tav* is given in the *Brit Hadasha*:

> *"Behold, he cometh with clouds; and every eye shall see him, and they also which pierced him: and all kindreds of the earth shall wail because of him. Even so, Amen. I am* [the] *Alpha and* [the] *Omega, the beginning and the ending, saith the Lord, which is, and which was, and which is to come, the Almighty. Saying, I am* [the] *Alpha and* [the] *Omega, the first and the last: ..."* (Revelation 1:7-8,11; also in Revelation 21:6, 22:13 with Zechariah 12:10.)

The Pierced One is the *Aleph-Tav*! The Lord Messiah Himself calls His Name "Aleph-Tav" in the *Hebrew* New Testament. The *Greek* translation is a combination of the first and the last letters of the *Greek* alphabet, (ΑΩ) *Alpha-Omega*! The comprehensive use of *Alpha* and *Omega* quoting from the Old Testament *Aleph-Tav* as an allusion to the Messiah, *identifies the entire Alphabet to Him*! It is His *symbol*!

Another outstanding instance of the Aleph-Tav is found in the names *Urim* and *Thummim* (see Exodus 28:30). In the Hebrew Text "Urim" begins with *Aleph* and "Thummim" with *Tav*. In the original text each word is preceded by the two letters *Aleph-Tav*! Example: Aleph-Tav [את] *Urim* and Aleph-Tav [את] *Thummim*. "Urim" means "Lights," "Thummim" means "Perfections." The combination of these two words signifies Wisdom and Glory. Our Lord Messiah Jesus is the true Urim and Thummim, the Light and Glory of God, the Perfections and Wisdom of Him who filleth all in all!

PICTOGRAPH OF ALEPH-RESH-TAV (ארת)

Egyptian Heiroglyph	Sinai Script	Aramaic	Moabite Stone	Phoenician	Hebrew Name	Hebrew Letter	English Equivalent
					Aleph	א	A
					Resh	ר	R
					Tav	ת	T

The pictograph (pictures) of the ancient Hebrew letters is another proof that the Aleph-Tav is the name of our Messiah-Jesus. The first and last letter of the *Sinai Script* shows the *ox* and the *cross*. The ox was the animal of sacrifice and many of these were killed on the altars in Jewish worship as commanded by God. Not only was this first letter drawn in the shape of the face of an ox, but the *name* of the letter (aleph) signifies "ox." The last letter of the Hebrew alphabet is "tav" meaning a "sign" or "symbol." In the ancient manuscripts this letter was pictured as an "X" or a cross! It is related of the synod of Chalcedon and other Oriental synods, that the bishops who could not write their names affixed the mark of a (lying-down) cross which looked like an X as their signature. This is common today for those who cannot sign their name. The cross stands for the name as well as for the person who makes it. Messiah is the Sacrificial Ox (Aleph) who died for our salvation, and He made His sign (Tav) with the blood of His Cross–this "sign" which represents His Name and His Person forever!

Numerical Value of "Hei" (ה)

The numerical value of the *fifth* letter of the Hebrew Alphabet (ה "Hei") is *five*. Its pictograph form shows arms raised in praise and prayer. It is the beginning letter of "Hallel"—"Praise" taken from

"Halo" or "Sun." "Hei" is a part of God's Name ("Yod-*Hei*—*Yah*) and is used to stand for His Person, His very breath. God uses the number FIVE in many instances when His *grace* is manifested to man in man's weakness. When He made an unconditional Covenant with Abraham and his seed *forever*, He commanded that *five* sacrifices were to be made: a heifer, a goat, a ram, a dove, and a pigeon (Genesis 15:9). It is striking too, that afterwards when God changed Abram's name (Genesis 7:5) He inserted in it the *fifth* letter of the Hebrew alphabet (*hei*) which is a part of His own Divine and personal Name and Abram became AbraHam! (In Hebrew there are *five* letters in the name *Abraham*!) God, as it were, breathed (*hei*) His grace and Holy Name into Abram and Abram was changed. This was done at a very important time—when God called Abram to "walk before" Him in a very special way! In this same Covenant Sarai's name was also changed. God placed the *fifth* letter of the Hebrew alphabet (which is a part of His own Name) at the end of hers and *Sarai* became "SaraH"! (Genesis 17:15).

The Yod (ˈ)

Though the *yod* (ˈ) is the smallest letter of the Hebrew alphabet it is very important. It is the embryo of all the other Hebrew letters. In other words, each of the 22 letters of the Hebrew alphabet contains and conceals a *yod*. "Yod" also begins the Divine Name, YHWH (Yehovah or Yahweh) and very often when the Tetragram (YHWH, yod hei waw [vav] hei) is by itself it is written with a double *yod* (ˈˈ).

From *A Treasury of Jewish Quotations* edited by Joseph L. Baron is the following:

> "A Jew is called 'Yud', for as the letter Yod is the only one in our alphabet which cannot be magnified (if written longer vertically it becomes a 'vav' ['waw'] and horizontally a 'daled' ['dalet'], so a Jew who magnifies himself ceases to be a Jew."[106]

GEMATRIA

Gematria (or numerology) is a mystical approach to the interpretation of words and numbers. This is a practice whereby words have mystical meanings based on their numerological equivalent, or numbers are given mystical meaning based on their verbal equivalent. This is because both the Hebrew and Greek alphabets are also their numerical systems. Therefore, whenever a number is written, letters must necessarily be used.

The Rabbis explain that *Gematria* is a hermeneutical system for interpreting the words or phrases of the Torah (Hebrew Scriptures)

---

[106]*Simha Bunam.q Imre Tsaddikim*, p. 7, No. 30.

on the basis of *numerical* equivalents. According to the *Kabbalah* ("doctrines received by traditions" the world was created through speech–that is, as the name was spoken, the thing came into being. Since the word spoken is composed of letters, and every letter (Hebrew) of the word has a *numerical* equivalent, then two words having the same value are considered as fundamentally related, etc.

PICTOGRAPH FORMS OF THE HEBREW ALPHABET

The following notes from a Jewish viewpoint (and in quote marks) are derived from Professor Shlomo Marenof of Brandeis University in the book entitled: *"A New Art For an Old Religion"* with illustrations by the Artist, A. Raymond Katz. (The spiritual significance and *Christian* applications preceded by an **arrow** are mine.)

"Some literary records, over two thousand years old, tell us that the alphabet played a great part in the emotional life of the Jewish people. The *'Sefer Yetzirah,'* ("Book of Creation") which is based on sources as far back as 200 BC deals with Cosmopolia and tells us how the letters were used by God to create the world and man. Another book, also very old, ascribed to the authorship of Rabbi Akiba who lived in the second century AD, called *'Otiot de Rabbi Akiba,'* ('The Letters of Rabbi Akiba') discussed the values of the letters in Creation and human behavior. A Midrashic legend tells us that 'Bezalel,' the artist of the Bible, inspired by the alphabet, created the Menorah and other objects of the Tabernacle."

Number Value	Letter	Name	Explanation
1	א	*(aleph)*	"The early pictographic sign expressed the idea of the ox—face, ears, and horns."

⇒As the OX is the patient, enduring servant of man, so Messiah Jesus is the patient, enduring Servant of Jehovah and is strong enough to pull us out of sin. The OX also was the sacrifice upon the Altar of God in ancient Israel. Messiah is the Supreme Sacrifice upon the Altar of Calvary.

2	ב	*(bayt)*	"The early pictographic form expressed the idea of 'a place to lodge' from which was derived the modern version of 'Bayit,' 'a House'."

⇒This also signified a tent in which the Israelites dwelt through their wilderness wanderings. It was prophesied that Messiah would dwell with His people. He tented among men. He is *God's* Dwelling Place, God's House (see Revelation 21:3)! Also He is *our* Dwelling Place, Psalm 90:1.

3	**ג**	*(gimmel)*	(The word for camel is "gammal.") Its ancient Phoenician form bears a resemblance to the camel's hump. A Camel signifies a journey through the desert.

⇒Messiah Jesus came into this world and journeyed in the unclean "desert" with us that we might enter at last into the Holy Place with Him!

4	**ד**	*(dalet)*	"Door"

⇒Messiah is the *Door* for the "whosoever" (4) of the world.

5	**ה**	*(hei)*	"The early pictographic sign depicts a man raising his hands in prayer toward the sun. This is the first letter of the word 'Hallelujah,' meaning 'Praise God'–its root is 'hallel' (Halo) meaning 'Sun'."

⇒The English "H" comes from this letter. Consider the two upper extensions on the "H" as hands raised in prayer and praise. This letter is a part of God's own name ("Yah." Psalm 68:4). Jesus is the Personification of Prayer. He is the Grace of God (5), the Sun, the Praise of God. Hallelujah! Also, incorporated in His Hebrew Name is the Name of the Lord; i.e., YAH-oshua or YEHshuah–*"The Lord is Salvation."*

6	**ו**	*(vav)*	"Nail-Hook"

⇒Messiah Yeshua is the Nail in a sure place, the Anchor of our soul!

7	**ז**	*(zayin)*	"Weapon"

⇒Messiah Jesus is the Word of God–the Weapon against the enemy.

8	**ח**	*(het)*	"Hedge-Fence"

⇒Messiah Jesus is our Protector, surrounding us as a fence against the world.

9	**ט**	*(tet)*	(uncertain)

10	**י**	*(yod)*	"Hand [*hand* in Hebrew is *yad*] is used in the Bible as a memorial sign."

⇒Messiah is the Hand of God extended to all mankind.

20	**כ**	*(kof)*	"The early pictographic sign is indicated by the palm of the hand."

⇒Messiah holds us in the "hollow" of His hand, the Hand that was bruised for us. The Word of God tells us that we are "written" in the palms of His hands.

30	**ל**	*(lamed)*	"Its early pictographic form indicated the yoke of the ox. Later, it came to mean 'guiding'."

⇒Messiah Jesus said His "yoke" was easy; His burden is light. He wants us to take His "yoke" upon us and learn of Him.

40	**מ** *(mem)*	"Water (*mayim*)—waves. Its early pictograph form expressed the waves of the sea."

⇒Messiah Jesus is the Living Water to satisfy the thirsty soul.

50   ‫נ‬ *(nun)*   "The early pictographic form indicated the 'fish'."

⇒Messiah Jesus is the Creator of the fish and all that are in the waters. (He is the great Fisherman as well).

60   ‫ס‬ *(samekh)* "Rest, Prop or Support."

⇒Messiah Jesus is our Rest. He supports us, holds us up that we might not fall.

70   ‫ע‬ *(ayin)*   Its early pictographic form indicated the 'eye,' also the mouth of a spring."

⇒Messiah is the Source of all our need and the Eye ever watching us so to supply.

80   ‫פ‬ *(pey)*   "Its early pictographic form expressed a 'mouth.' According to an ancient legend the mouth was created for prayer."

⇒Messiah Jesus is God's Mouth, His Voice to speak and be heard. He is the PRAY-er, our Intercessor.

90   ‫צ‬ *(tzadi)*   "Its pictograph expressed a two-handed sickle."

⇒Messiah Jesus is the Sickle of God's Word who reaps the twofold harvest: the sinner to be cast away, the righteous, to life eternal.

100   ‫ק‬ *(kuf)*   (Its early pictograph form is uncertain.)

200   ‫ר‬ *(resh)*   "Its early pictographic form represented a head. In ancient lore the Resh played a great part because it is the first letter of the word 'reshith' meaning 'beginning'," [of creation].

⇒Messiah Jesus is the "Head" of the Body, His Church. He is the Beginning, not only of the First Creation, but of the New!

300   ‫ש‬ *(sheen)*   "This letter begins the word 'Shekinah' which means 'the presence of God' and 'Shaddai' which is a name signifying the all-sufficiency of God."

⇒Messiah Jesus is the "Shekinah." He is the Manifestation of God's Presence. He is also the All-Sufficient One.

400   ‫ת‬ *(tav)*   "Its early pictographic form" [a lying-down cross, the X] "was used as a sign or brand. It also indicated the 'completion' of something."

⇒Messiah Jesus is the Crucified One. His mark or sign is the Cross! He *finished* the work God gave Him to do on earth. By His Cross He completed or fulfilled the Old Testament, the Hebrew Scriptures.

THE HEBREW NEW TESTAMENT

It is believed that the language of the original New Testament was Hebrew. This was translated into Greek and from the Greek into the many languages of today. The thought patterns behind the entire New Testament are Hebrew, not Aramaic nor Greek. There is conclusive evidence for Hebrew being the language of the New Testament for it is filled with semitisms such as Hebrew vocabulary, Hebrew syntax, Hebrew idioms, Hebrew thought patterns, and Hebrew theology (see Exodus 20:7; Leviticus 24:15-23). Hebrew idioms became clouded and unclear when they were translated in the First Century from the Hebrew into the Greek. Since the New Testament was originally written in Hebrew it can only be understood correctly from a *Hebrew* perspective!

Greek was used exclusively for many years as the language of the New Testament until recently.

"The newly-released translation of the New Testament in *modern* Hebrew was displayed at the International Book Fair in Jerusalem by the Israel Agency of the United Bible Societies. James Payne, Chairman of the Executive Committee of the United Bible Societies, was present for a special service of dedication on April 16 when the first copies were presented to representatives of different Hebrew-speaking Christian communities throughout Israel. The publication of the New Testament in *Modern* Hebrew is the culmination of efforts that began in early 1969. The standard Hebrew text for many years has been *Franz Delitzsch's translation* first published in 1877 by the British and Foreign Bible Society."
—*The Jerusalem Post*, 1977

THE RESURRECTION OF THE HEBREW LANGUAGE

The resurrection of the Hebrew language, which for over 18 centuries was not spoken in everyday life, is as remarkable as the revival of Israel itself. Indeed, it is a most important factor in cementing the Jews into a united nation.

In the process of learning a common language the Jew has undergone a revolutionary change, casting off his 2,000-year shroud of exile, taking on a new aspect and mentality. Once again the language of Abraham, Isaac, and Jacob is heard throughout the hills and cities of the ancient homeland which has opened its arms to receive the ingathering of their descendants.

A hundred years ago Hebrew was considered a dead language. Actually, however, the Jews never considered it so. It was the language of their Bible and the language of their prayers; and although they did not use it in secular life they always felt that at some time they would return to Zion and speak Hebrew. It remained for *Eliezer Ben-Yehuda,* a European Jew, to demonstrate that the time for doing so was now, not in some distant future.

So God raised up this man, born near Vilna in 1858, to lead the Jews back to a common language. The people were scattered abroad throughout the nations; they spoke the languages of the people among whom they dwelt. Many Jews in Europe spoke *Yiddish,* a language based on Medieval German. Others spoke Ladino, based on Medieval Spanish. In the spring of 1879 Ben-Yehuda (formerly known by the name Perlman) published an article in which he proposed that a Jewish state be founded in Palestine and that the language of that state be Hebrew. The more pious Jews were shocked at the suggestion: to them it was sacrilegious to think of using the language of the Bible in everyday conversation. A few of them spoke Hebrew, but only on the Sabbath. But Ben-Yehuda was a determined man and he was convinced his idea was right.

Driven by a supernatural force (though doubtless unaware of the fact) this young man laid aside his medical studies at the Sorbonne in Paris and, to the consternation of relatives and friends, made off with all his belongings toward Jerusalem. In 1880, on his way to Palestine, he wrote, "Today we are speaking foreign languages, tomorrow we shall speak Hebrew."

Jerusalem, the holy city, was at that period a hub of medieval fanaticism and obscurantism [making obscure], unpenetrated by any ray of modernity. A few thousand pious Jews, old men for the most part, had come from all corners of the earth to live there, or rather to vegetate and die there. They concentrated in the area near the Wailing Wall and spent most of their time praying and bemoaning the loss of the Temple. There in the insalubrious Jewish quarter Eliezer Ben-Yehuda made his home and raised his family. He was the first man in Jerusalem to teach his children to speak Hebrew.

From the start he faced opposition from the ultra-orthodox Jews among whom he established himself. To them this young Jew was a heretic from the modern Sodom, who profaned the sacred tongue. How dare he speak of common things in Hebrew! He even addressed an "impure creature" (his wife) in that language, as well as his child! To them he was an enemy of God, a false messiah who ought to be obliterated, so he became an object of hatred and persecution. He and his family endured much suffering. Denunciations, threats, even the hardships of a Turkish prison became his lot. One of his children died–a little girl, the first child to "stutter" Hebrew words in Jerusalem. The orthodox saw in this the hand of God–it was punishment from heaven–and they refused to let him bury her in the Jewish cemetery. The father, crushed with grief, had to bury the child himself next to his house; but he persevered with stoic determination and courageously withstood all opposition.

He succeeded in establishing the first Hebrew-speaking family in Palestine after a span of 18 centuries. Soon a few other families who were newcomers followed his example. Little by little Hebrew became a language of conversation in various Jewish centers until its use became widespread. By 1918 some 40 percent of the Jews in Palestine spoke Hebrew. By 1948 the number had grown to 80 percent. Today (1968) it is estimated that 95 percent can carry on their daily business in Hebrew, although many still speak other languages at home and they may read daily newspapers in non-Hebrew languages.

Eliezer Ben-Yehuda created the first nonreligious Hebrew school where all subjects were taught in Hebrew. He also founded and operated four Hebrew newspapers, and was instrumental in establishing the Hebrew language council which in 1954 became the government's official Academy of the Hebrew Language. His chief work, however, was gathering material for a 17-volume Hebrew dictionary now widely used.

In reviving the Hebrew language it was necessary to create many new words for modern use, particularly in industrial, technological, and professional areas. The Hebrew vocabulary has been multiplied several times over. The Academy of the Hebrew Language has fixed the use of some 30,000 words.

The task of teaching the language to Jewish immigrants has been gigantic, but the Israelis, with characteristic vigor and resourcefulness, have devised rapid methods of learning. By means of these modern methods the immigrants are able to learn the language in five months. Among the 17 daily newspapers in Israel which are published in Hebrew there is one which uses simplified, voweled Hebrew for the benefit of immigrants who cannot yet read the regular Hebrew in which most vowels are omitted. Also Hebrew lessons and news bulletins in easy Hebrew are broadcast over the national radio.

Every Jew in Israel is urged to learn Hebrew and it is the language of instruction in all the Jewish schools, but Arabic is used by teachers in Arab schools. Arab citizens of Israel are not forced to learn Hebrew. There is full liberty for each race to maintain its own culture and traditions. Stamps, coins, and currency bear both Jewish and Arabic inscriptions.

The resurrection of the Hebrew language is a modern miracle. Never before in human history has a "dead" language come to life again. The advance of Hebrew, to which Ben-Yehuda dedicated his life, became a triumphal march which today overflows the frontiers of the promised land reaching toward every corner of the globe. Again

Hebrew is a modern tongue which proclaims the power of God and His faithfulness to fulfill His promises—the miraculous accomplishment of His will in the past, in our time as well, and also in times to come. To Him be all the glory!

Supplemental Notes:

When Israel would return to her land God promised that the *Hebrew* language would be restored:

> *"For then will I turn to the people a **pure** language, that they may all call upon the name of the LORD, to serve him with one consent."*
> (Zephaniah 3:9; see Isaiah 19:18 where the Hebrew is called "the language of Canaan").

In the centuries following the Reformation, the Jews adopted the languages of the countries in which they lived along with their development of a peculiar speech known as *Yiddish.* Today (1992) Hebrew is the language of Israel and is the only language in which lectures are delivered in the Hebrew University. All the road signs are in Arabic, Hebrew and English, and now there is a whole new literature in Hebrew; in fact, over *one thousand new books* are published every year in Israel in the Hebrew language.

—Z. Kofsmann (Jerusalem, Israel 1968

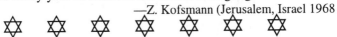

THE SACRED TETRAGRAMMATON

Known as the *Tetragrammaton,* the Hebrew characters shown here is how the Lord's name appears in *ancient* manuscripts of our Bible. The Tetragrammaton traces its origin to the Fifth Century AD. The present-day Hebrew letters are shown as יהוה or "Yahweh."

Ancient Hebrew Letters of the Tetragrammaton.

Tetragrammaton is a Greek term meaning "word of four letters," which Josephus applied to the Sacred Name of Deity (YHWH). In his *Wars* (V.v.7) Josephus states that the high priests' golden crown "was engraven (with) the sacred name: *it consists of four vowels.* "[108] This Name (JHVH, or more correctly, YHWH[109]) is used approximately 6,823 times in the Hebrew Old Testament. It was translated as JeHoVaH when the vowel signs of *Adonay* were added to it as found in Martini's manuscript (Pugio Fidel) in 1278 AD and in the year 1518 in the manuscript of Petrus Galatinus. The word *Jehovah* for

---

[108]In ancient Hebrew there were no vowel signs but the consonants YHWH were used as **vowels**.
[109]There is no letter **J** in the Hebrew alphabet. The *yod* י (y) is used instead.

YHWH is a misapplication to these 4 Hebrew letters. Many Hebrew scholars feel that *Yahweh* would be more correct. However, the root of the Name "Jehovah" is the verb "havah," "to be," or "being," signifying God exists, that He is the "I AM."

In Exodus 3:14, *"I am that I am"* [*ehyeh asher ehyeh*] is translated correctly as *"I will be what I will be,"* or "I shall be what I AM," a Semitic idiom meaning "I will be all that is necessary as the occasion will arise." (Compare with Revelation 1:4, 8.) This is a familiar Old Testament idea (cf. Isaiah 7:4, 9; Psalm 23). Rabbi Joseph Albo declared that "the JHVH expresses necessary being" (*Ikkarim*, part 2, C.28). YHWH is the personal proper name *par excellence* of Israel's God. He is the God of revelation, the Ever-Becoming One.

In the Old Testament the name of God appears very often in the plural, *Elohenu* or *Elohim*. The singular is *Eloah* or *El*. The plural term, Elohenu or Elohim, is sometimes used in the Old Testament in reference to heathen gods, while the singular El, is sometimes applied to a hero. But the *Tetragrammaton*, YHWH, is always used in the singular and *only* of the Supreme Being, not of any heathen gods or of man.

RABBIS AND THE TETRAGRAM

Exodus 3:14 with verse 15: *"This is my name forever,"* refers to The Tetragrammaton. Rashi says that the Hebrew *leolam* (forever) is written defective, without the letter *waw* (*vav* ו) and can be read as *leallem*, "to conceal." The Rabbis found in this rule that the Name of four letters should not be read as written, but be "concealed," i.e., another word was to be substituted for it (see *Soncino Chumash*, p. 332). Thus, in reading the Tetragrammaton, devout Jews will pronounce "Adonai" which also means "Lord."

According to the Rabbis, the pronunciation of the Name (YHWH) was forbidden; only the High Priest used it on the Day of Atonement (It was required he pronounce it 10 times on that Day), and in the priestly benediction (Numbers 6:27) after the daily sacrifice in the Temple. No Jew would say this Name for various reasons: for fear the heathen might hear it and desecrate it and that the Name might be incorrectly pronounced thereby breaking the commandment: that of taking the Name of the Lord in vain (see Exodus 20:7; Leviticus 24:15, 23). Too, it was their belief that this Name held magical powers exercised in its use which was strictly prohibited by Jewish law.

The Mishnah (with Gemara form the Talmud) warns of severe punishment to those who utter the Holy Name: "He who pronounces the Name with its own letters has no share in the future world" (*Sanhedrin* x,i.).

It is said that scribes, when coming to that holy Name in their writing, would remove their clothes, take a bath, put on clean apparel, and use a new pen to inscribe it on the parchment scrolls. The Kabbalists (who received their doctrines by traditions) claimed to know the Name and performed miracles by it.

> "It was employed by healers, exorcists and magicians and is found on many magical papyri. It is asserted by Philo that only priests might pronounce it and by Josephus that those who knew it were forbidden to divulge it." —*Encyclopaedia Britannica*

Jewish writings prohibit the pronunciation of the Name of the Lord and substitute the name "Adonai" which also means "Lord." Jews today (and some Gentiles) leave out a letter to the name of God or Lord out of respect to the sacredness of that Name which they feel was not to be pronounced.

However, that Sacred Name was known and used in the Holy Scriptures as we read in the following portion:

> *"And Moses said unto God, Behold, when I come unto the children of Israel, and shall say unto them, The God of your fathers hath sent me unto you; and they shall say to me, What is his name? what shall I say unto them? And God said unto Moses, I AM THAT I AM* [Yahweh]*: and he said, Thus shalt thou say unto the children of Israel, I AM* [Yahweh] *hath sent me unto you"* (Exodus 3:13-14).

At first Moses did not know God's Name. When Moses asked God to tell him His Name so he could inform the children of Israel of the Name, God did not hesitate one moment to reveal that Holy Name to Moses. So then this Name was known by him and by Israel to whom he was sent! God didn't command them to hide that Name nor use a substitute Name neither to leave out any letter but distinctly gave His Holy Name in it entirety—*Yahweh* יהוה YHWH. And in the times of Messiah Yeshua the Divine Name of the Lord was used by Messiah of Himself and in the working of His miracles as well as used by His disciples when they performed miracles also.

Combinations of the Tetragram

Intimated in Psalm 23

YeHoVaH-Roi—"The Lord is *my Shepherd.*"

YeHoVaH-Yireh—"I shall *not want*" ("The Lord will provide").

YeHoVaH-Shalom—"He leadeth me beside the *still* waters" ("The Lord is peace").

YeHoVaH-Ropheka (Rapha)–"He *restoreth* my soul." ("The Lord is Healer").

YeHoVaH-Tsidkenu–"He leadeth me in paths of righteousness" ("The Lord our Righteousness").

YeHoVaH-Shammah—"Thou art with me" ("The Lord is *There-Present*").

YeHoVaH-Nissi—"A table before me *in the presence of my enemies*" ("The Lord, my Banner").

SOME DEFINITIONS OF THE TETRAGRAM

"Tetragrammaton" (Gk., 'four' and 'letter'). The four letters, usually referring to the four which compose the name of the Deity. The Jews of olden time never pronounced the name of Jehovah, composed with four Hebrew letters YeHoVaH [or YaHWeH], which are the tetragrammaton usually referred to."

—E. Royston Pike, *Encyclopaedia of Religion and Religions*

"Tetragrammaton, the four-lettered name for the Hebrew God pronounced Jehovah through misapplication, dating back to 1270, of the vowels of Adonai (Lord) to the consonants J,H,V,H. The correct pronunciation is probably Yahweh or Jahveh (German). To avoid repetition of the name Yahweh, when the word Adonai precedes it, Yahweh is written by the Massoretes with the vowels of Elohim (God) and is read Elohim."   —*Encyclopedia Britannica*

"JEHOVAH—The common English pronunciation of the Hebrew *tetragram,* YHWH one of the names of God (Exodus 17:15). ... It seems that out of reverence for the divine name, there had grown up around 300 BC the custom among the Jews in reading to pronounce the word *adonay* (my Lord or LORD) in its stead or, when it follows 'adonay,' to pronounce *elohim*, God (Genesis 15:2). When the vowel points were added to the Hebrew consonantal text, the vowels of 'adonay' and 'elohim' were accordingly given to the tetragram. This pointing gave rise to the Eng. pronunciation, *Jehovah*, current since the days of Petrus Galatinus, confessor of Leo X, AD 1518 ... The Tetragram is generally believed to have been pronounced *Yahweh*, because the divine name *Jah* (Psalms 89:8, R.V. marg.) and the forms Yeho, Yo and Yah, Yahu, which occur constantly in proper names, ... can all be derived from Yahweh."—John D. Davis, *The Westminster Dictionary of the Bible*

"The Divine Name here originally was Jah or Yah. This came to be represented in verbal form by the Hebrew letters YHWH– that is to say Yahweh or Jahweh, which means 'He causes to be.' The word 'Jehovah' is a later creation which came about by pointing the vowels of the Greek 'Adonai' or Lord. Original is Yahweh or Jahweh as it is written in the Lachish Letters dated BC 600. January 29, 1935 is the date the Lachish Letters were found in the debris of the gate tower of the city. They are written documents of the time of Jeremiah. The constant use of the Divine Name is another feature of this most ancient correspondence. The Lachish Letters are contemporary correspondence between orthodox Jews, written in the last days of the kingdom of Judah. There is much significance in the fact that in these Letters the Divine Name, always used, and constantly appealed to, is 'Yahweh'."[110]

"No reasonable scholar, of course, objects to the use of the term Jehovah in the Bible [although this is an incorrect translation]. But

---

[110]Sir Charles Marston, *The Bible Comes Alive*, excerpts from pp. 191-194.

since only the Hebrew consonants YHVH appear without vowels, pronunciation is at best uncertain, and dogmatically to settle on Jehovah is straining at the bounds of good linguistics. ... All students of Hebrew know that any vowel can be inserted between the consonants (YHWH or JHVH) so that theoretically the divine name could be any combination from JoHeVaH to JiHiViH without doing violence to the grammar of the language in the slightest degree."[111]

MESSIAH AND THE TETRAGRAMMATON

In using the words "I AM," the Messiah Jesus identified Himself with the Covenant Personal Name of the Lord in the Old Testament. The Jews recognized His claim to Deity when He said, *"Before Abraham was, I AM,"* and they took up stones to stone Him, considering it as blasphemy, which by law was punishable by death (Leviticus 24:16; John 8:58). See also John 8:24 *"... if ye believe not that I AM he, ye shall die in your sins."* The personal pronoun "he" is not here in the original Greek text. It has been supplied by the translators. The Greek for "I am" is *eimi* and in John 8:58 is really absolute. It is a statement by Messiah Jesus not only of His pre-existence, but of His eternal being.

> "Why did He not say, —before Abraham was I *was*, but I *am*? because He uses this word, 'I am,' as His Father uses it; for it signifies perpetual existence, independent of all time."[112]

> "What the Jews thought of the assertion appeared in their action ... Believing that He was speaking sheer blasphemy and claiming equality with the great 'I Am,' they sought to stone Him."[113]

The Tetragram (intimated) in the Gospel of John

"I AM He, the Messiah (4:26)—meets our need of a Divine Saviour.
I AM the Bread of Life (6:35)—meets our soul-hunger.
I AM the Light of the World (8:12)—meets our darkness.
I AM the Door of the Sheep (10:7)—meets our need of shelter.
I AM the Good Shepherd (10:11)—meets our helplessness.
I AM the Resurrection and the Life (11:25)—meets our death.
I AM your Master and Lord (13:13)—meets our dependence.
I AM the Way, the Truth, and the Life (14:6)—meets our need of salvation.
I AM the True Vine (15:1)—meets our need of union with Himself.
I AM Jesus of Nazareth (18:5)—meets our need of a human Saviour, who is also Divine."

—Author Unknown

---

[111]Martin and Klann, *Jehovah of the Watchtower*, p. 146.
[112]Chr. Wordsworth, *The New Testament with Introduction and Notes,* Vol. I, p. 315.
[113]*The Expositor's Greek Testament*, Vol. I, p. 782.

According to a **Rabbinical tradition** when Jesus was about 30 years of age He secretly stole the letters of the Divine Name which had been written on the Foundation Stone of the Holy of Holies in the Temple and sewed them under his skin! Another story is that He stole the true pronunciation of the Sacred Name from the Temple Scroll and inserted it in His thigh. This was the reason for His supernatural power which the religious leaders of the Jews considered as blasphemy of which they accused Him. According to these religious leaders, with the power of the Divine Name Jesus began to heal the sick and eventually gathered 310 young men as His followers. He also performed such "tricks" as enabling a millstone to float on the Sea of Galilee and causing clay birds to fly as well as Himself on occasion (see *The Jewish Toledot, Yeshu*—"History of Jesus").

On the other hand, according to the Talmud, there was a man called the *Besht* "Baal Shem Tov" (Master of the Good Name) who, it was claimed, knew the correct pronouncement of that Divine Name and worked miracles by it. However, he was not accused of blasphemy in using that Name but instead was honored!

How significant is the revelation of Messiah Jesus coming in glory as related in Revelation 19:16 which corresponds with the Rabbinical *tradition* of the Divine Name *written on His thigh*: On His *thigh* will be a name written: "The King of Kings, and Lord of Lords"!

The Tetragram Combinations

There are 10 distinct combinations of the Tetragram in the Old Testament (besides those indistinct) which are:

1. *YeHoVaH-Yireh*—Genesis 22:14
   "The Lord will see or provide"
2. *YeHoVaH-Ropheka* (Rapha)—Exodus 15:26
   "The Lord that healeth" (See article following this list.)
   "The Lord is Healer"
3. *YeHoVaH- Nissi*—Exodus 17:15
   "The Lord, my Banner"
4. *YeHoVaH-Meqaddeshkem*—Exodus 31:13
   "The Lord that doth sanctify you"
5. *YeHoVaH-Elyon*—Psalm 7:17
   "The Lord Most High"
6. *YeHoVaH-Roi* (Ra-ah)—Psalm 23:1
   "The Lord, my Shepherd"
7. *YeHoVaH-Shalom*—Judges 6:24
   "The Lord is Peace"

8. *YeHoVaH-Tsabaoth*—1 Samuel 1:3
   "The Lord of Hosts"
9. *YeHoVaH-Tsidkenu*—Jeremiah 23:6
   "The Lord, our Righteousness"
10. *YeHoVaH-Shammah*—Ezekiel 48:35
    "The Lord is There (present)*"*

THE LORD THAT HEALETH
Yehovah-Ropheka

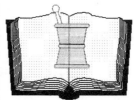

God's Medicine-chest
(Graphic by Duane Bagaas)

Most everyone is familiar with the "Red Cross Society" and their Red Cross symbol. In Christian countries (so-called) all doctor's cars, hospitals, ambulances, etc., bear this Red Cross as a sign of first aid and healing. But the Jews did not want to adopt a symbol of what they have rejected for 1,900 years so they use a red Mogen David (Shield of David) or Star of David instead of a red cross. Their first aid society is called the "Red Mogen David Service" and today, in Israel, doctor's cars, ambulances, hospitals, etc. bear the insignia of a red Mogen David in the center of which is a picture of a serpent on a pole, signifying the healing of Israel while they journeyed in the wilderness. (However, the first meeting to consider the organizing of the American Red *Cross* was held in the home of Adolphus Salomon, a *Jew!*)

God Promised Healing to Israel

> *"And said, If thou wilt diligently hearken to the voice of the LORD thy God, and wilt do that which is right in his sight, and wilt give ear to his commandments, and keep all his statutes, I will put none of these diseases upon thee, which I have brought upon the Egyptians: for I am the LORD that **healeth** thee"* (Exodus 15:26).

Thank God! He still heals today! He is the same miracle-working Lord. He is able to deliver from every power of the devil *now*. Our God has not changed His covenant or His Name!

Isaiah, the Jewish prophet, asks a question in the 53rd chapter of his book concerning the Lord that heals. *"Who has believed our report? And to whom is the arm of the Lord revealed?"* This question is answered in the second part of the Bible (the New Covenant) after the Lord's arm was revealed through Messiah Yeshua (Jesus):

*"But though he had done so many miracles before them, yet they believed not on him: That the saying of Esaias [Isaiah] the prophet might be fulfilled, which he spake, **Lord, who hath believed our report? and to whom hath the arm of the Lord been revealed?**"* (John 12:37-38).

Isaiah saw the suffering Messiah and exclaimed:

"Surely he hath borne our sicknesses and carried our pain; but he was wounded for our transgressions, he was bruised for our iniquities, the chastisement of our peace was upon him; and by his bruise [singular case] was healing granted unto us" (Isaiah 53:4, 5; Isaac Leeser's translation).

We read of the fulfillment of this prophecy in the *Brith Hadasha*:

*"When the even was come, they brought unto him [Yeshua] many that were possessed with devils: and he cast out the spirits with his word, and **healed** all that were sick: That **it might be fulfilled** which was spoken by Esaias the prophet, saying, **Himself took our infirmities, and bare our sicknesss"*** (Matthew 8:16-17).

David knew the Great Physician. His heart welled up in praise to Him as he spoke to his own soul: *"Bless the LORD, O my soul, and forget not his benefits: Who forgiveth all thine iniquities; who **healeth all thy diseases;**"* (Psalm 103:2-3).

Moses knew the Great Physician. He was commanded by God to raise a brazen serpent upon a pole, so that the Israelites who had been poisoned *in their bodies*, looking upon it would *be healed*! And as Moses lifted up the serpent in the wilderness, so must the Son of Man be lifted up that those who were poisoned by sin and disease looking upon Him (that is, believing in Him) could be healed (John 3:14-15).

In the time of the Babylonian ruler Nimrod there was the worship of the serpent called *Aescalapius* which means "healer."[114] The heathen believed that this serpent entwined himself around a dead tree stump to bring renewed life to Nimrod. (The ancient pagans pictured Nimrod as the tree that had died.) The doctor's emblem today is a serpent entwined around a pole. It signifies healing.

Caduceus

*"And the LORD said unto Moses, Make thee a **fiery serpent**, and set it upon a pole: and it shall come to pass, that every one that is bitten, when he looketh upon it, shall live. And Moses made a serpent of brass [copper], and put it upon a pole, and it came to*

[114]*Aescalapius* was the ancient Greek god of *medicine* which was made into the form of *one snake on a staff*. Some medical groups use the *Caduceus* (*two* snakes on a staff shown here) originally called the "wand of Hermes (Mercury)" which stood for *medicine* and for *commerce*.

pass, that if a serpent had bitten any man, when he beheld the **serpent of brass** [the antidote], *he lived"* (Numbers 21:8-9).

At the time of the first Passover, the Israelites were commanded to take a Lamb, kill it, shed its blood, and eat its meat. Not only was the blood given for redemption of the soul, but the meat of the lamb was to be eaten for strength and health for the journey into the Promised Land.

God expects every child of His who has applied the blood of the Lamb (Yeshua) to their hearts' door in faith for deliverance from soul bondage, to also partake, by faith, of the meat of that Lamb for strength and health through this wilderness (world) journey into the Promised Land! Not only was the blood of the Lamb shed for remission of our sins, but His body was bruised and broken for our *physical health!*

Yeshua was made a curse in order to redeem us from the curse of the law. He who knew no sin was made sin so that we, believing upon Him, might be delivered from sin. He who knew no sickness, was made sick that we, believing on Him, might be delivered from sickness.

Dear Jewish people, it was for *you* (as well as the Gentile) that the Messiah paid the price for our deliverance and healing. Take Him today not only as your Messiah who has redeemed your soul, but also as "The Lord That Healeth."

Our God is still able–and willing–and eager to extend His mercy to all those who call upon Him in faith. All things are possible to him that believes!

HEALING BY THE TONGUE

(When I was an Instructor at Seattle Bible College I gave the following message on **healing** in Chapel, January, 1984.)

The Contrary and Consecrated Tongue

Leshon Ha-Ra ("The Evil Tongue")
Leshon Ha-Kodesh ("The Sanctified Tongue")

One instance where "Leshon Ha-Ra" ("the tongue of evil") is found is in Leviticus 19:16 (*"You shall not go up and down as a slanderer among your people"*).

Rabbis say that slander, talebearing, and evil talk are worse than the three cardinal sins of murder, immorality, and idolatry.

"And Miriam and Aaron spake against Moses because of the Ethiopian woman whom he had married: ..." (Numbers 12:1).

We learn in the order of events after this that God called Moses, Aaron and Miriam to the Tabernacle of the Congregation and spoke to them about this *sin of the tongue.* He asked *"Were ye not afraid to speak against my servant Moses?"* God then departed from them and Miriam became leprous. She was mentioned first in the "speaking against" as if to imply that she was instrumental in swaying Aaron to agree with her in this sin. Aaron confesses their sin of evil speaking and Moses intercedes for Miriam's healing. Miriam was shut out from the camp for seven days after which she was brought back healed. The people did not journey on until first Miriam was brought in again.

Do you not see that the *tongue* affected Miriam's physical and spiritual *health*? According to the Jewish disciple, James, the tongue is an unruly member and it sets on fire the whole course of our natural bodies (James 3:6-10). How very true! Doctors have discovered that the digestion is affected, nerves burn, the brain is inflamed by a word of temper or of anger. The tongue speaks that which is within. Words of envy, fault-finding, complaining, resentment will affect the body. "Speaking against," in the case of Miriam, was a sin which was manifested in leprosy, affecting every member of her body. "Death and life are in the power of the tongue," the Word of God tells us. Also there is suffering and destruction as well as health in this little organ of our mouth: *"There is that speaketh like the piercings of a sword: but the tongue of the wise is **health**"* (Proverbs 12:18). Miriam criticized her brother Moses. Her *tongue* was the cause of her leprosy. It brought disease with the sentence of death.

Notice: Miriam didn't say anything false about Moses or criticize him for any sin. She spoke only that of which she did not approve. God calls this "speaking against." The greater part of speaking against is either from habit of criticism or from wrong motives.

Miriam was not the only one affected by her unruly member but also the body of God's people. They were delayed in the progress of their journey seven days because of Miriam's transgression of the tongue. One person's evil speaking–the wrong use of this little member–can affect the whole local body of God's people or the body to which that member is related.

On another occasion Israel murmured against Moses and Aaron in connection with the rebellion of Korah and Abiram and because of this use of their tongues in murmurings, disease was sent among them in judgment and 14,700 people died. When Aaron made atonement for the people, the disease was halted.

The Word of God says that the tongue is full of deadly poison (James 3:8). In Numbers 21:5-6 we see this poison experienced by the Israelites in the wilderness. God's people, redeemed from Egypt, saw the miracles of God, experienced His blessings—yet their tongues were full of deadly poison. They murmured and complained against their God.

What was the result of their evil speaking? It affected their physical bodies. The poison of the serpents was injected into their blood stream and their bodies began to swell. Much of the people died as a result. Doctors know that that which poisons the mind, also poisons the blood and produces various forms of disease. There is death and life in the power of the tongue. This poisonous tongue affected *all* of God's people. It, no doubt, was started by *one* member of their group. Not only do we poison ourselves with this unruly member but by the wrong use of our tongues we bring others into condemnation.

Praise God, there is a remedy of healing for the contrary tongue and it can become a "consecrated" tongue. What was the beginning of healing for the criticizing tongue of Miriam? First of all, confession of that sin, then the sanctified and consecrated tongue of Moses who interceded on her behalf and she was healed. What was the beginning of healing for the poisonous, murmuring tongues of the Israelites? First of all, a confession of that sin, and then the sanctified, consecrated tongue of Moses who interceded on their behalf. And this is the same procedure today!

Notice that Moses did not criticize Miriam nor condemn her, though she spoke against him; he simply interceded for her. Moses did not condemn the Children of Israel but simply interceded for them. This is *Leshon haKodesh*, a consecrated tongue, a sanctified, controlled tongue!

The Holy Spirit through James said that no man can tame this little member of the body. No *man* can, but the Holy Spirit can control it if we turn it over to Him. He enables us to do that which we cannot do without Him! Do you want your tongue to be tamed–to be delivered–to be controlled–to be a consecrated tongue? Be filled with God's Holy Spirit, the Dove of Peace and Love!

–End of Message

Interesting Note: Not only is the tongue of *man* used in the case of healing but also the tongue of a *dog*! Healing qualities are found in both.

> Archaeologists discovered in their excavations located in the area of Ashkelon (1991) that there were many dog burials related to the worship of the Phoenician *healing deities* Eshmoun and Resheph-Mukol. Perhaps because of the *curative powers* exhibited by dogs licking their sores and wounds, these animals were associated with *healing* in the ancient Near East. Their tongues held healing properties. —*Biblical Archaeology Review*, 1997

We notice the story told by Messiah about the experience of the beggar Lazarus who lay at the rich man's gate full of sores (Luke 16:19-21). The rich man ignored the beggar (as everyone did) but the dogs *licked his sores*. Thus the dogs were more compassionate toward him than anyone. They healed him with their tongue!

Be Strong

Another message connected to *healing* follows. I gave this brief exhortation to the graduating class of SBC (Seattle Bible College) in June of 1980.

At the end of each year Jewish people recite a salutation to each other in Hebrew: *Hazak, hazak, vinit hazak* חֲזַק חֲזַק וְנִתְחַזֵּק (which means) *Be strong, be strong, and let us strengthen one another.* At the conclusion of some books of the *T'nakh* (the Hebrew Scriptures) this exhortation is found such as in *Kings,* the book of *Chronicles,* the books of *Jeremiah* and *Isaiah,* but they are hidden to most of us because they are *not translated!*

Then, at the conclusion of each of the books of Moses, there is only *one* word in *large Hebrew letters:* **Hazak** (be strong)! It also means "hold fast," "be of good courage," "be steadfast," "be strengthened." At the conclusion of *ten* other books of the Old Testament we also find this word ***Hazak*** *which is not translated.* (Look in your Hebrew Bible and see חֲזַק—*Hazak!*)

We do find that this word *Hazak* is translated in the following verses:

> *"Be ye* strong [hazak] *therefore, and let not your hands be weak: for your work shall be rewarded"* (2 Chronicles 15:7).

> *"Be* strong [hazak] *and of a good courage, fear not, nor be afraid of them: for the LORD thy God, he it is that doth go with thee; he will not fail thee, nor forsake thee"* (Deuteronomy 31:6).

> *"Yet now be strong* [hazak], *O Zerubbabel, saith the LORD; and be strong* [hazak], *O Joshua, son of Josedech, the high priest; and be strong* [hazak], *all ye people of the land, saith the LORD, and work: for I am with you, saith the LORD of hosts:* (Haggai 2:4).

> *"Have not I commanded thee? Be strong* [hazak] *and of a good courage; be not afraid, neither be thou dismayed: for the LORD thy God is with thee whithersoever thou goest"* (Joshua 1:9).

> *"Strengthen* [hazak] *ye the weak hands, and confirm the feeble knees. Say to them that are of a fearful heart, Be strong* [hazak], *fear not: ...*
>
> Strengthen [hazak] *ye the weak hands, and confirm the feeble knees. Say to them that are of a fearful heart, be strong* [hazak], *fear not: ..."* (Isaiah 35:3-4).

In the Hebrew NT: *"Thou therefore, my son, be strong* [hazak] *in the grace that is in Christ Jesus."* (2 Timothy 2:1).

My exhortation to you, graduating class of 1980, is:

חֲזַק = *Hazak! Be Strong!*

APPENDIX I:

IS CHRISTIANITY THE OFFSPRING OF JUDAISM?

Not at all; instead of Christianity is the fulfillment and sequence of the *religion of ancient Israel* as expressed in the Law, the Prophets and the Writings; whereas Judaism is the *adjustment* to 70 AD and a defense against Jesus as the Messiah and as the Son of God in a unique sense.

The 613 commandments of the Torah (the Law of Moses) are characterized by Peter (Acts 15:10) as that *"... which neither our fathers nor we were able to bear ... "* The commandments placed upon the Jew by the **system of Judaism** include much more than Scripture, for the *Talmud* with its *Mishnah*, and *Gemara* amplifies those commandments and lays a far greater burden upon the people. The sense of sin in the Jewish mind is most frequently found to be fear of breaking the law of Kosher or the law of the Sabbath, but the system is very capable of rationalizing any infringement of the law.

Is There a Conflict Between Jewish Faith and Christianity?

There is no conflict between the *true* Jewish faith as recorded in the Tenach [OT] and *true* Christianity as expressed in the New Testament. Christianity is the fulfillment of the faith of ancient Israel; *It is not the outcome of Talmudic Judaism*. Indeed, the Judaism of today is *not* the faith of ancient Israel. Judaism is an elaborate adjustment to the tragedy of 70 AD when both Jerusalem and the second Temple were destroyed by the Romans.

True Christianity is *Jewish*. Jesus, the disciples, and all the writers of the New Testament except Luke [some say], were Jews. Furthermore, the first Christian church, founded at Jerusalem, was composed of Jews, and the missionary movement which swept the Roman empire was Jewish-inspired. Therefore, original Christianity as reflected in the New Testament was *Jewish*. In later centuries pagan elements crept into the church doctrine and ritual; however, these were largely eliminated during the Protestant reformation.

Christianity cannot be the offspring of *Judaism*; but instead Judaism is the attempt to adjust to 70 AD, and, we would add, to defend itself from New Testament teaching.

—Reverend Frederick J. Berger, D.D.

~ 353 ~

APPENDIX II:

JACOB, THE JEW[115]

(I prepared the following article for a young lady who had been ridiculed for naming her son "Jacob." Those who use the Scriptures as supporting their *derogatory* view of this name should be advised also.)

It seems to be the opinion of some persons that the Jacob of the Bible depicts the Jewish people, that as Jacob was a cheat, a usurper, a crook, so are all Jews. This is a form of anti-semitism or Jew-hatred. However, we will look into the Scriptures for a true description of the Jew, Jacob.

First of all we find that Jacob was the strongest man in the Bible! The story is told in Genesis 32:24, 26, 28-30 that Jacob wrestled with *God*! God Himself said that Jacob had wrestled with Him and *won*! It is written in Hosea 12:3-4: *"By his strength Jacob overcame God"*! Notice that Jacob's name was still *Jacob* when he wrestled with the Lord!

God, speaking of Jacob, said: *"He took his brother by the heel in the womb, and by his strength he had power with God. Yea, he had power over the angel, and prevailed"* (Hosea 12:3-4). The Angel (who was the Lord) had to say to Jacob: *"Let me go."*

God Himself honored the name of *Jacob*. There is no place recorded in the Bible where God found any fault with him! On the contrary, the Bible boldly declares Jacob *a perfect man*! See Genesis 25:27 where the word "plain" is a mis-translation. The Revised Version gives it as *quiet* man. But the Hebrew text is *ish tam* or *perfect man*. (*Tam* rhymes with *Tom*.)

The word "perfect" (*tam*) appears 7 times in Scripture.

    a.   Of Noah—Genesis 6:9
    b.   Of Abram—Genesis 17:1
    c.   Of Job, three times—Job 1:1, 8 and 2:3
    d.   And once of the *work* of God—Deuteronomy 32:3-4 (The plural of *tam* is *tammim* here.)

In all instances *tam* is translated as perfect, upright, sincere, innocent, righteous except when the translators came to the man, Jacob. Here they translated it by *plain*! Clearly "ish tam" in the biblical idiom usually refers to a man whose character is beyond reproach. And yet, *in the case of Jacob*, translators have often avoided the plain meaning of this idiom, providing instead ingenious substitutes.

---

[115]Also in my book entitled *My Jewish People*, pp. 193-196.

"And the boys grew: and Esau was a cunning hunter, a man of the field; and Jacob was a plain man, dwelling in tents" (Genesis 25:27).

The King James Version of the Bible says Jacob was a "plain man"; the Revised Standard Version and the Jerusalem Bible say he was a "quiet man"; the new translation of the Jewish Publication Society says a "mild man." Speiser in the Anchor Bible translates the term as a "retiring man"; the New English Bible says Jacob "led a settled life." The list could go on and on. (The word "perfect" does not mean sinlessness but describes those who sincerely sought *to please God*.)

The names "Jacob" and "Israel" are used in the Bible more than any other name, except the name of God! *Jacob* is mentioned 332 times in the Old Testament, 26 times in the New Testament equalling 358 occurrences altogether.

It is *Esau* who is called a supplanter, a fornicator or profane person (by God)! See Hebrews 12:16 where Esau is called a profane man. The Bible "profane" means "outside the sphere of religious things." It is the opposite of "perfect." Esau despised his birthright so can be called "profane."

Was Jacob a supplanter? See Genesis 27:36 where Esau said: *"... is not he rightly named Jacob? for he hath supplanted me these two times: he took away my birthright: and, behold, now he hath taken away my blessing."* Keil and Delitzsch translates this verse: "Is it that they have named him Jacob (over-reacher), and he has over-reached me twice?" i.e., has he received the name Jacob from the fact that he has twice *outwitted* me? It has been erroneously translated as "supplanter." (Jacob's name was given him at birth, not after he "outwitted" Esau!)

Esau *gave away* his birthright for a mess of pottage. The blessing really belonged to Jacob. This was a promise of God even before they were born. Jacob, who loved the birthright did not usurp or deceive Esau for—it belonged to him! Esau was the actual usurper, deceiver and trickster but he called Jacob the usurper!

Why do people go by what the real usurper, trickster called Jacob instead of what God called him? Because Satan hates the Jews and has painted Jacob as an example of all Jews! Why do not we call Abraham, Isaac, Moses, David, Job and classify *them* as a picture of the Jew, when they were liars, adulterers, murderers, etc. Yet God called each of them as an *ish tam*, a perfect man. Why only pick on Jacob?

So, what is the true meaning of the name, *Jacob*? It comes from the circumstance at the time of his birth. It does not denote his character as is so popularly accepted. When Jacob was born he was grasping the *heel* of his brother Esau. This is what the name, *Jacob,* means: *heel,* "heel-catcher," "overtaker," "over-reacher." Jacob, *Ya'aqobh,* is here derived from the verb *'agabh* which is formed from the noun *'aqebh,* "heel" thus the verb connotes "to grasp by the heel" or, by extension, "to overreach."

Strong's Exhaustive Concordance explains the name Jacob further: "to restrain (as if holding to the heel)." Simply stated, Jacob's name was given to him because he took hold of Esau's heel.

It is true that Jacob did some crooked things. He suffered for these dearly, but this did not express his character and was not the meaning of his name! Abraham and David did some crooked things but this did not express their character, it only expressed their failures and their sins. Abraham, David, and Jacob all yearned for holiness and purity. God covered them with perfection and righteousness. Abraham became "The Friend of God"; David became "A Man After God's Own Heart," Jacob became "Israel, A Prince With God."

I repeat: it is said that Jacob "stole" the birthright from Esau. But as we study the story we learn that Jacob did not unlawfully steal Esau's birthright! *The birthright really belonged to Jacob in the first place!* Before they were born it was said that *Jacob was like the firstborn!* The elder (Esau) would serve the younger (Jacob; see Genesis 27). So the truth is: *Esau had Jacob buy his own birthright!*

God loved Jacob (Malachi 1:2, 3 with Romans 9:12-13). That is, God preferred Jacob over Esau because Jacob valued the birthright. He wanted it more than anything else. Jacob loved God more than Esau did. The blessing which Jacob sought was not material wealth, but the right of Messianic succession. The Messianic line must come either from Jacob or Esau. To be the forefather of the Messiah, *Jacob was ready to pay any price.*

Jacob is forever a name of honor! God calls Himself by this Name! He said that this would be His Name *forever!* Even after Jacob's name was changed at Peniel, God called Himself "The God of ... *Jacob*"! It was 400 years after Jacob's name was changed, when God spoke to Moses out of the burning bush, He declared *"I am the God of Abraham, the God of Isaac and the God of Jacob."* The Lord Jesus did not correct this name but He referred to it. He quoted it to the Pharisees and Sadducees of His day.

The most remarkable fact of all about the name, *Jacob* is that it is applied to God Himself! The Scriptures declare: *"This is the generation of them that seek him, that seek Thy face, O Jacob. Selah"* (Psalm 24:6). From the Hebrew text God is called *Jacob.* In some translations it is: *God of Jacob.* But the words "God of" are not found in the *Hebrew* text. Some translations give it as "the generations of Jacob"; i.e., who called on God as Jacob did.

Jacob foreshadowed Messiah. He fought Satan and won. With His heel He, the true Jacob, crushed Satan's head and won a victory for us!

(Note: I was pleased to learn via TV in 1995 according to statistics recorded in the United States that the most popular name given to newborn baby boys was *Jacob*!)

"Pastor Stearns of Germantown asked his large Philadelphia Bible Class *what the difference was between Esau and Israel*? There were many answers given by the class, and some of them to the point. But Pastor Stearns said there was yet another one, and that was, that 'Esau saw, as *he-saw*, but what Israel saw, *is-real*'."[116]

Jacob
by Mrs. Butterfield

For Esau the paths
Of the desert forever must be
Life's loftiest way,
Full of freedom and wild ecstasy;
For Jacob the purpose of God
Was the aim which would bear
His will's most courageous endeavor,
His heart's deepest care.
He saw what from others was hidden;
He heard in his soul
What other men heard not,
Responded to unseen control."

Symbols of the 12 tribes of israel

---

[116]Mark Lev, *Lectures on Messianic Prophecy*, p. 85.

BIBLIOGRAPHY

Apisdorf, Shimon. *Passover Survival Kit.* Columbus, Ohio, Leviathan Press, c1994.

Ausubel, Nathan. *The Book of Jewish Knowledge*, New York, Crown Publishers, c1964 by Nathan Ausubel.

Bates, Barbara. *Bible Festivals and Holy Days*, Nashville, Tennessee, Broadman Press, c1968.

Bertinoro, Maimonides. *Mishnayoth with the two greatest commentaries and complete English translation of the Mishnah.* New York, Yavne Press, Inc., 1965.

Blech, Benjamin. *The Secrets of Hebrew Words.* Northvale, New Jersey, London, Jason Arson, Inc., c1991 by Benjamin Blech.

Brooks, Keith L. *The Jews and the Passion For Palestine.* Grand Rapids, Michigan, Zondervan, c1937.

Burney, C.F. *Outlines of Old Testament Theology.* New York, Edwin S. Gorham, 1904.

Cohen, A. (ed.). *The Soncino Chumash.* London, The Soncino Press, 1956.

_____. *Everyman's Talmud.* New York: Schocken Books, 1949.

Daube, David. *The New Testament and Rabbinic Judaism.* Peabody, Massachusetts, Hendrickson Publishers, c1956 by School of Oriental and African Studies, The University of London.

Davis, John D. *The Westminster Dictionary of the Bible.* Philadelphia, Westminster Press, c1944.

Danby, Herbert (ed.). *The Mishnah.* London, Oxford University Press, 1938.

DeHaas, Jacob (ed.). *The Encyclopedia of Jewish Knowledge.* New York, Longmans, Green and Company, 1904.

Edersheim, Alfred. *The Life and Times of Jesus the Messiah, Vol. I & II.* New York, Longmans, Green and Company, 1904.

Edidin, Ben M. *Jewish Holidays and Festivals.* New York, Hebrew Publishing Company, c1941.

_____. *Jewish Holidays and Festivals.* New York, Hebrew Publishing Company, c1940.

Elias, Rabbi Joseph. *The Haggadah / Passover Haggadah* with translation and a New Commentary based on Talmudic, Midrashic and Rabbinic Sources. New York, Mesorah Publications, Ltd. c1977, 1980, 1994.

Encyclopedia Judaica, Vol. 15, Article, *Reading the Torah.* p. 1254.

Enelow, H.G. *A Jewish View of Jesus.* New York, Bloch Publishing Company, 1931.

Engle, Fannie and Gertrude Blair. *The Jewish Festival Cookbook.* New York, Paperback Library, Inc., c1954 by Fannie Engle and Gertrude Blair.

Freehof, Solomon B. *Preface to Scripture.* Cincinnati, Ohio, Union of American Hebrew Congregations, c1950.

Gaster, Theodor H. *The Holy and the Profane, Evolution of Jewish Folkways*, New York, William Morrow and Company, Inc., c1955, 1980 by Theodor H. Gaster.

Gift, Joseph L. *Life and Customs of Jesus' Time*. Cincinnati, Ohio, The Standard Publishing Foundation, c1947.

Gilbert, Arthur and Oscar Tarcov. *Your Neighbor Celebrates*. New York, Friendly House, c1957.

Glazerson, Mattityahu. *The Secret of the Haggadah*, Jerusalem, New York. Feldheim Publishers, Shvat 5749 [1989].

_____. *Sparks of the Holy Tongue*. Jerusalem/New York, Feldheim Publishers Ltd., Printed in Israel, c1975, 1981 by M. Glazerson.

Goldstein, David, LL.D. *Jewish Panorama*. St. Paul, Minnesota, Radio Replies Press, c1940 by David Goldstein.

Goodman, Philip. *The Passover Anthology*. Philadelphia, Jerusalem c1961 by The Jewish Publication Society of America and 1993 by Philip Goodman.

Grant, F.C. *Ancient Judaism and the New Testament*. New York, Macmillan, 1959.

Harkavy, Alexander (trans.). *The Holy Scriptures*. Hebrew Publishing Company, c1916.

Heller, Abraham Mayer. *The Vocabulary of Jewish Life*. New York, Hebrew Publishing Company, c1942.

Hertz, Joseph H., ed. *Authorized Daily Prayer Book*. New York, Block Publishing Co., 1948.

Heydt, Dr. Henry J. *The Chosen People Question Box II*, Englewood Cliffs, New Jersey. American Board of Missions to the Jews, c1976 by American Board of Missions to the Jews.

Holy Scriptures of the Old Testament, Hebrew and English. London, The British and Foreign Bible Society, 1963 Printed in Great Britain by Lowe and Brydone (Printers) Limited, London, N.W.10.

Howard, George. *The Name of God in the New Testament*, Article in Biblical Archaeology Review, March 1978, p. 12.

Ice, Thomas and Randall Price. *Ready to Rebuild*, Eugene, Oregon. Harvest House Publishers, c1992 by Harvest House Publishers.

Ironside, H.A. *The Four Hundred Silent Years*. Neptune, New Jersey, Loizeaux Brothers, 1914.

Jocz, Jakob. *The Jewish People and Jesus Christ,* 3rd edition. Grand Rapids, Baker Book House, 1979.

Kertzer, Rabbi Morris N. *What is a Jew?* New York, The Macmillan Company, 1960.

Klinck, Arthur W. *Home Life in Bible Times*. St. Louis, Missouri, Concordia, 1947.

Larkin, Clarence. *Dispensational Truth*. Glenside, Pa., Rev. Clarence Larkin Est. © 1918 & 1920.

LaSor, William Sanford. *Daily Life in Bible Times*. Cincinnati, Ohio, Standard Publishing Company, 1956.

Leeser, Isaac (trans.). *The Holy Bible*. New York, Hebrew Publishing Co., c1916.

Lev, Mark. *Lectures on Messianic Prophecy.* Philadelphia, 1917.

Lindberg, Milton B. *The Jew and Modern Israel.* Chicago, Illinois, Moody Press c1969, Milton B. Lindberg, Revised, 1970.

Lipman, Eugene J. (trans.) *The Mishnah.* New York, Shocken Books, c1970, (*Oral Teachings of Judaism*).

Livingston, Sigmund. *Must Men Hate.* New York, The World Publishing Company, c1944 by Harper & Brothers.

Mackie, George M. *Bible Manners and Customs.* New York, Fleming H. Revell Company, n.d.

Mozeson, Isaac E. *The Word, The Dictionary That Reveals the Hebrew Source of English.* New York, Shapolsky Publishers, c1989 by Isaac Mozeson.

Myers, Jack M. *The Story of the Jewish People, Vol. III.* with a prefatory note by the Very Rev. The Chief Rabbi. London, Kegan Paul, Trench, Trubner & Co. Ltd. New York, The Bloch Publishing Co. 1925.

Newman, Louis I., Translator and Arranger. *The Hasidic Anthology.* New York, Bloch Publishing Company, 1934, Fourth Printing, 1946.

Newman, Yacov and Gavriel Sivan. *Judaism A-Z,* Jerusalem, Ahva Cooperative Press, 1980.

Pentecost, J. Dwight. *Things to Come.* Grand Rapids, Michigan, Zondervan Publishing House. c1958 by Dunham Publishing Company.

Philips, Dr. A. *Prayer Book For the Day of Atonement.* New York, Hebrew Publishing Company, 1913.

Pike, E. Royston. *Encyclopaedia of Religion and Religions.* New York, Meridian Books, Inc., c1958.

Powell, Frank J. *The Trial of Jesus Christ.* Grand Rapids, Michigan, c1948 by The Paternoster Press.

Pierson, A.T. *Knowing the Scriptures.* New York, Gospel Publishing House, 1910.

Prichard, Augustus Bedlow. *Christ in Psalm CXIX.* Los Angeles, California, Bible House of Los Angeles, c1938 by Augustus B. Prichard.

Robinson, Edward. (trans.) *Hebrew and English Lexicon of the Old Testament* (*including the Biblical Chaldee from the Latin of William Gesenius*) *23rd Edition.* Boston, Houghton Mifflin and Company, 1882.

Rosenau, William. *Jewish Ceremonial Institutions and Customs.* New York, Bloch Publishing Company, c1925 by William Rosenau.

Scherman, Rabbi Nosson/Rabbi Meir Zlotowitz, General Editors. *Pesach/ Its Observance, Laws, and Significance.* Brooklyn, New York, Noble Book Press, c1994 by Mesorah Publications, Ltd.

Schonfield, Hugh. *A Popular Dictionary of Judaism.* New York, c1962 by Hugh J. Schonfield.

Siegel, Richard; Michael and Sharon Strassfield. *The Jewish Catalog, Number I.* Philadelphia, The Jewish Publication Society of America, c1976.

Steingroot, Ira. *Keeping Passover.* San Francisco, New York. Harper Collins Publishers, c1995 by Ira Steingroot.

Tan, Paul Lee. *The Interpretation of Prophecy*. Rockland, Maryland, Assurance Publishers, c1974, eighth printing, 1988, Printed in Hong Kong.

Torrey, R.A. *Difficulties in the Bible*. Chicago, Illinois, The Moody Press, c1907.

Unger, Merrill F. *Unger's Bible Dictionary*; Chicago, Moody Press, 1966.

Wehl, Rabbi Yaakov. *The Haggadah With Answers: The Classic Commentators Respond to Over 200 Questions*. Brooklyn, N.Y., Noble Book Press, c1997 by Mesorah Publications, Ltd. and Rabbi Yaakov Wehl.

Whitsell, Faris Daniel. *Evangelistic Preaching and the Old Testament*. Chicago, Illinois, Moody Press, c1947.

Wilkerson, David. *Sipping Saints*. Old Tappan, New Jersey. Fleming H. Revell Company, c1978 by World Challenge, Inc. and Fleming H. Revell Company.

Wilson, Marvin R. *Our Father Abraham, Jewish Roots of the Christian Faith*. Grand Rapids, Michigan, Eerdmans Publishing Co., c1989 by Marvin R. Wilson.

Wouk, Herman. *This Is My God*. New York, Pocket Books, 1970.

Yaseen, Leonard C. *The Jesus Connection*. New York, Crossroad, 1985.

Young, Brad. *The Jewish Background to the Lord's Prayer*. Austin, Texas, Center for Judaic-Christian Studies, c1984 by Brad Young.

General Index

A

Aaronic benediction, 45
abaye, 32
abiding place, 176
Abihail, 218
Aboda, 54
abomination of desolation, 226
accension, 184
accomplice, 278, 280
Acre, 37
acrostic, 193, 218, 219, 254, 310, 311
Adar, 219, 295
adhesions, 23
adultery, 10
adversity, 15
Aescalapius, 348
aesophagus, 23
afflict the soul, 188
Akdamuth, 170
Akko, 37
akros, 310
alam, 259
alamoth, 261
aleph, 34, 214, 333, 335
Alexandria, 8, 179
alien, 123
Allies, 68
allusion, 15, 332
almanac, 48
Alpha, 2, 126, 328, 330, 332
alpha privative, 208
alter, 233

American Red Cross, 347
Amoraim, 49
ample, 144
amulet, 28
Anan, 325
anatomical, 34
animosity, 222
ankles, 200
Annas, 278
anniversary, 70
anteroom, 10, 189
anthem, 59, 60
anti-Roman, 324
Antiochus, 220, 226, 232
Antiochus Epiphanes, 225, 226, 324
antithesis, i
Apis, 143
Apocrypha, 218
apparition, 288
apple, 206
Arabia, 64
Aravot, 205
Arba Minim, 205
aristocrats, 278
ark, 11, 111, 188
army, 184, 193, 225, 276
Artaxerxes, 307
asah, 272
asceticism, 325
ashes, 69, 143, 201
Ashkenazi, 101, 129
Ashkenazic, 76, 170
asphyxiation, 273
assimilation, 67

Assyrian, 75, 327
Astronomy, 147
atrophied lobes, 23
attic, 128
auditorium, 13, 211, 214
Avram, 323

B

Baal Shem Tov, 325
babirusa, 20
Babli, 49
Babylon, 48, 49, 216
Babylonian Exile, 8
backbiting, 155
bain-ha-arbaiim, 14, 153
baking soda, 129
Balfour Declaration, 297
Baltokia, 182
bands of females, 102
banquets, 133
baptism, 83, 84
Bar Kochba, 240
Bar Kozba, 241
Barabbas, 280
Barcelona, 182
barren, 65, 72, 98
bars, 129, 161
baru, 75
Baruch habah, 146
Barukh habah, 75
Basel, Switzerland, 300
Bashan, 24
basin, 189, 203, 284
bath house, 189

BaZillion, 318
beheading, 274
Ben Elohim, 87
berachoth, 113
berches, 113
bereaved, 69
berith, 75
Besamim, 112
beseiged, 63
Besht, 325, 346
bet medresh, 214
Beth ha-Knesset, 9
betrothal, 97
Bible Chronology, 90
biblical, 39, 42, 47,
     102, 121, 354
Biblical Sabbath, 110
biceps, 30
bicycle, 169
Bi'er Hametz, 128
Bimah, 7
biritu, 75
bishops, 333
bitters, 133, 148
blasphemy, 279, 345,
     346
bleeding, 24, 273
bloodshed, 201
bloody, 200, 285
blue shawl, 92
Boaz, 170, 303
boils, 143
bolt, 24
bonnet, 10
Book of Death, 320
Book of Life, 180,
     185, 188, 190, 202,
     323
Book of Remem-
     brance, 188
booty, 131
bosor echad, 44

Boston, 300, 360
braid of dough, 113
Bread from Heaven,
     131
breed, 107
bricklayers, 150
brickmaking, 150
Bride of Christ, 99
Britons, 276
Brogez Tanz, 102
brotherhood, 28, 41,
     99
Bruchot Nessuin, 98
bugle, 193
Bul, 295
bull, 143, 180, 196
bullock, 198, 202
bulls, 24, 196, 197
burning bush, 73
byssus, 189

C

Cabalistic, 302
Cabalists, 159
Caduceus, 348
Caesar, 275
Caiaphas, 279
calories, 206
camel, 19, 90, 131,
     336
camel's hump, 336
Cana, 140
Canaan, 138, 146, 174
Canaanites, 247, 329
candelabrum, 7, 126,
     206
canon, 136, 312
canopy, 94, 95, 96
cantaloupe, 205
cantillation, 145
Cantor, 7

carnival, 223
carol, 227
casebook, 48
catastrophe, 215, 226,
     297
cathedrals, 177
cattle dealers, 278
cemetery, 215, 339
Certificate, 131
certified, 131
Chabad, 311
Chag, 122
Chair of Glory, 37
Chalcedon, 333
Chaldee, 47, 139, 328,
     360
chalk, 224
challah, 113, 159
charity, 15, 188, 222
chastened, 64
chattel, 91
chew the cud, 18, 19,
     20
chicks, 123
chief honour, 137
Cholee, 95
cholesterol, 206
chorus, 102, 103
Chumash, 87, 169,
     342, 358
cider, 140
cipher, 91
citizenship, 73, 190
citron, 205
citrus fruit, 205
Civil Year, 121
clay, 150, 178
clay birds, 346
clear glass, 95
cloven, 18, 19, 20
co-equal, 45

co-eternal, 45
coat of mail, 19
coats, 183, 200, 283, 325
coined, i, 8, 330
comity, 297, 298
commemorate, 106, 118, 223, 226, 256
commemoration, 102, 169
community rabbi, 127
companion, 278
compensation, 89
Computer, 318, 319
conceived in sin, 82
congeal, 197
congratulations, 85
connotation, 45
connubial, 100
conoid, 180
consoled, 105
Constantine, 167
constellations, 146
consummation, 90, 96, 103, 210
conversion, 78
convert, 78, 84, 195, 215
corpse, 10
couches, 133, 136, 137
Court of the Priests, 189
Credo, 30, 216
creed, 41
crevice, 11
crib, 84
crippled, 155
cross-shaped stand, 153
crossbreeds, 20
crosspiece, 153

crumbs, 127, 183
curse, 72, 91, 221, 244, 273, 349

D

dagesh, 199
daily devotions, 32, 37
Dat Jehudit, i
Dat Moshe, i
debauchery, 140, 226
Decalog, 115
defilement, 10, 226
deformed, 155
den of thieves, 279
desertion, 273
dessert, 157
Destroying Angel, 138, 150, 200
diadem, 189, 287
diamond, 11, 176
Diaspora, 37, 299
didaskale, 251
diglycerides, 17
disguised, 223
dismounted, 90
dissipation, 140
divan, 137
divination, 198
document, 75
dogmas, 34
dogs, 24, 275
Douai, 218
dove, 148, 250, 334
Dragon, 220
drainboard, 23
drunkenness, 140, 226
dummy camp, 225
Dung Gate, 216
duplication, 175

E

eagle, 38, 71
ears, 192, 262, 319, 335
earthquake, 171, 294
Easter Sunday, 121
Eastern wall, 59
Ecclesiastical Latin, 109
Echad, 160
echad, ii, 42, 44, 45
ecstasy, 325
edible, 20
edifices, 177
ehyeh asher ehyeh, 342
El Shaddai, 21, 45, 176
electric shock, 23
Eliezer, 90
Eliezer Ben-Yehuda, 339, 340
Elijah's Chair, 75
Elijah's Cup, 134
Eloah, 342
Emancipation, 123, 153
Emancipator, 125, 162
embodiment, 25, 41
emissaries, 239
emptied, 147, 176
empty chair, 134
encircled U, 18
encompass, 233
encompassed, 63
enemy armies, 63
ensign, 68, 300
Eostre, 167
Ephrathah, 252
epikomos, 157

Epimanes, 225
Epiphanes, 220
epitaphs, 311
epithet, 242
Ereb Shabbat, 109
Eretz Israel, 68
Eretz Yisroel, 64, 144
eschol echad, 44
Eskol Ha-Kofer, 303
espousal, 121
espoused, 122, 245
Essenes, 83, 324
Ethanim, 295
ethics, 47
Etrog, 205, 206
etymologists, 327
Etz Hayyim, 307
Even Ha'ezer, 329
everlasting fires, 188
evetishri, 179
evil eye, 158
evil speaking, 350
Examining Board,
   278
execution, 127, 273,
   274, 275, 282, 284
exegesis, 47
exhibited joy, 326
exile, 41, 47, 69, 149,
   151, 338
expiation, 206
expunged, 320
extinction, 67
extinguish, 110
Ezra, 329

F

fairs, 17
famine, 220
fat, 16, 17, 18, 20,
   206

Feast of Dedication,
   228, 234
Feast of Ingathering,
   203
feeble, 152
feeding-trough, 84
fellowlabourers, 321
ferment, 126, 129,
   130
fermentation, 129,
   130, 138, 139
fertility, 149, 252
Fido, 131
figures, 219, 315
fingertips, 27
fins, 18, 19
First Zionist Con-
   gress, 297
firstling, 152, 200
five silver dollars, 81
flattened tube, 180
Flavius Josephus,
   307, 308
flayed, 24
fleishig, 20
fleshly tables, 28
flogged, 110
floods, 184
foe, 224
food restrictions, 18
forehead, 11, 24, 29,
   30, 31
foreigners, 26, 178,
   274, 275
foreskin, 78, 79
Forest Ranger, 147
fornicator, 355
foursquare, 95
fowl, 190, 191, 196,
   202
fragile, 100
French, 9, 276

fringe, 37, 39, 40
fringed robe, 38
frontlets, 29
frustration, 219
furnace, 221
furry hats, 325

G

Gabriel, 180
Galatia, 117, 281
gallnut, 213
gallows, 219, 221,
   222
Gamaliel, 49, 240
garage, 127
garbage cans, 131
Garden of Eden., 38,
   99, 174, 206
Gauls, 276
geber, 233
Gedolah, 181
gelatin, 17
Gemara, 49, 139, 342
Gematria, 228, 334
Gemiluth Chasadim,
   54
generosity, 222
gennao, 233
gennesis, 233
Gentile property, 67
George Jessel, 59
George Washington,
   225, 303
Germans, 276
gever, 191
Gezer Calendar, 329
ghost, 288
gloves, 10
gluttony, 22, 193
goat skin, 138
goblets, 97

365

goddess, 143, 167
Gog, 206
Golden Calf, 103, 180
golden thread, 166, 173
gragers, 224
Great Hosannah, 211
Great Husbandman, 65
Great Purifier, 128
Great Synagogue, 49
Grecian, 8, 232
Greek customs, 226
Greek Islands, 327
grotesque, 102, 223
groves, 203
Gut Woch, 112
gutters, 111

H

habitation, 28, 59, 177
Hadar tree, 205
Hadassah, 217, 302
Hadassim, 205
Hader, 214
hades, 161
haftorah, 85
Hag Hashofaret, 179
Hag-ha-Asif, 203
Hagadot, 184
Hagiographa, 310
hairgrowth, 29
half-shekel, 17, 223
Hallel, 145, 204, 205, 211, 333
hallot, 113, 114
hallowed, 82, 97
Halo, 334, 336
halof, 23
Hamantaschen, 223
hametz, 127, 129, 131, 138

Hammerer, 225
hamsters, 131
handkerchief, 99
handmaidens, 222
Hanu, 225
Hanukat Habayit, 28
Haroseth, 147, 150
hasid, 323, 324
Hasideans, 324
Hasidic, 31, 156, 324, 325, 326, 360
Hasidic Movement, 31, 156
Hasmoneans, 226
Hassidic Rabbi, 68
Hathor, 143
Hatikvah, 59, 60
hauteur, 100
havah, 342
Havdalah, 112
Hazan, 95, 99
Headstone of the Corner, 146
Heavenly Isaac, 90, 94
Hebraism, 308
Hebrew idiom, i
Hebrew-Phoenician alphabet, 327
heifer, 334
hell, 74, 161, 188, 286
Hellenism, i, 324
hen, 123, 190
hermeneutical system, 334
Herod, 254, 276
hesitate, 123
Hesychius, 328
Hethlon, 64
hexagon, 303
High Being, 325
High Commissioner, 68

hind quarter, 18
hinuma', 96
Hislahavus, 324
hiss, 184, 224
holiness sect, 102
Holy of Holies, 7, 13, 14, 15, 59, 144, 198
holy people, 18, 25
honey combs, 139
hooves, 19, 20
Horah, 102
Hoshana Rabba., 211
Hoshannah Rabbah, 204
Hoshen, 307
hospitality, 122
house of prayer, 279
howl, 141
humiliation, 73, 142, 286
hut, 204
hygiene, 22
hymn, 112, 145, 170, 227
hypocritical, 39
hypotheses, 46
hyssop, 148, 149

I

ibex, 19
idolatrous, 18
idolatry, 21, 79, 143, 274, 324, 349
ikneomai, 157
ikomen, 157
ill omen, 99
illegitimate, 251
immaculate, 147
immaculate conception, 247
immersion, 84, 182
immortality, 320

imprimatur, 152
imprinting, 79
imputed, 196
inattentive, 158
incantations, 325
incense, 112, 113, 189
incest, 247
Indonesia, 20
inflation, 16, 175, 270
inhumane, 23
insalubrious, 339
intermarriage, 87
interpreter, 191
intestines, 319
intoxicant, 139, 140
inverted, 147
ish echad, 44
Ishtar, 167
Isis, 143
Italians, 276
Ivreit, 327
Iyar, 121, 294, 295

J

Jabne, 49
jam, 139
jasper, 95
jaw, 319
Jeconiah, 244, 246
Jehoiakim, 244
Jehovah-Jireh, 21
Jeremy, 270
Jericho, 184
jerked, 15
Jesse, 43, 244, 250
jest, 224
Jewess, 218, 221, 222, 223, 250
Jewish calendar, 121, 167, 188, 213, 232, 294, 295

Jewish revivalists, 31
Jewishness, 76
Jewry, 25, 34, 170
jig, 102
jubilee, 90
Judaea, 275
Judah ha-Nasi, 49
Judah Maccabeus, 228
Judas Maccabeus, 225, 232
Julian, 167

K

Kabbalah, 129, 335
Kabbalists, 343
kaddish, 69
Kadesh, 64
kah, 225
Kallah, 99
kaphar, 188
kappel, 10
Karaim, 325
Karaites, 325
karath, 75
Kareth, 188
kashering, 23, 24
Kashrut, 22, 51
kashruth, 20
Katzotske, 102
kematzlif, 199
keriah, 68
kettle, 139
khatsoserah, 182
Kiddush, 112, 138, 141, 142
Kiddushin, 50, 98
Kidron, 203
kindled, 110, 113, 255
King of Israel, 244, 245
Kingship, 244

kipah, 10
kippur, 188
Kittel, 132, 323
klaf, 27
kneading, 130
kneeling, 114
knife, 22, 23, 24
Kohanim, 13
Kohen, 81, 189
Kol Nidre, 191, 192, 193
koots, 73
Korah, 350
kosher, 17, 19, 20, 22, 23, 24, 180
kosher pig, 20
Koso Shel Eliyahu, 134
Kotel, 215, 216, 240
kraspedon, 39
Kreplach, 169

L

Laban, 96
Lachish Letters, 344
lacteals, 319
ladder, 113
Ladino, 339
lashes, 155
Last Adam, 88
Last Supper, 133, 135, 141, 145, 159
laver, 10
Lazarus, 74, 279
League of Nations, 297
Leah, 31, 96
leap year, 295
leg bones, 155, 273
legal code, 49
Lehem ha-Panim, 114

Lehem Mishnah, 159
Lehem Oni, 159
leprosy, 14, 266, 350
leprous, 350
Leshanah Tovah, 320
Leshon ha-Kodesh, 328
Leshon Ha-Ra, 349
Lesser Sanhedrin, 277
Levites, 16, 145, 159, 169, 204, 211
liberation, 138
lightnings, 177
lime, 213
limp, 123
lintels, 150
lion, 41, 275, 300
lion-strength, 41
lions, 6
liquor, 139
litter, 95, 96
little books, 47
liturgy, 170
loan, 144
locusts, 18, 143, 184
loins, 133
lomad, 47
longitudinal pole, 153
Lover, 90, 93, 94, 98, 103, 121, 125
lower lights, 227
Lulav, 205, 210
lulavs, 204
Lydda, 49

M

maaser, 15, 16
Maccabean, 226, 324
Machzor, 8
magical formulae, 325
Magog, 206
mai-av, 247

Maimonides, 1, 9, 30, 42, 182, 358
maize, 129
major evening oblation, 153
MaKHBiY, 226
makkabhah, 225
Malach, 257
malefactors, 155
Malloula, 327
mamzer, 251
Manoah, 237
mantles, 214
manure, 140
Many-Breasted, 21, 30
Maoz Tsur, 227
ma'pilim, 297
marjoram, 148
Marranos, 191
marriage broker, 89
Marriage Supper, 93, 96, 123, 144
martyr's, 160
Masoretic Text, 329
masquerading, 223
massacre, 297
massektot, 223
massektoth, 47
Master of the Good Name, 325, 346
match, 89, 227, 258
matrimonial, 89
Matstsah, 129
mattresses, 137
matza, 131
Matza Tash, 159
matzah, 123, 131
matzah formula, 130
Matzah Tash, 156
matzot-machine, 130
Meah Shearim, 326
medieval Spanish, 339

meditation, 19
Mediterranean Sea, 37
Megiddon, 293
Megillah, 50, 222, 223, 224
Meir ben Isaac Nahorai, 170
Melchizedek, 17, 241, 263
Memra, 216
Mesha, 327
Meshiah ben David, 239
Meshiah ben Joseph, 239
mess of pottage, 355
Messiah-Lord, 80
Messiahnist, 17
Messiahship, 293
Messianic Kingdom, 65, 207, 208, 209
messianic pretender, 241
Metatron, 183
microscopic, 126
Midrash, 49, 206, 307
Migdal Edar, 254, 255
mikvah, 83, 84
milchig, 20
Millennium, 119
minor evening oblation, 153
mint, 148
Minyan, 12
minyan, 85
miqva'ot, 83
mirth, 99
Mishnah-Gamara, iii
Mishnaic, 49, 324
mitre, 10
Mitsveh, xii
Mitsvos aseh, xii

Mitsvos lo-saaseh, xii
mitzvah, 33, 122
mizrak, 14
Moabite Stone, 327
moan, 181
mockery, 64, 273
modernist, 200
modes, 46
Mohammedan, 241
Mohel, 76
molasses, 139
moldy bread, 140
monetary, 223
money lenders, 278
Mono, 17
Moralism, 55
Mordekai, 89
Morocco, 158
Mosaic, 17, 30, 178
Moses Maimon, 72
Moses' seat, 251
Moslem, 327
Moslems, 20
motif, 11
Mount Lebanon, 201
mourner, 69
mourning for the
     Temple, 100
mud, 19
murder, 274, 276, 280,
     349
mysterious, 46

N

Nachash Ha-
     Kadmoon, 53
nashku bar, 87
National Seal, 303
nationhood, 297
natural science, 47
Nazarene, 32, 178,
     268

Nazareth, 77, 79, 254,
     268, 345
Nazi halocaust, 298
Nazi Party, 219
needle, 79
Ner Tamid, 7
Ner Tomid, 11, 226,
     227
nerve center, 65
nest, 38
New Moon, 183
new wine,, 96
Nicaean Council, 167
Nicodemus, 77
Night of Vigil, 121
nikudah, 329
nikudit, 328, 329
Nimrod, 348
nonsense, 208
northern fringe, 254
nose, 31, 319
notches, 23
NSDAP, 220
nudity, 10
numerology, 228, 334

O

obligation, 13, 75
obscurantism, 339
oinos, 140
olive oil, 227
Olivet Discourse, 68
Omega, 2, 126, 330,
     332
omen, 99
omer, 169, 170, 171
Omud, 7
Or Zarua, 89
orchards, 203
Oriental, 89, 333
Oron Hakodesh, 7, 9
Osiris, 143

oth, 233, 258
outwitted, 355
over-reacher, 355

P

padded paw, 19
pagan, 26, 103, 231
paganism, 232
pain, 152, 155, 166,
     192, 215, 268, 348
palace, 174, 253
Palestine Mandate, 68
palm branches, 204,
     205
paper scroll, 27
papyri, 343
parabolic, 180
parallelogram, 136
Parasceve, 109
parchment, 6, 27, 28,
     29, 170, 343
parekhet, 7
Paris, 339
parthenos, 260
parve, 20
Paschal Lamb, 155,
     167
Passover Matzot, 131
peanuts, 129
peculiar, 25, 88, 267,
     268, 341
Peniel, 256, 356
penny, 98
Pentateuch, 23, 113
perforated, 156
perforator, 130
performers, 102
perjury, 273
permanent, 174, 176,
     178, 204
permeating, 148
Persia, 217, 218, 294

pertinence, 154
peruk, 10
perverted, 39
Pesahim, 50, 138, 139
Petrus Galatinus, 342
Petty Court, 277
peyah, 323
Philistina, 327
Philistines, 96
Philo, 179, 343
philosophy, 41, 47, 325
Phoenicians, 326, 329
phulakterion, 29
physiognomy, 100
pictographs, 327
piglike, 20
Pilgrim Fathers, 204
pilgrimage, 223
pilgrims, 90, 330
pillows, 133, 158
pious, 27, 33, 34, 39, 53, 89, 123, 259, 323, 324, 339
piracy, 273
Pirke Abboth, 13
pistols, 224
pitch, 188
pitched, 176
Pithom, 150
pivot of piety, 34
piyutim, 8
placard, 31
plaintive melody, 215
plaque, 59
Pliny, 140
plundered, 63
plurality, 43
pockets, 127, 183, 223
Podolia, 325
poison, 350
Polish, 323, 325

Polish-Turkish, 325
polluted, 100, 225, 228
pomegranate, 139, 307
Pontius Pilate, 276, 284
Pool of Siloam, 203
poppy-seeds, 223
Poroches, 7
portico, 234
pouf, 71
Prayer Shawl, 32, 69
pre-existence, 345
pregnant, 158, 190
preservative, 29
Prince Metatron, 183
prison house, 280
profanation, 143, 279
profane, 312, 355
profligacy, 140
Promised Land, 66, 152, 166, 172, 203, 349
propagate, 247
propulsion, 19
proselyte, 83
proselytes, 83
prosperity, 15, 16, 17, 28
protein-rich, 206
pseudo, iii
Pugio Fidel, 341
purification, 82, 83, 84, 250
purified, 82, 83, 87, 250
purify, 25, 201
purtenance, 154
Puss, 131

Q

queen, 91
Queen Esther, 221, 222, 223, 224
quill, 170
quorum, 12
quwts, 73

R

Raamses, 150
Rabbi Akiba, 240, 335
Rabbi Hillel, 49
rabbinical hermeneutics, 49
Rabbinics, 52
Rachab, 247
ram, 8, 334
Rambam, 1
ram's horn, 68, 179, 180, 182, 193
Ras Shamra Tablets, 21
ratification, 75
rattles, 224
Recording Angel, 180
Red Cross Society, 302, 347
Red Mogen David, 347
reference encyclopedia, 48
relaxation, 108, 111
renascence, 330
revelry, 223
reverence, 69, 328, 344
reversed, 222, 259
revolution, 121, 295
riedel, 130
rimmonim, 307

ripped, 15
river of death, 178
Roman Empire, 231
Rome, 253, 274, 275, 276, 295, 302, 311
roofed colonnade, 234
rooster, 190, 191
rotten, 140, 141
rotten fish, 140
Ruach ha-Kodesh, 325
ruins, 63
rushing wind, 172
Russian army, 287

S

Sabbath Day's journey, 111
saccharine, 139
sack, 68, 220
sack-cloth, 259
Sacrament, 125
sacrilege, 10
sacrilegious, 339
Sadducees, 31, 278, 279, 281, 282
Sages, 100
Samson, 96
sanction, 141
sandek, 75
Sanhedrin of Poland, 89
sanitary, 22
Sapa, 140
Sar Shalom, 64
sash-belt, 323
satin, 94, 95, 132
saucer, 112
savav, 233
scales, 18, 19
scapegoat, 199
scarecrow, 112
scepter, 222, 287

schisms, 155
scholar-rabbi-sages, 48
scrambled, 179, 327
scribe, 170, 218
Second Adar, 295
Second Commonwealth, 215
Second Law, 49
security, 64
sedition, 273, 280
Sefer ha-Hayyim, 320
Seir, 201
self-affliction, 325
semitisms, 338
Sephardi, 85, 102
Sephardic, 76, 92, 101
Serapis, 143
servitude, 150, 166
sex, 91, 152
Shabbos-Goy, 110
Shadchan, 89, 90
Shaloch Monos., 223
Shalom, 64, 242, 343, 346
Shammas, 227
shamrock, 46
shankbone, 147, 150, 151, 165
Shebethai Zvi, 241
Sheep Gate, 152
sheital, 10
shekalim, 81
shekar, 139
Shem, 225, 327, 346
shema, 41, 251
Shemini Atzeres, 206
sheol, 72, 286
Shereleh, 102
Sheva Berachot, 98
Shevarim, 181, 182, 193

shevarim, 181
Shiloh, 97, 242, 254, 258
Shimchas Torah, 206
shivah, 69
shochet, 23, 24
shtreiml, 323
Shulkhan Arukh, 51
Siddur, 37
side parts, 88
sidepost, 27
Sidon, 302
sikera, 139
Silk, 95
silk, 32, 94
silverware, 127, 134
Simeon, 43, 82, 252
Simhat Bet Hasho'eva, 203
Simon, 240
Sinai Script, 333
sinew, 20
sinful nation, 195
slantwise, 182
slave, 26, 38, 48, 91
Slavic-Tartarian, 10
sledgehammer, 24
sojourn, 138
Solomon's Porch, 228, 234
Song of Songs, 121, 223, 310
sop, 135, 137, 143, 148
Sorbonne, 339
sounds of alarm, 182
Spain, 215
Spanish Inquisition, 191
spectre, 220
sperm, 260
sphere, 176

spit, 153
splinters, 100
sport, 224
St. Patrick, 46
stable, 84, 244, 253, 254, 268
staccato, 181, 193
staff, 133, 153, 242
State of Israel, 59, 60, 66, 300, 326
stichos, 310
stink, 107
stoic, 340
strangers, 26, 90, 178, 275
strangulation, 274
straw, 150
streetcar, 169
stubble, 150
stunned, 23
stylus, 213
subsistence, 45
sugar, 22, 139
sukkah, 204
super-soul, 325
superstitious, 21, 219
supplanter, 355
surefooted walk, 19
surgeon, 76
symphony, 11
symposiums, 48
synod, 333
syntax, 338
Syria, 226, 327
syrup, 138

T

Ta'anis B'horim, 153
Talmudic Judaism, i, 84
Talmudic dialect, 191
Tamar, 247

Tannaim, 49
target, 20, 280
Targum Ha-Shibim, xii, 260
Tarquin the Proud, 274
tarry, 30, 177, 216
Tashlich, 183
tassel, 39
tattooing, 79
T'chum Shabbos, 111
tefillah shel rosh, 31
tefillah shel yad, 31
Tekia, 181, 182
tekia, 181
Telos, 272
Temple Court, 59
tent life, 95
tent of flesh, 176
tenting, 176
Tephilla, 54
terephah, 22, 24
Teru'ah, 181
Teshuva, 53, 54
tesovav, 233
Tetelestai, 272, 274
T'fillah, 188
t'fillah shel rosh, 29
t'fillah shel yad, 29
Thanksgiving Day, 204
The Big Dipper, 146
The Greater Sanhedrin, 278
The Six-Day War, 111
Theodor Herzl, 297
theology, 47, 183, 287, 338
Theudus, 240
three-pronged letter, 31
threefold, 47, 165

threshold, 284
thunderings, 172, 177
Tiberius, 329
Tikkun Hatzot, 216
tikosev, 320
timbrels, 261
Tisha B'Av,, 7
tithers, 16
token, 93, 102, 268
tomb, 74, 161, 171, 172, 286
Tomb of David, 215
Tosefta, 312
totaphoth, 29
Tower of the Flock, 254, 255
tower of the flock, 255
toy, 91, 224
trachea, 23
Tractate, 96, 185, 223
tractates, 47
traditional Jew, 127
train, 60, 90, 169
traitor, 137, 278
transcripts, 48
Transformer, 253
transitory, 100
treachery, 137, 193
treason, 273
treasure, 25, 111
treasurer, 135, 277
tree trunk, 244
treif, 22, 24
trek, 300
trembling, 8, 172, 182
Trendel, 228
Tri-personal God, 46
Tri-unity, 46, 160
Triplicate, 169
Triune God, 46, 47, 304
trope, 145

tru'a, 181
Tsafon, 157
tsafon, 158
Tsedaka, 54
T'sedekah, 188
Tsedokeh, 15
T'shuvah, 188, 190
tuba, 180
Turkish prison, 339
tzitzith, 69

U

ultra-orthodox, 339
un-intoxicating, 140
unblemished, 24, 127
undeveloped, 67
unfermented, 129, 140
uni-plurality, 44
unitary entity, 46
universe, 65, 102, 182, 205
unkosher, 24
unquenchable, 325
Upper Room, 117, 172, 177
urine, 140
Ur'sa Major, 146

V

vandalism, 203
Varro, 295
veil, 7, 36, 96, 161
veins, 38, 100, 201, 283
velvet, 94, 95, 214
Venus, 217

vernal equinox, 121, 167
vestry, 85
vetechosem, 320
vicarious, 73
Vilna, 339
vinegar, 271, 273, 284
violent shaking, 170
virgin bride, 96
vows, 92, 93, 191, 269

W

war, 175
watchword, 41
water tower, 189
Water-Drawing, 203
water-libation, 203
wedding dress, 92
Week of Weeks, 161, 169, 170
welded, 41
whistle, 184
wig, 10
willow, 205, 211
willows, 205
wind instrument, 180
windows, 59
Wisdom, 1, 333
witchcraft, 279
withered arm, 279
woe, 91, 93
womb of the world, 84
World Zionist Organization, 300, 306
worms, 107
wrested, 171, 172
wrestling, 18, 20

Y

Ya'aqobh, 356
yachid, 42, 44
yaez, 19
yahrzeit, 70
Yahweh Rapha, 39
yarmulkah, 10
yayin, 139
yeast, 129
Yenon, 201, 258
Yerushalmi, 49
yetzer ha-rah, 53
Yinon, 253, 254
yom echad, 44
Yom Tru'a, 179
Yom-tov, 169
Yoma, 50, 52, 191
Yosef ben Mattiyahu, 307
youngest, 80, 133, 323

Z

Zaddik, 325
zakar, 108
Zebub, 143
Zebulun, 252
Zeus, 226
Zionist flag, 300
Zionward, 69
Ziv, 295
Zohar, 43, 183
zoologists, 147